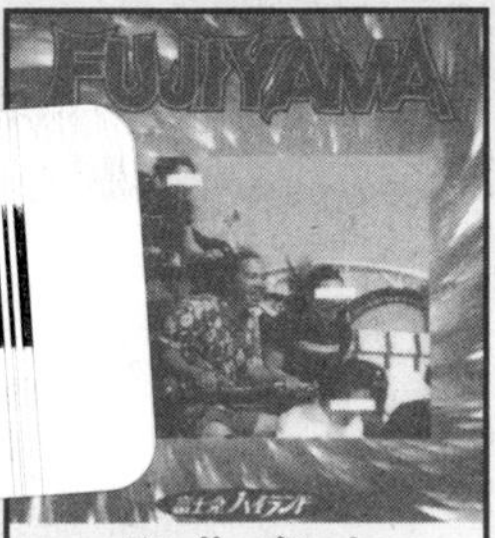
FUJIYAMA

武井宏之

I hate roller coasters. They're really tall, they're fast, you'll die if you fall, and I don't even want to think what happens if they break down. But to find out what lies beyond the terror, I ended up going on one...the world's best roller coaster...Fujiyama. What was it that I found on the other side of the terror? What's the deal with the big grin on my face in the picture?

—Hiroyuki Takei, 1999

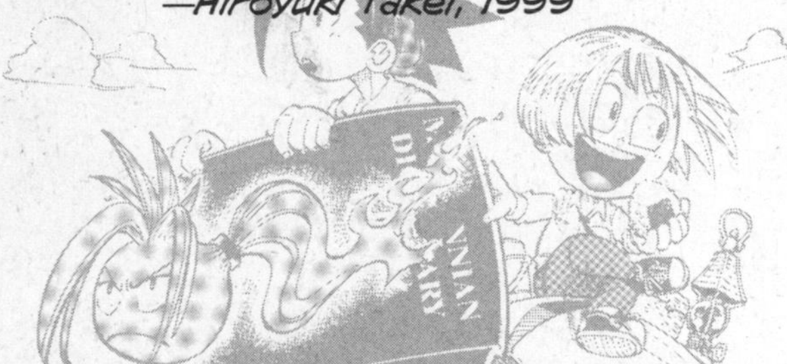
MANTANNIAN

Unconventional author/artist Hiroyuki Takei began his career by winning the coveted Hop Step Award (for ne manga artists) and the Osamu Tezuka Award (named after the famous artist of the same name). After work as an assistant to famed artist Nobuhiro Watsuki, Ta debuted in **Weekly Shonen Jump** in 1997 with **Butsu Zone**, an action series based on Buddhist mythology multicultural adventure manga **Shaman King**, which debuted in 1998, became a hit and was adapted int anime TV series. Takei lists Osamu Tezuka, America comics and robot anime among his many influence

SHAMAN KING VOL.5
The SHONEN JUMP Manga Edition

This graphic novel contains material that was originally published in
English in **SHONEN JUMP** #19-23.

STORY AND ART BY
HIROYUKI TAKEI

English Adaptation/Lance Caselman
Translation/Lillian Olsen
Touch-up Art & Lettering/Kathryn Renta
Design/Sean Lee
Editor/Jason Thompson

Editor in Chief, Books/Alvin Lu
Editor in Chief, Magazines/Marc Weidenbaum
VP of Publishing Licensing/Rika Inouye
VP of Sales/Gonzalo Ferreyra
Sr. VP of Marketing/Liza Coppola
Publisher/Hyoe Narita

Printed in the U.S.A.

Published by VIZ Media, LLC
P.O. Box 77010
San Francisco, CA 94107

SHONEN JUMP Manga Edition
10 9 8 7 6 5
First printing, December 2004
Fifth printing, May 2008

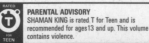

THE WORLD'S
MOST POPULAR MANGA

www.shonenjump.com

SHONEN JUMP MANGA

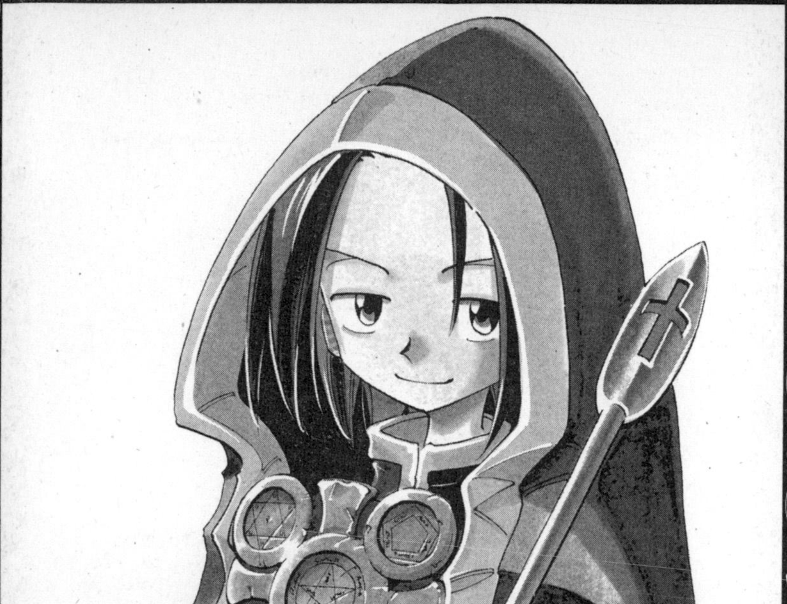
Shaman King

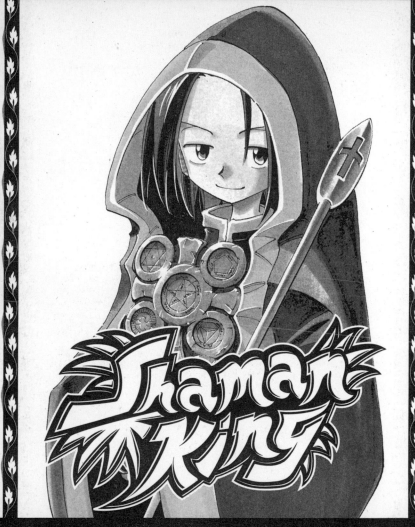

VOL. 5

THE ABOMINABLE DR. FAUST

STORY AND ART BY

HIROYUKI TAKEI

阿弥陀丸

AMIDAMARU
Known in legends as "the fiend," Amidamaru was a samurai who died in Japan's Muromachi Era (1334-1467). His soul haunted Funbari Hill for 600 years, until he became Yoh's ghost companion. His name is based on a Buddhist prayer.

麻倉 葉

YOH ASAKURA
Cheerful and easygoing, Yoh seems to be a slacker, but he is actually the heir to a long line of Japanese shamans. His first name means "leaf."

阿弥陀丸

AMIDAMARU v.2
Spirit Flame mode.

オーバーソウル

AMIDAMARU v.3
Over Soul mode. In this mode, Amidamaru possesses his sword, giving it magical powers.

小山田まん太

MANTA OYAMADA
An easily panicked student who always carries a huge dictionary. He has enough sixth sense to see ghosts, but not enough to control them. In the anime he's named "Mortimer."

恐山アンナ

ANNA KYOYAMA
Yoh's no-nonsense fiancée (it's an arranged marriage). She is an *itako* (a traditional Japanese village shaman).

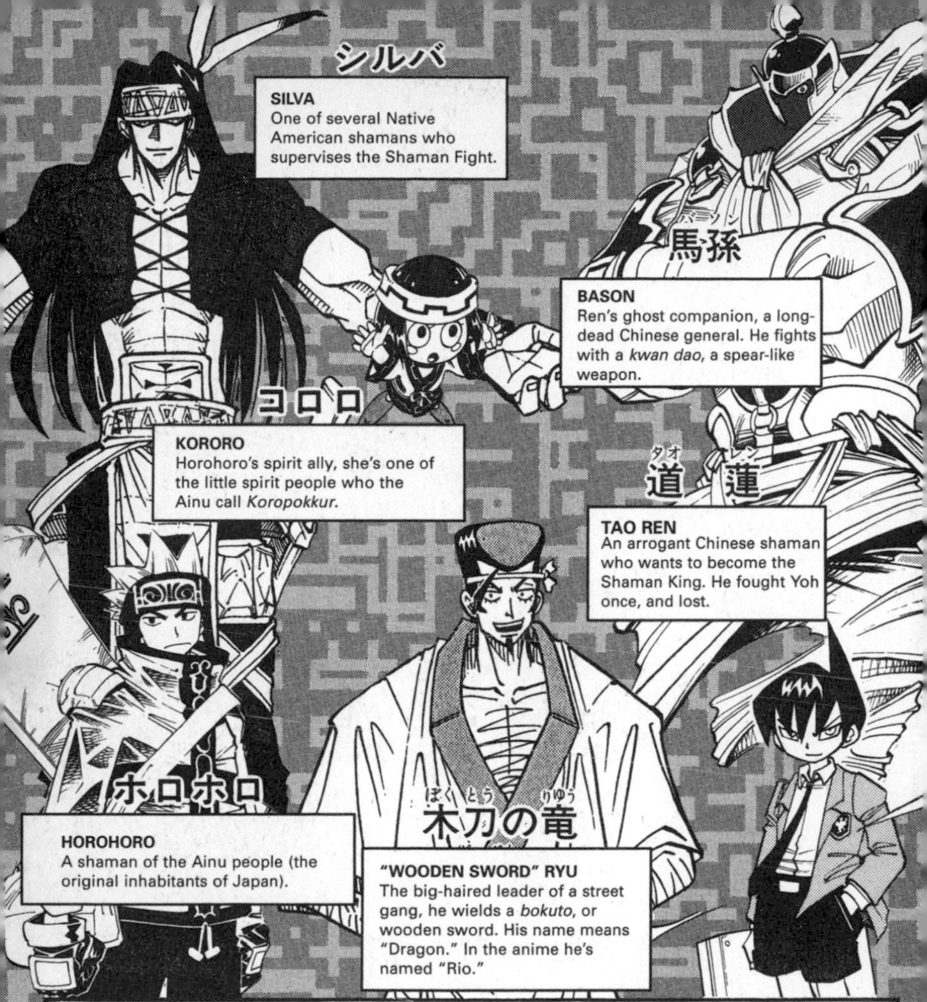
シルバ
SILVA
One of several Native American shamans who supervises the Shaman Fight.
馬孫
BASON
Ren's ghost companion, a long-dead Chinese general. He fights with a *kwan dao*, a spear-like weapon.
コロロ
KORORO
Horohoro's spirit ally, she's one of the little spirit people who the Ainu call *Koropokkur*.
道蓮
TAO REN
An arrogant Chinese shaman who wants to become the Shaman King. He fought Yoh once, and lost.
ホロホロ
HOROHORO
A shaman of the Ainu people (the original inhabitants of Japan).
木刀の竜
"WOODEN SWORD" RYU
The big-haired leader of a street gang, he wields a *bokuto*, or wooden sword. His name means "Dragon." In the anime he's named "Rio."

THE STORY SO FAR...

Yoh Asakura is a shaman--one of the gifted few who, thanks to training or talent, can channel spirits that most people can't even see. With the help of his fiancée Anna, Yoh is in training for the ultimate shaman sports event: the "Shaman Fight in Tokyo," the once-every-500-years tournament to see who can shape humanity's future and become the Shaman King. Now, Yoh's first official Shaman Fight has begun. His opponent: the Ainu shaman Horohoro, who wants to use the power of the Shaman King to save the environment!

VOL. 5:
THE ABOMINABLE DR. FAUST

CONTENTS

Reincarnation 36	Great Ghost, Great Sword	7
Reincarnation 37	Decision	27
Reincarnation 38	A Hot Bath and a Starry Sky	47
Reincarnation 39	Backbone	66
Reincarnation 40	Spill Your Guts	87
Reincarnation 41	Natural Bone Killers	107
Reincarnation 42	The Atrocity Exhibition	127
Reincarnation 43	Regarding Yoh	149
Reincarnation 44	The Pale Lover	169
Bonus: Funbari Stories		188
Previews		191

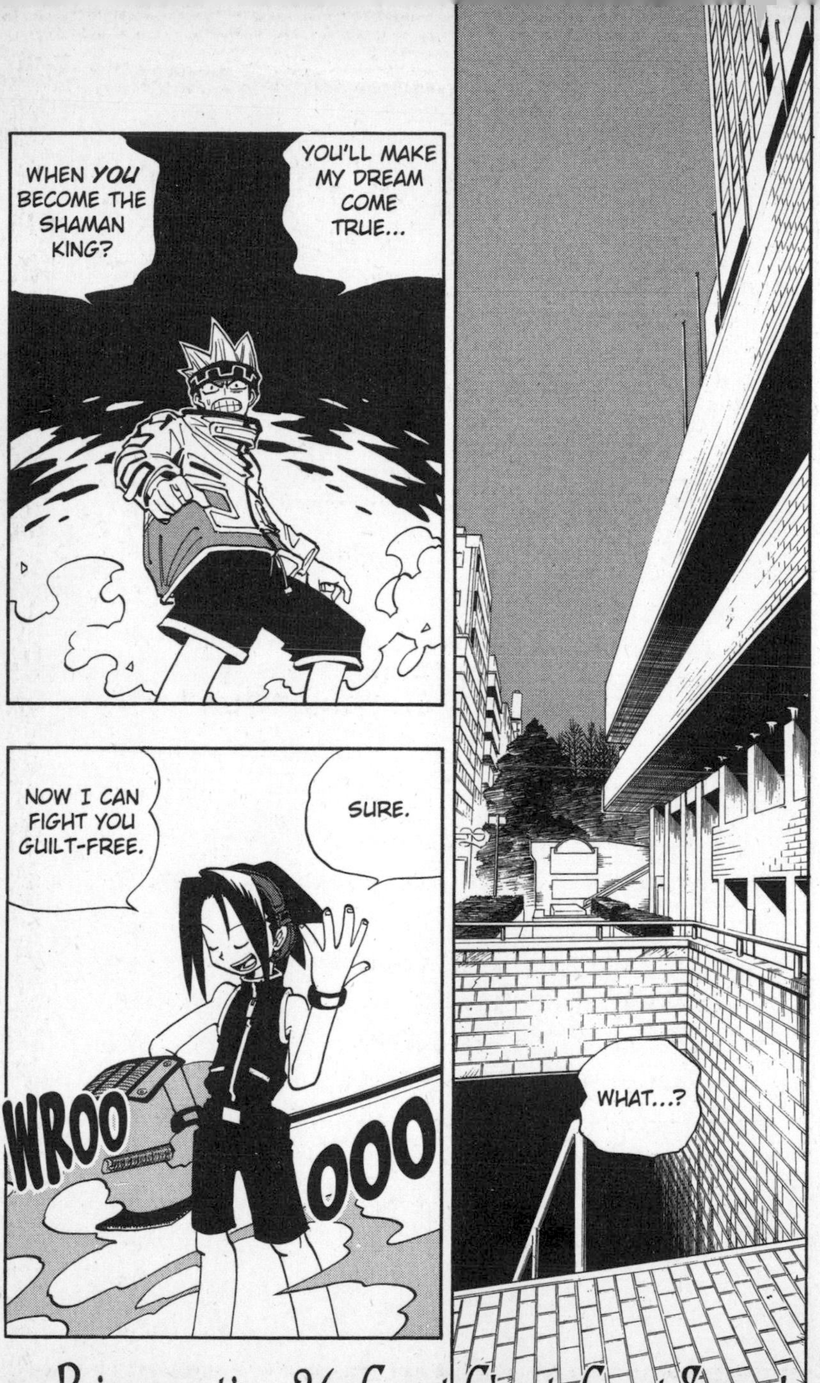
WHAT...?
YOU'LL MAKE MY DREAM COME TRUE...
WHEN *YOU* BECOME THE SHAMAN KING?
SURE.
NOW I CAN FIGHT YOU GUILT-FREE.
WROO OOO

Reincarnation 36: Great Ghost, Great Sword

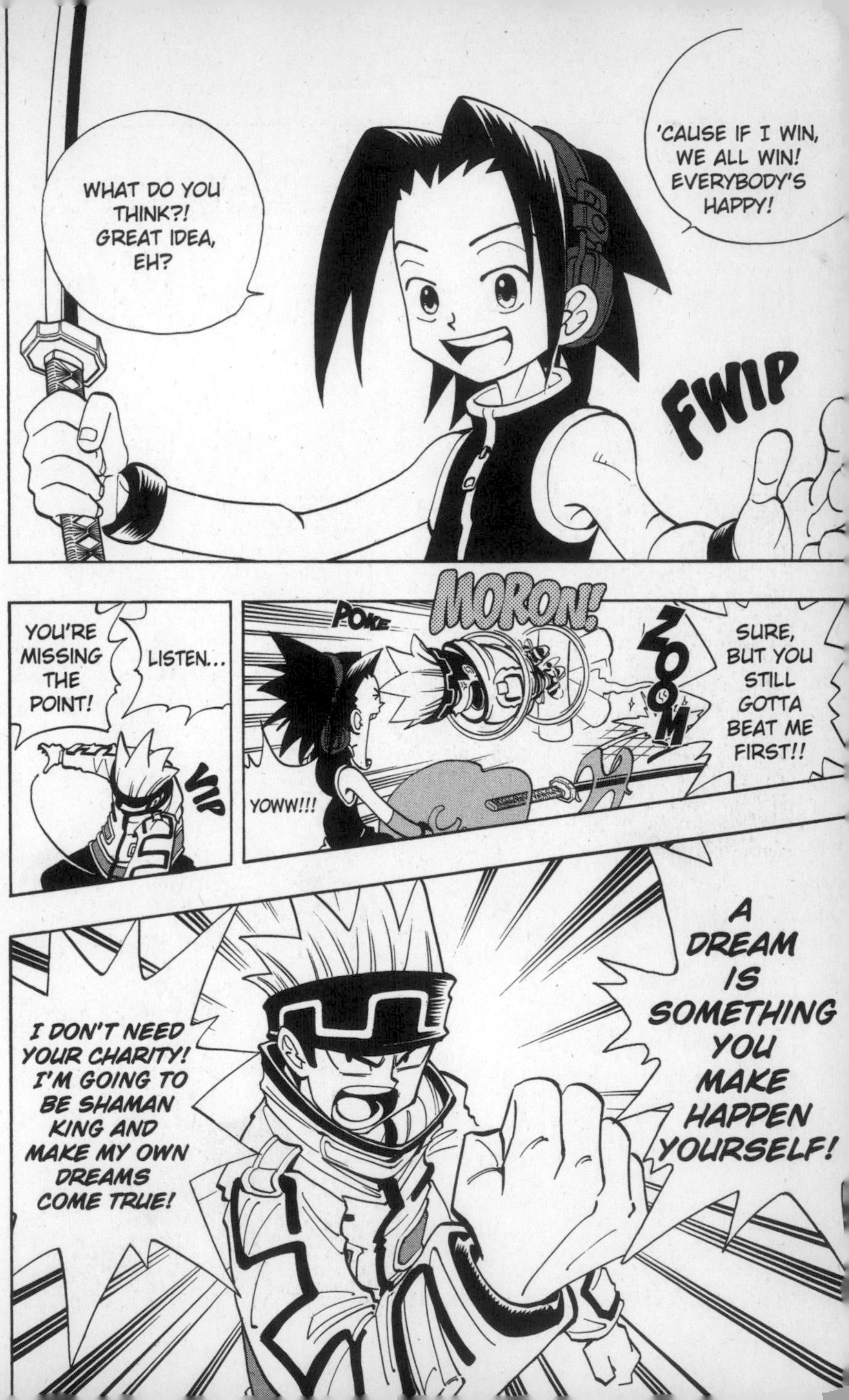

'CAUSE IF I WIN, WE ALL WIN! EVERYBODY'S HAPPY!
WHAT DO YOU THINK?! GREAT IDEA, EH?
FWIP
SURE, BUT YOU STILL GOTTA BEAT ME FIRST!!
ZOOM
MORON!
POKE
YOWW!!!
LISTEN...
YOU'RE MISSING THE POINT!
VIP
A DREAM IS SOMETHING YOU MAKE HAPPEN YOURSELF!
I DON'T NEED YOUR CHARITY! I'M GOING TO BE SHAMAN KING AND MAKE MY OWN DREAMS COME TRUE!

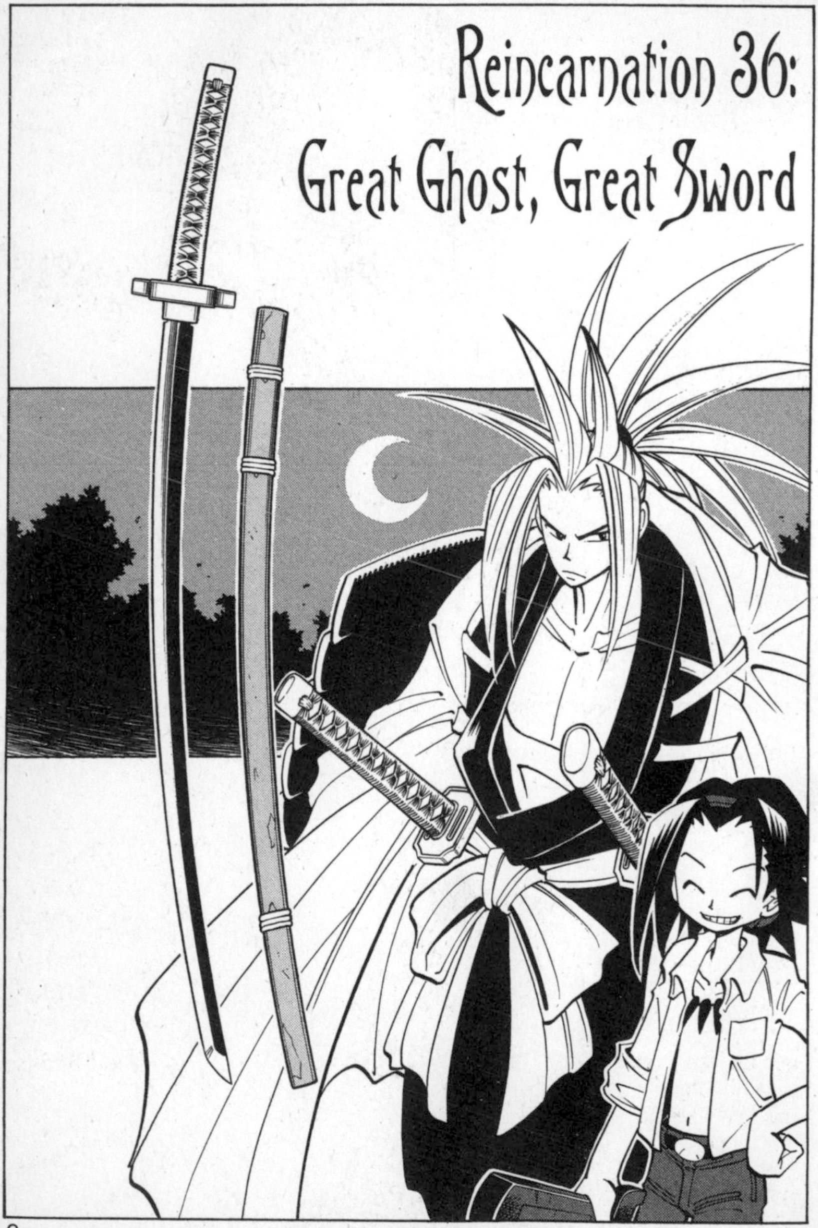
Reincarnation 36:
Great Ghost, Great Sword

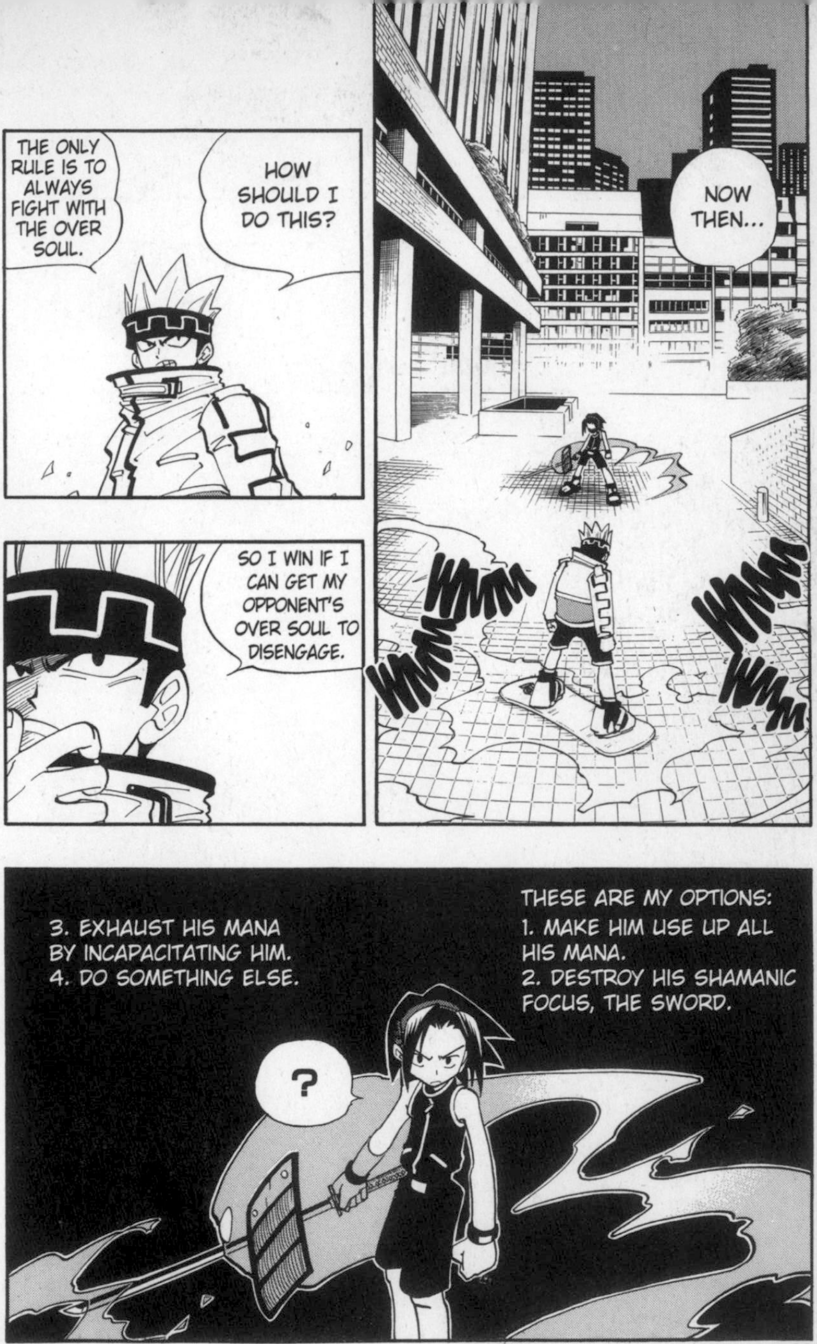
NOW THEN...
HOW SHOULD I DO THIS?
THE ONLY RULE IS TO ALWAYS FIGHT WITH THE OVER SOUL.
SO I WIN IF I CAN GET MY OPPONENT'S OVER SOUL TO DISENGAGE.
THESE ARE MY OPTIONS:
1. MAKE HIM USE UP ALL HIS MANA.
2. DESTROY HIS SHAMANIC FOCUS, THE SWORD.
3. EXHAUST HIS MANA BY INCAPACITATING HIM.
4. DO SOMETHING ELSE.
?

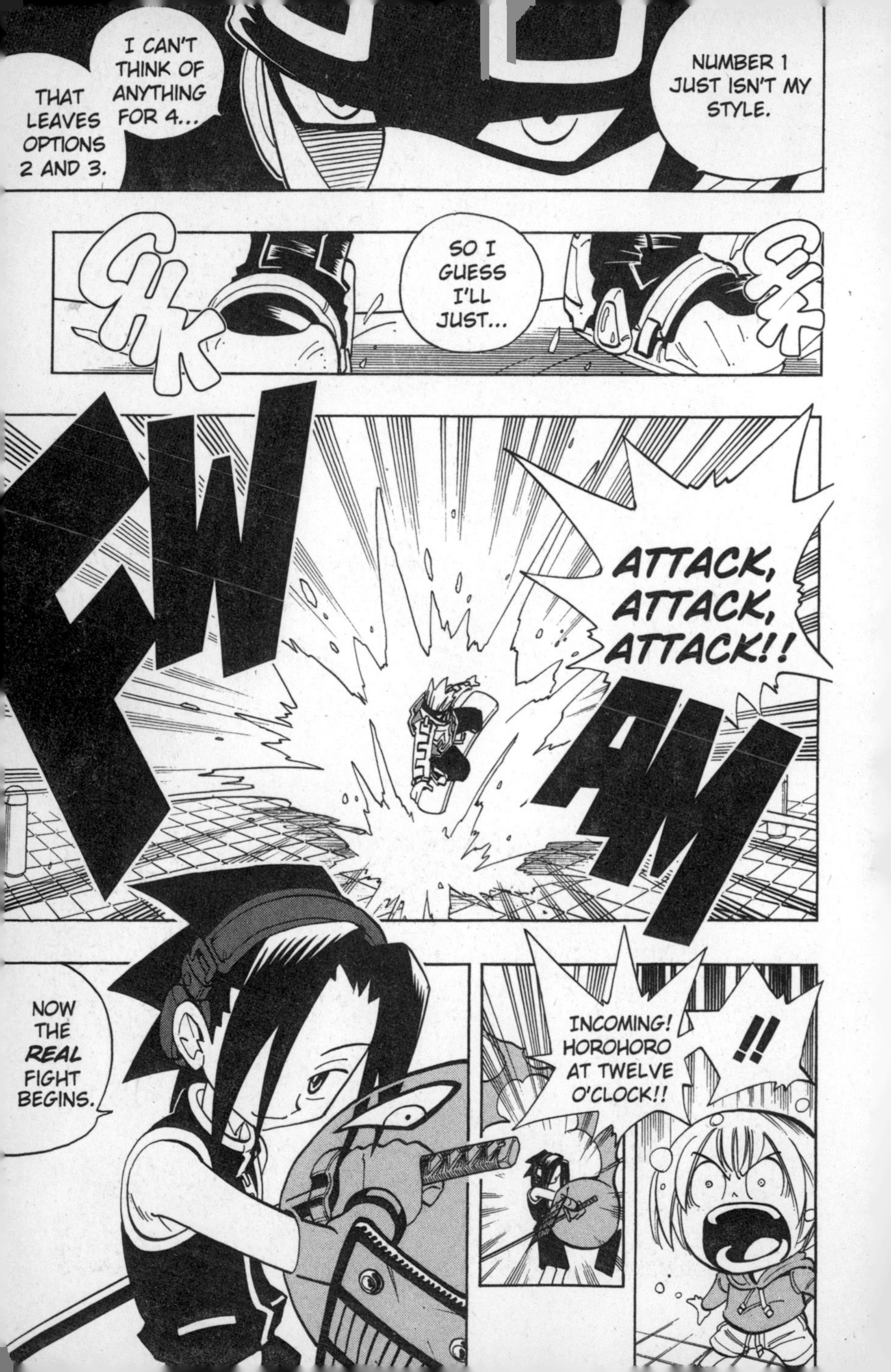
NUMBER 1 JUST ISN'T MY STYLE.
I CAN'T THINK OF ANYTHING FOR 4...
THAT LEAVES OPTIONS 2 AND 3.
CHK
SO I GUESS I'LL JUST...
CHK
ATTACK, ATTACK, ATTACK!!
!!
INCOMING! HOROHORO AT TWELVE O'CLOCK!!
NOW THE *REAL* FIGHT BEGINS.

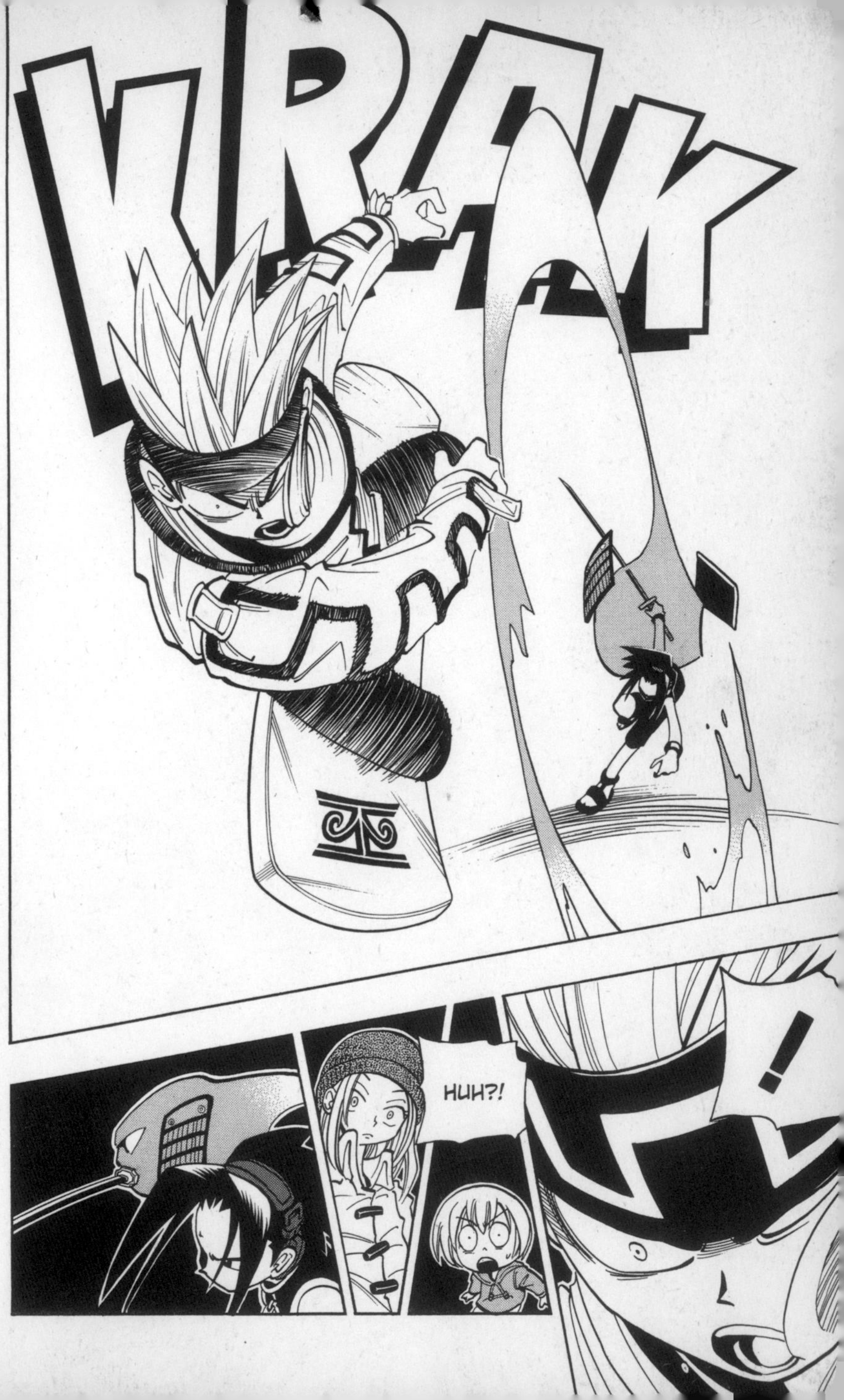
VRAK
!
HUH?!

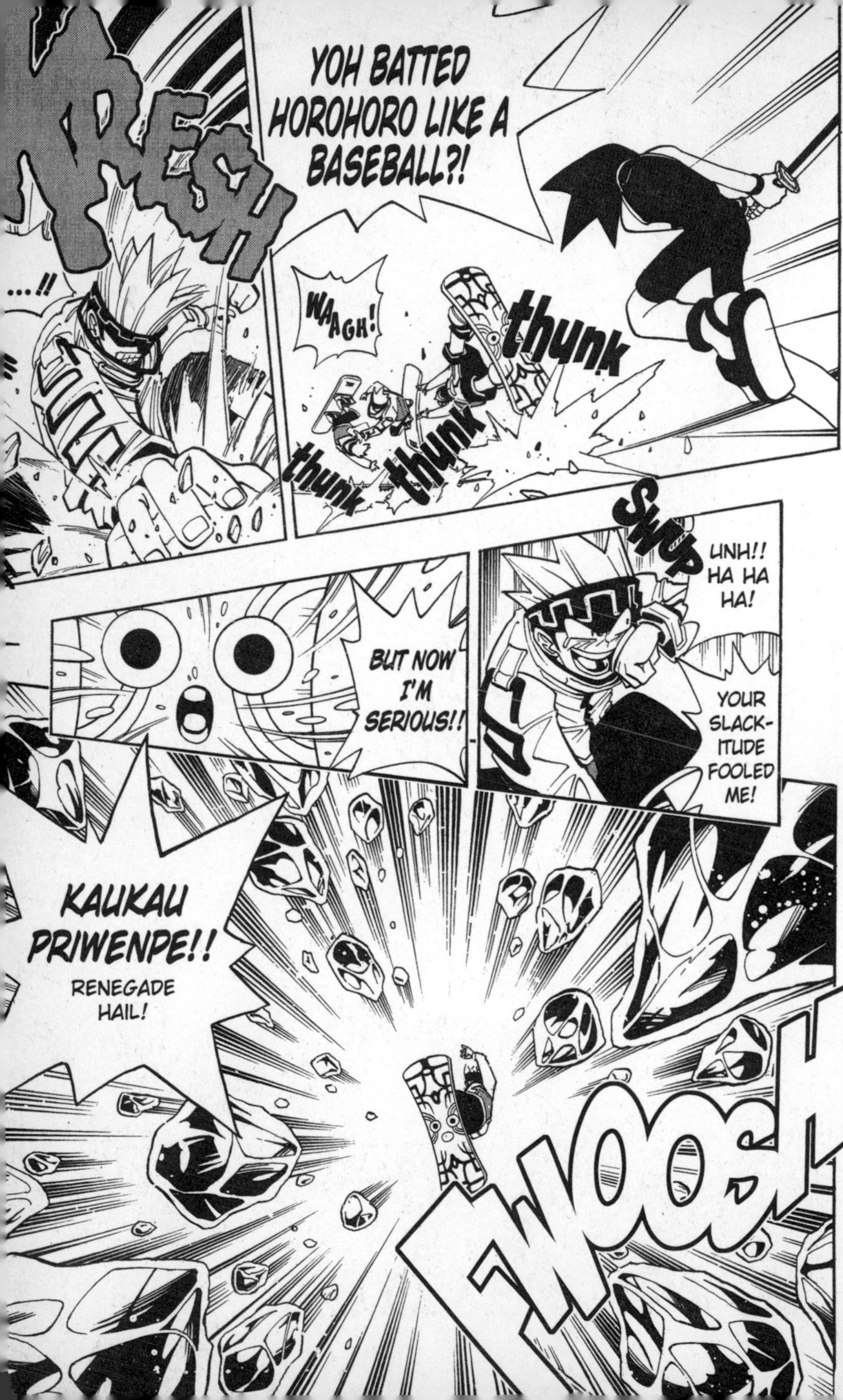
YOH BATTED HOROHORO LIKE A BASEBALL?!
WAAGH!
thunk
thunk
thunk
KRESH
...!!
SWUP
UNH!! HA HA HA!
YOUR SLACK-ITUDE FOOLED ME!
BUT NOW I'M SERIOUS!!
KAUKAU PRIWENPE!!
RENEGADE HAIL!
WOOSH

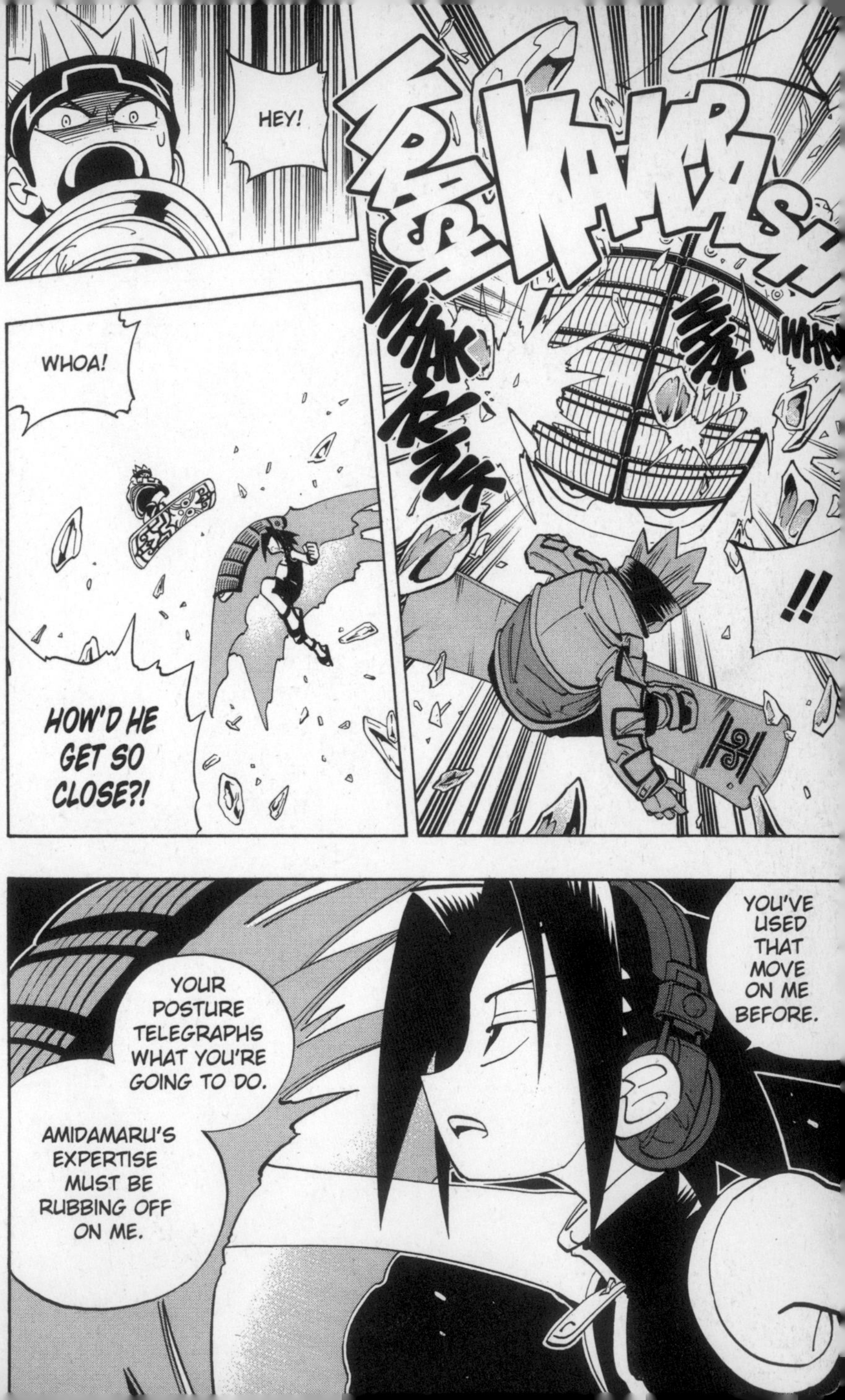
WHAK
WHAK
!!
HEY!
WHOA!
HOW'D HE GET SO CLOSE?!
YOU'VE USED THAT MOVE ON ME BEFORE.
YOUR POSTURE TELEGRAPHS WHAT YOU'RE GOING TO DO.
AMIDAMARU'S EXPERTISE MUST BE RUBBING OFF ON ME.

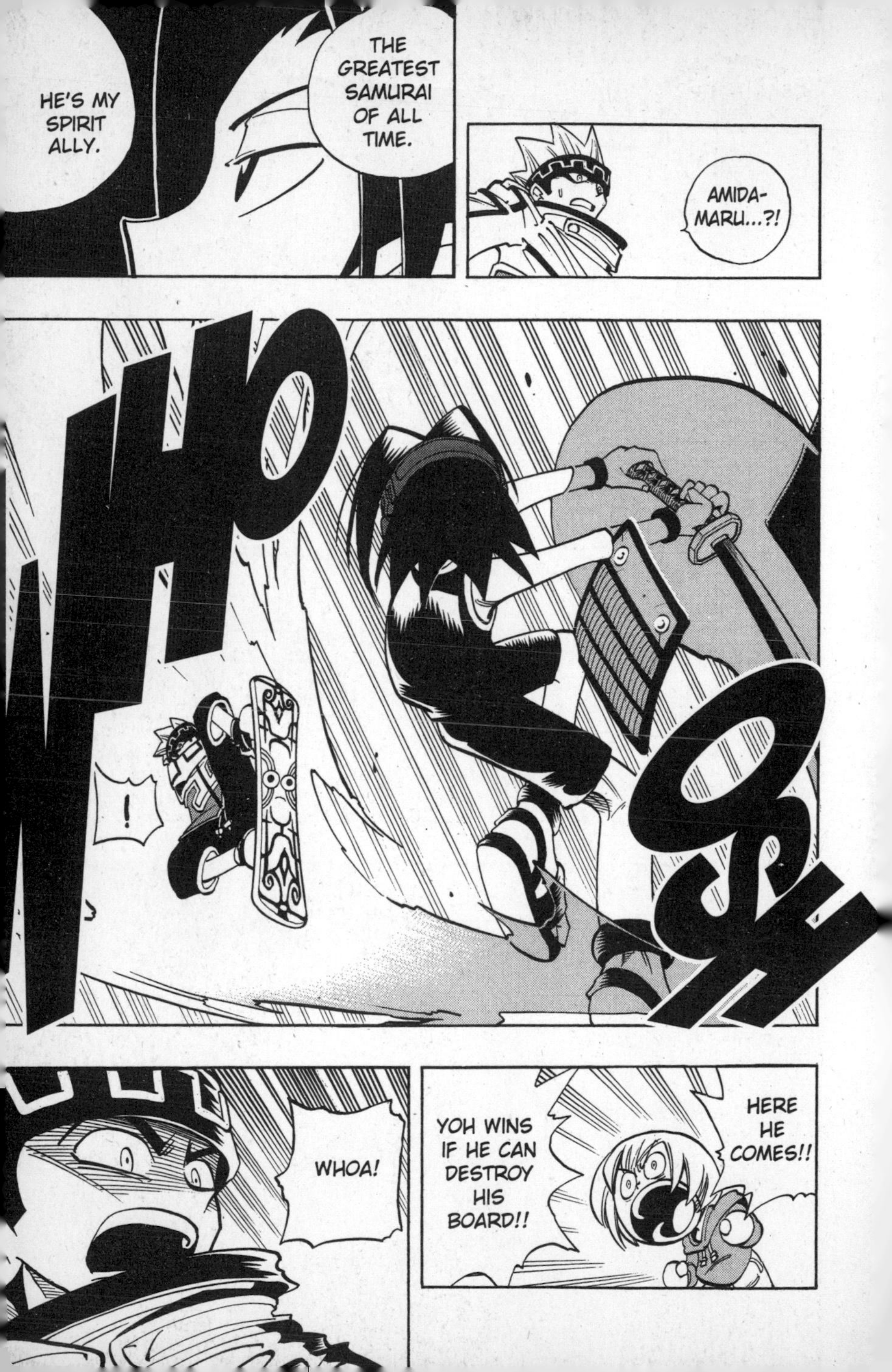
AMIDA-MARU...?!
THE GREATEST SAMURAI OF ALL TIME.
HE'S MY SPIRIT ALLY.
WHOOSH
!
HERE HE COMES!!
YOH WINS IF HE CAN DESTROY HIS BOARD!!
WHOA!

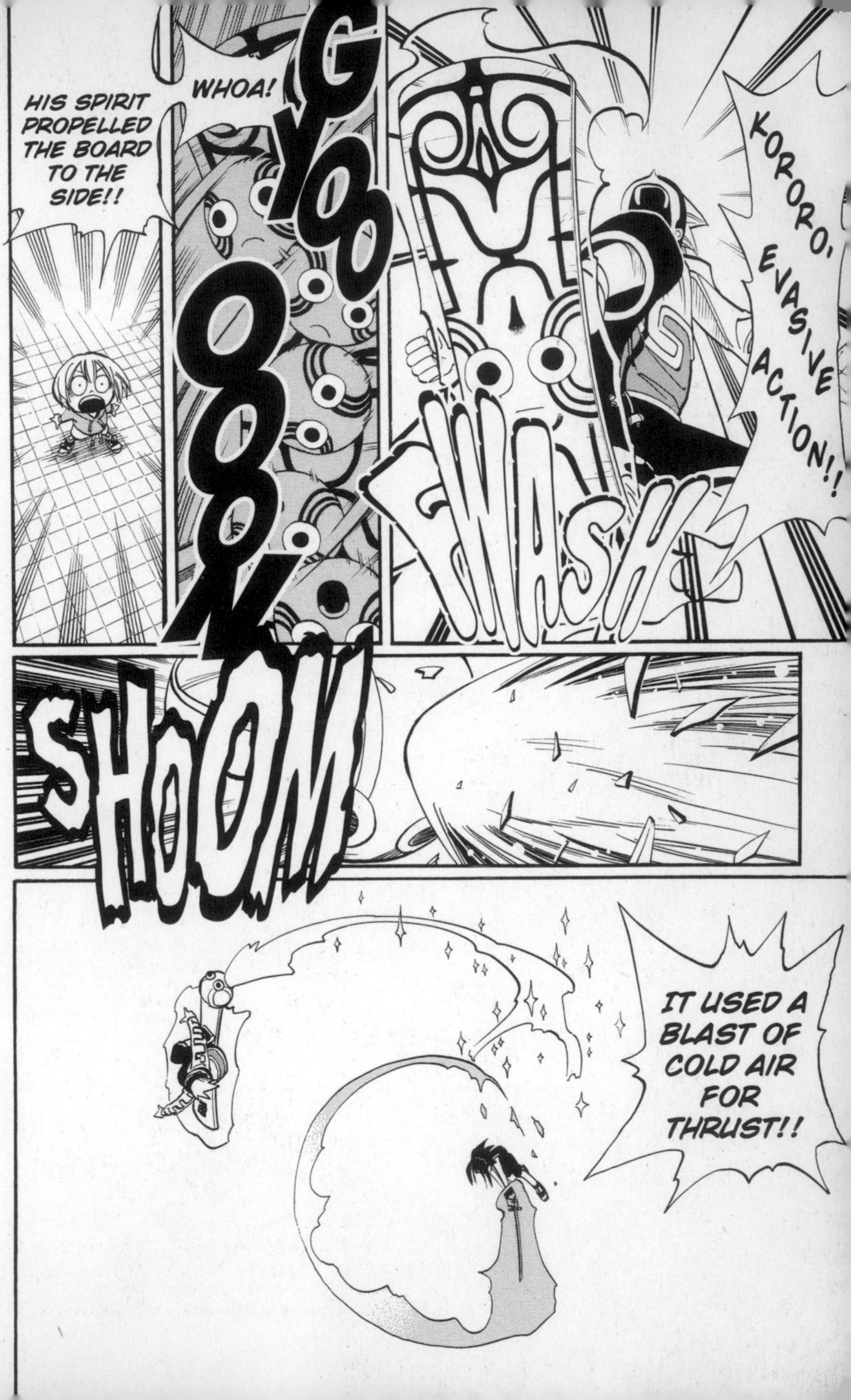
KORORO, EVASIVE ACTION!!
WASH
WHOA!
HIS SPIRIT PROPELLED THE BOARD TO THE SIDE!!
SHOOM
IT USED A BLAST OF COLD AIR FOR THRUST!!

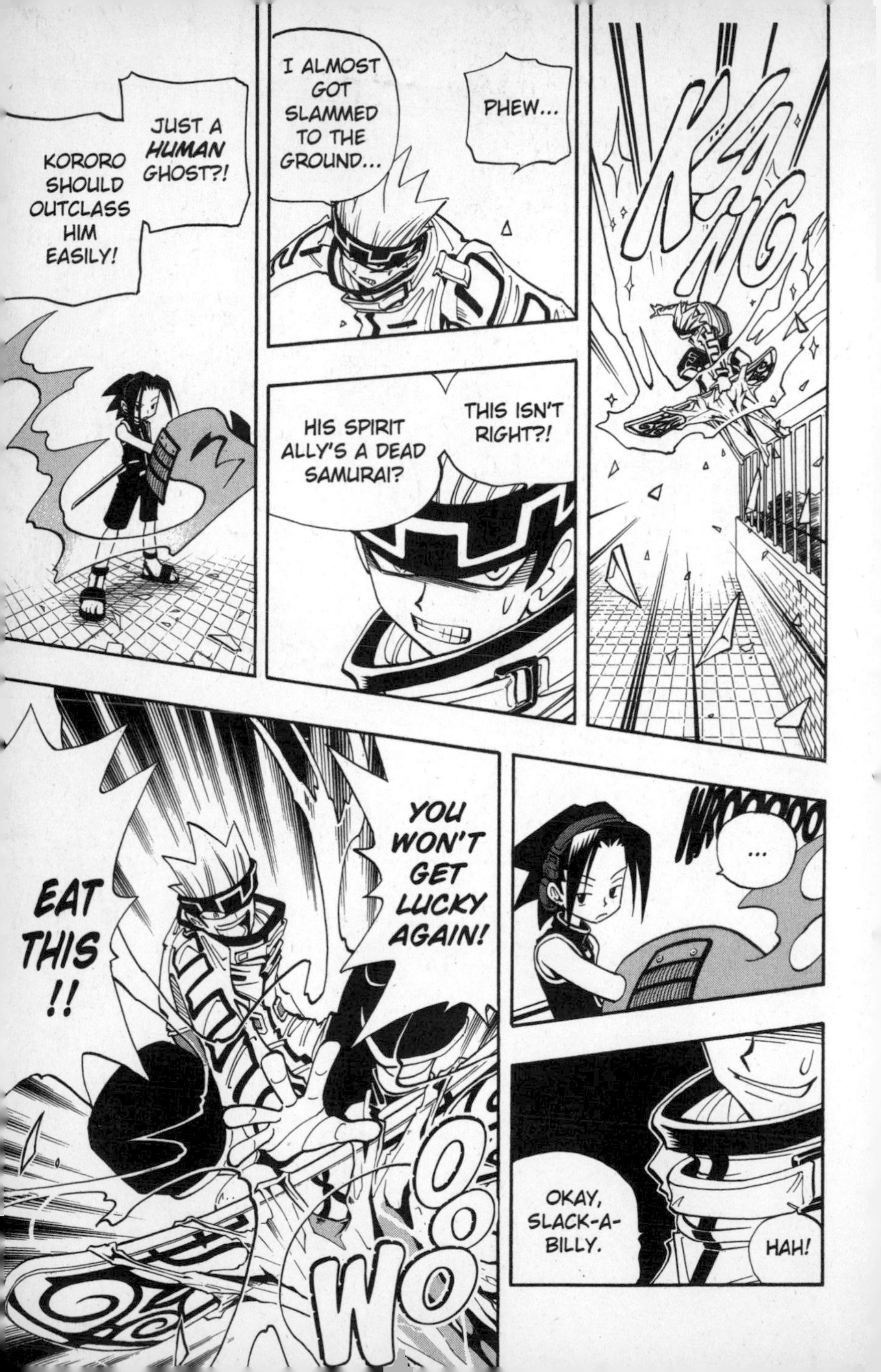
PHEW...
I ALMOST GOT SLAMMED TO THE GROUND...
THIS ISN'T RIGHT?!
HIS SPIRIT ALLY'S A DEAD SAMURAI?
JUST A *HUMAN* GHOST?!
KORORO SHOULD OUTCLASS HIM EASILY!
...
HAH!
OKAY, SLACK-A-BILLY.
YOU WON'T GET LUCKY AGAIN!
EAT THIS!!
WOOOO

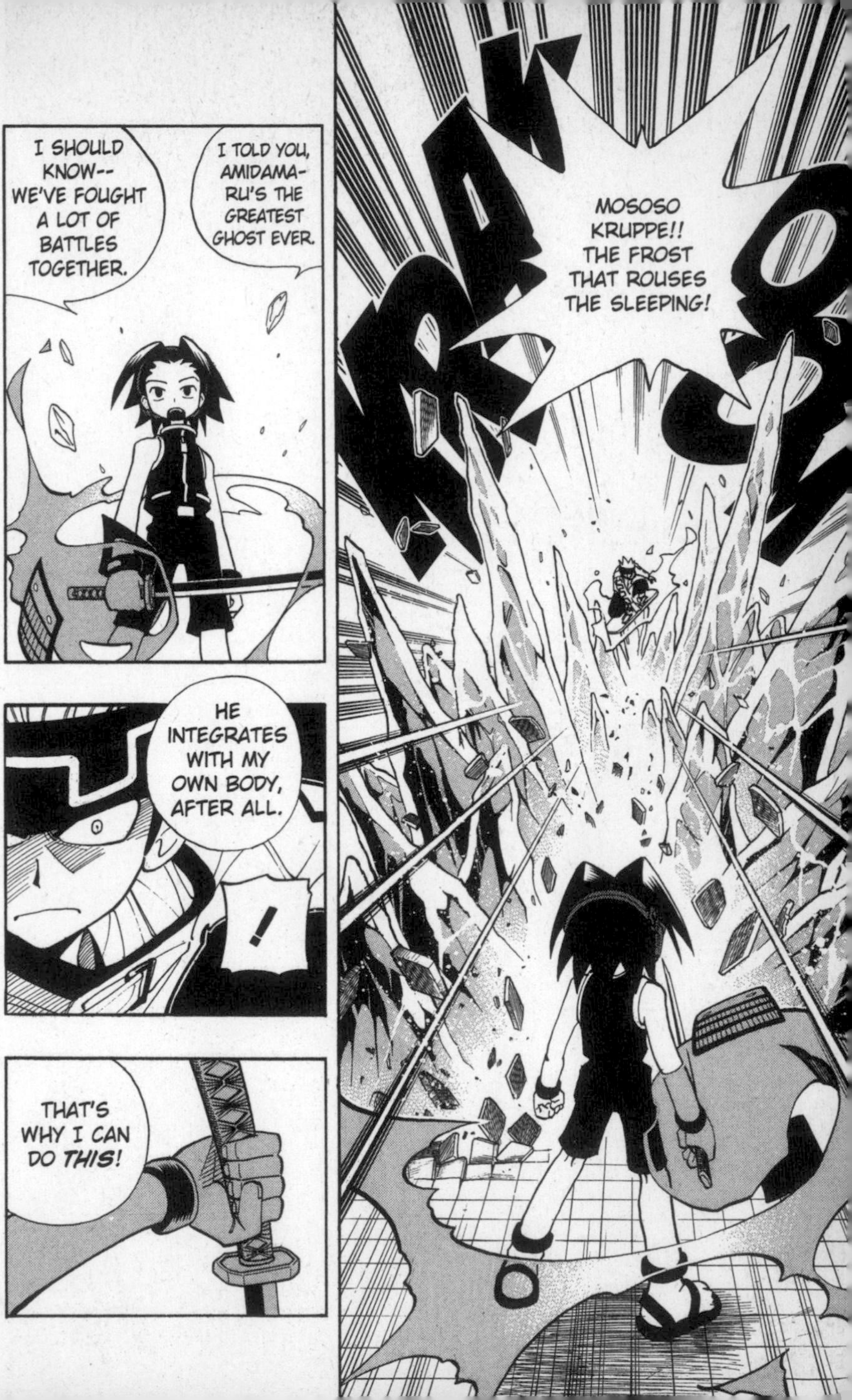
MOSOSO KRUPPE!! THE FROST THAT ROUSES THE SLEEPING!
I TOLD YOU, AMIDAMA-RU'S THE GREATEST GHOST EVER.
I SHOULD KNOW-- WE'VE FOUGHT A LOT OF BATTLES TOGETHER.
HE INTEGRATES WITH MY OWN BODY, AFTER ALL.
!
THAT'S WHY I CAN DO *THIS*!

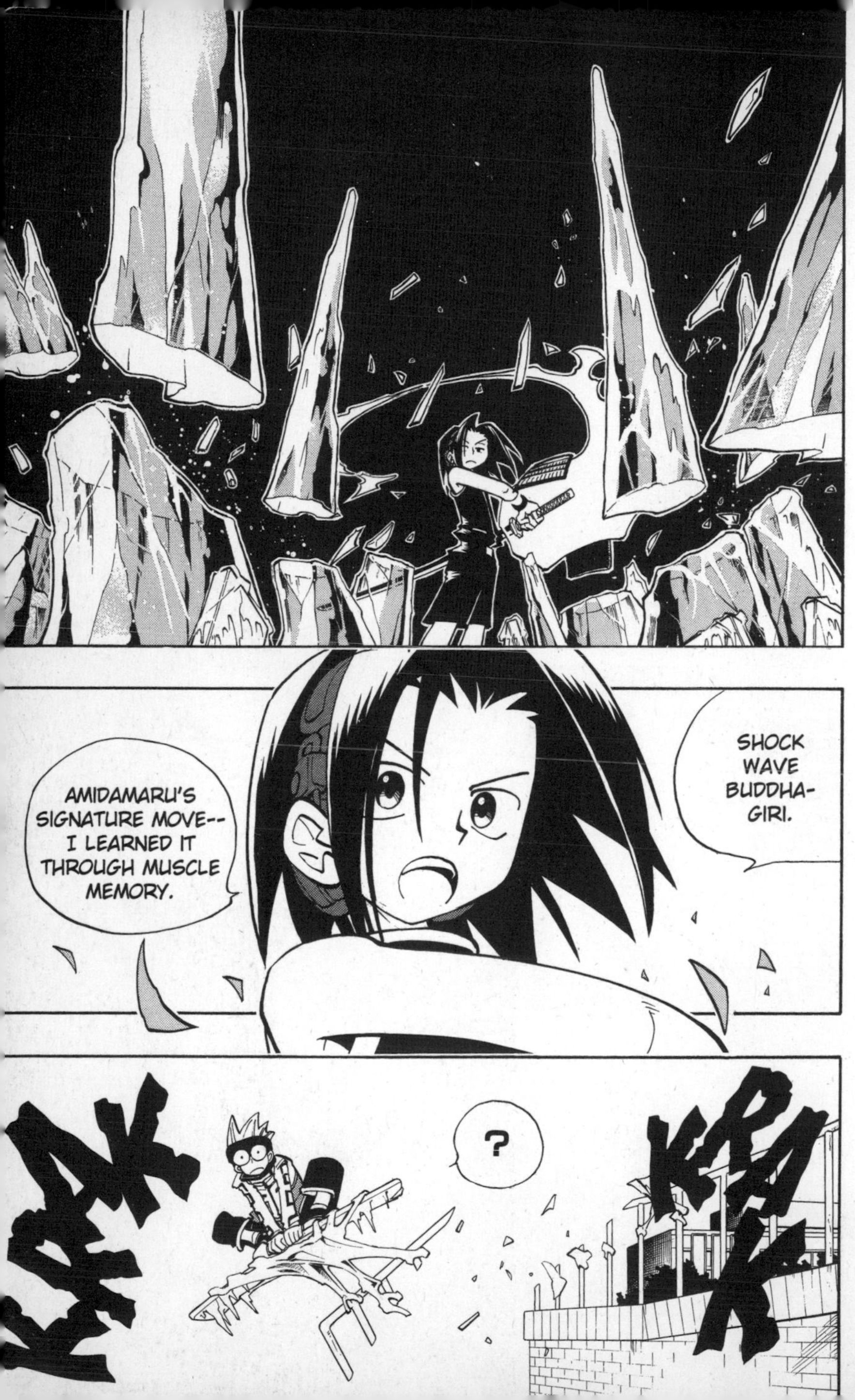
SHOCK WAVE BUDDHA-GIRI.
AMIDAMARU'S SIGNATURE MOVE--I LEARNED IT THROUGH MUSCLE MEMORY.
KRAK
?
KRAK

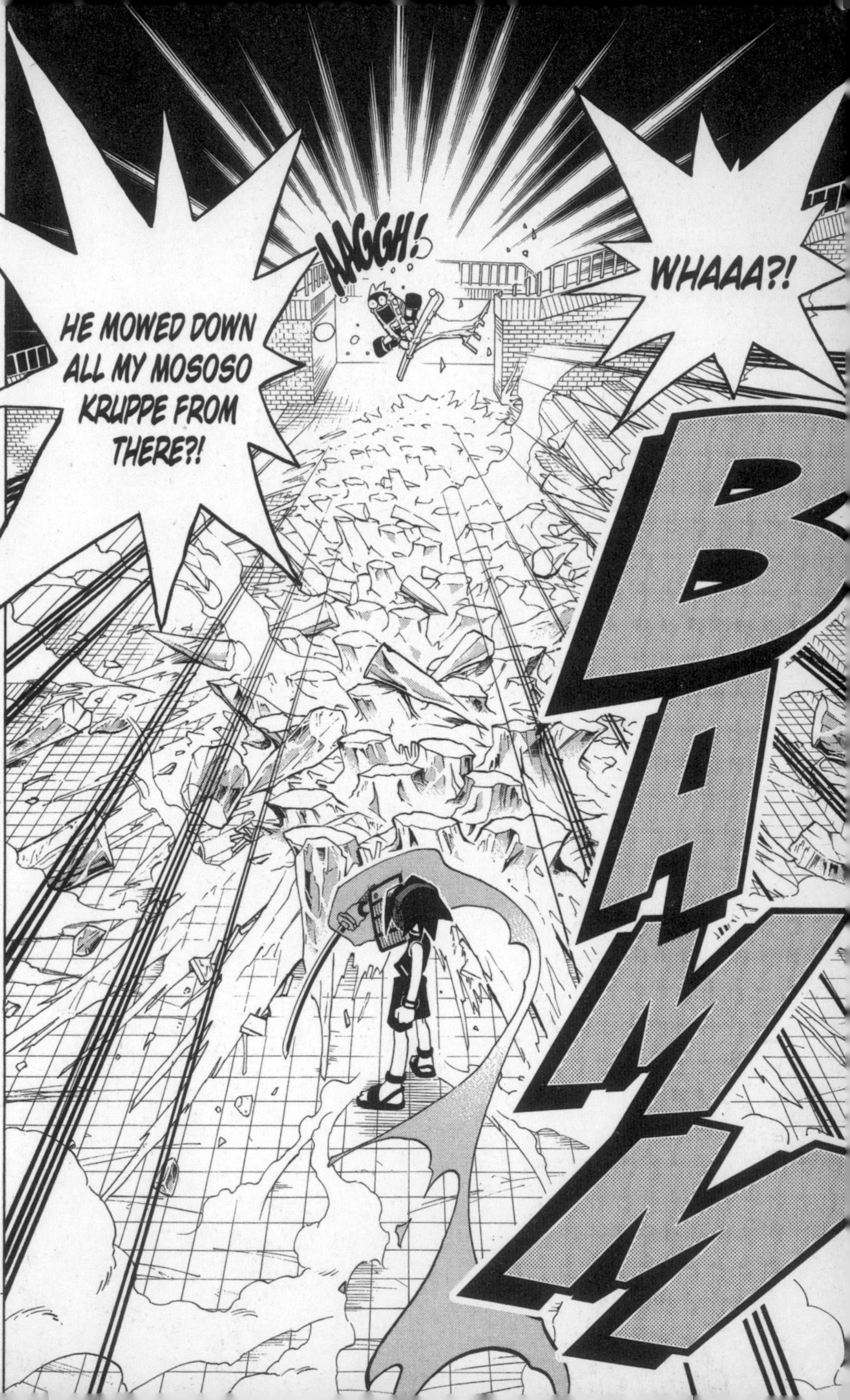
WHAAA?!
AAGGH!
HE MOWED DOWN ALL MY MOSOSO KRUPPE FROM THERE?!
BLAMM

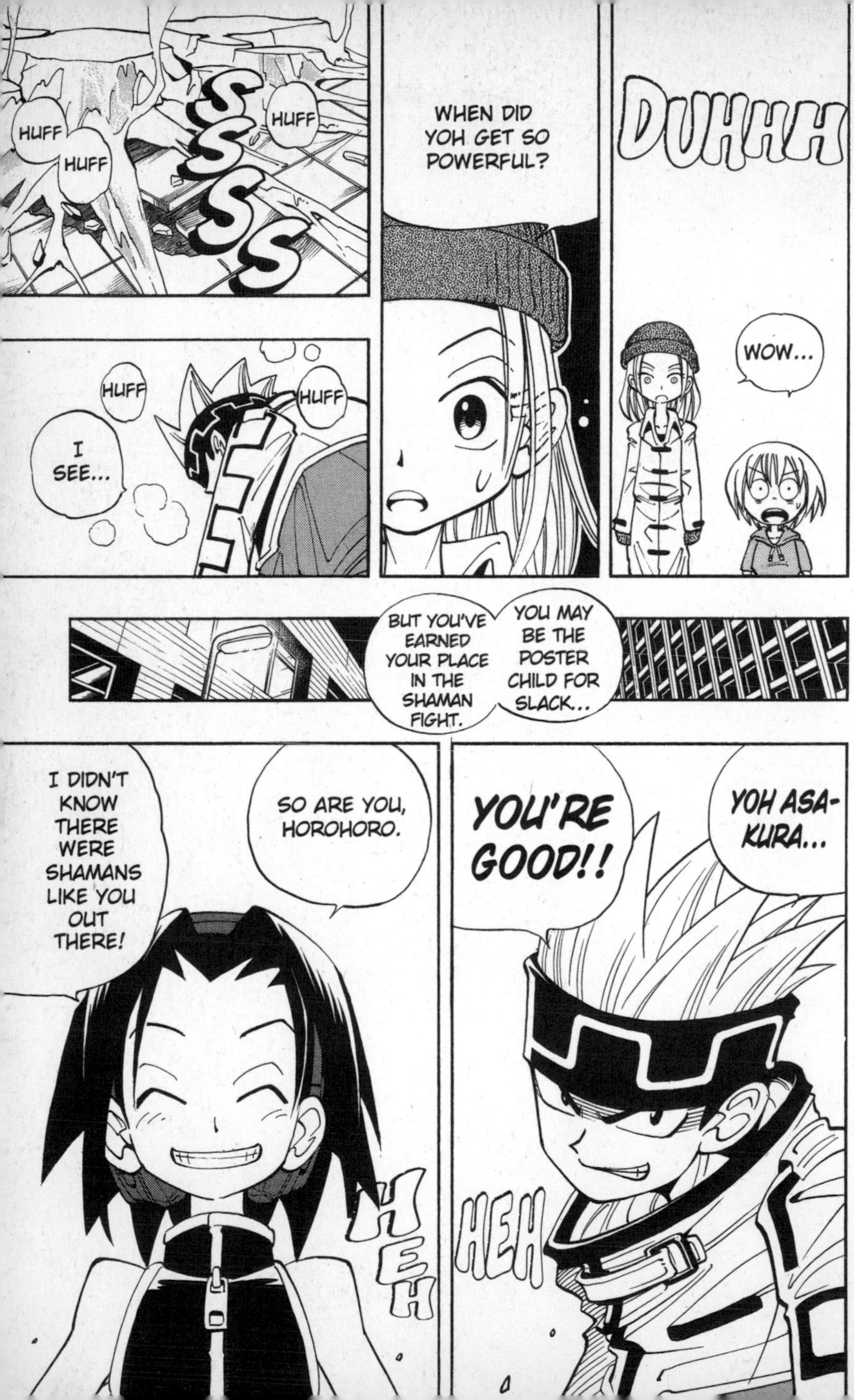
DUHHH
WOW...
WHEN DID YOH GET SO POWERFUL?
HUFF
SSSSS
HUFF
HUFF
HUFF
HUFF
I SEE...
YOU MAY BE THE POSTER CHILD FOR SLACK...
BUT YOU'VE EARNED YOUR PLACE IN THE SHAMAN FIGHT.
YOH ASA-KURA...
YOU'RE GOOD!!
HEH
SO ARE YOU, HOROHORO.
I DIDN'T KNOW THERE WERE SHAMANS LIKE YOU OUT THERE!
HEHEH

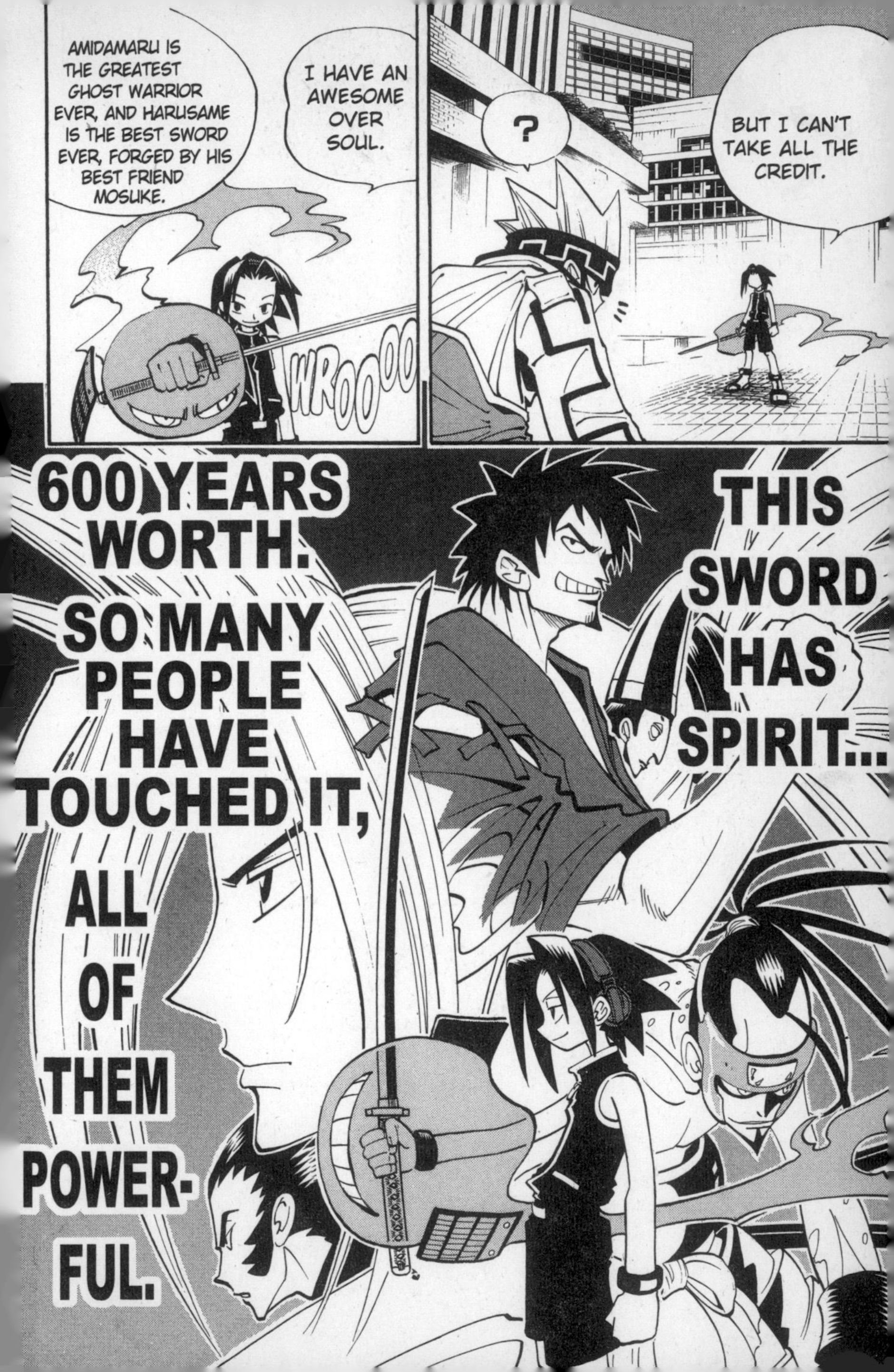
BUT I CAN'T TAKE ALL THE CREDIT.
?
I HAVE AN AWESOME OVER SOUL.
AMIDAMARU IS THE GREATEST GHOST WARRIOR EVER, AND HARUSAME IS THE BEST SWORD EVER, FORGED BY HIS BEST FRIEND MOSUKE.
WROOOO
THIS SWORD HAS SPIRIT...
600 YEARS WORTH.
SO MANY PEOPLE HAVE TOUCHED IT,
ALL OF THEM POWER-FUL.

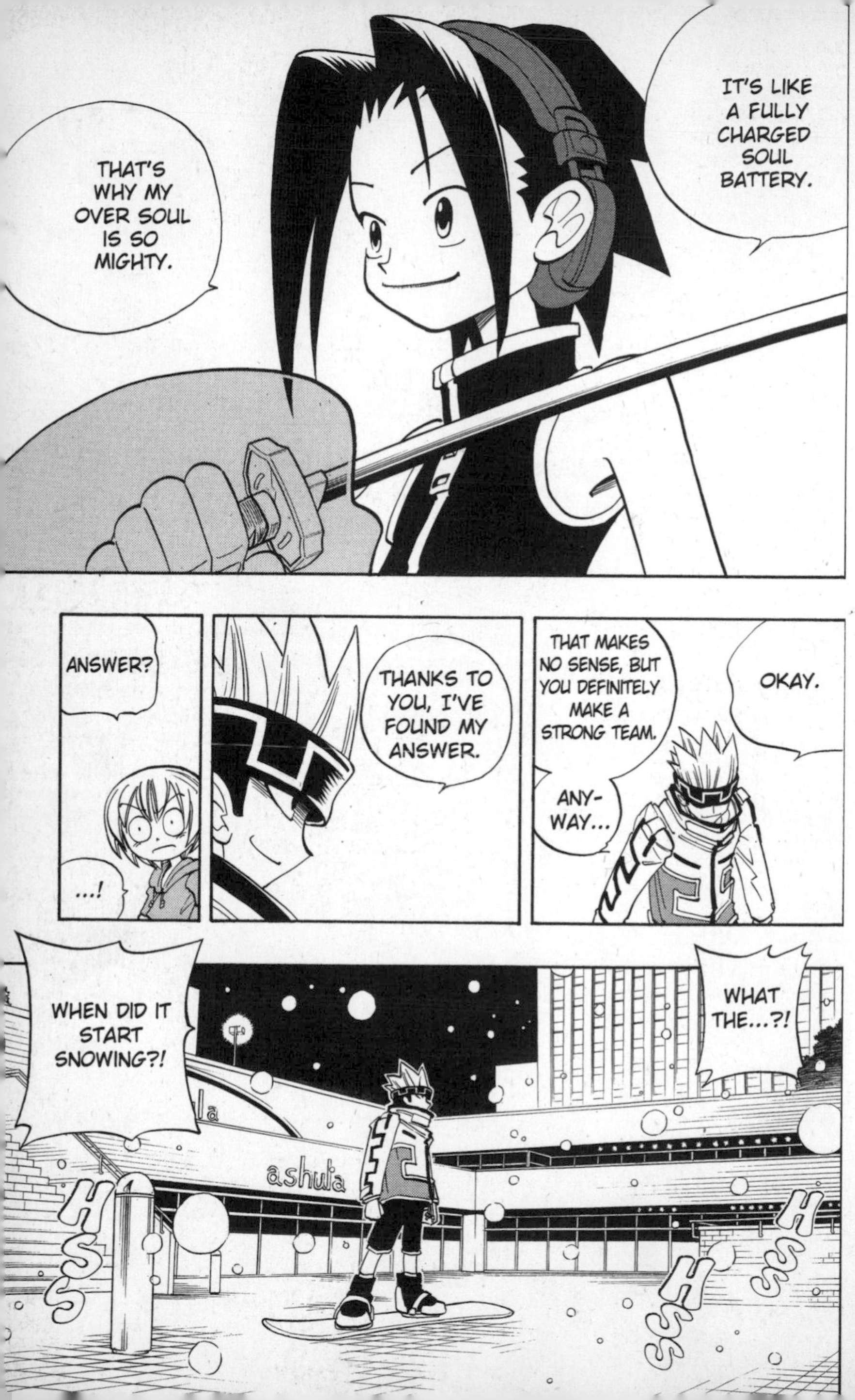
IT'S LIKE A FULLY CHARGED SOUL BATTERY.
THAT'S WHY MY OVER SOUL IS SO MIGHTY.
OKAY.
THAT MAKES NO SENSE, BUT YOU DEFINITELY MAKE A STRONG TEAM.
ANY-WAY...
THANKS TO YOU, I'VE FOUND MY ANSWER.
ANSWER?
...!
WHAT THE...?!
HSSS
HSSS
WHEN DID IT START SNOWING?!
ashula
HSSS

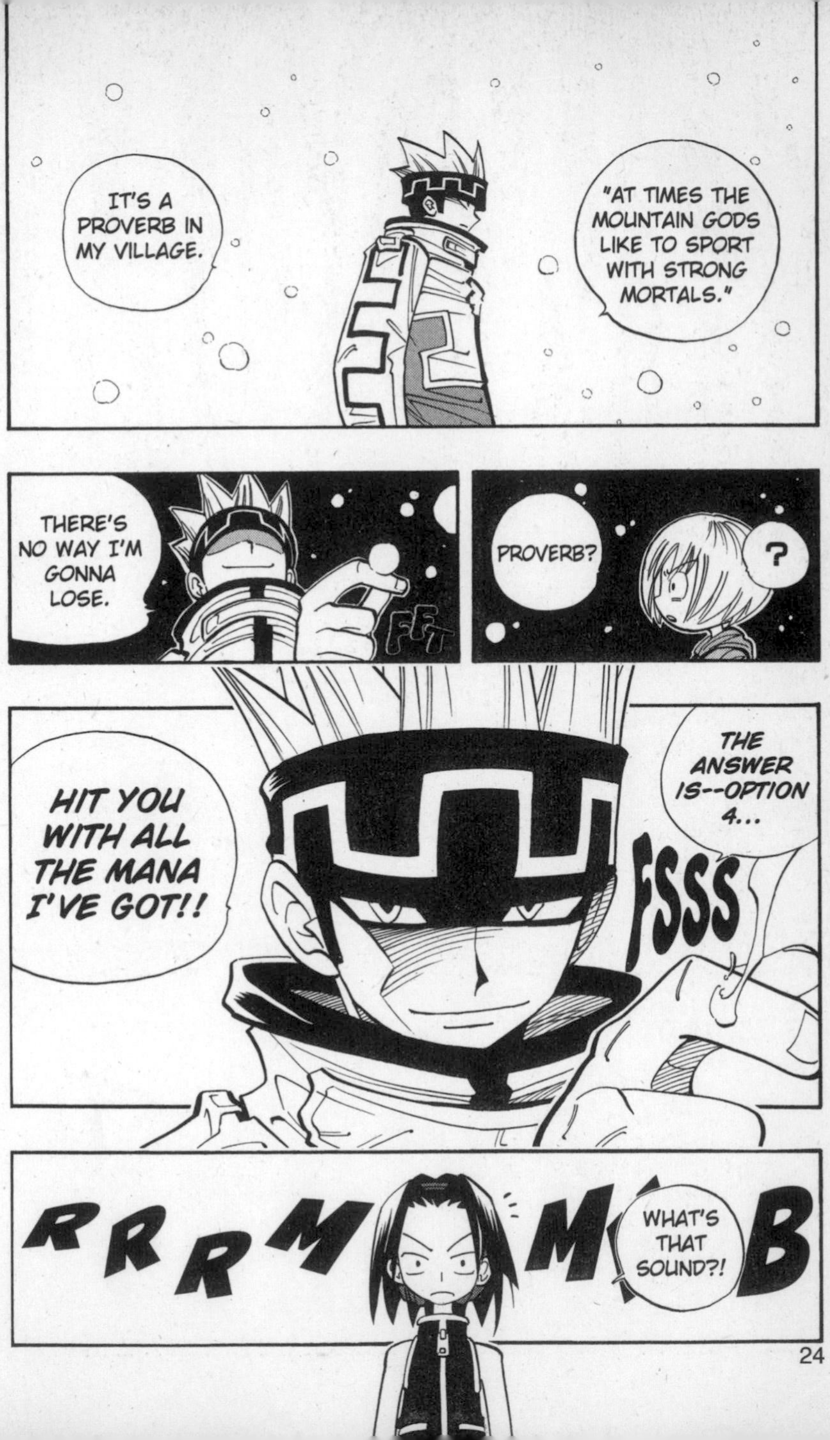
"AT TIMES THE MOUNTAIN GODS LIKE TO SPORT WITH STRONG MORTALS."
IT'S A PROVERB IN MY VILLAGE.
?
PROVERB?
FFT
THERE'S NO WAY I'M GONNA LOSE.
THE ANSWER IS--OPTION 4...
FSSS
HIT YOU WITH ALL THE MANA I'VE GOT!!
WHAT'S THAT SOUND?!
RRRM
M
B

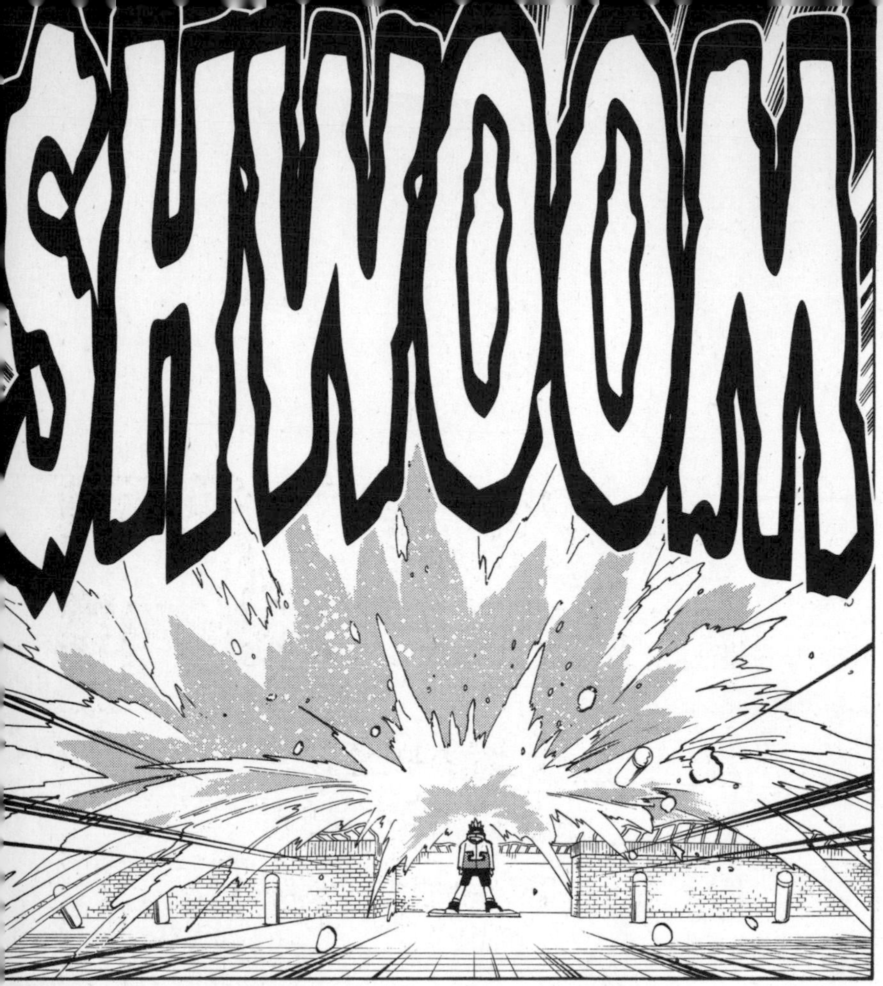
SHWOOM

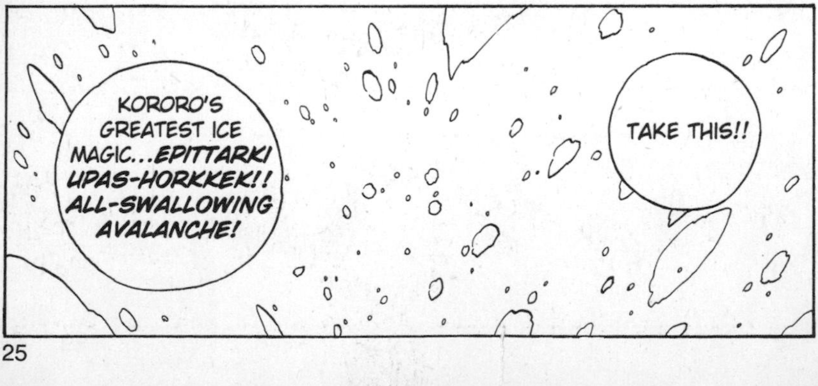
TAKE THIS!!
KORORO'S GREATEST ICE MAGIC...EPITTARKI UPAS-HORKKEK!! ALL-SWALLOWING AVALANCHE!

SHAMAN KING CHARACTER FILE No.20

ホロホロ

HOROHORO

1999
(AUG)

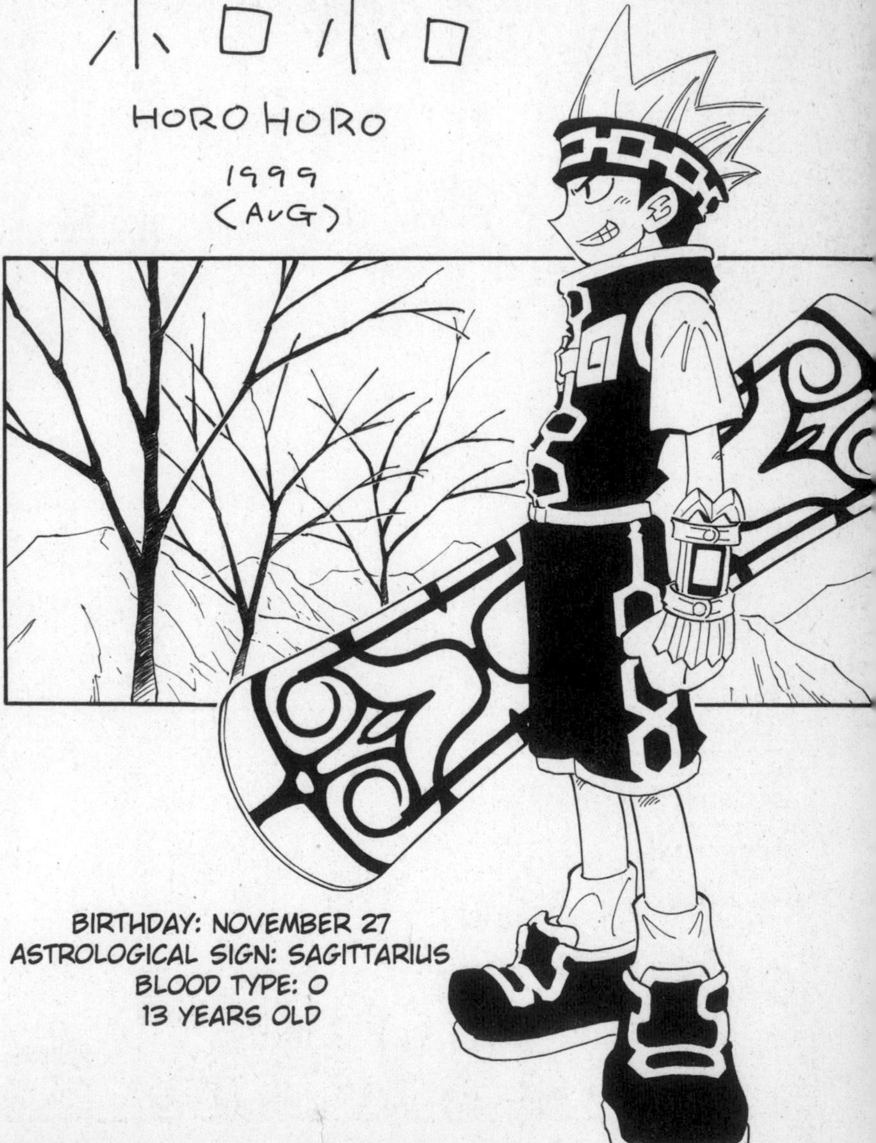

BIRTHDAY: NOVEMBER 27
ASTROLOGICAL SIGN: SAGITTARIUS
BLOOD TYPE: O
13 YEARS OLD

Reincarnation 37: Decision

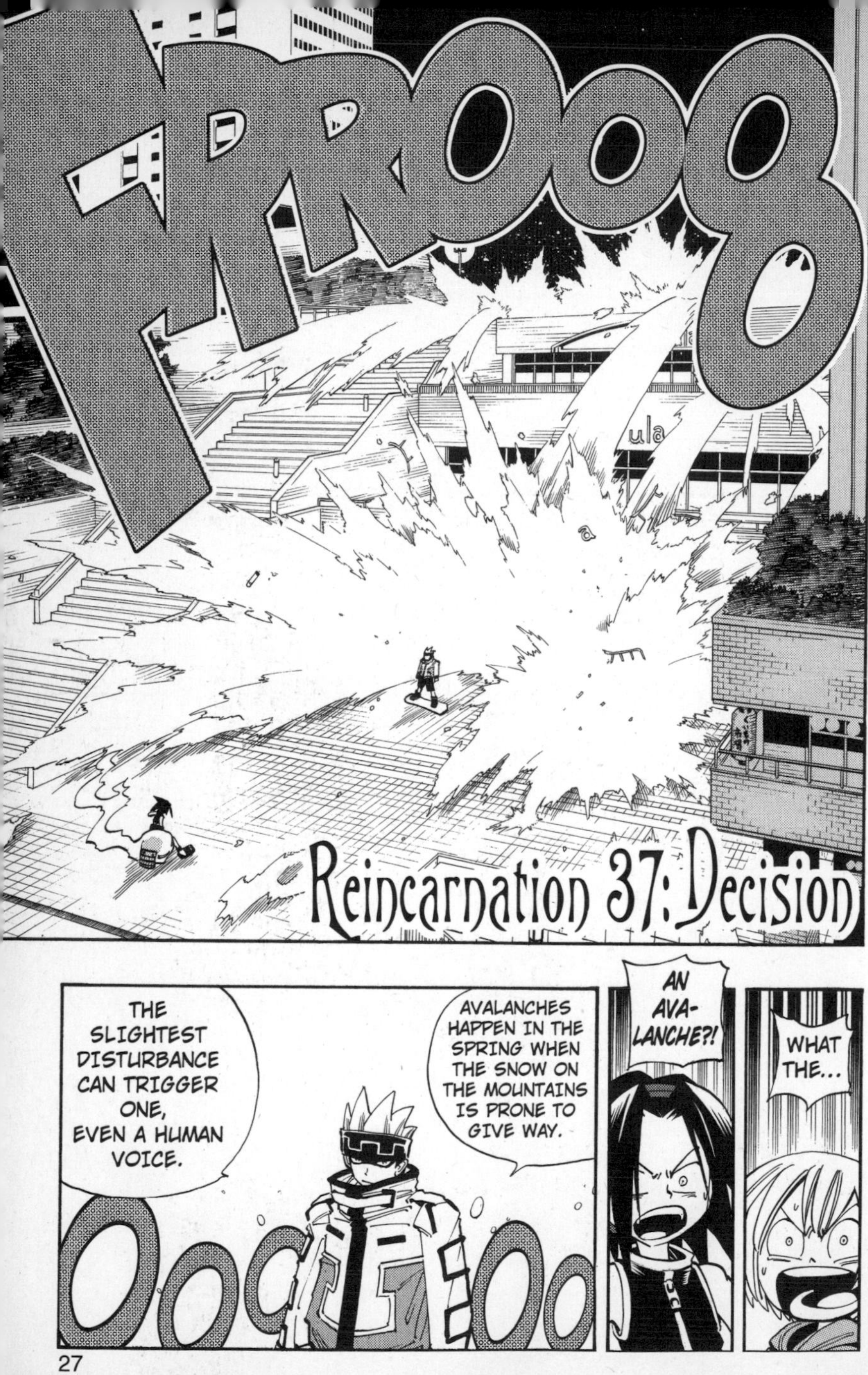

WHAT THE...
AN AVA-LANCHE?!
AVALANCHES HAPPEN IN THE SPRING WHEN THE SNOW ON THE MOUNTAINS IS PRONE TO GIVE WAY.
THE SLIGHTEST DISTURBANCE CAN TRIGGER ONE, EVEN A HUMAN VOICE.

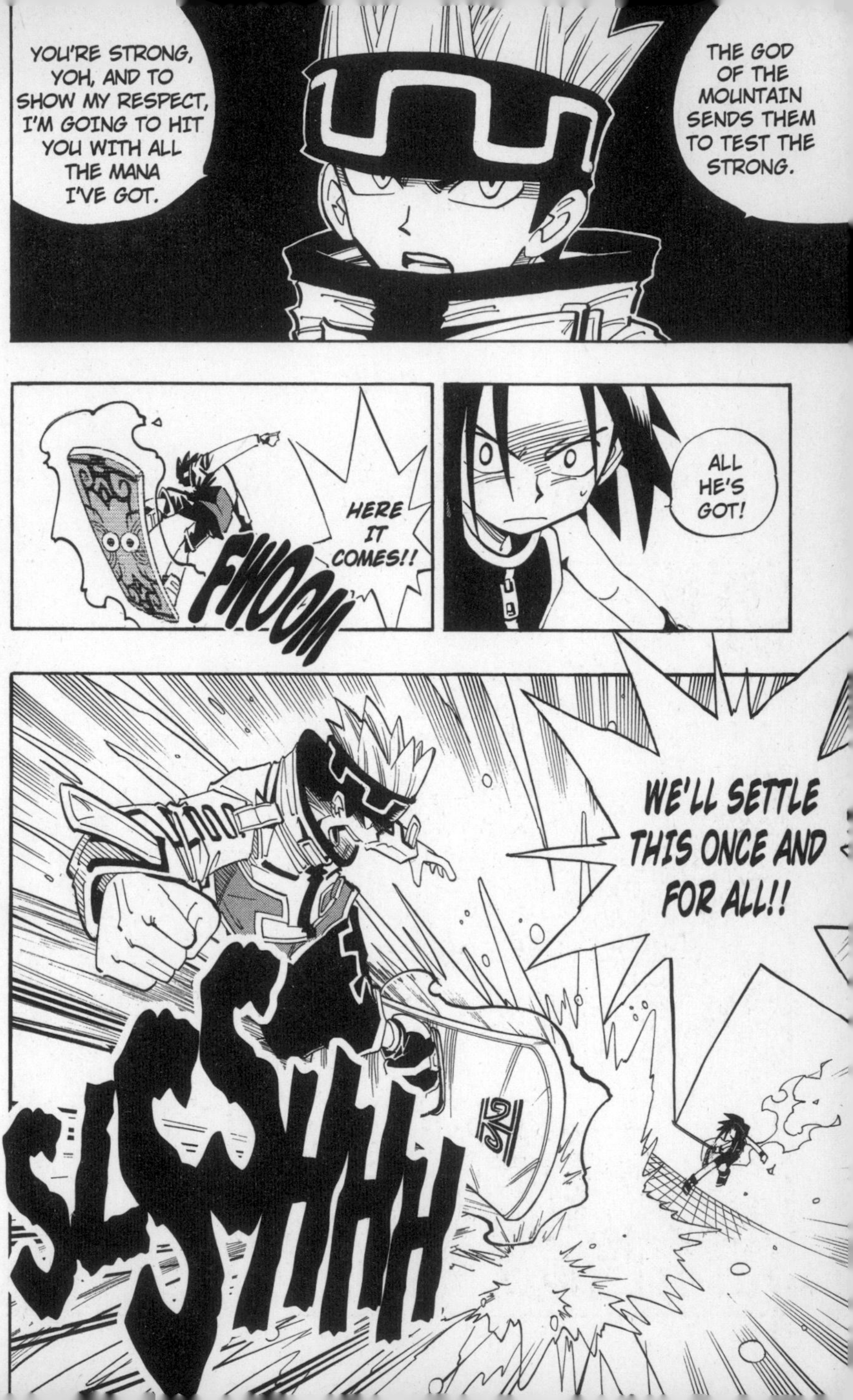
THE GOD OF THE MOUNTAIN SENDS THEM TO TEST THE STRONG.
YOU'RE STRONG, YOH, AND TO SHOW MY RESPECT, I'M GOING TO HIT YOU WITH ALL THE MANA I'VE GOT.
ALL HE'S GOT!
HERE IT COMES!!
FWOOM
WE'LL SETTLE THIS ONCE AND FOR ALL!!
SLSHHH

Reincarnation 37: Decision

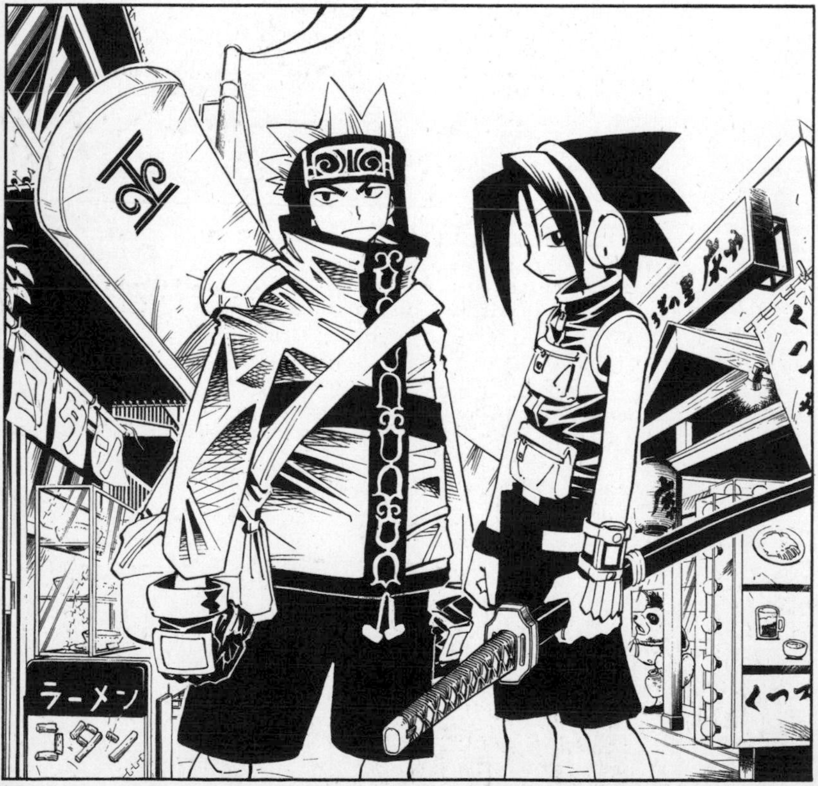
ラーメン
コタン

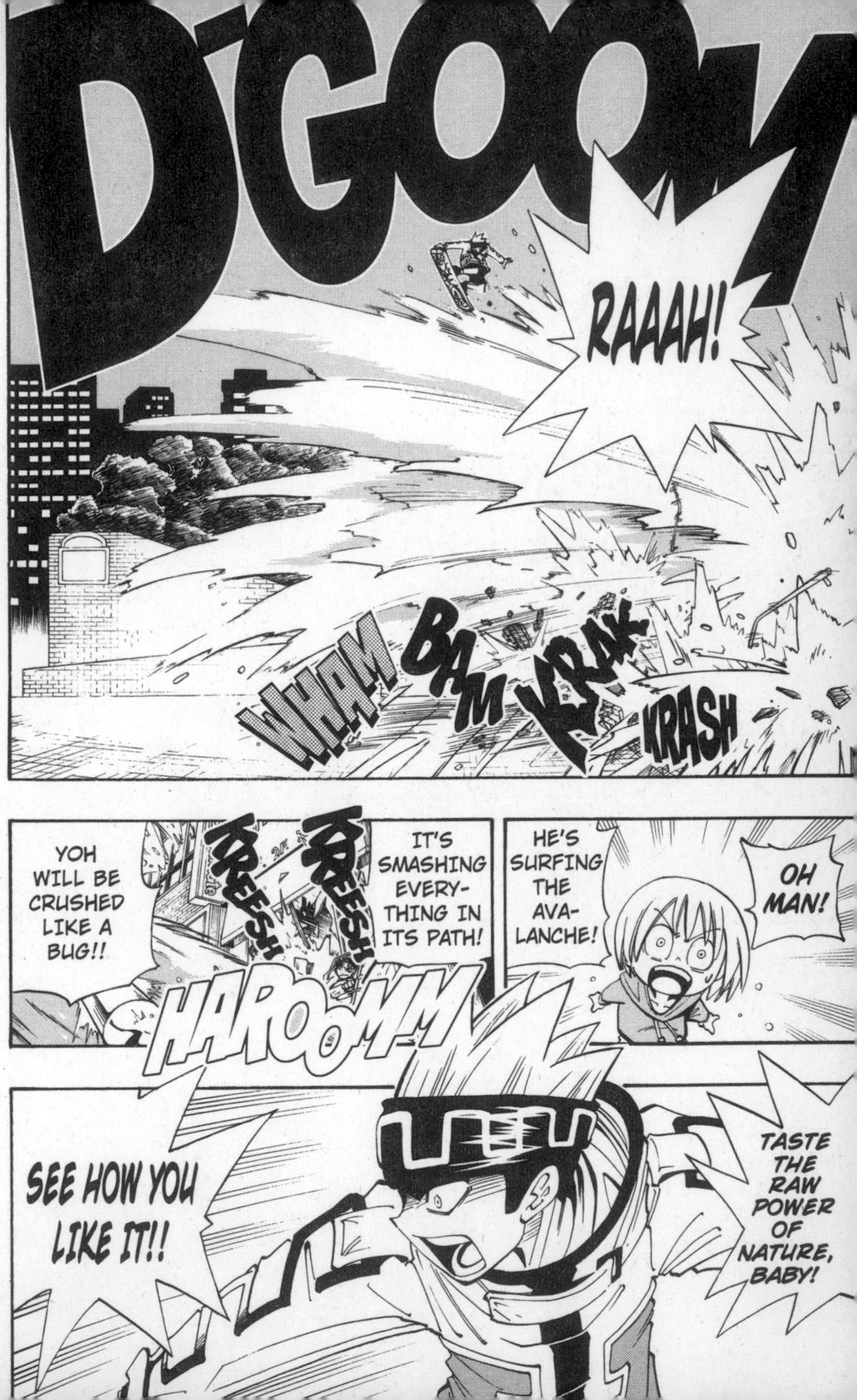
D'GOOM
RAAAH!
WHAM
BAM
KRAK
KRASH
OH MAN!
HE'S SURFING THE AVA-LANCHE!
IT'S SMASHING EVERY-THING IN ITS PATH!
KREESH
KREESH
YOH WILL BE CRUSHED LIKE A BUG!!
HAROOMM
TASTE THE RAW POWER OF NATURE, BABY!
SEE HOW YOU LIKE IT!!

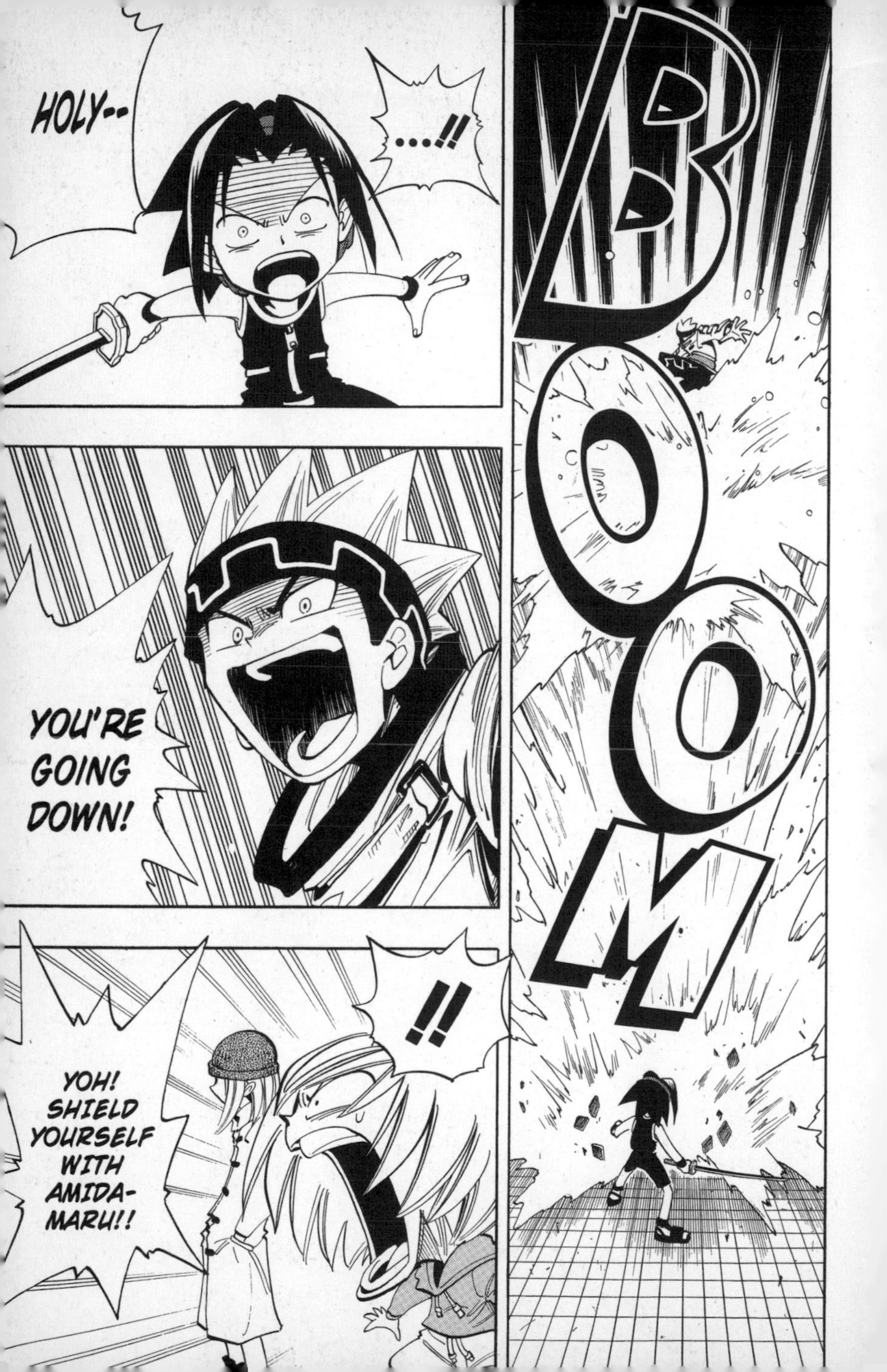
BOOM
....!!
HOLY--
YOU'RE GOING DOWN!
!!
YOH! SHIELD YOURSELF WITH AMIDA-MARU!!

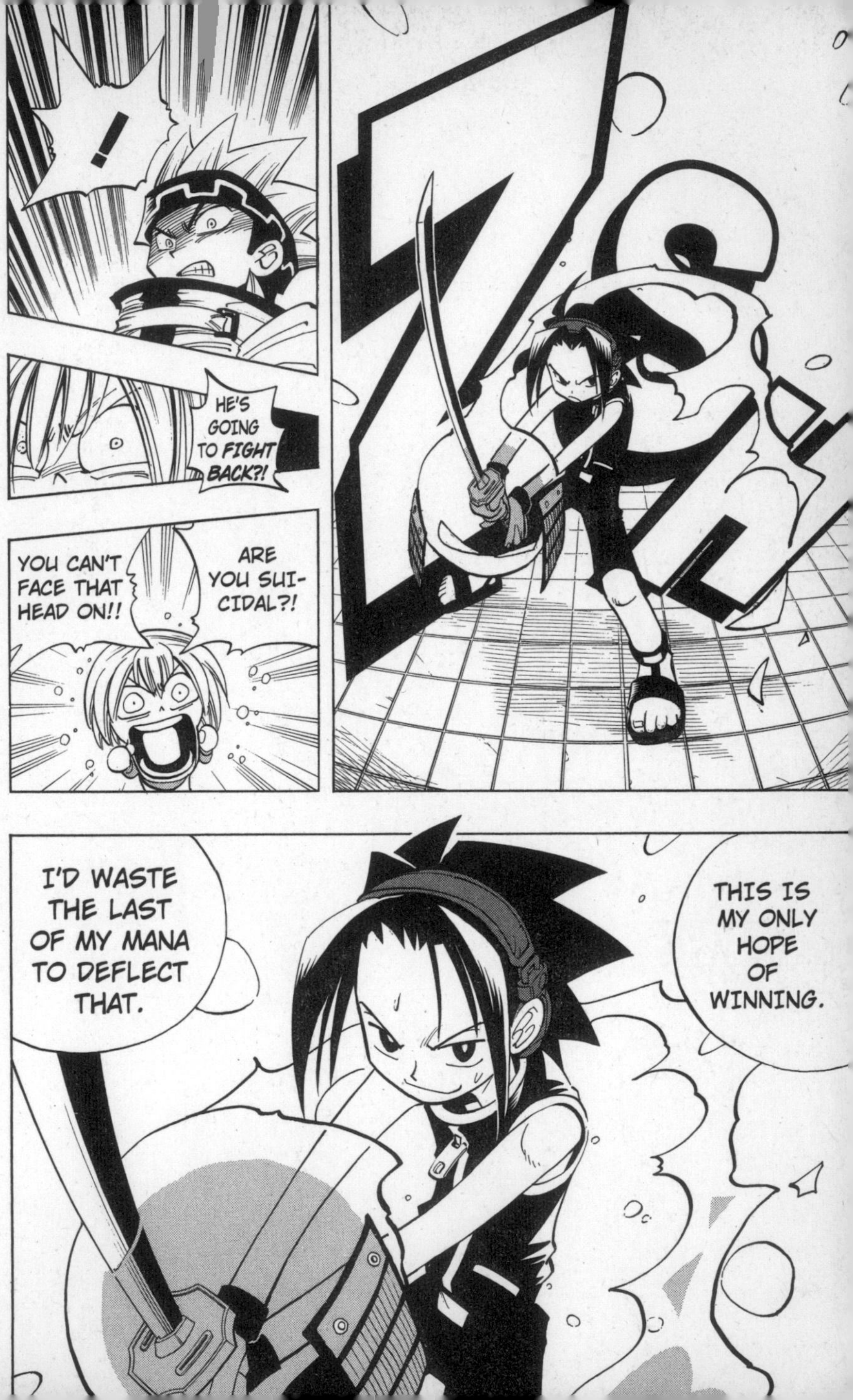
!
HE'S GOING TO FIGHT BACK?!
ARE YOU SUI-CIDAL?!
YOU CAN'T FACE THAT HEAD ON!!
THIS IS MY ONLY HOPE OF WINNING.
I'D WASTE THE LAST OF MY MANA TO DEFLECT THAT.

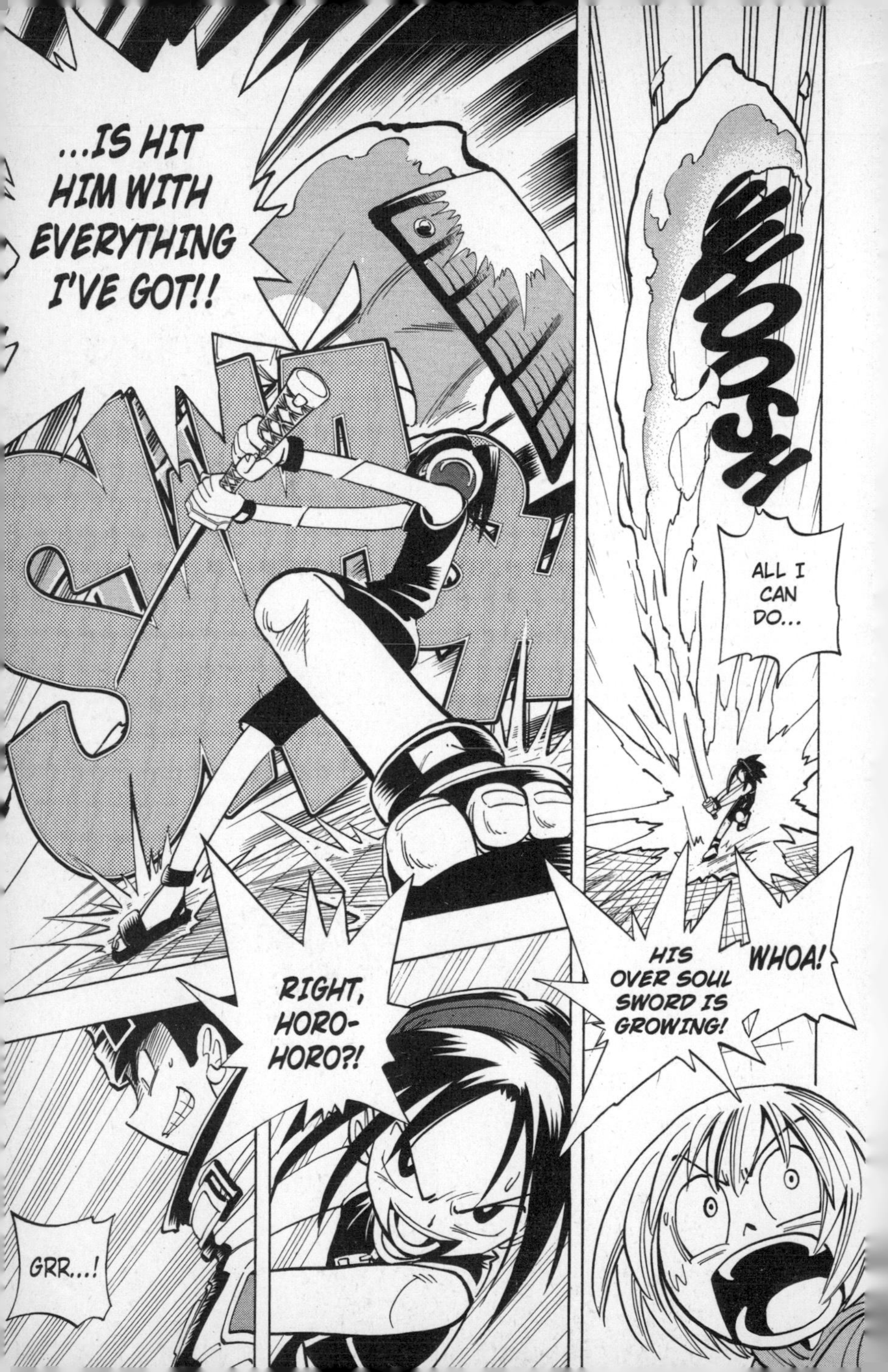
WHOOSH
ALL I CAN DO...
...IS HIT HIM WITH EVERYTHING I'VE GOT!!
WHOA!
HIS OVER SOUL SWORD IS GROWING!
RIGHT, HORO-HORO?!
GRR...!

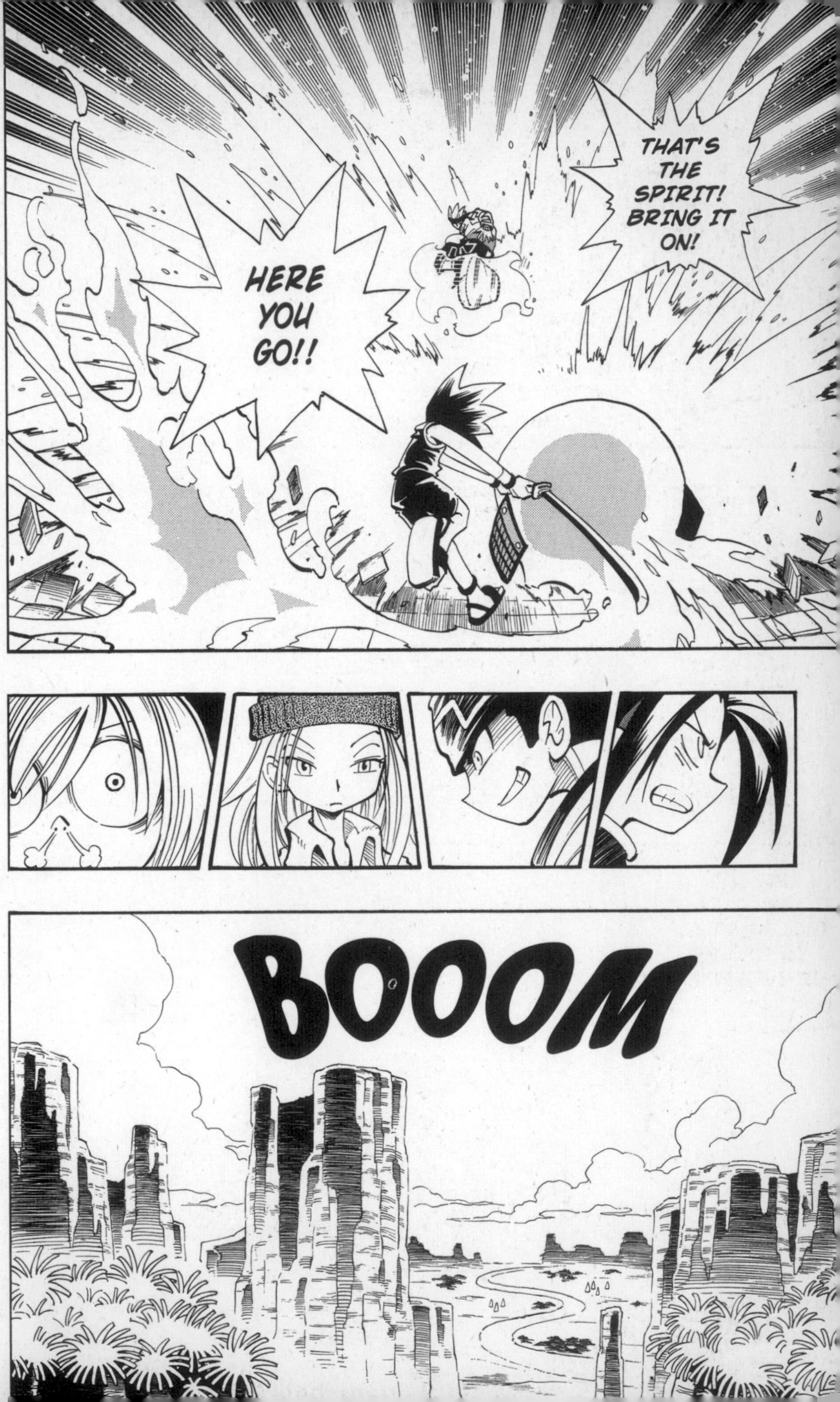
THAT'S THE SPIRIT! BRING IT ON!
HERE YOU GO!!
BOOOM

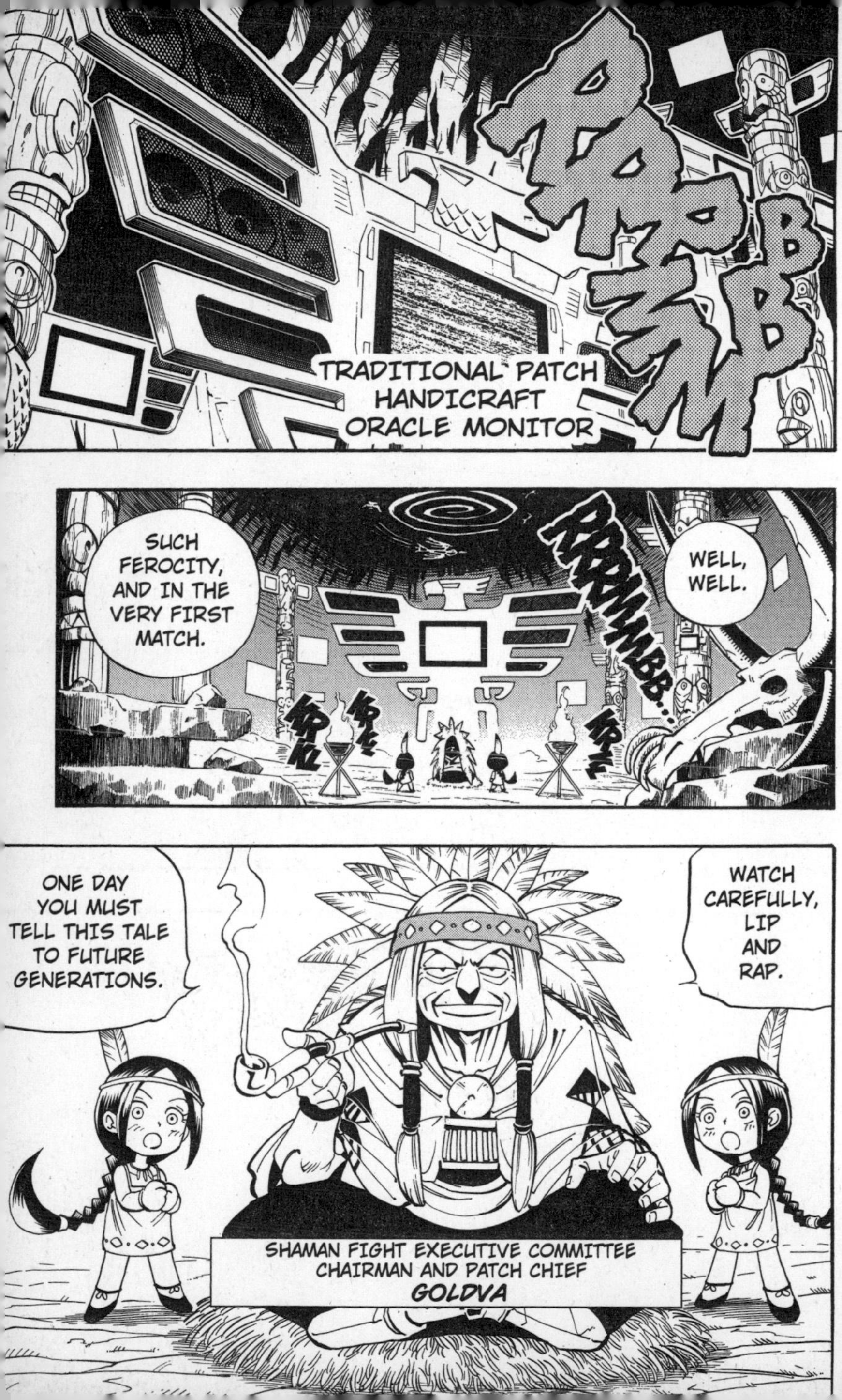
TRADITIONAL PATCH HANDICRAFT ORACLE MONITOR
WELL, WELL.
SUCH FEROCITY, AND IN THE VERY FIRST MATCH.
WATCH CAREFULLY, LIP AND RAP.
ONE DAY YOU MUST TELL THIS TALE TO FUTURE GENERATIONS.
SHAMAN FIGHT EXECUTIVE COMMITTEE CHAIRMAN AND PATCH CHIEF
GOLDVA

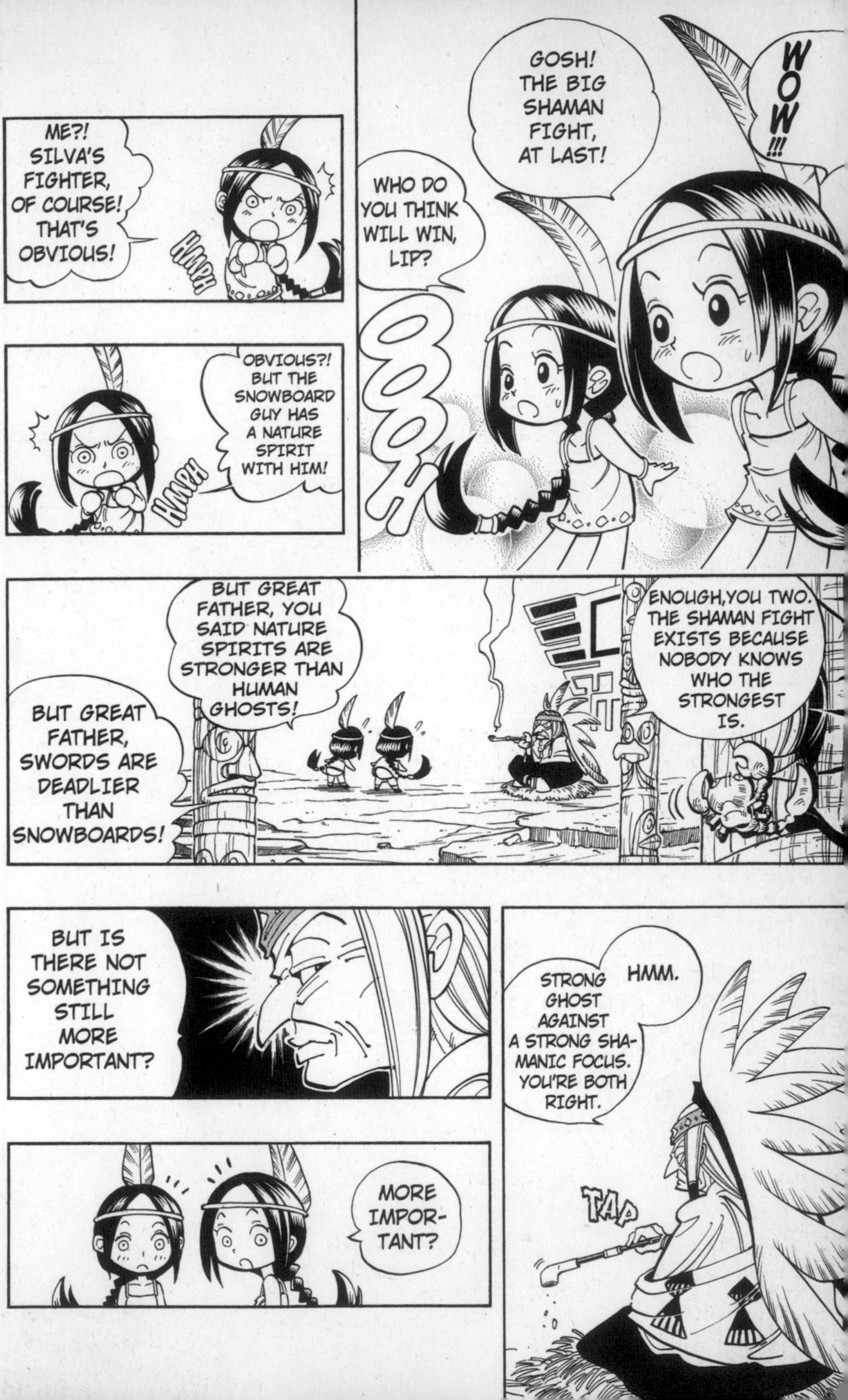
WOW!!!
GOSH! THE BIG SHAMAN FIGHT, AT LAST!
WHO DO YOU THINK WILL WIN, LIP?
OOOH
ME?! SILVA'S FIGHTER, OF COURSE! THAT'S OBVIOUS!
HMPH
OBVIOUS?! BUT THE SNOWBOARD GUY HAS A NATURE SPIRIT WITH HIM!
HMPH
ENOUGH,YOU TWO. THE SHAMAN FIGHT EXISTS BECAUSE NOBODY KNOWS WHO THE STRONGEST IS.
BUT GREAT FATHER, YOU SAID NATURE SPIRITS ARE STRONGER THAN HUMAN GHOSTS!
BUT GREAT FATHER, SWORDS ARE DEADLIER THAN SNOWBOARDS!
HMM.
STRONG GHOST AGAINST A STRONG SHA-MANIC FOCUS. YOU'RE BOTH RIGHT.
TAP
BUT IS THERE NOT SOMETHING STILL MORE IMPORTANT?
MORE IMPOR-TANT?

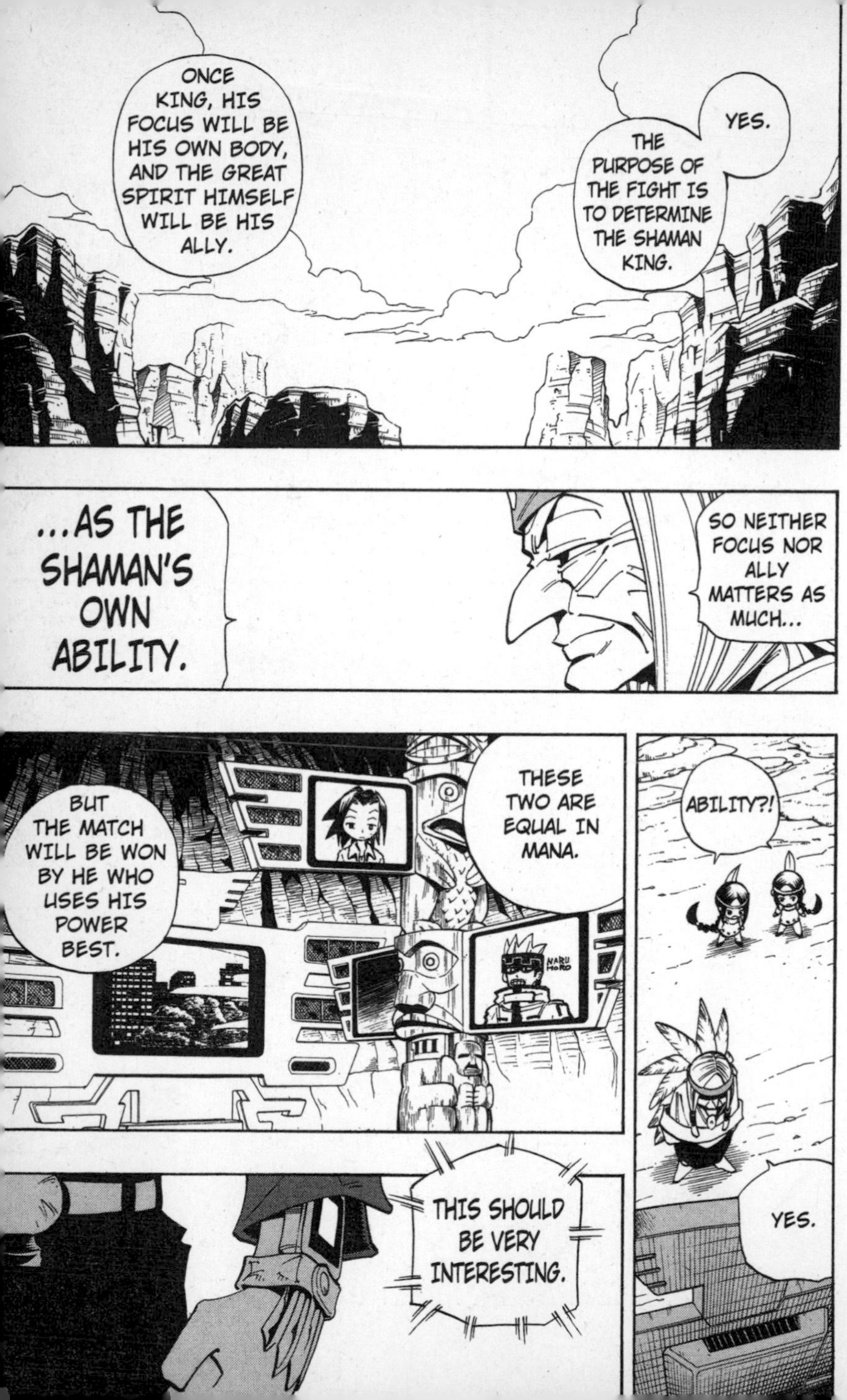
YES.
THE PURPOSE OF THE FIGHT IS TO DETERMINE THE SHAMAN KING.
ONCE KING, HIS FOCUS WILL BE HIS OWN BODY, AND THE GREAT SPIRIT HIMSELF WILL BE HIS ALLY.
SO NEITHER FOCUS NOR ALLY MATTERS AS MUCH...
...AS THE SHAMAN'S OWN ABILITY.
ABILITY?!
YES.
THESE TWO ARE EQUAL IN MANA.
BUT THE MATCH WILL BE WON BY HE WHO USES HIS POWER BEST.
NARU HORO
THIS SHOULD BE VERY INTERESTING.

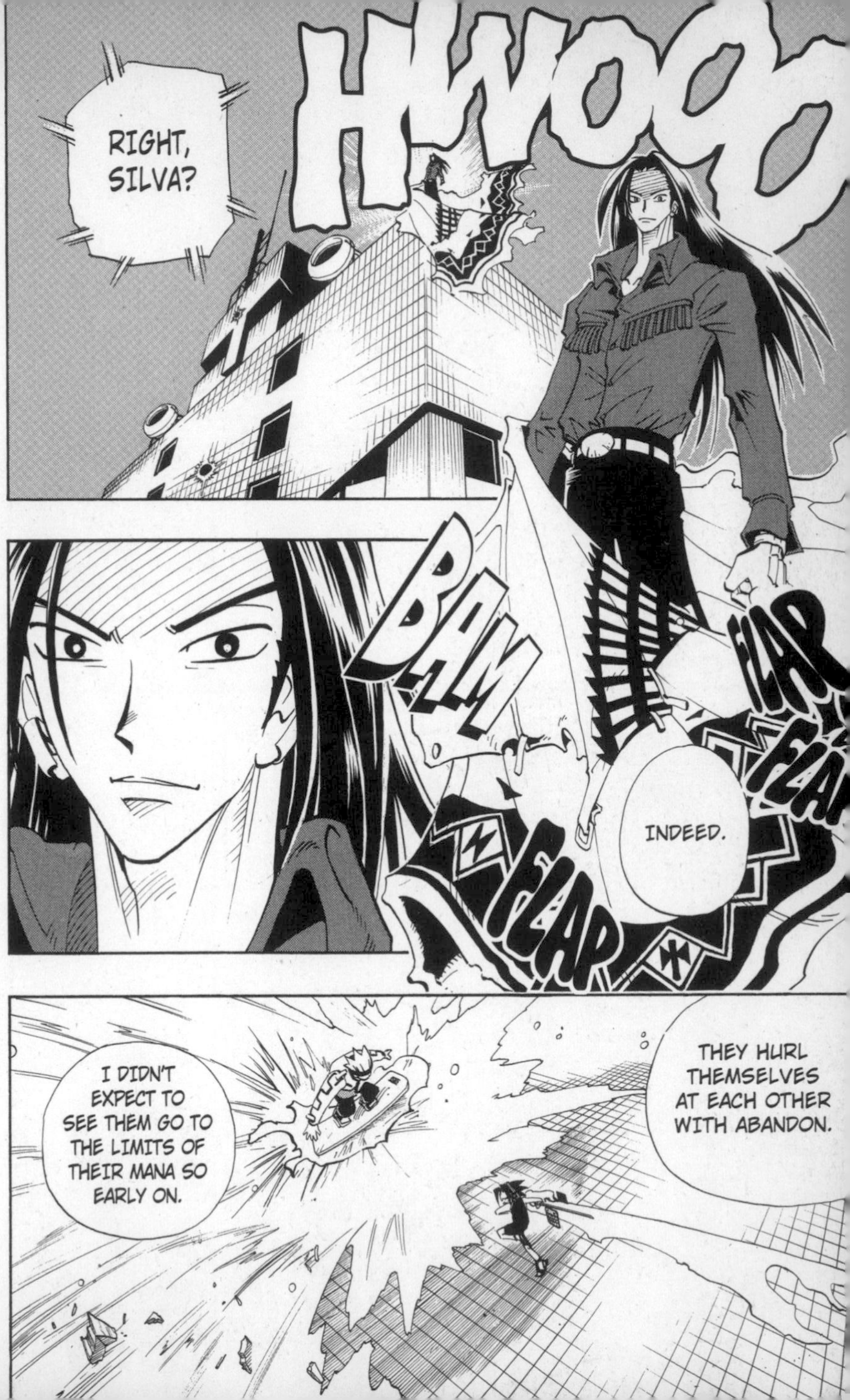
HWOOO
RIGHT, SILVA?
BAM
FLAP FLAP
FLAP
INDEED.
THEY HURL THEMSELVES AT EACH OTHER WITH ABANDON.
I DIDN'T EXPECT TO SEE THEM GO TO THE LIMITS OF THEIR MANA SO EARLY ON.

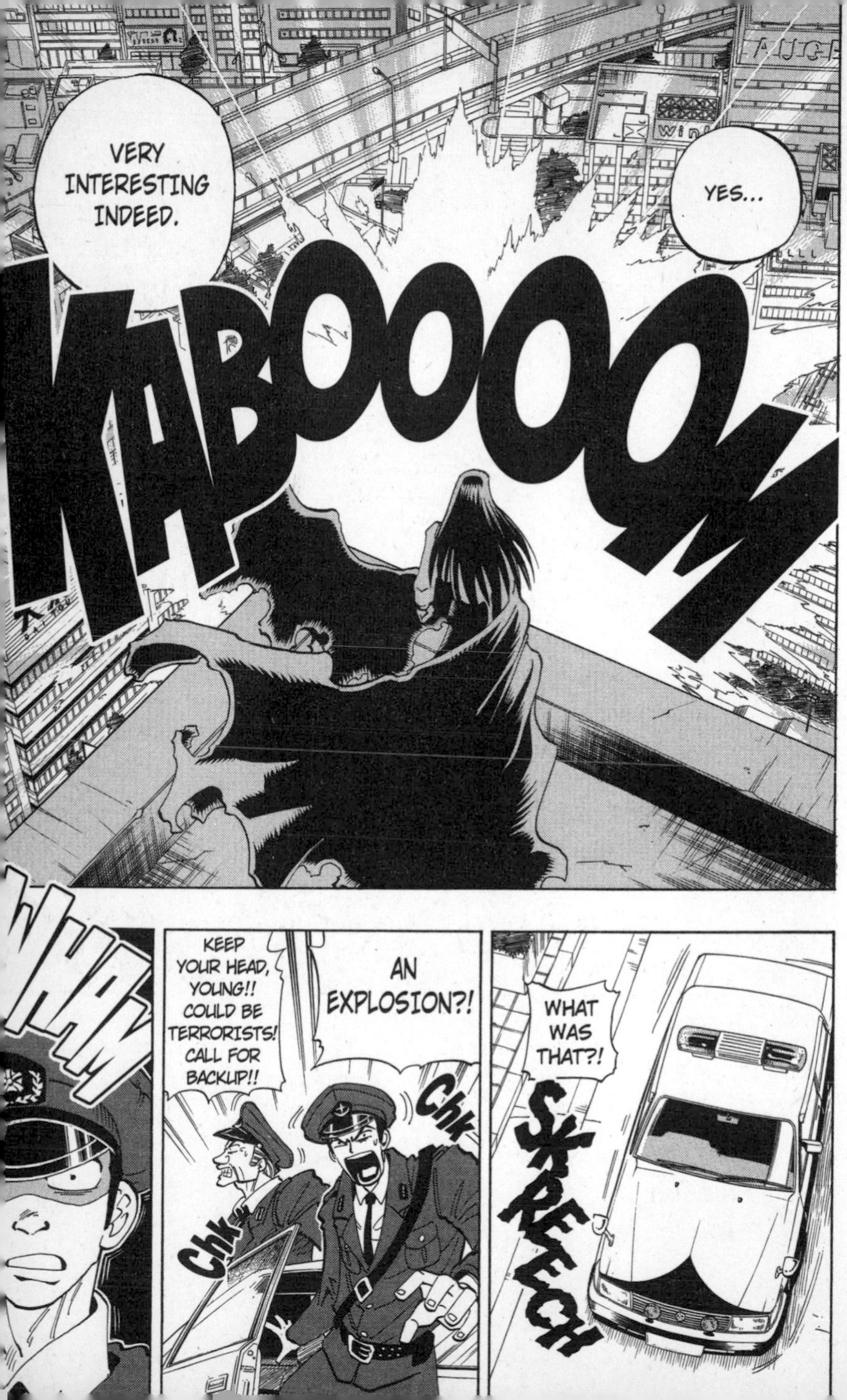
YES...
VERY INTERESTING INDEED.
KABOOOM
WHAT WAS THAT?!
SKREECH
AN EXPLOSION?!
KEEP YOUR HEAD, YOUNG!! COULD BE TERRORISTS! CALL FOR BACKUP!!
Chk
Chk
WHAM

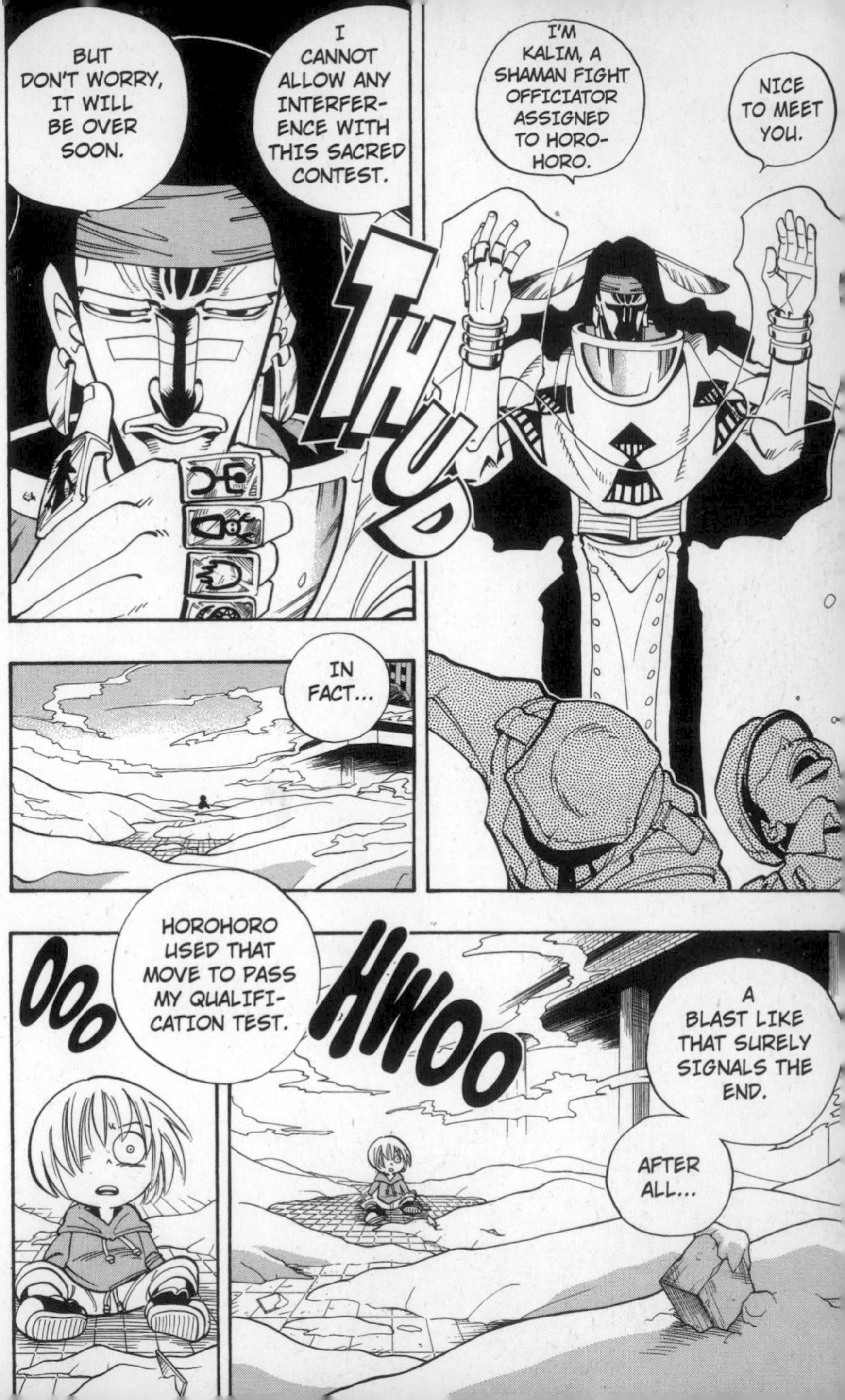
NICE TO MEET YOU.
I'M KALIM, A SHAMAN FIGHT OFFICIATOR ASSIGNED TO HORO-HORO.
I CANNOT ALLOW ANY INTERFER-ENCE WITH THIS SACRED CONTEST.
BUT DON'T WORRY, IT WILL BE OVER SOON.
THUD
IN FACT...
A BLAST LIKE THAT SURELY SIGNALS THE END.
AFTER ALL...
HWOO
HOROHORO USED THAT MOVE TO PASS MY QUALIFI-CATION TEST.
OOO

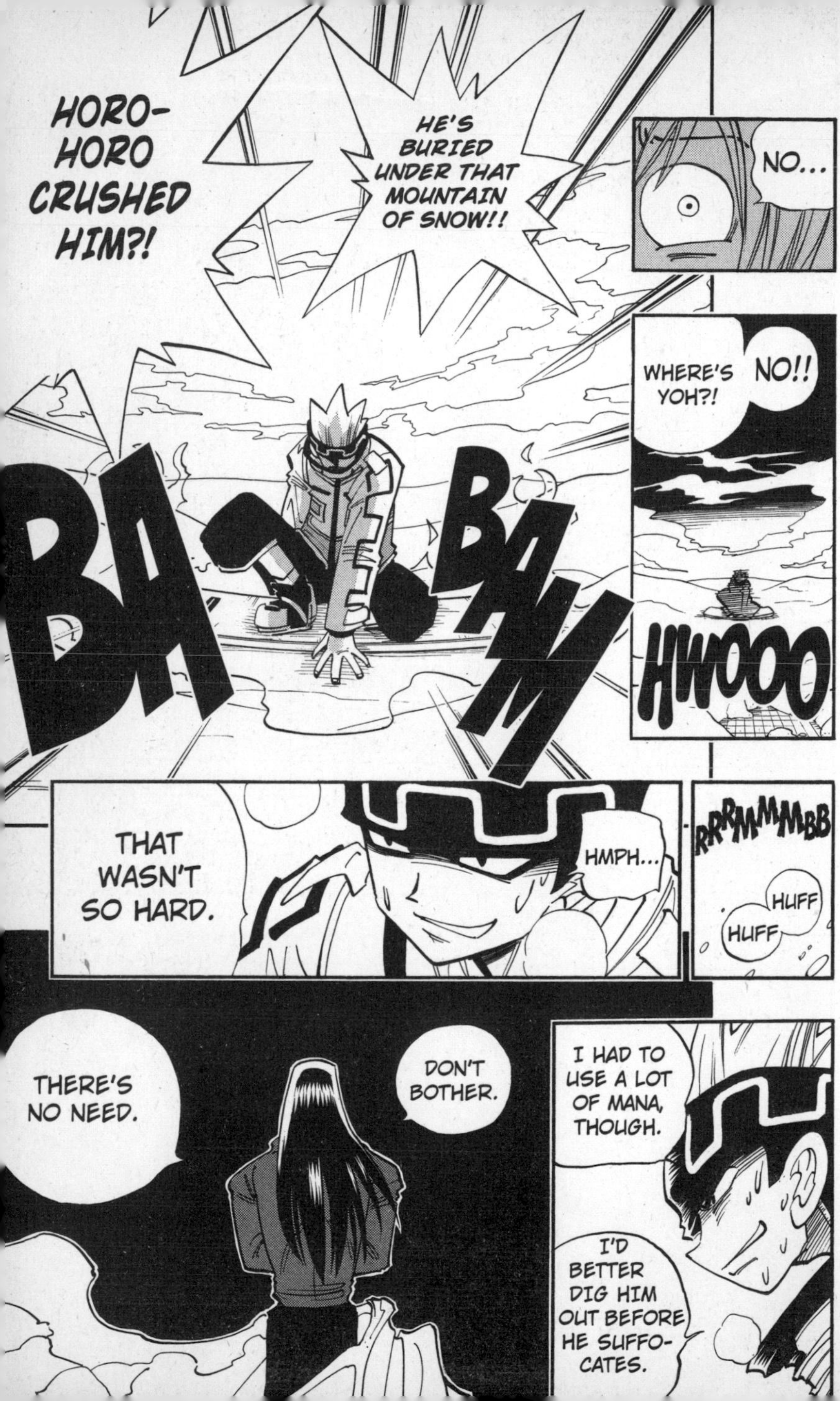
NO...
NO!!
WHERE'S YOH?!
HWOOO
HE'S BURIED UNDER THAT MOUNTAIN OF SNOW!!
HORO-HORO CRUSHED HIM?!
BABAM
RRRMMMBB
HUFF
HUFF
HMPH...
THAT WASN'T SO HARD.
I HAD TO USE A LOT OF MANA, THOUGH.
I'D BETTER DIG HIM OUT BEFORE HE SUFFOCATES.
DON'T BOTHER.
THERE'S NO NEED.

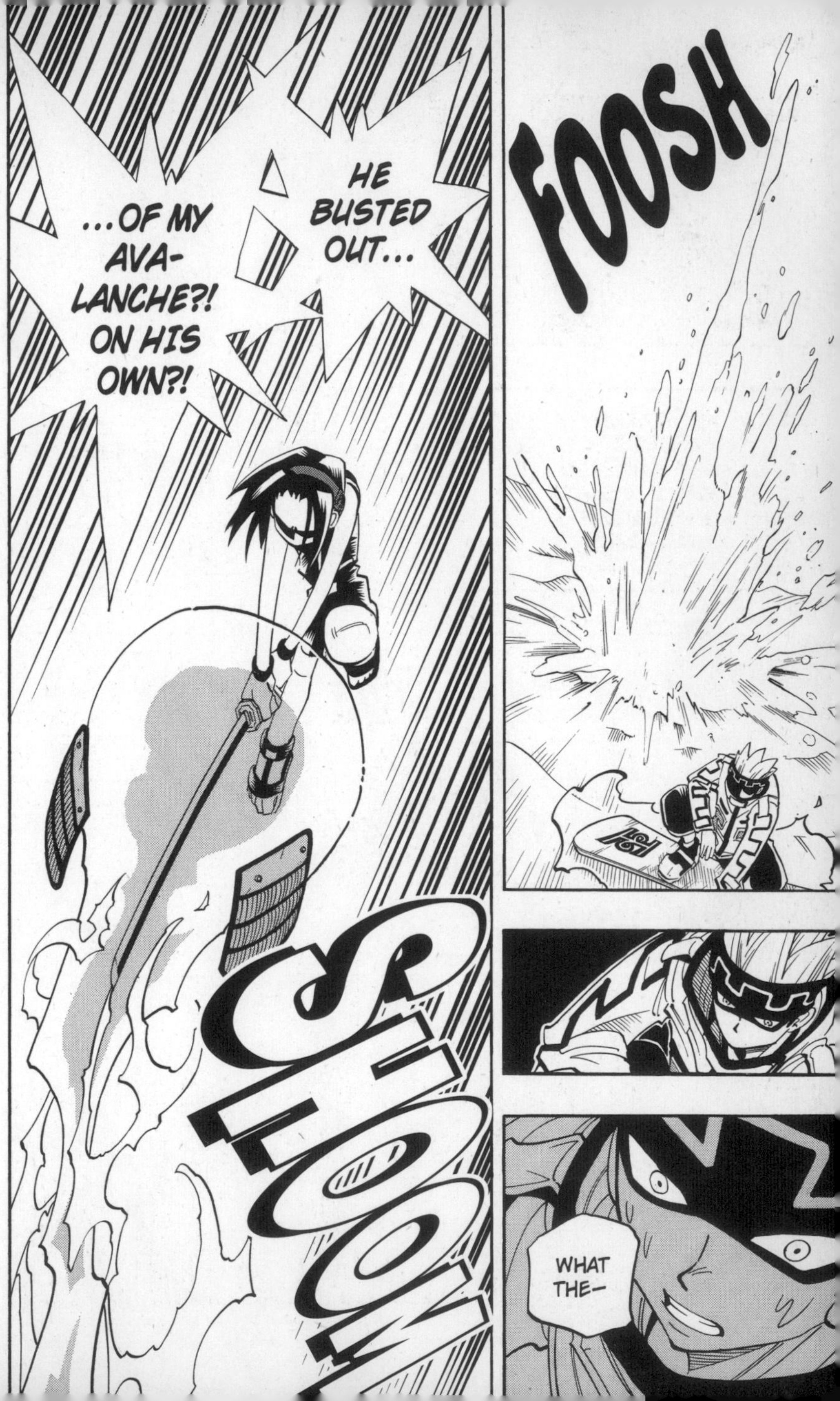
FOOSH
WHAT THE—
HE BUSTED OUT...
...OF MY AVA-LANCHE?! ON HIS OWN?!
SHOOM!

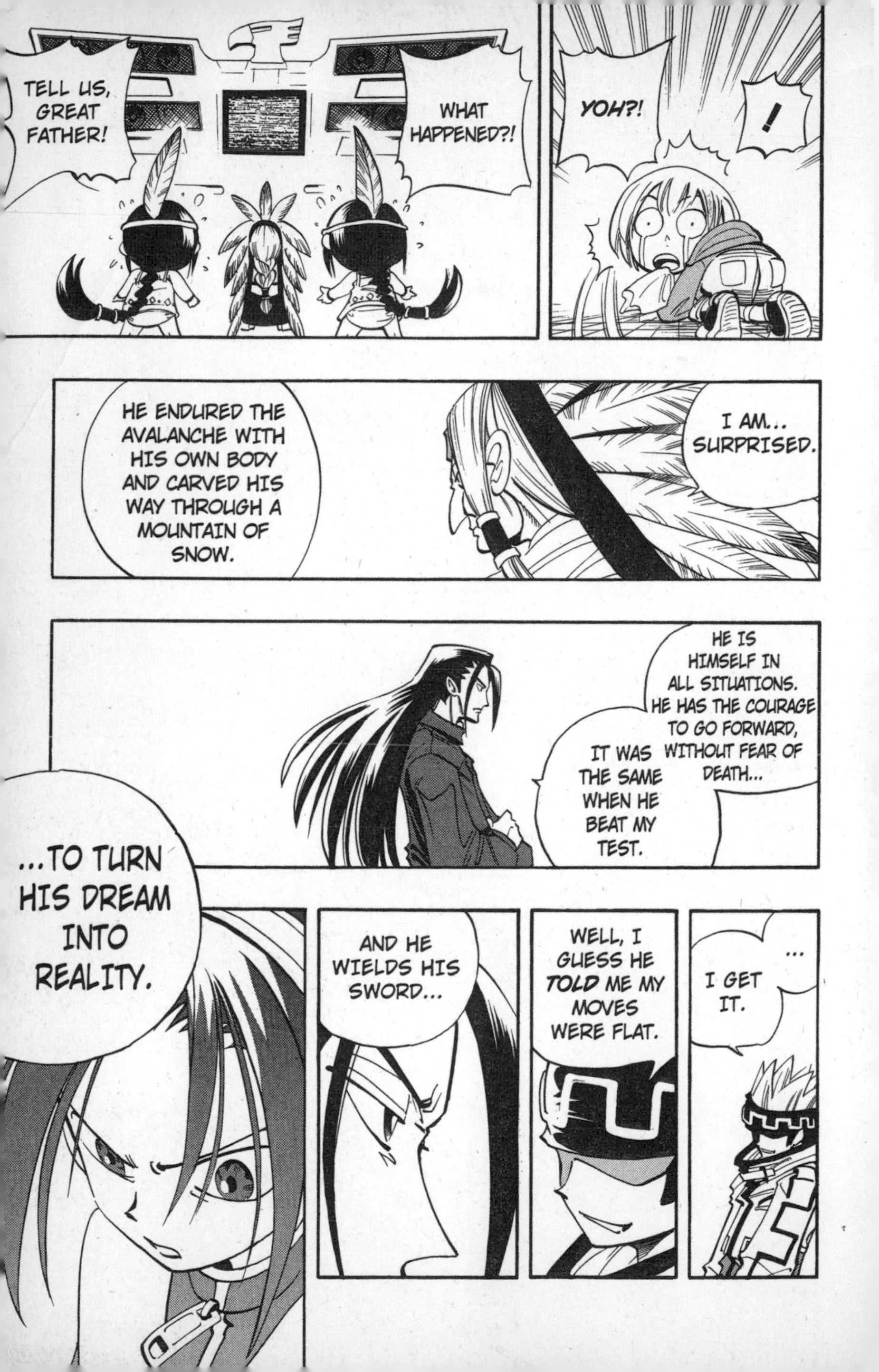
!
YOH?!
WHAT HAPPENED?!
TELL US, GREAT FATHER!
I AM... SURPRISED.
HE ENDURED THE AVALANCHE WITH HIS OWN BODY AND CARVED HIS WAY THROUGH A MOUNTAIN OF SNOW.
HE IS HIMSELF IN ALL SITUATIONS. HE HAS THE COURAGE TO GO FORWARD, WITHOUT FEAR OF DEATH...
IT WAS THE SAME WHEN HE BEAT MY TEST.
...
I GET IT.
WELL, I GUESS HE ***TOLD*** ME MY MOVES WERE FLAT.
AND HE WIELDS HIS SWORD...
...TO TURN HIS DREAM INTO REALITY.

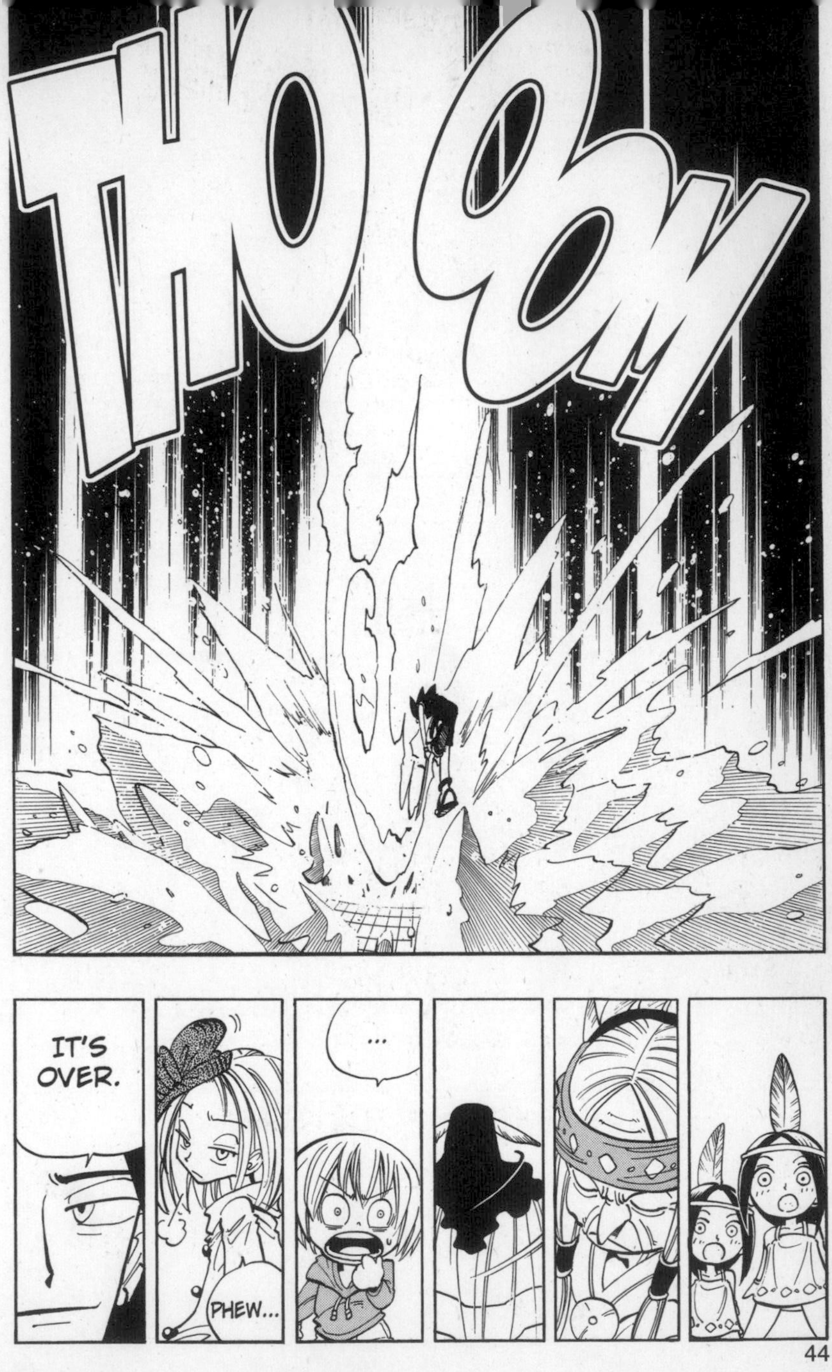
THOOM
...
PHEW...
IT'S OVER.

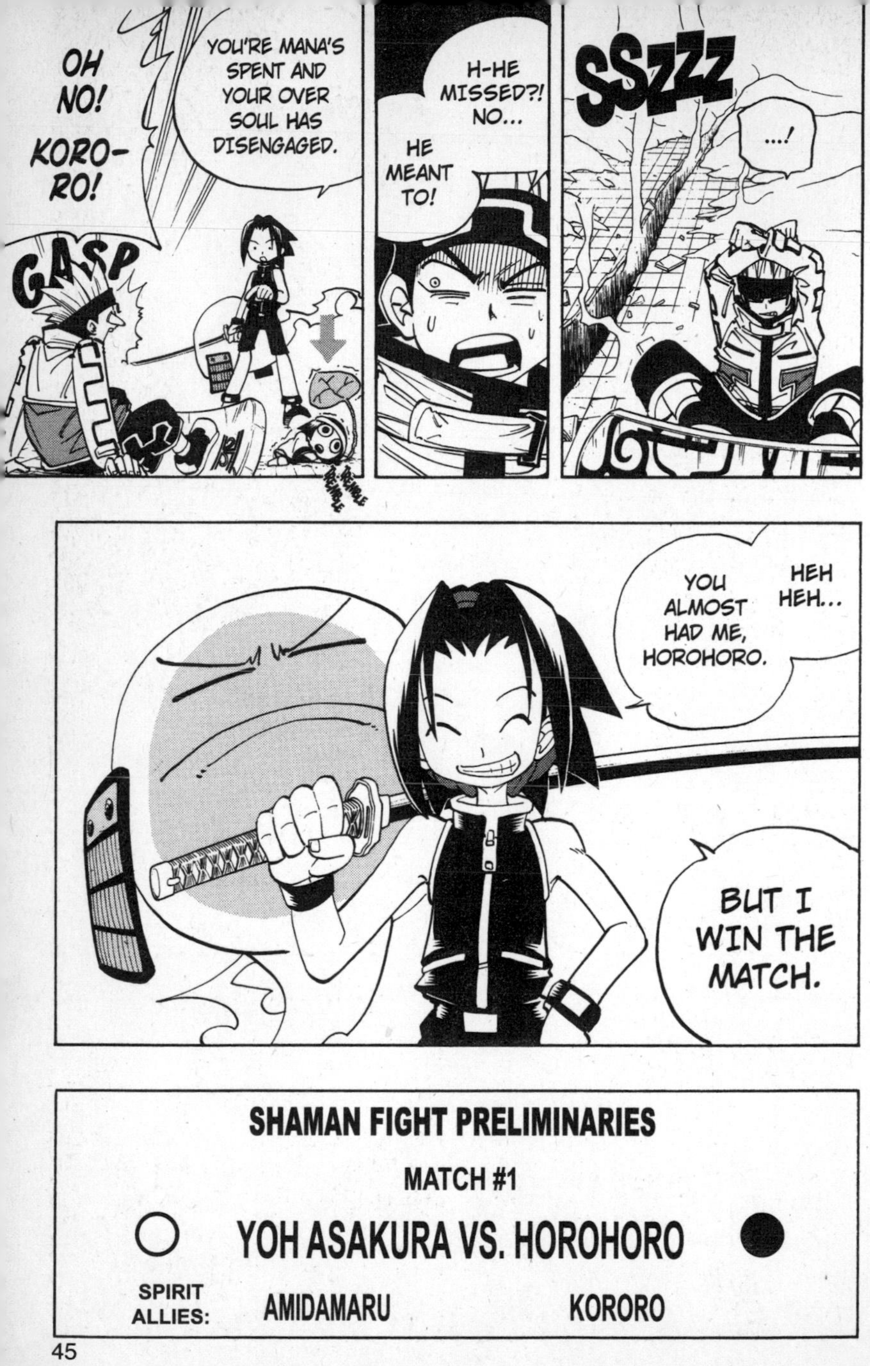
SSZZZ
....!
H-HE MISSED?! NO...
HE MEANT TO!
YOU'RE MANA'S SPENT AND YOUR OVER SOUL HAS DISENGAGED.
OH NO! KORORO!
GASP
TREMBLE TREMBLE
HEH HEH...
YOU ALMOST HAD ME, HOROHORO.
BUT I WIN THE MATCH.

SHAMAN FIGHT PRELIMINARIES

MATCH #1

○ **YOH ASAKURA VS. HOROHORO** ●

SPIRIT ALLIES:	**AMIDAMARU**	**KORORO**

SHAMAN
KING
5

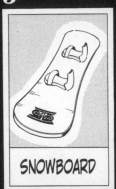

SNOWBOARD

Reincarnation 38: A Hot Bath and a Starry Sky

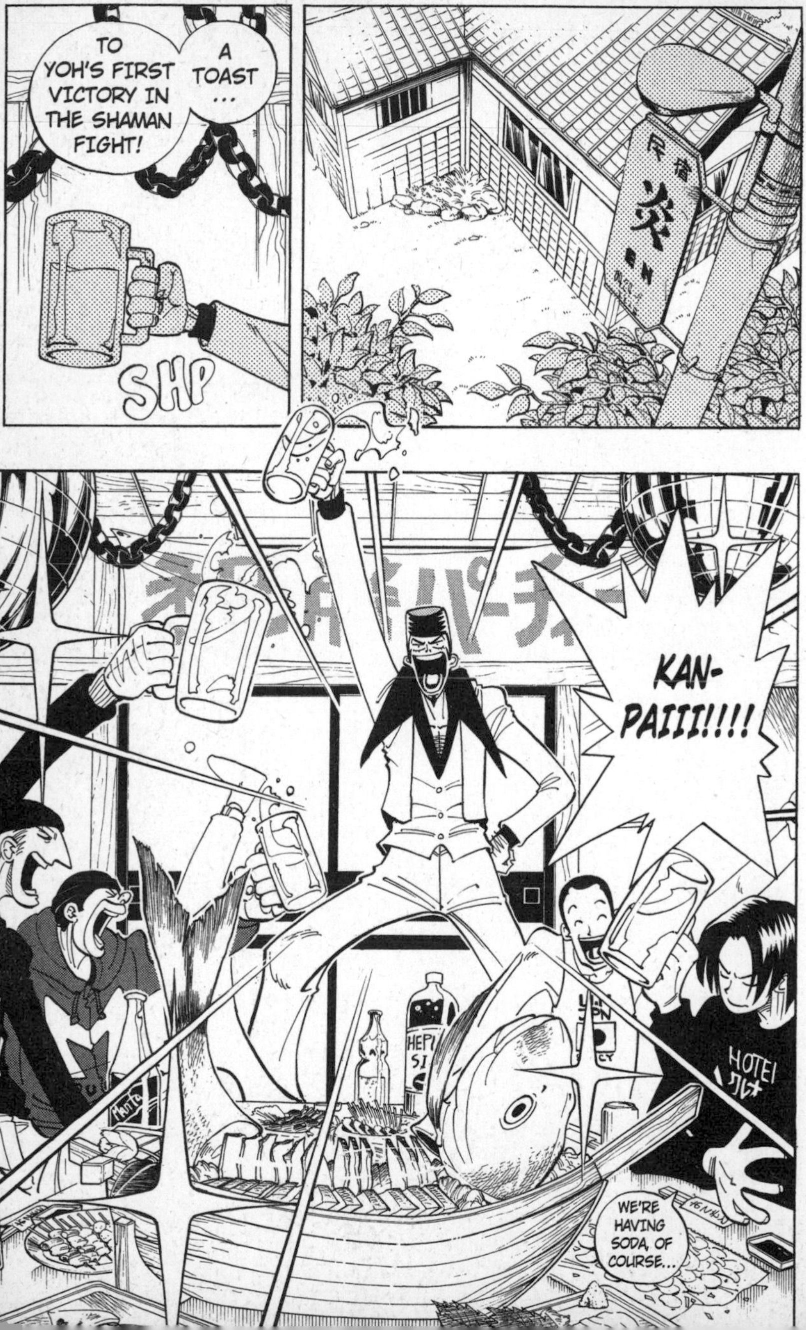

A TOAST...
TO YOH'S FIRST VICTORY IN THE SHAMAN FIGHT!
SHP
KAN-PAIII!!!!
WE'RE HAVING SODA, OF COURSE...

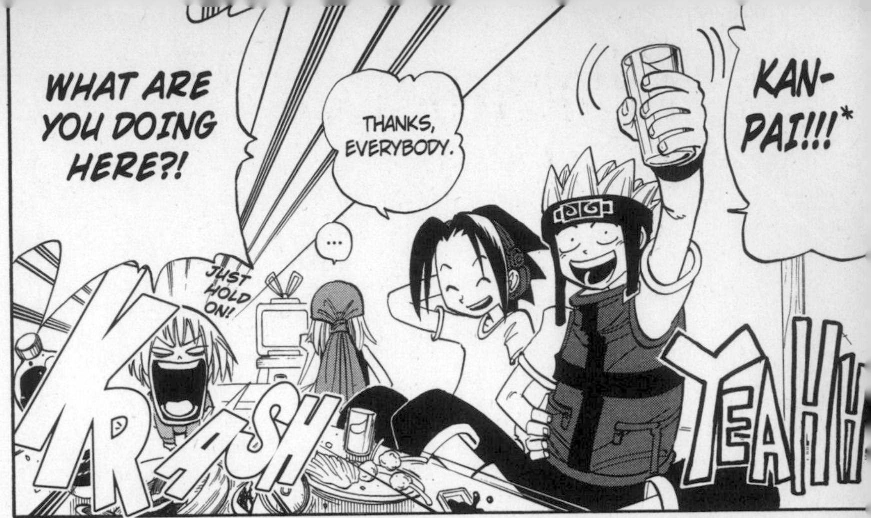
KAN-PAI!!!*
YEAHH
THANKS, EVERYBODY.
WHAT ARE YOU DOING HERE?!
...
JUST HOLD ON!
KRASH

*"KANPAI" IS WHAT YOU SAY WHEN YOU DRINK A TOAST IN JAPANESE.

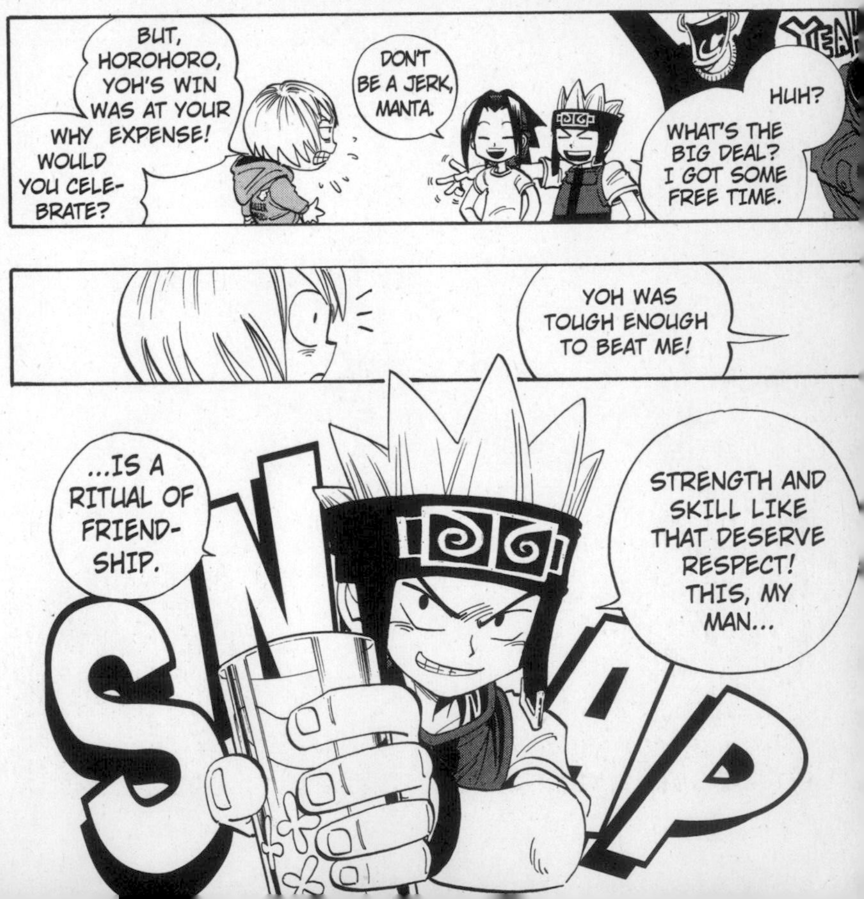
YEAH
HUH? WHAT'S THE BIG DEAL? I GOT SOME FREE TIME.
DON'T BE A JERK, MANTA.
BUT, HOROHORO, YOH'S WIN WAS AT YOUR EXPENSE! WHY WOULD YOU CELEBRATE?
YOH WAS TOUGH ENOUGH TO BEAT ME!
STRENGTH AND SKILL LIKE THAT DESERVE RESPECT! THIS, MY MAN...
...IS A RITUAL OF FRIENDSHIP.
SNAP

Reincarnation 38:
A Hot Bath and a Starry Sky

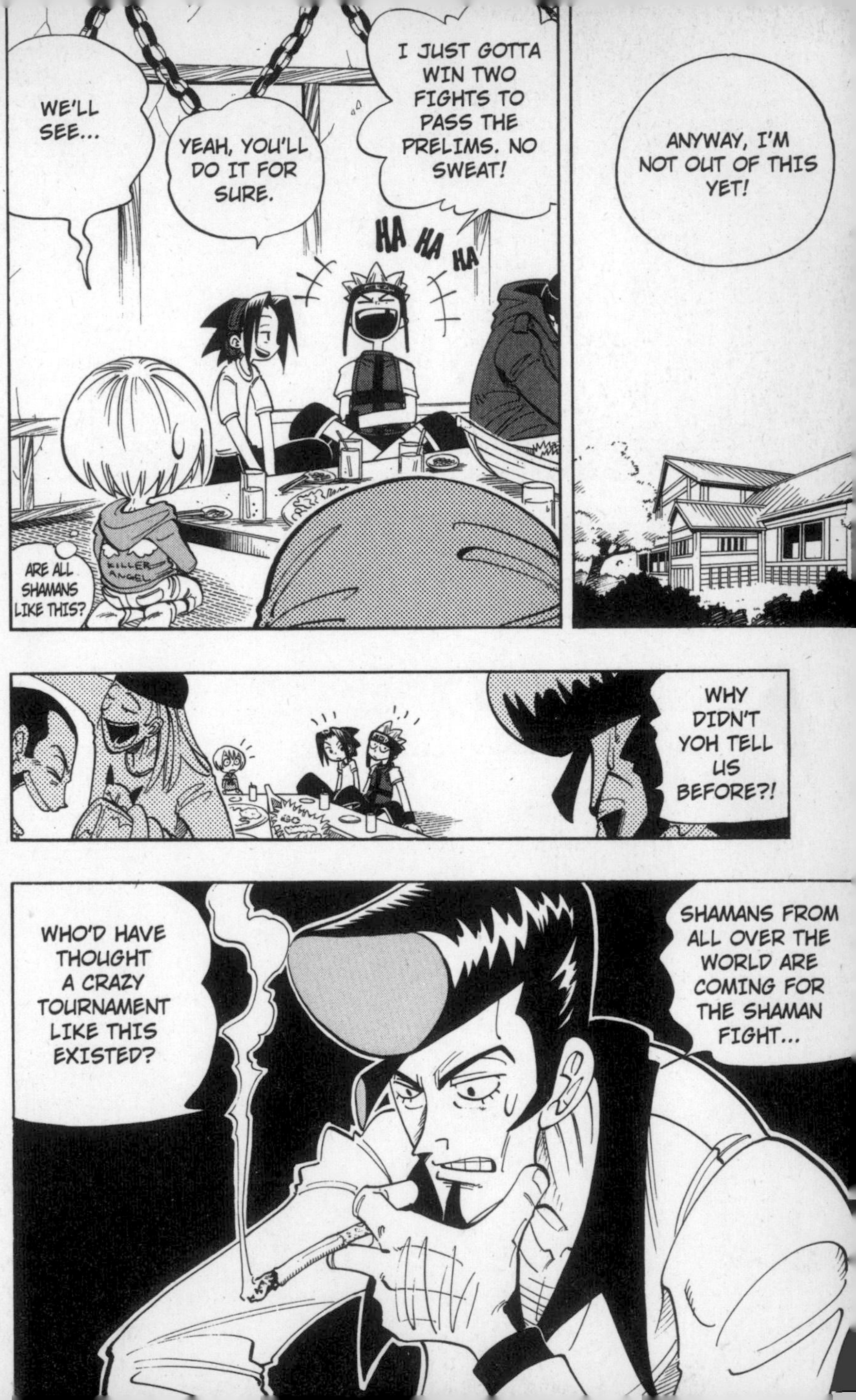
ANYWAY, I'M NOT OUT OF THIS YET!
I JUST GOTTA WIN TWO FIGHTS TO PASS THE PRELIMS. NO SWEAT!
HA HA HA
YEAH, YOU'LL DO IT FOR SURE.
WE'LL SEE...
ARE ALL SHAMANS LIKE THIS?
KILLER ANGEL
WHY DIDN'T YOH TELL US BEFORE?!
SHAMANS FROM ALL OVER THE WORLD ARE COMING FOR THE SHAMAN FIGHT...
WHO'D HAVE THOUGHT A CRAZY TOURNAMENT LIKE THIS EXISTED?

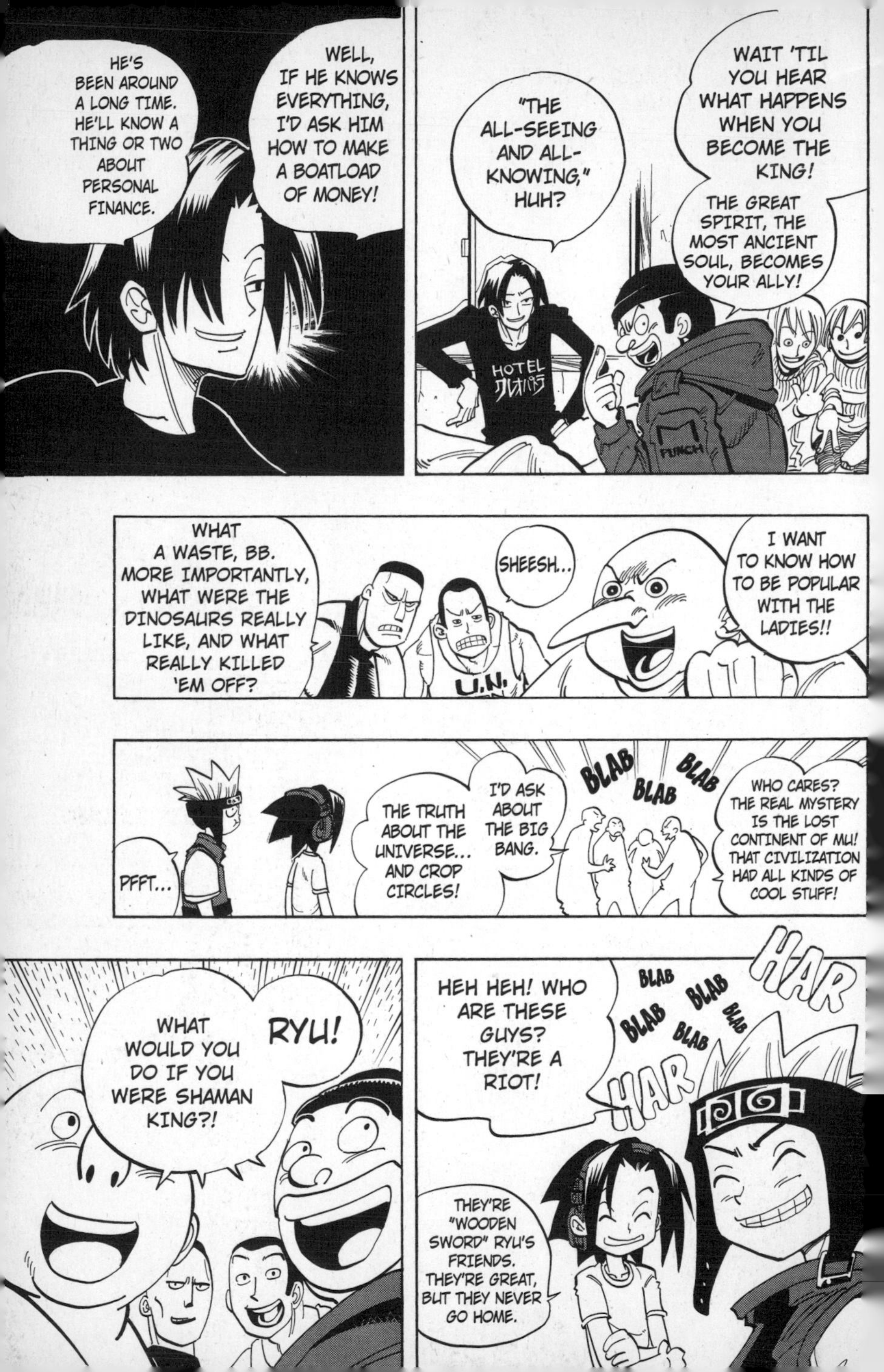
WAIT 'TIL YOU HEAR WHAT HAPPENS WHEN YOU BECOME THE KING!
THE GREAT SPIRIT, THE MOST ANCIENT SOUL, BECOMES YOUR ALLY!
"THE ALL-SEEING AND ALL-KNOWING," HUH?
HOTEL
PUNCH
WELL, IF HE KNOWS EVERYTHING, I'D ASK HIM HOW TO MAKE A BOATLOAD OF MONEY!
HE'S BEEN AROUND A LONG TIME. HE'LL KNOW A THING OR TWO ABOUT PERSONAL FINANCE.
I WANT TO KNOW HOW TO BE POPULAR WITH THE LADIES!!
SHEESH...
U.N.
WHAT A WASTE, BB. MORE IMPORTANTLY, WHAT WERE THE DINOSAURS REALLY LIKE, AND WHAT REALLY KILLED 'EM OFF?
WHO CARES? THE REAL MYSTERY IS THE LOST CONTINENT OF MU! THAT CIVILIZATION HAD ALL KINDS OF COOL STUFF!
BLAB
BLAB
BLAB
I'D ASK ABOUT THE BIG BANG.
THE TRUTH ABOUT THE UNIVERSE... AND CROP CIRCLES!
PFFT...
HAR
BLAB
BLAB
BLAB
BLAB
BLAB
HEH HEH! WHO ARE THESE GUYS? THEY'RE A RIOT!
HAR
THEY'RE "WOODEN SWORD" RYU'S FRIENDS. THEY'RE GREAT, BUT THEY NEVER GO HOME.
RYU!
WHAT WOULD YOU DO IF YOU WERE SHAMAN KING?!

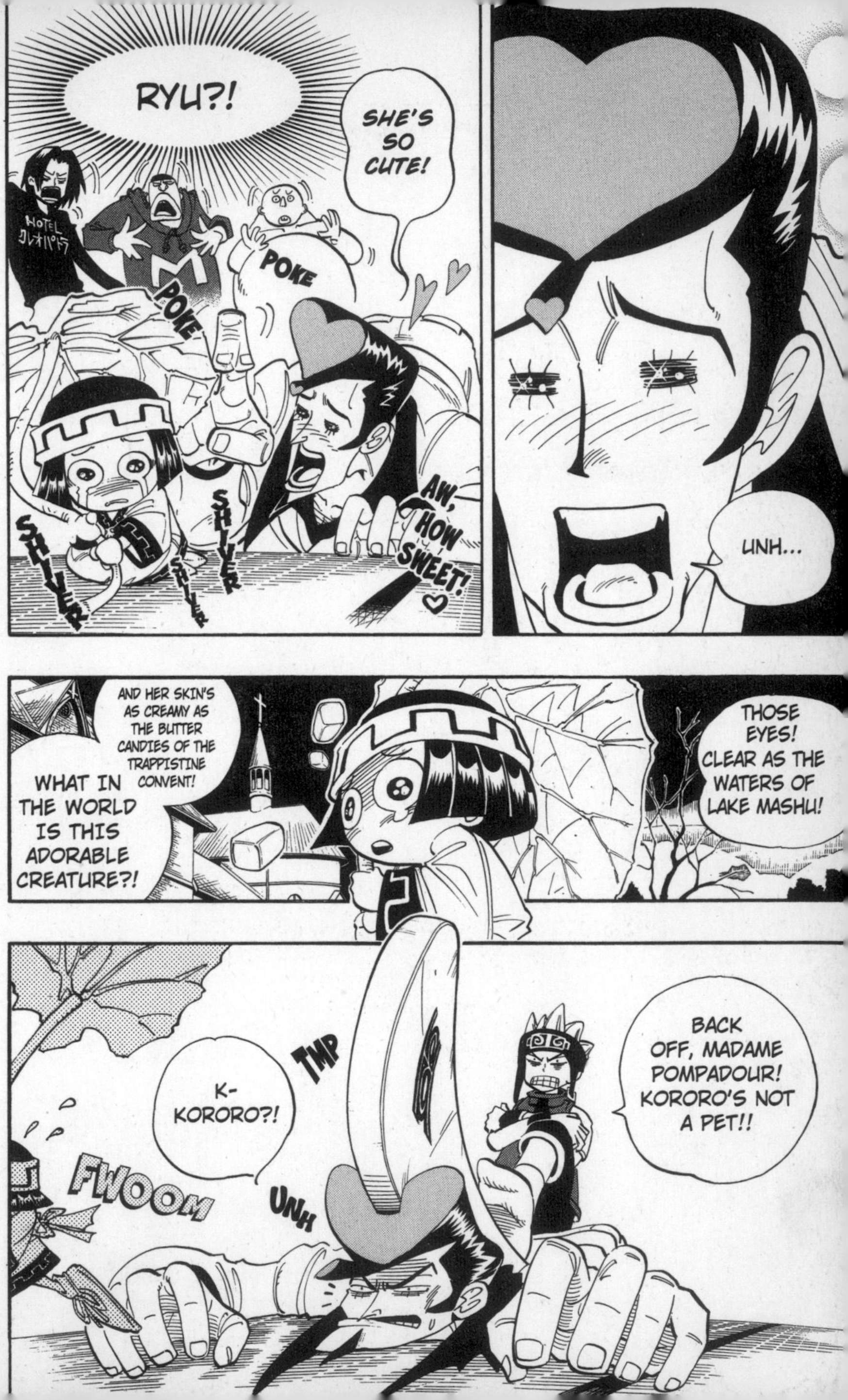
UNH...
SHE'S SO CUTE!
RYU?!
HOTEL クレオパトラ
POKE
POKE
AW, HOW SWEET!
SHIVER
SHIVER
SHIVER
THOSE EYES! CLEAR AS THE WATERS OF LAKE MASHU!
AND HER SKIN'S AS CREAMY AS THE BUTTER CANDIES OF THE TRAPPISTINE CONVENT!
WHAT IN THE WORLD IS THIS ADORABLE CREATURE?!
BACK OFF, MADAME POMPADOUR! KORORO'S NOT A PET!!
TMP
K-KORORO?!
UNH
FWOOM

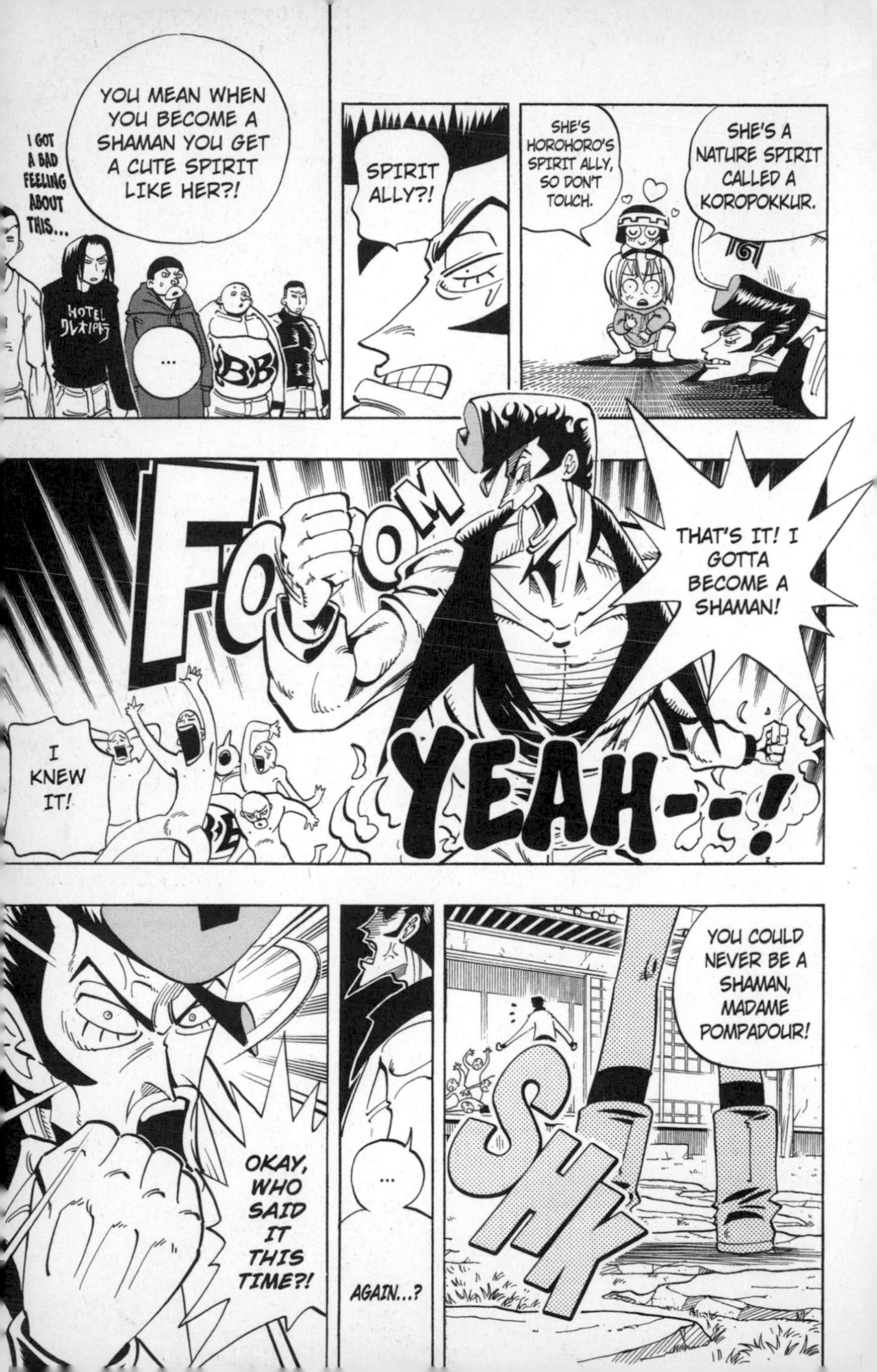
SHE'S A NATURE SPIRIT CALLED A KOROPOKKUR.
SHE'S HOROHORO'S SPIRIT ALLY, SO DON'T TOUCH.
SPIRIT ALLY?!
YOU MEAN WHEN YOU BECOME A SHAMAN YOU GET A CUTE SPIRIT LIKE HER?!
I GOT A BAD FEELING ABOUT THIS...
...
THAT'S IT! I GOTTA BECOME A SHAMAN!
FOOOM
YEAH--!
I KNEW IT!
YOU COULD NEVER BE A SHAMAN, MADAME POMPADOUR!
SHK
...
AGAIN...?
OKAY, WHO SAID IT THIS TIME?!

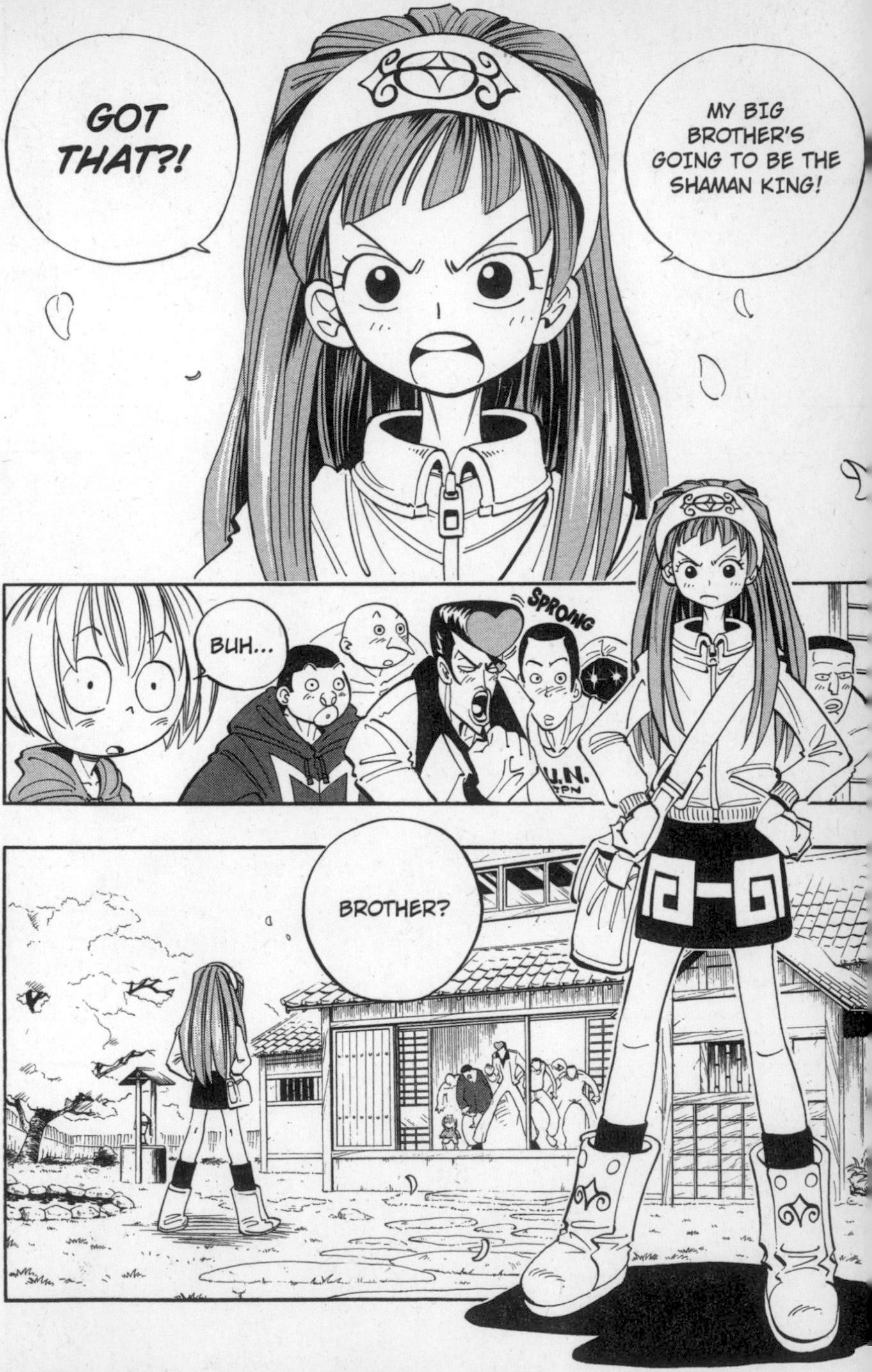
MY BIG BROTHER'S GOING TO BE THE SHAMAN KING!
GOT THAT?!
SPROING
BUH...
BROTHER?

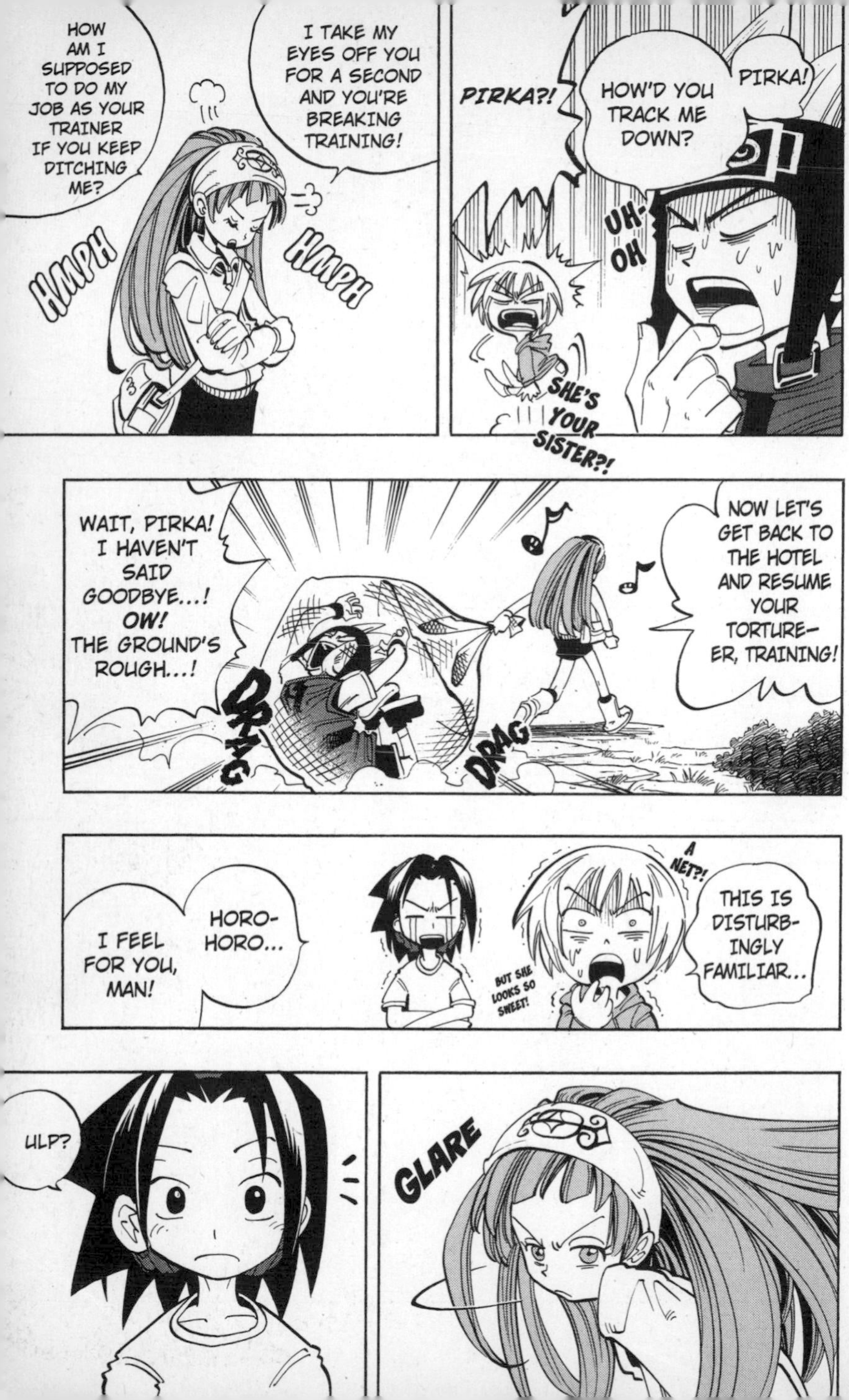
PIRKA!
HOW'D YOU TRACK ME DOWN?
PIRKA?!
UH-OH
SHE'S YOUR SISTER?!
I TAKE MY EYES OFF YOU FOR A SECOND AND YOU'RE BREAKING TRAINING!
HOW AM I SUPPOSED TO DO MY JOB AS YOUR TRAINER IF YOU KEEP DITCHING ME?
HMPH
HMPH
NOW LET'S GET BACK TO THE HOTEL AND RESUME YOUR TORTURE- ER, TRAINING!
DRAG
WAIT, PIRKA! I HAVEN'T SAID GOODBYE...! OW! THE GROUND'S ROUGH...!
DRAG
A NET?!
THIS IS DISTURBINGLY FAMILIAR...
BUT SHE LOOKS SO SWEET!
HORO-HORO...
I FEEL FOR YOU, MAN!
GLARE
ULP?

READ THIS WAY

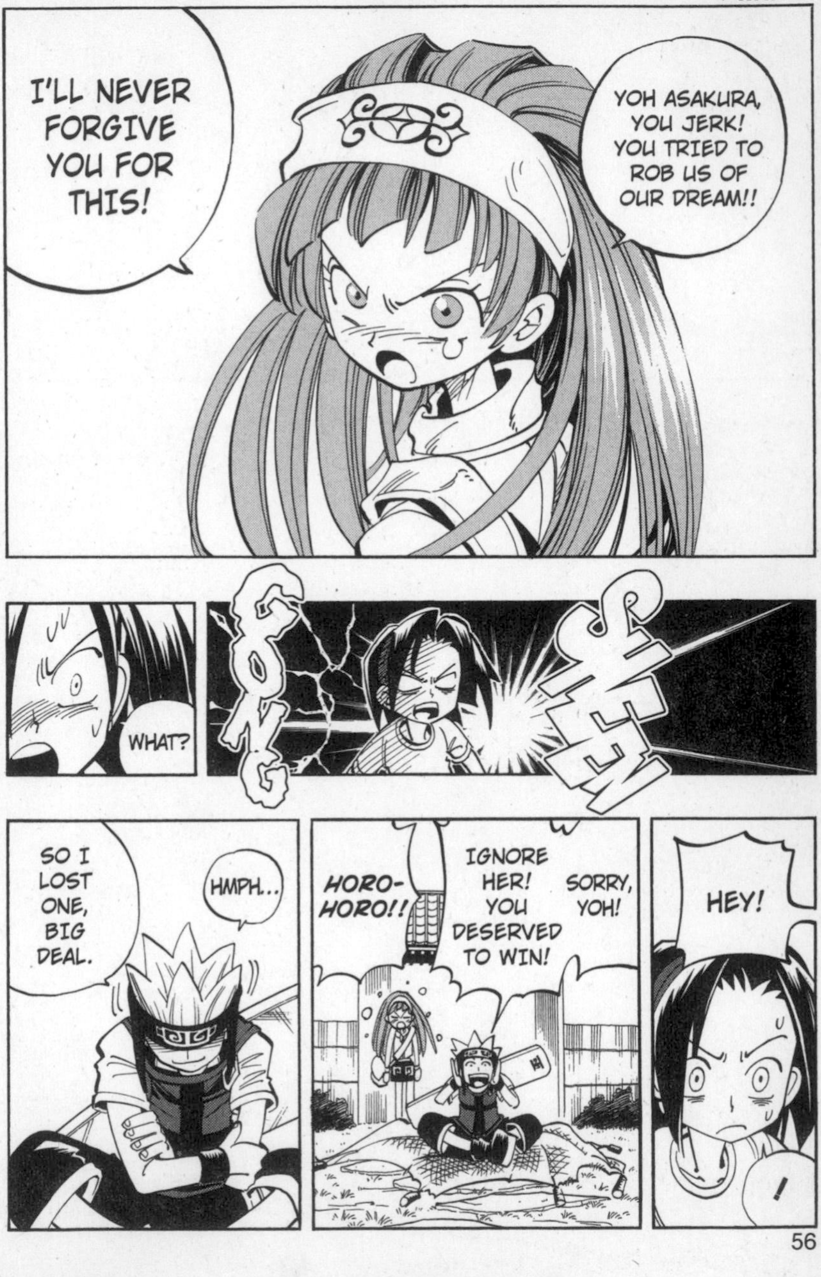
YOH ASAKURA, YOU JERK! YOU TRIED TO ROB US OF OUR DREAM!!
I'LL NEVER FORGIVE YOU FOR THIS!
WHAT?
HEY!
!
SORRY, YOH!
IGNORE HER! YOU DESERVED TO WIN!
HORO-HORO!!
HMPH...
SO I LOST ONE, BIG DEAL.

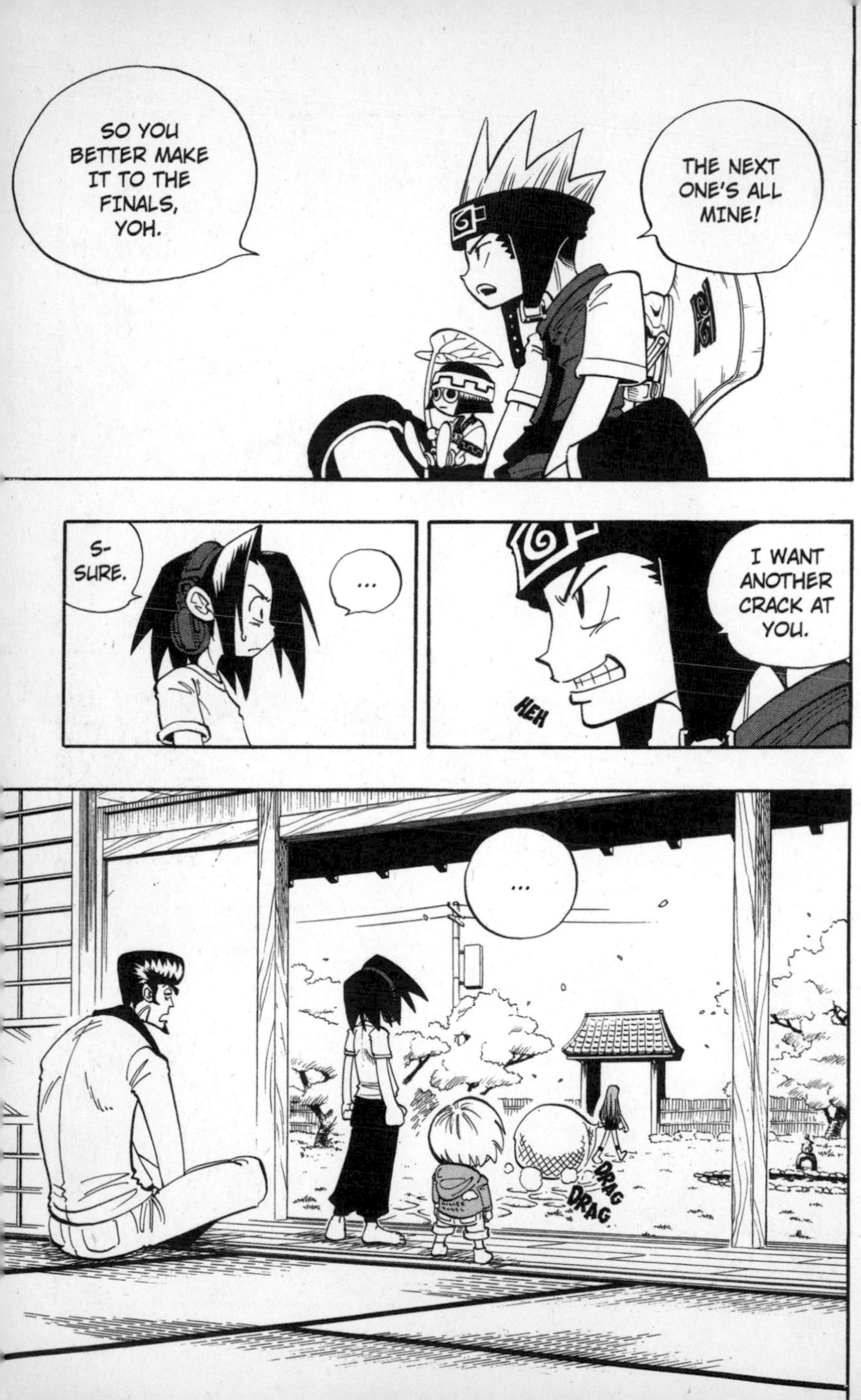
THE NEXT ONE'S ALL MINE!
SO YOU BETTER MAKE IT TO THE FINALS, YOH.
I WANT ANOTHER CRACK AT YOU.
HEH
...
S- SURE.
...
DRAG
DRAG

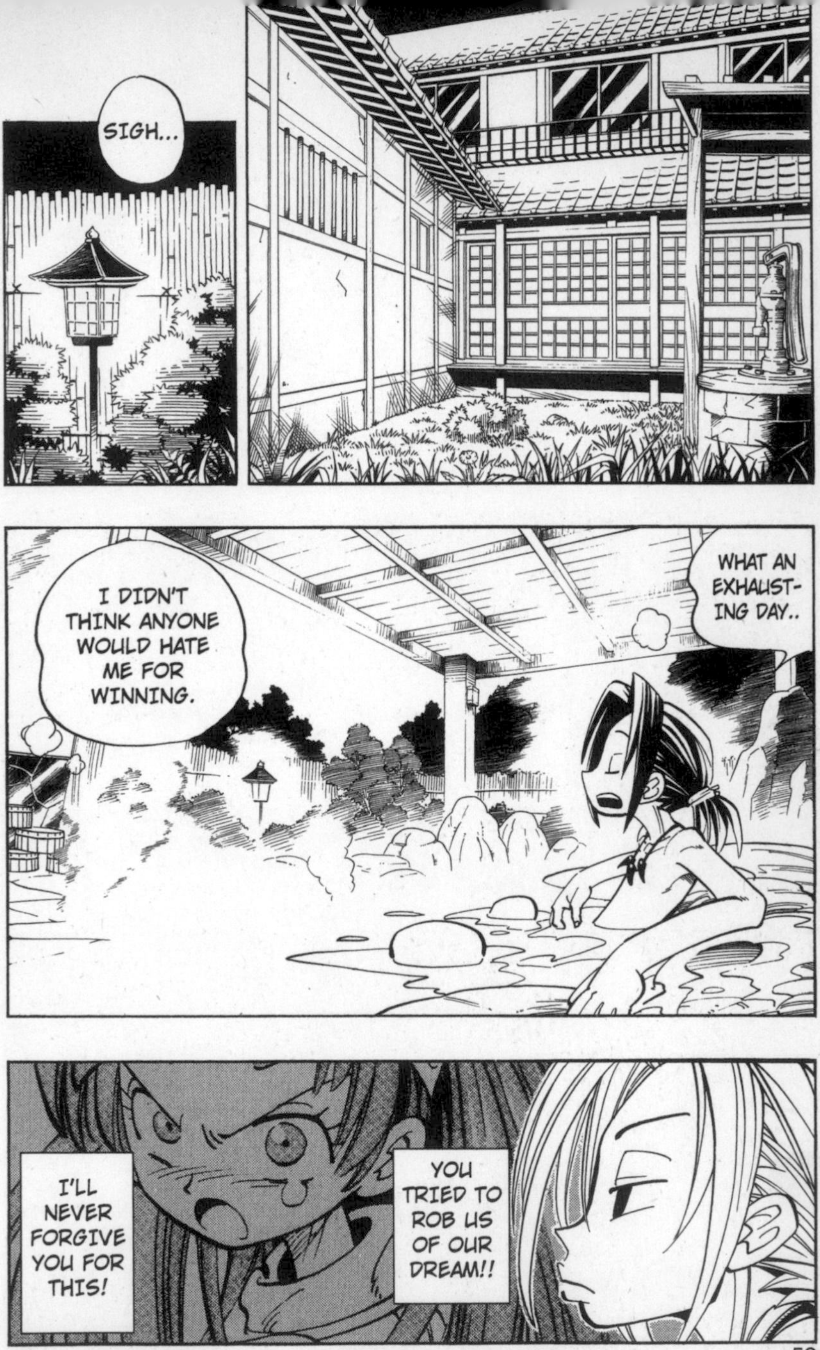
SIGH...
WHAT AN EXHAUST-ING DAY..
I DIDN'T THINK ANYONE WOULD HATE ME FOR WINNING.
YOU TRIED TO ROB US OF OUR DREAM!!
I'LL NEVER FORGIVE YOU FOR THIS!

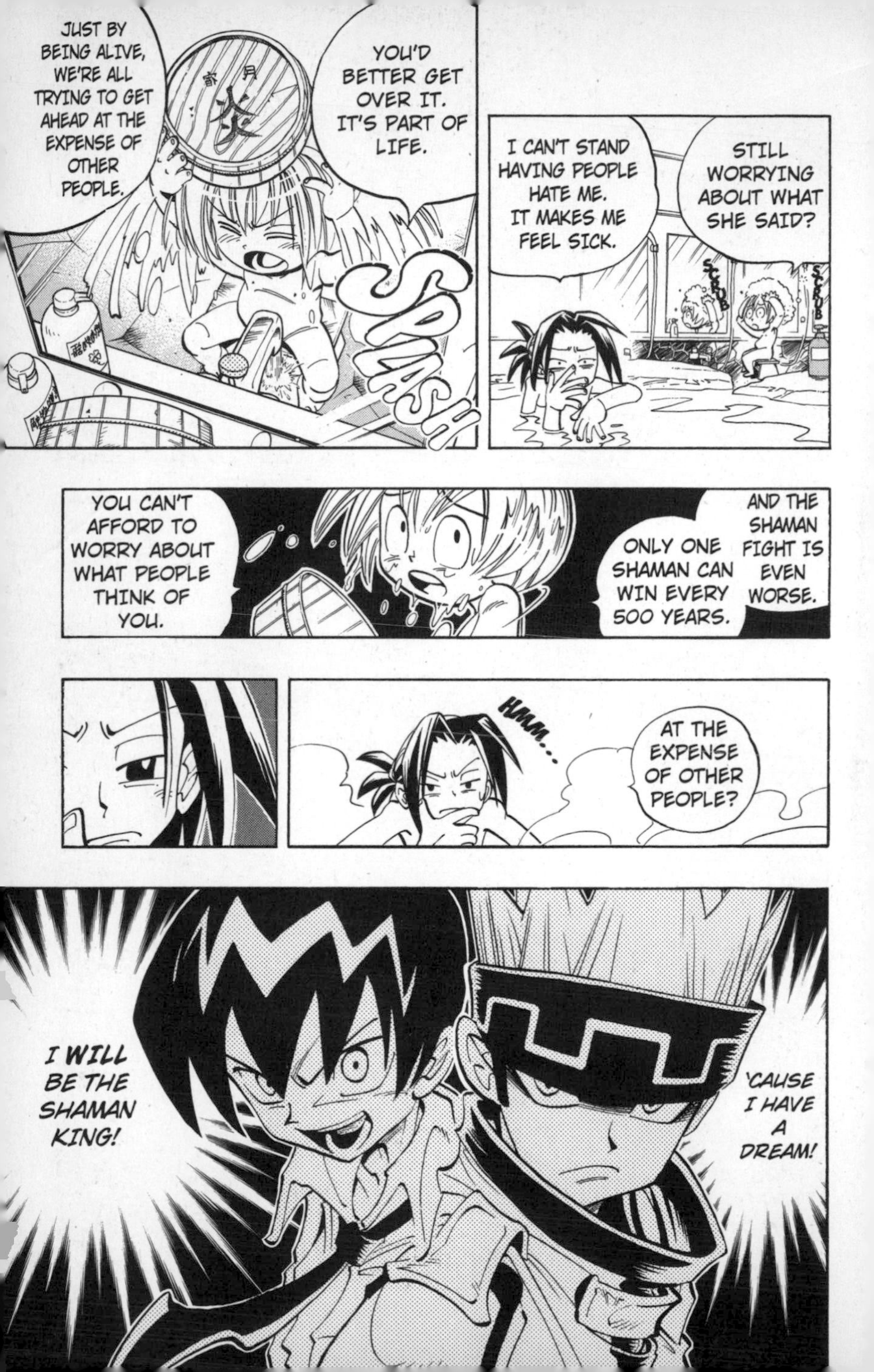
STILL WORRYING ABOUT WHAT SHE SAID?
I CAN'T STAND HAVING PEOPLE HATE ME. IT MAKES ME FEEL SICK.
SCRUB
SCRUB
YOU'D BETTER GET OVER IT. IT'S PART OF LIFE.
JUST BY BEING ALIVE, WE'RE ALL TRYING TO GET AHEAD AT THE EXPENSE OF OTHER PEOPLE.
SPLASH
AND THE SHAMAN FIGHT IS EVEN WORSE.
ONLY ONE SHAMAN CAN WIN EVERY 500 YEARS.
YOU CAN'T AFFORD TO WORRY ABOUT WHAT PEOPLE THINK OF YOU.
HMM...
AT THE EXPENSE OF OTHER PEOPLE?
'CAUSE I HAVE A DREAM!
I WILL BE THE SHAMAN KING!

READ THIS WAY

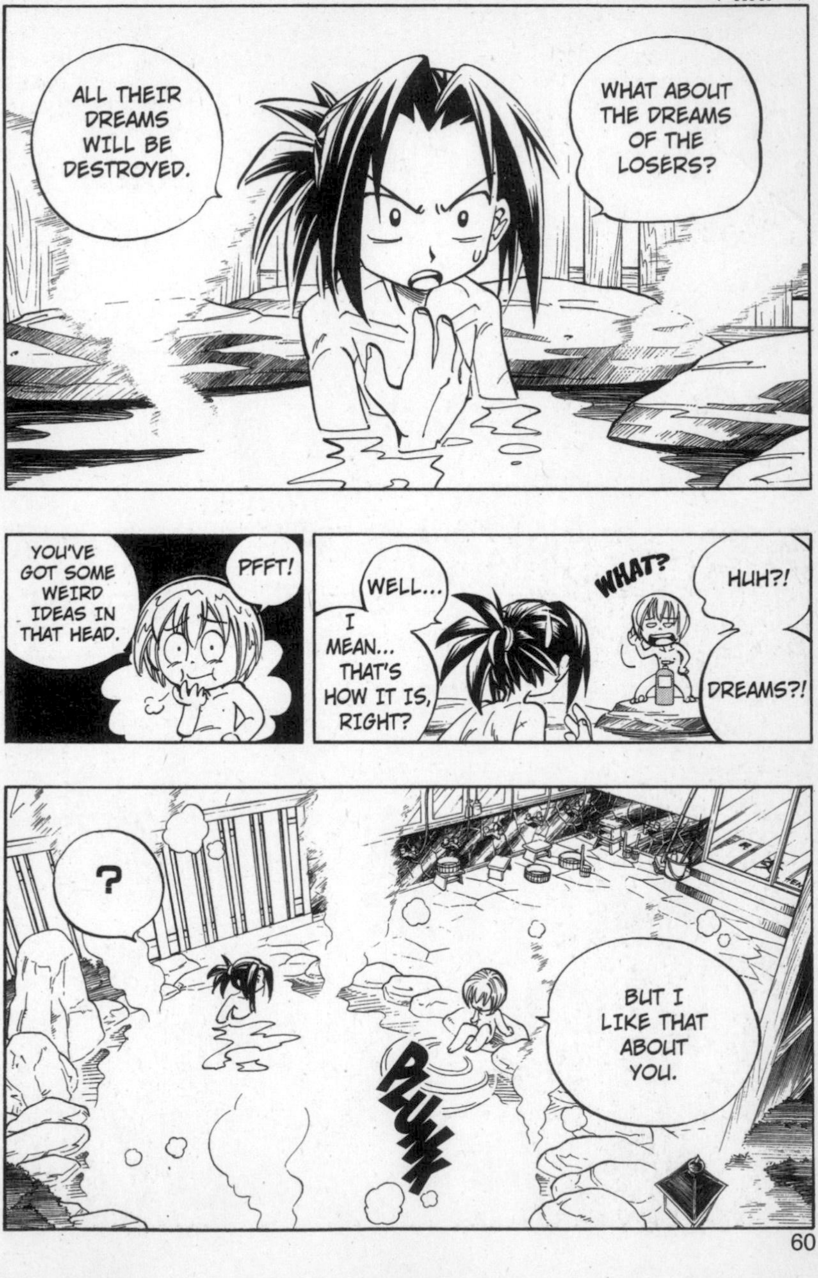
WHAT ABOUT THE DREAMS OF THE LOSERS?
ALL THEIR DREAMS WILL BE DESTROYED.
HUH?!
DREAMS?!
WHAT?
WELL...
I MEAN... THAT'S HOW IT IS, RIGHT?
PFFT!
YOU'VE GOT SOME WEIRD IDEAS IN THAT HEAD.
BUT I LIKE THAT ABOUT YOU.
PLUNK
?

READ THIS WAY

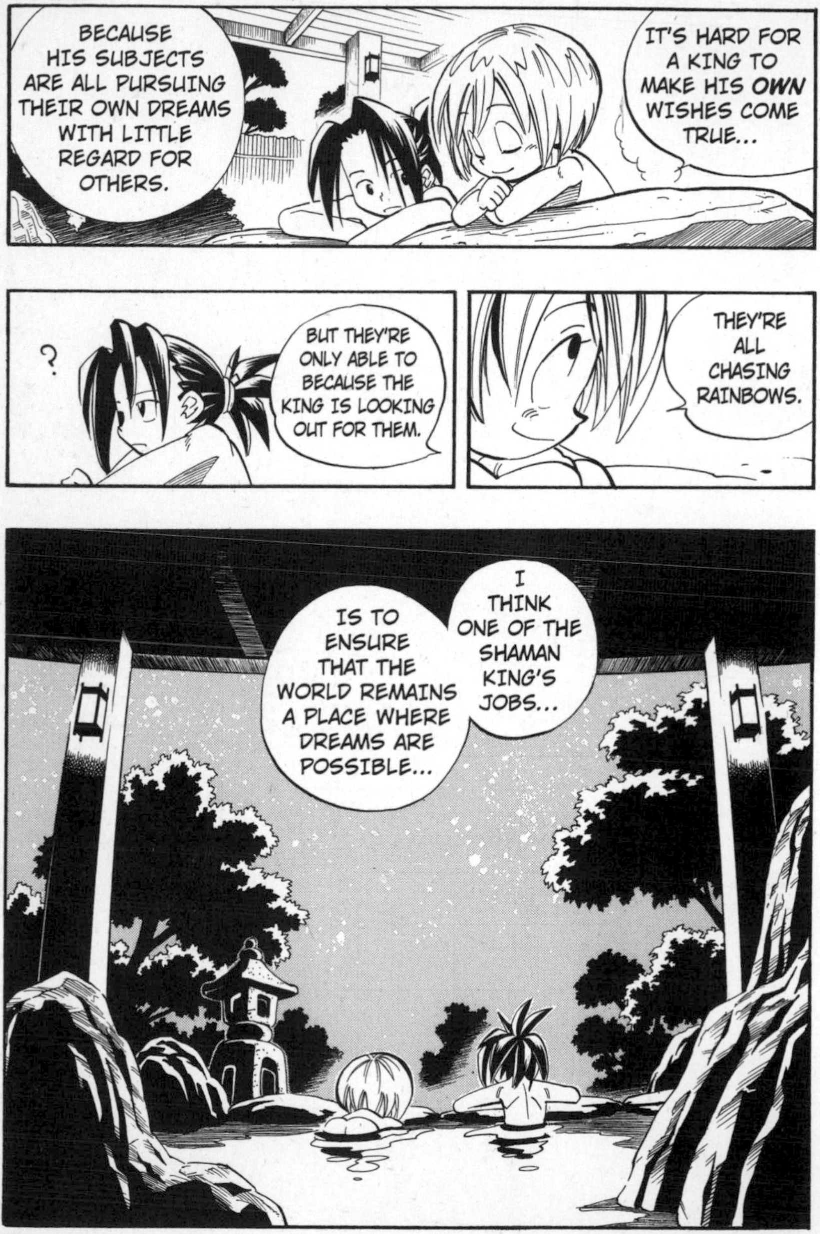
IT'S HARD FOR A KING TO MAKE HIS *OWN* WISHES COME TRUE...
BECAUSE HIS SUBJECTS ARE ALL PURSUING THEIR OWN DREAMS WITH LITTLE REGARD FOR OTHERS.
THEY'RE ALL CHASING RAINBOWS.
BUT THEY'RE ONLY ABLE TO BECAUSE THE KING IS LOOKING OUT FOR THEM.
?
I THINK ONE OF THE SHAMAN KING'S JOBS...
IS TO ENSURE THAT THE WORLD REMAINS A PLACE WHERE DREAMS ARE POSSIBLE...

READ THIS WAY

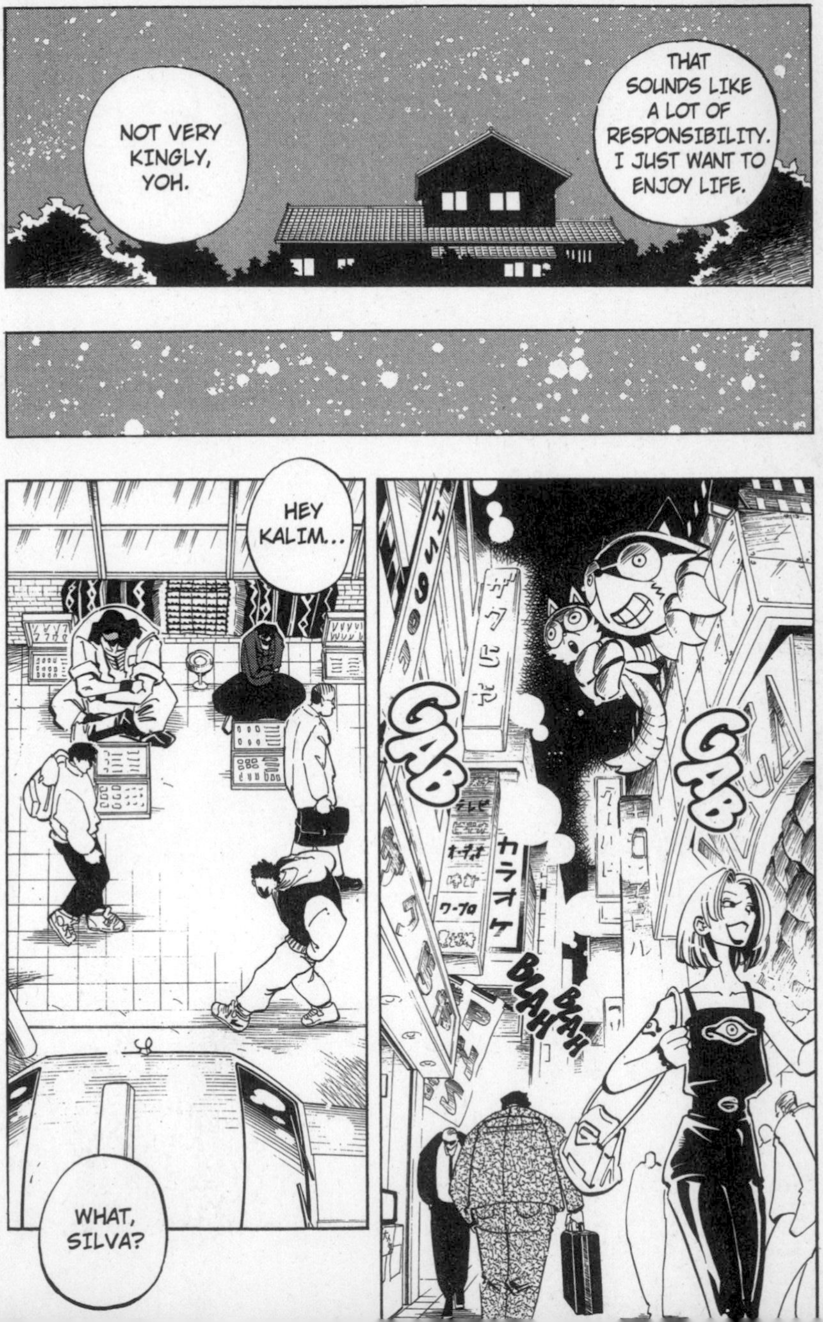
THAT SOUNDS LIKE A LOT OF RESPONSIBILITY. I JUST WANT TO ENJOY LIFE.
NOT VERY KINGLY, YOH.
GAB
GAB
カラオケ
ワープロ
BLAH BLAH
HEY KALIM...
WHAT, SILVA?

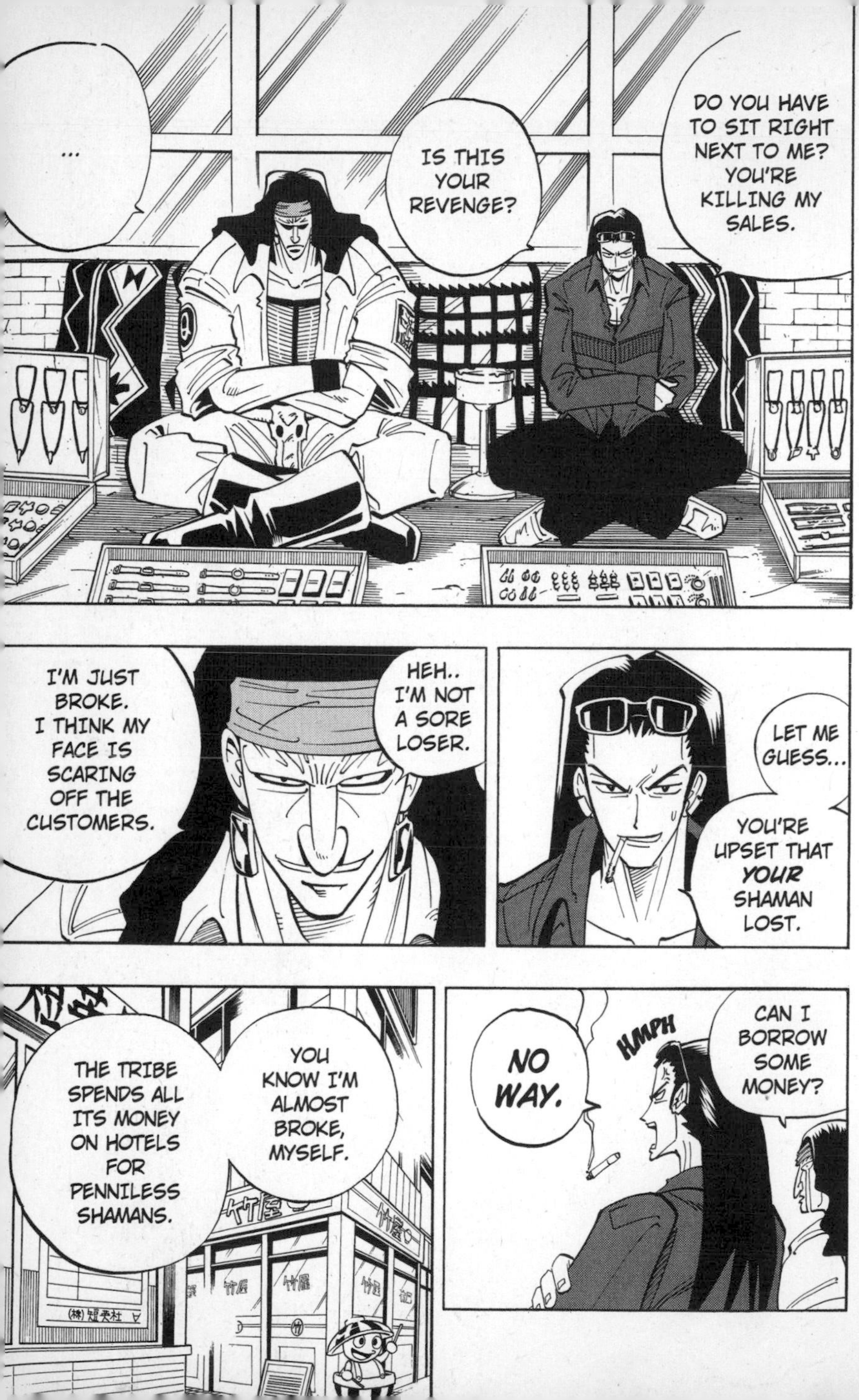
DO YOU HAVE TO SIT RIGHT NEXT TO ME? YOU'RE KILLING MY SALES.
IS THIS YOUR REVENGE?
...
LET ME GUESS...
YOU'RE UPSET THAT *YOUR* SHAMAN LOST.
HEH.. I'M NOT A SORE LOSER.
I'M JUST BROKE. I THINK MY FACE IS SCARING OFF THE CUSTOMERS.
CAN I BORROW SOME MONEY?
HMPH
NO WAY.
YOU KNOW I'M ALMOST BROKE, MYSELF.
THE TRIBE SPENDS ALL ITS MONEY ON HOTELS FOR PENNILESS SHAMANS.

READ THIS WAY

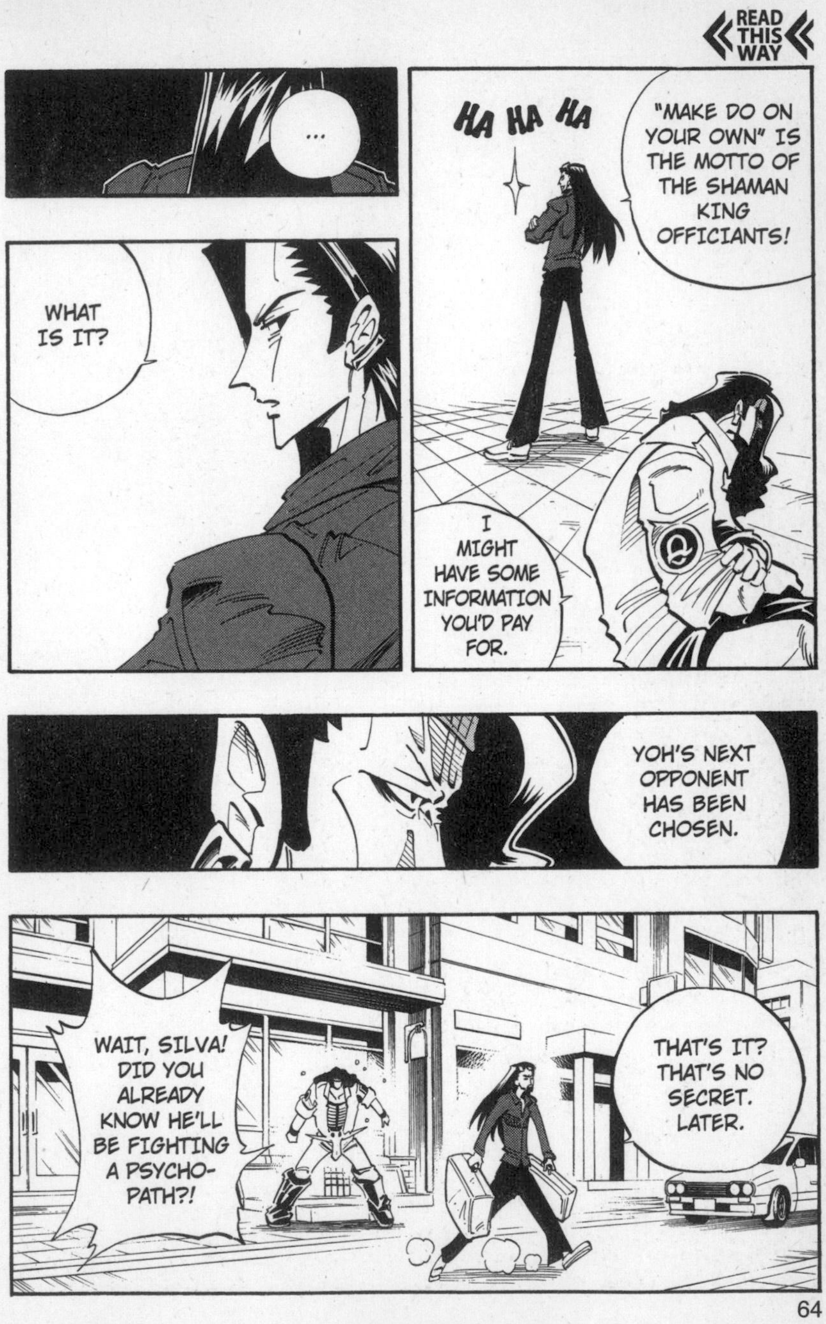
HA HA HA
"MAKE DO ON YOUR OWN" IS THE MOTTO OF THE SHAMAN KING OFFICIANTS!
I MIGHT HAVE SOME INFORMATION YOU'D PAY FOR.
...
WHAT IS IT?
YOH'S NEXT OPPONENT HAS BEEN CHOSEN.
THAT'S IT? THAT'S NO SECRET. LATER.
WAIT, SILVA! DID YOU ALREADY KNOW HE'LL BE FIGHTING A PSYCHO-PATH?!

READ THIS WAY

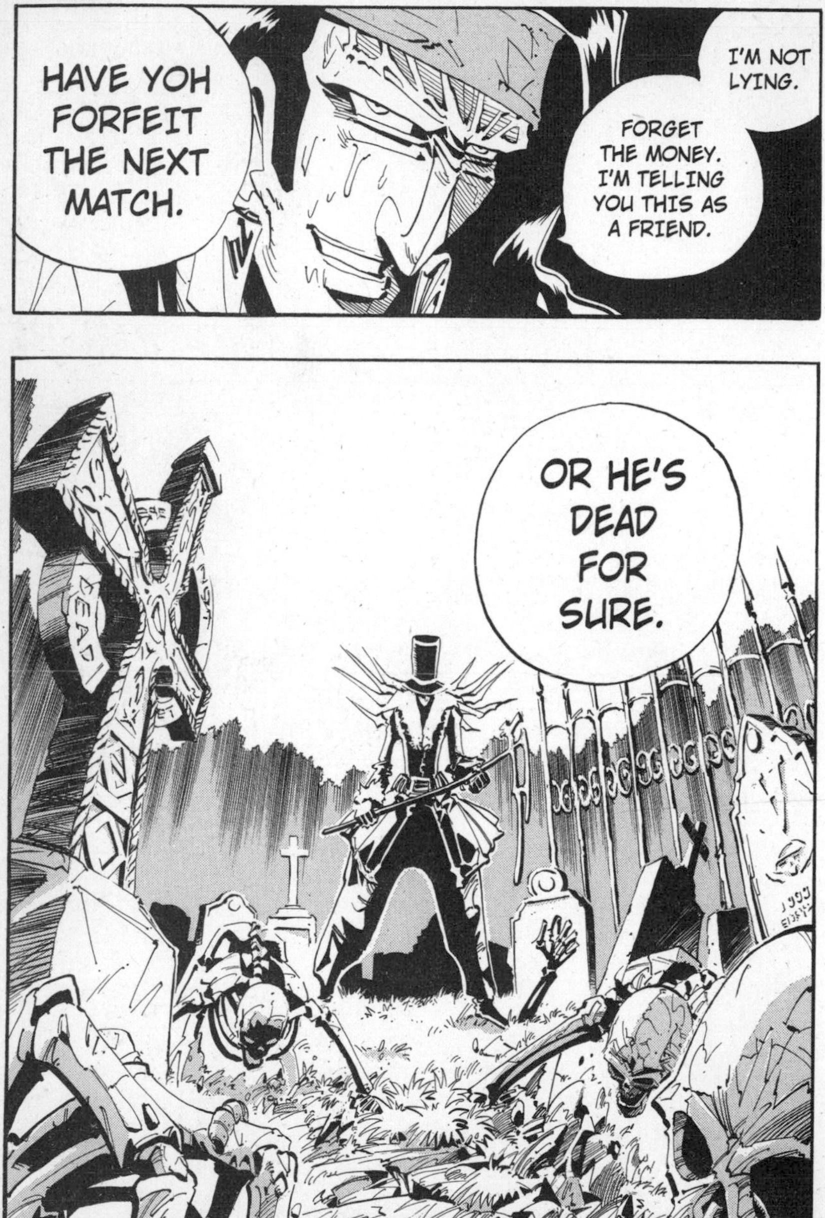

I'M NOT LYING.
FORGET THE MONEY. I'M TELLING YOU THIS AS A FRIEND.
HAVE YOH FORFEIT THE NEXT MATCH.
OR HE'S DEAD FOR SURE.
DEAD

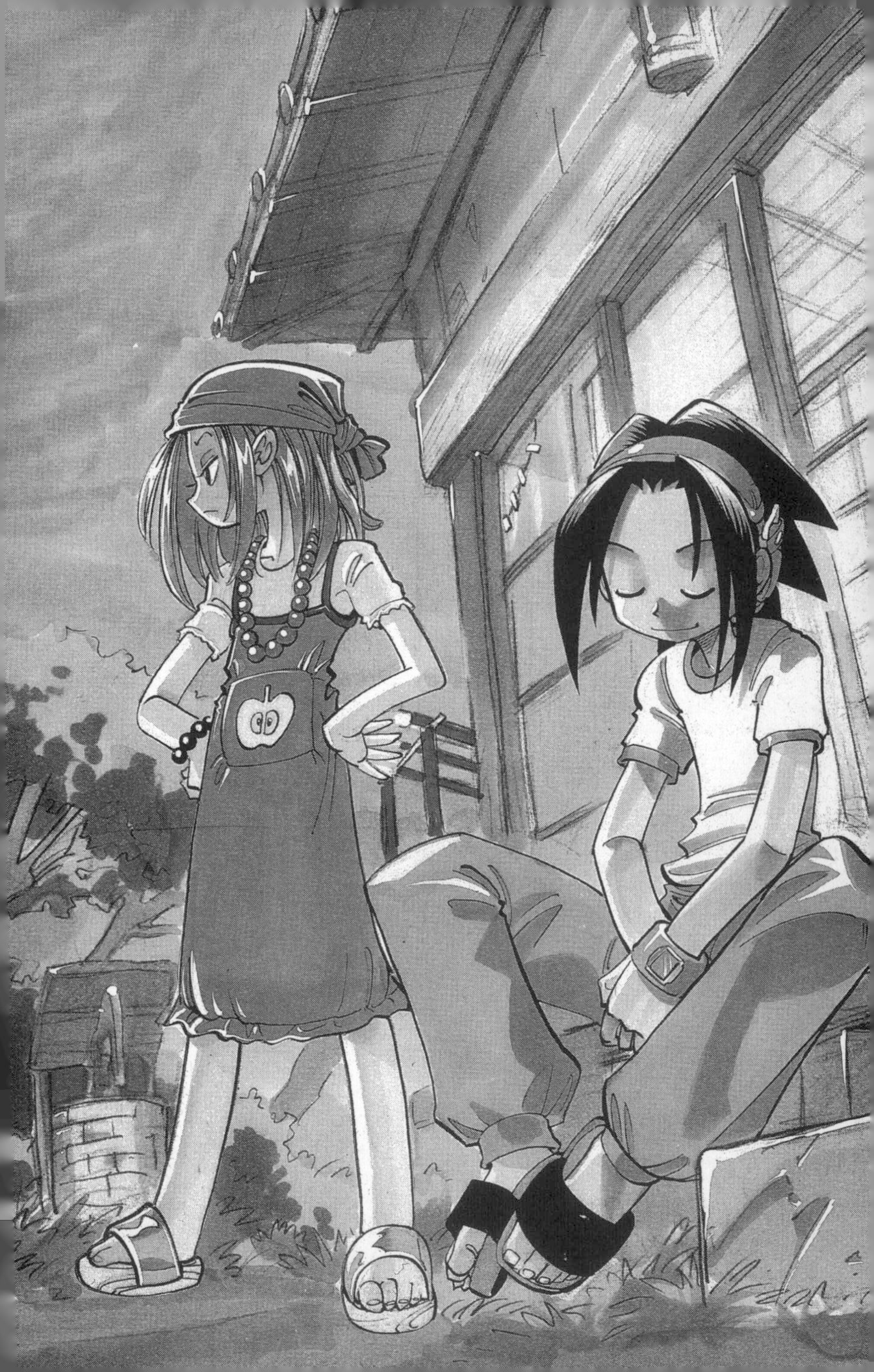

Reincarnation 39: Backbone

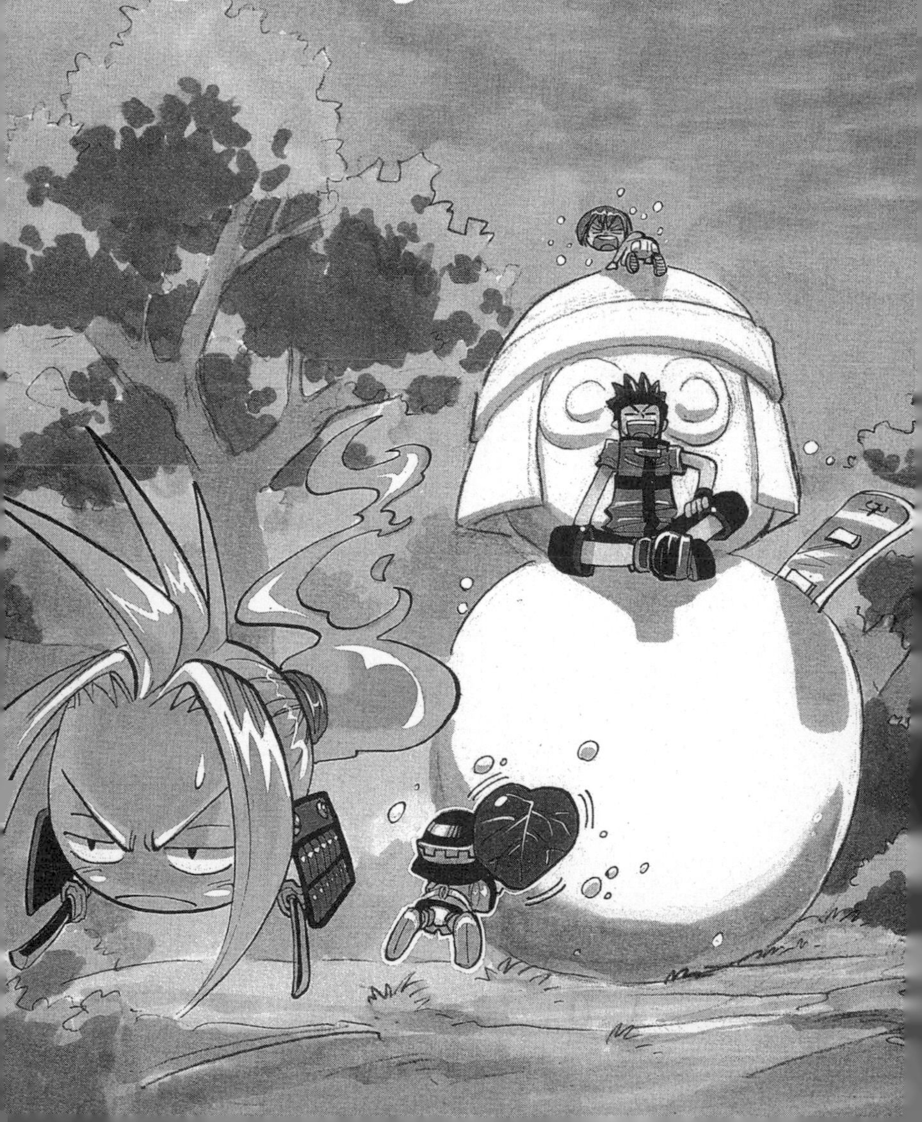

SHAMAN KING CHARACTER FILE No.21

コロロ

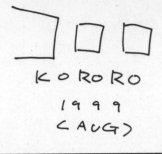

KORORO

1999
(AUG)

?

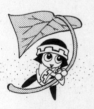

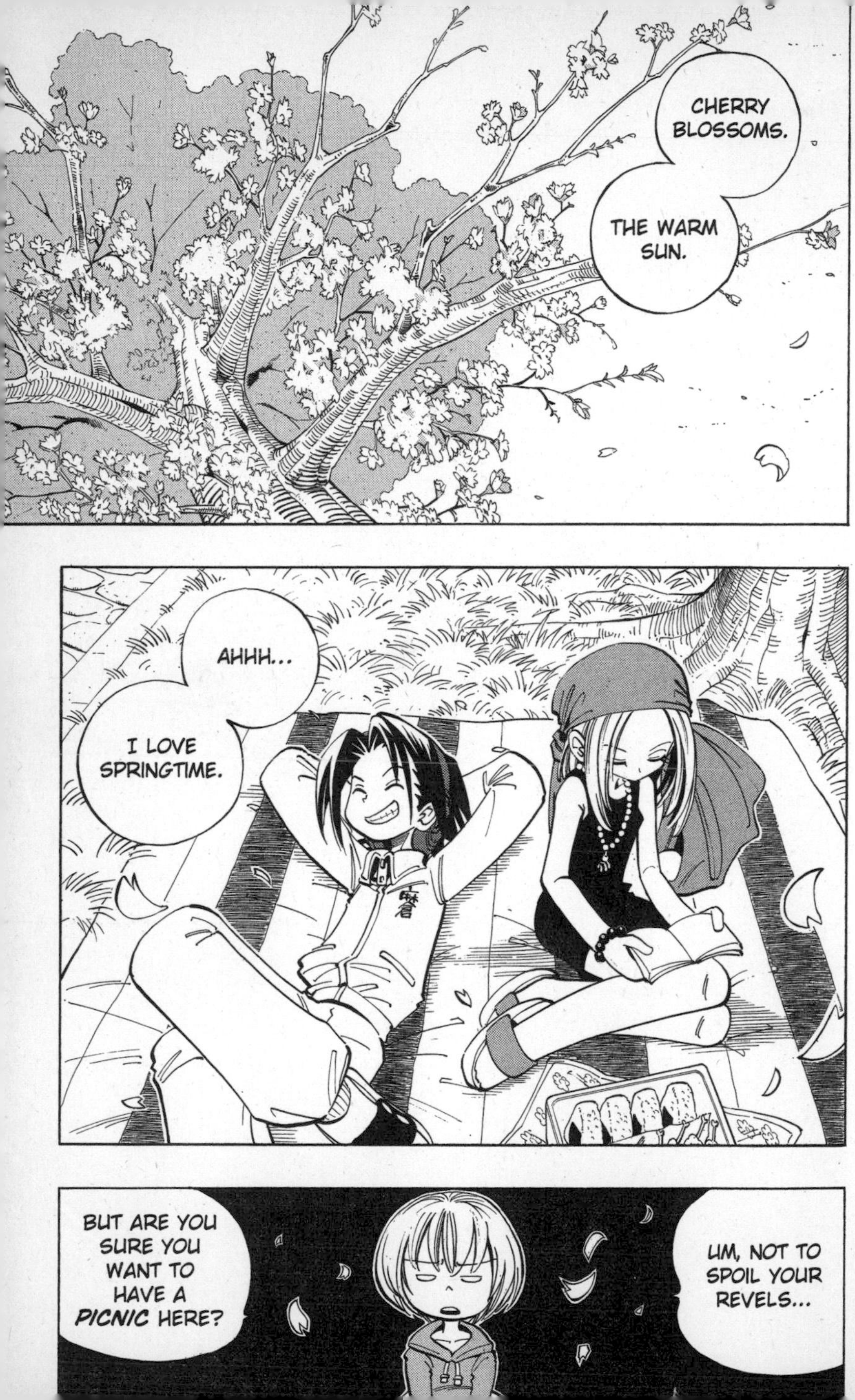
CHERRY BLOSSOMS.
THE WARM SUN.
AHHH...
I LOVE SPRINGTIME.
UM, NOT TO SPOIL YOUR REVELS...
BUT ARE YOU SURE YOU WANT TO HAVE A *PICNIC* HERE?

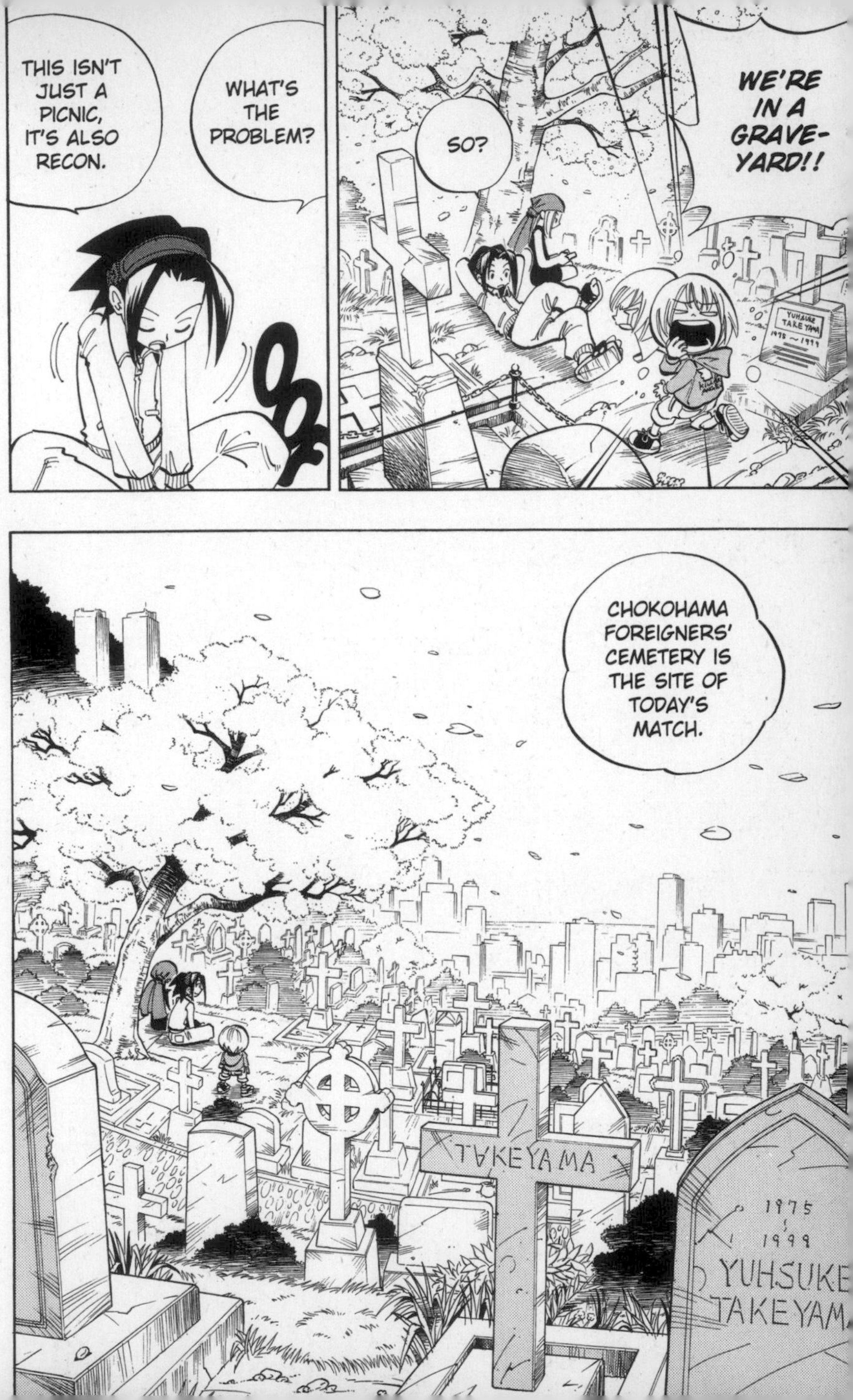
WE'RE IN A GRAVE-YARD!!
SO?
WHAT'S THE PROBLEM?
THIS ISN'T JUST A PICNIC, IT'S ALSO RECON.
CHOKOHAMA FOREIGNERS' CEMETERY IS THE SITE OF TODAY'S MATCH.
TAKEYAMA
1975
1999
YUHSUKE

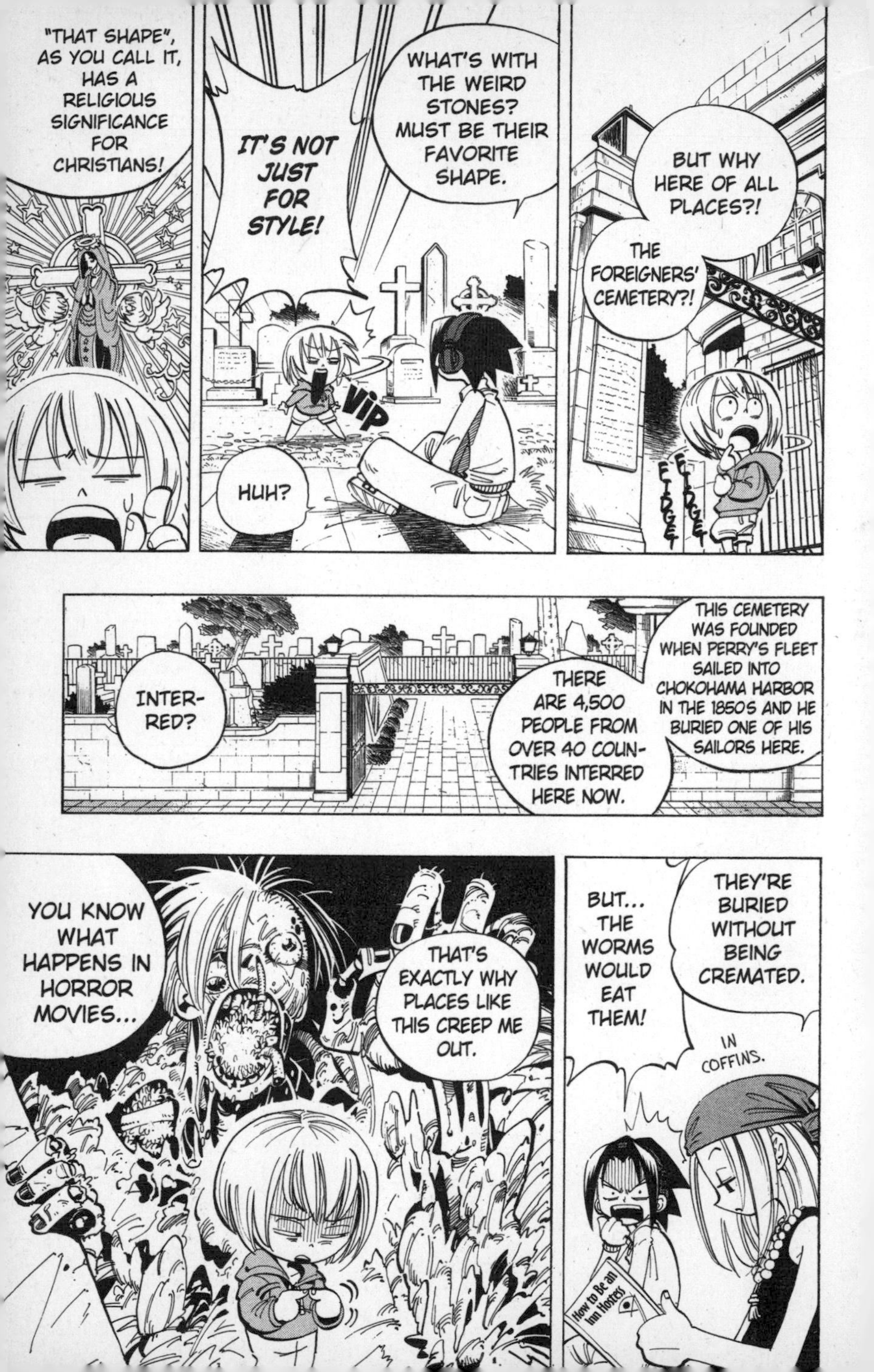
BUT WHY HERE OF ALL PLACES?!
THE FOREIGNERS' CEMETERY?!
FIDGET
FIDGET
WHAT'S WITH THE WEIRD STONES? MUST BE THEIR FAVORITE SHAPE.
IT'S NOT JUST FOR STYLE!
HUH?
"THAT SHAPE", AS YOU CALL IT, HAS A RELIGIOUS SIGNIFICANCE FOR CHRISTIANS!
THIS CEMETERY WAS FOUNDED WHEN PERRY'S FLEET SAILED INTO CHOKOHAMA HARBOR IN THE 1850S AND HE BURIED ONE OF HIS SAILORS HERE.
THERE ARE 4,500 PEOPLE FROM OVER 40 COUNTRIES INTERRED HERE NOW.
INTER-RED?
THEY'RE BURIED WITHOUT BEING CREMATED.
BUT... THE WORMS WOULD EAT THEM!
IN COFFINS.
How to Be an Inn Hostess
YOU KNOW WHAT HAPPENS IN HORROR MOVIES...
THAT'S EXACTLY WHY PLACES LIKE THIS CREEP ME OUT.

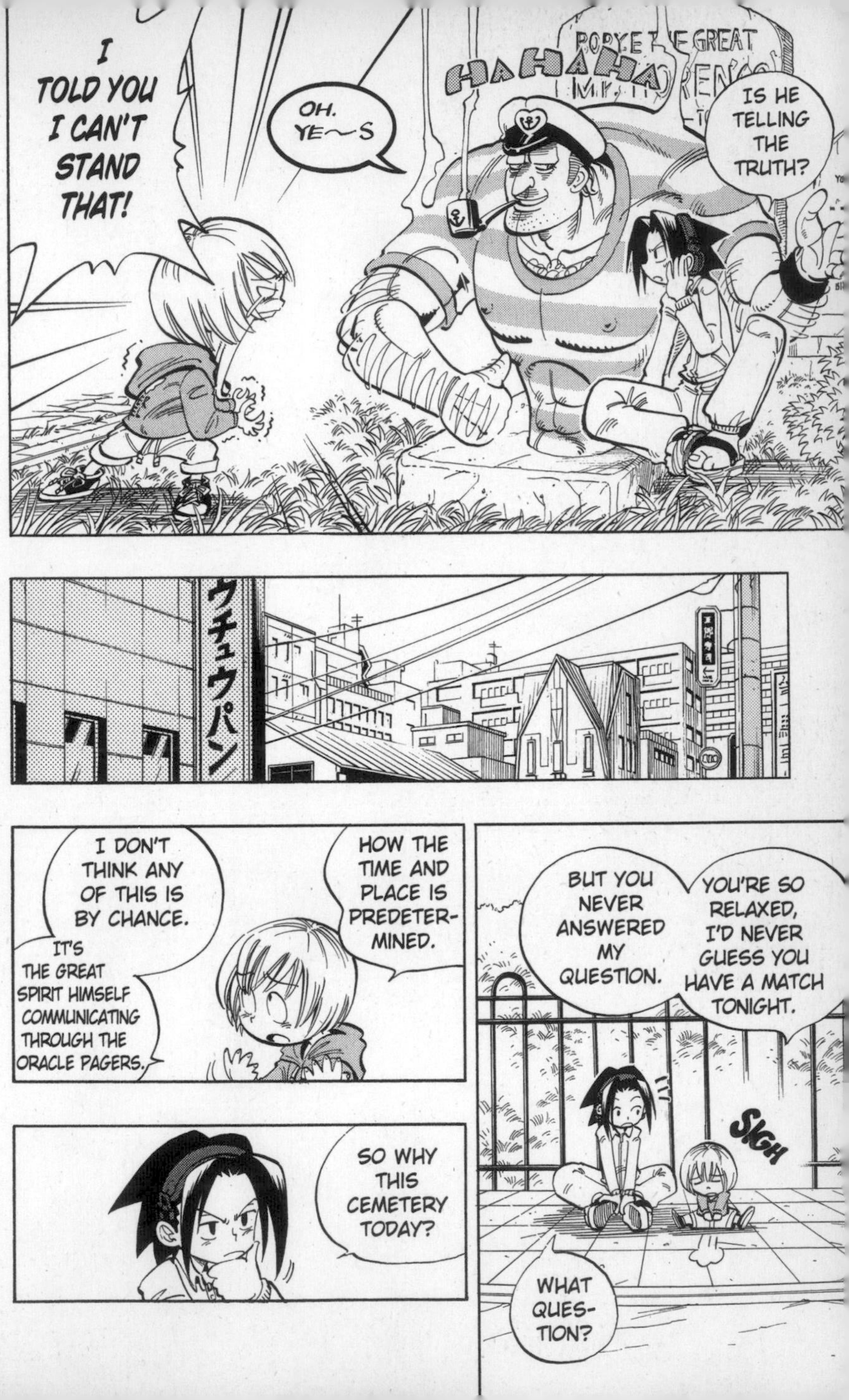

IS HE TELLING THE TRUTH?
HAHAHA
OH. YE~S
I TOLD YOU I CAN'T STAND THAT!
ウチュウパン
YOU'RE SO RELAXED, I'D NEVER GUESS YOU HAVE A MATCH TONIGHT.
BUT YOU NEVER ANSWERED MY QUESTION.
SIGH
WHAT QUES-TION?
I DON'T THINK ANY OF THIS IS BY CHANCE.
IT'S THE GREAT SPIRIT HIMSELF COMMUNICATING THROUGH THE ORACLE PAGERS.
HOW THE TIME AND PLACE IS PREDETER-MINED.
SO WHY THIS CEMETERY TODAY?

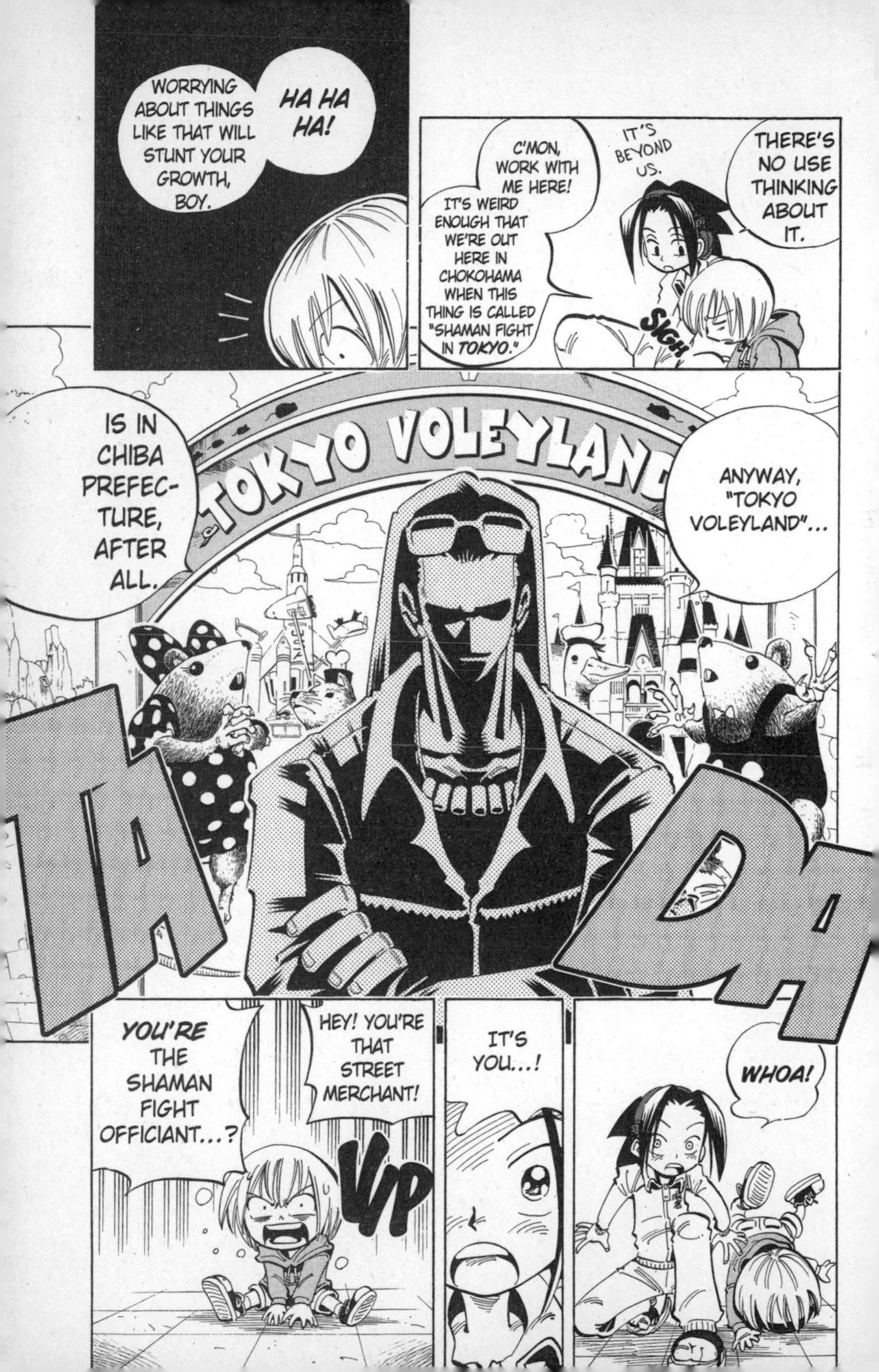
THERE'S NO USE THINKING ABOUT IT.
IT'S BEYOND US.
C'MON, WORK WITH ME HERE!
IT'S WEIRD ENOUGH THAT WE'RE OUT HERE IN CHOKOHAMA WHEN THIS THING IS CALLED "SHAMAN FIGHT IN TOKYO."
SIGH
HA HA HA!
WORRYING ABOUT THINGS LIKE THAT WILL STUNT YOUR GROWTH, BOY.
TOKYO VOLEYLAND
ANYWAY, "TOKYO VOLEYLAND"...
IS IN CHIBA PREFECTURE, AFTER ALL.
TA DA
WHOA!
IT'S YOU...!
HEY! YOU'RE THAT STREET MERCHANT!
YOU'RE THE SHAMAN FIGHT OFFICIANT...?

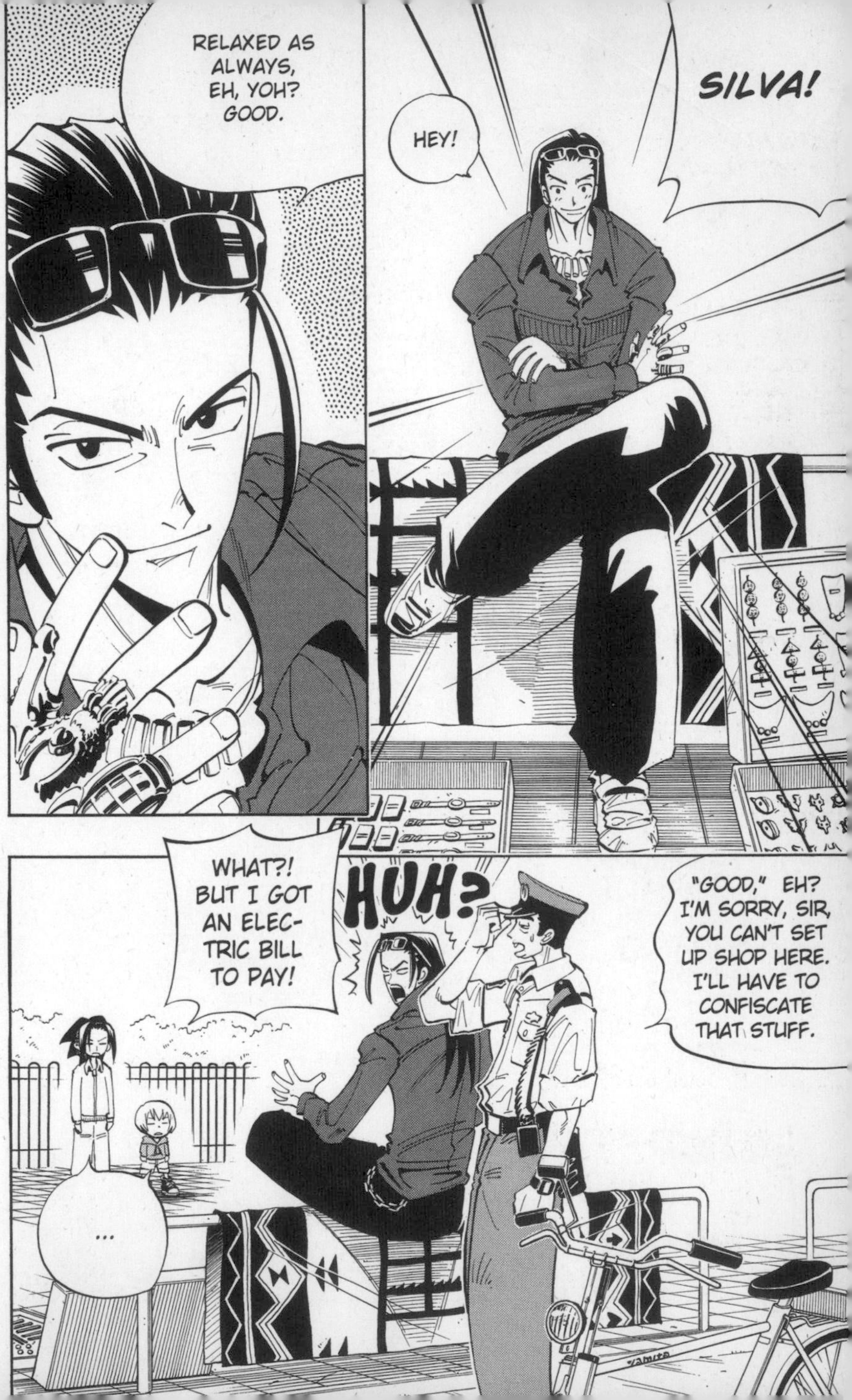
SILVA!
HEY!
RELAXED AS ALWAYS, EH, YOH? GOOD.
"GOOD," EH? I'M SORRY, SIR, YOU CAN'T SET UP SHOP HERE. I'LL HAVE TO CONFISCATE THAT STUFF.
HUH?
WHAT?! BUT I GOT AN ELEC-TRIC BILL TO PAY!
...

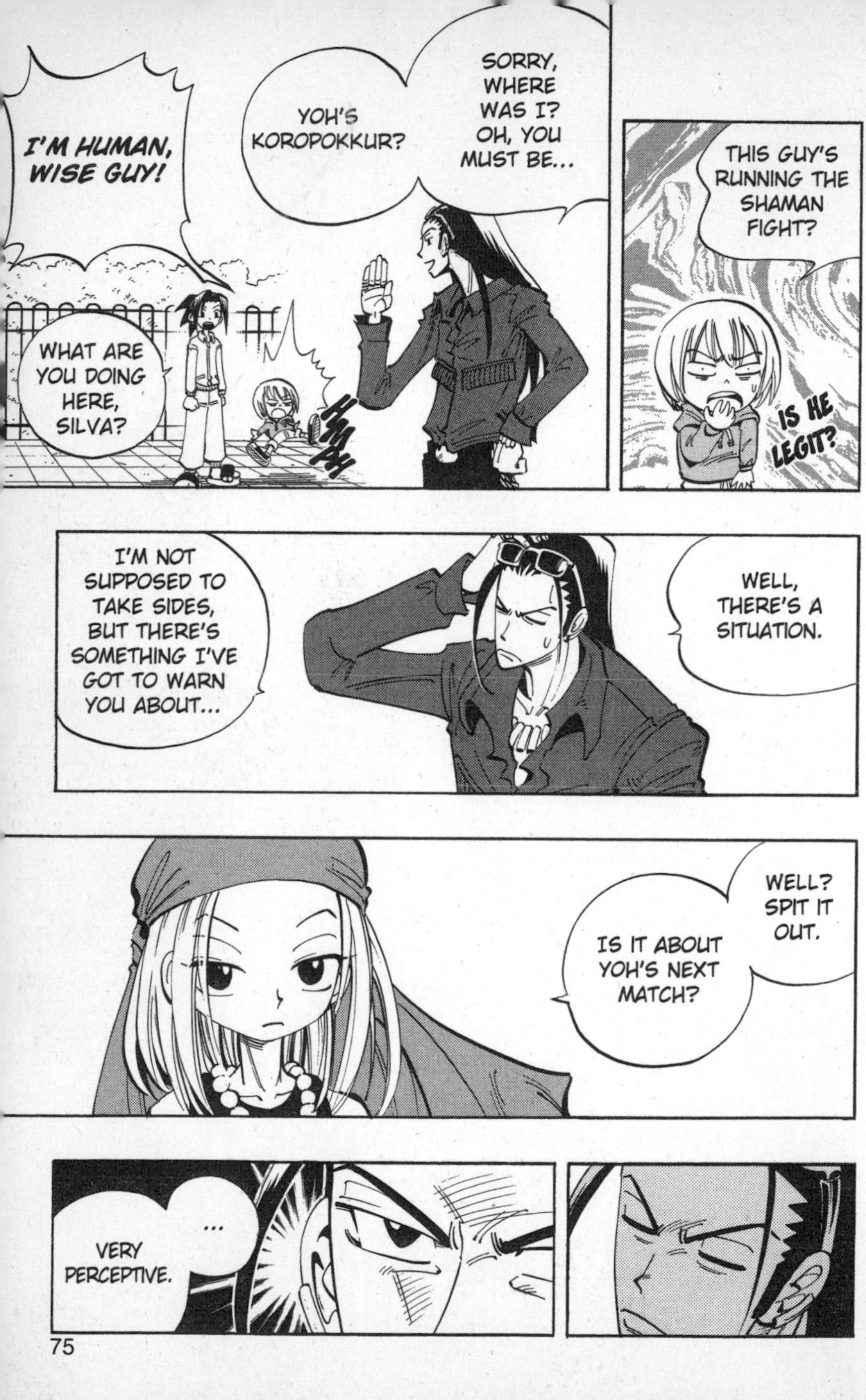
THIS GUY'S RUNNING THE SHAMAN FIGHT?
IS HE LEGIT?
SORRY, WHERE WAS I? OH, YOU MUST BE...
YOH'S KOROPOKKUR?
I'M HUMAN, WISE GUY!
HMMPH
WHAT ARE YOU DOING HERE, SILVA?
WELL, THERE'S A SITUATION.
I'M NOT SUPPOSED TO TAKE SIDES, BUT THERE'S SOMETHING I'VE GOT TO WARN YOU ABOUT...
WELL? SPIT IT OUT.
IS IT ABOUT YOH'S NEXT MATCH?
...
VERY PERCEPTIVE.

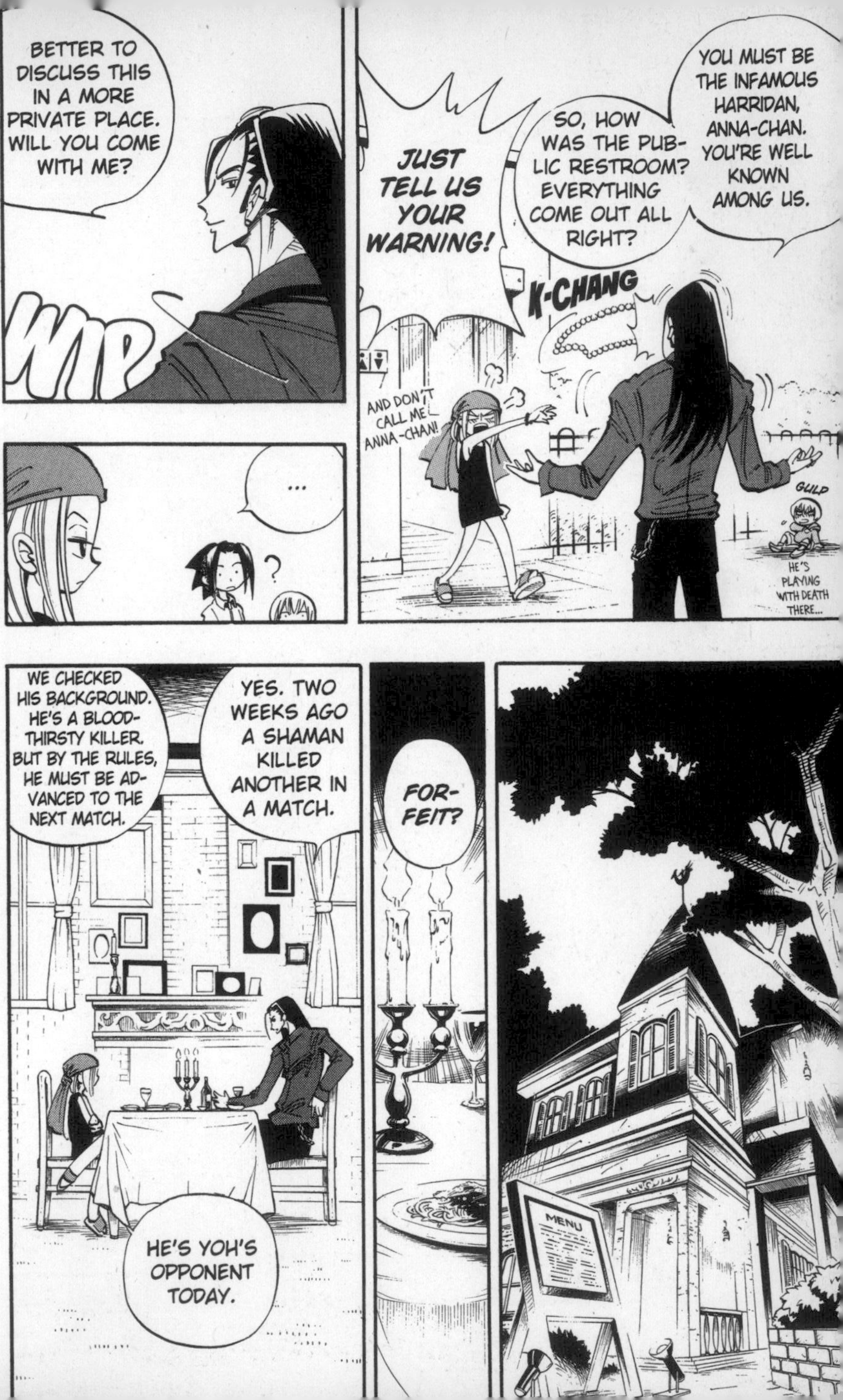
YOU MUST BE THE INFAMOUS HARRIDAN, ANNA-CHAN. YOU'RE WELL KNOWN AMONG US.
SO, HOW WAS THE PUB- LIC RESTROOM? EVERYTHING COME OUT ALL RIGHT?
JUST TELL US YOUR WARNING!
K-CHANG
AND DON'T CALL ME ANNA-CHAN!
GULP
HE'S PLAYING WITH DEATH THERE...
BETTER TO DISCUSS THIS IN A MORE PRIVATE PLACE. WILL YOU COME WITH ME?
WIP
...
MENU
FOR- FEIT?
YES. TWO WEEKS AGO A SHAMAN KILLED ANOTHER IN A MATCH.
WE CHECKED HIS BACKGROUND. HE'S A BLOOD- THIRSTY KILLER. BUT BY THE RULES, HE MUST BE AD- VANCED TO THE NEXT MATCH.
HE'S YOH'S OPPONENT TODAY.

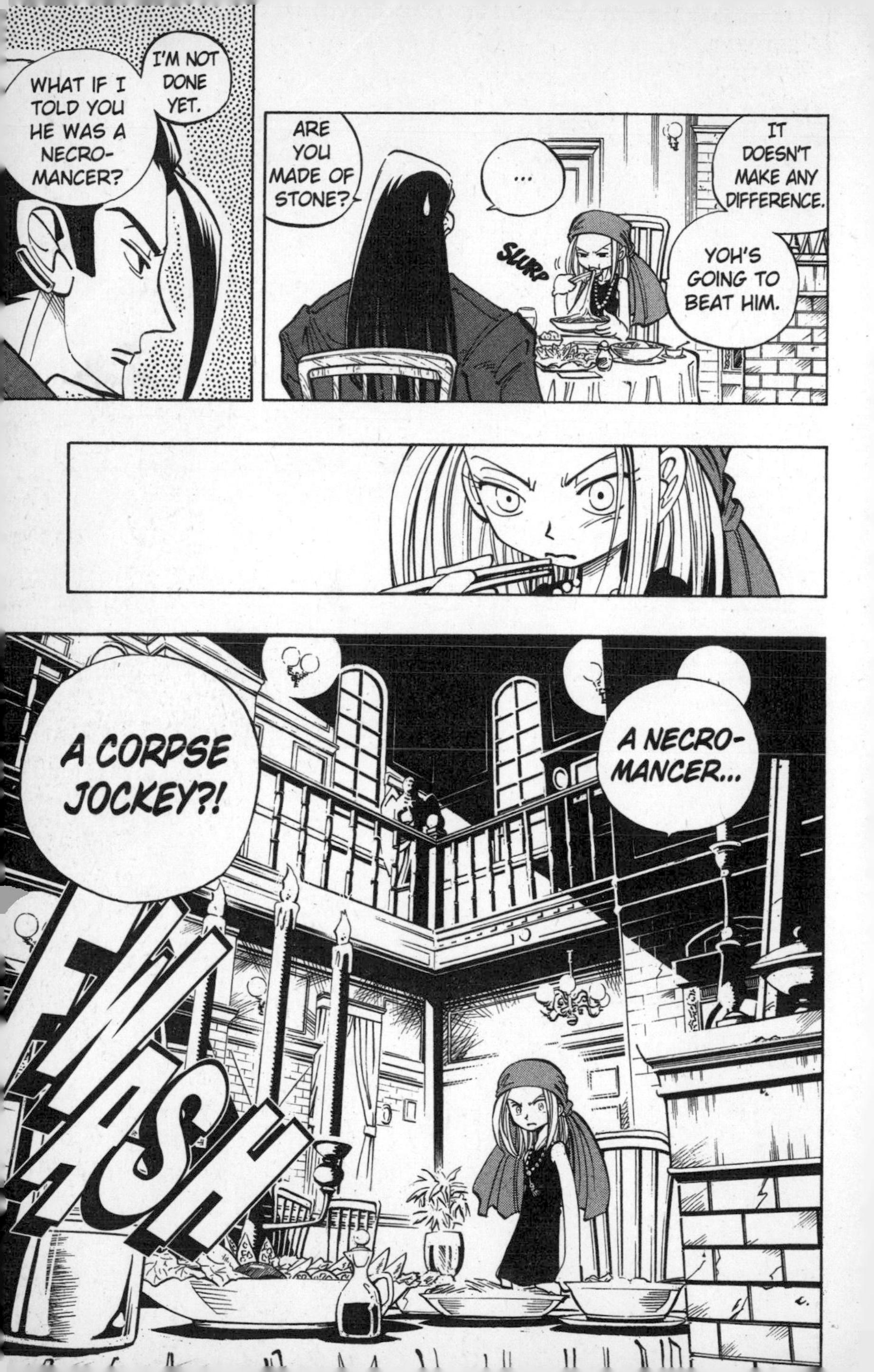
IT DOESN'T MAKE ANY DIFFERENCE.
YOH'S GOING TO BEAT HIM.
...
SLURP
ARE YOU MADE OF STONE?
I'M NOT DONE YET.
WHAT IF I TOLD YOU HE WAS A NECRO-MANCER?
A NECRO-MANCER...
A CORPSE JOCKEY?!
WASH

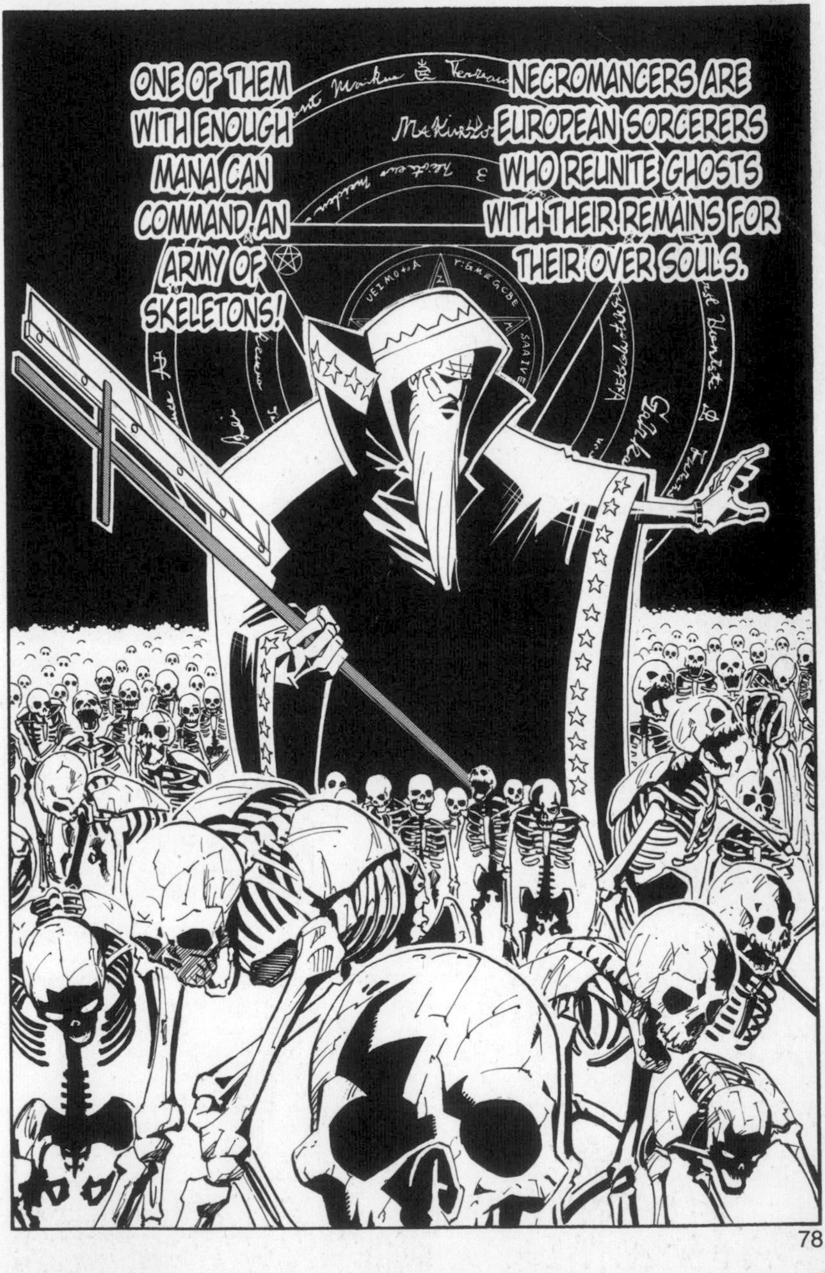
NECROMANCERS ARE EUROPEAN SORCERERS WHO REUNITE GHOSTS WITH THEIR REMAINS FOR THEIR OVER SOULS.
ONE OF THEM WITH ENOUGH MANA CAN COMMAND AN ARMY OF SKELETONS!

READ THIS WAY

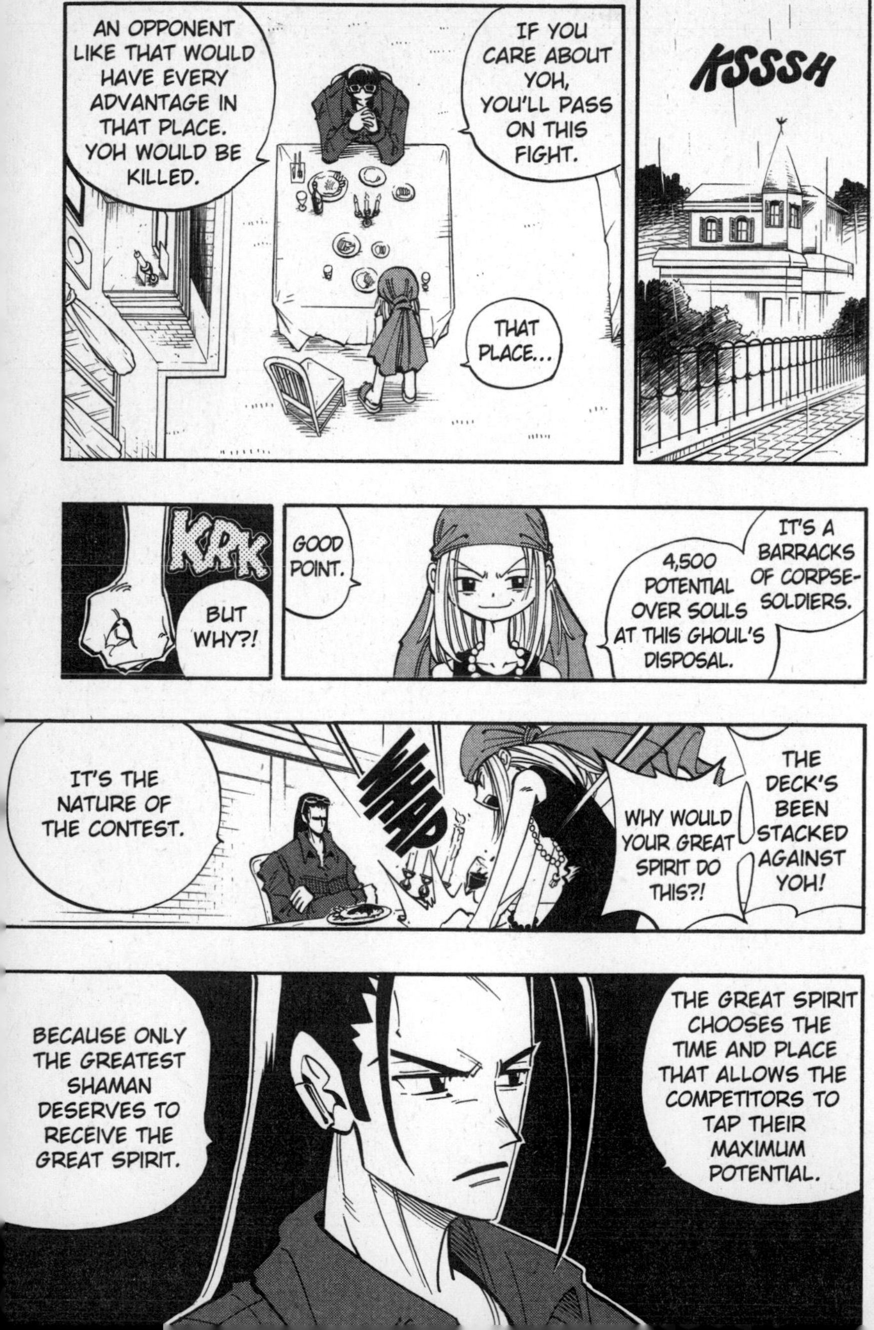
KSSSH
IF YOU CARE ABOUT YOH, YOU'LL PASS ON THIS FIGHT.
AN OPPONENT LIKE THAT WOULD HAVE EVERY ADVANTAGE IN THAT PLACE. YOH WOULD BE KILLED.
THAT PLACE...
IT'S A BARRACKS OF CORPSE-SOLDIERS.
4,500 POTENTIAL OVER SOULS AT THIS GHOUL'S DISPOSAL.
GOOD POINT.
KRK
BUT WHY?!
THE DECK'S BEEN STACKED AGAINST YOH!
WHY WOULD YOUR GREAT SPIRIT DO THIS?!
WHAP
IT'S THE NATURE OF THE CONTEST.
THE GREAT SPIRIT CHOOSES THE TIME AND PLACE THAT ALLOWS THE COMPETITORS TO TAP THEIR MAXIMUM POTENTIAL.
BECAUSE ONLY THE GREATEST SHAMAN DESERVES TO RECEIVE THE GREAT SPIRIT.

READ THIS WAY

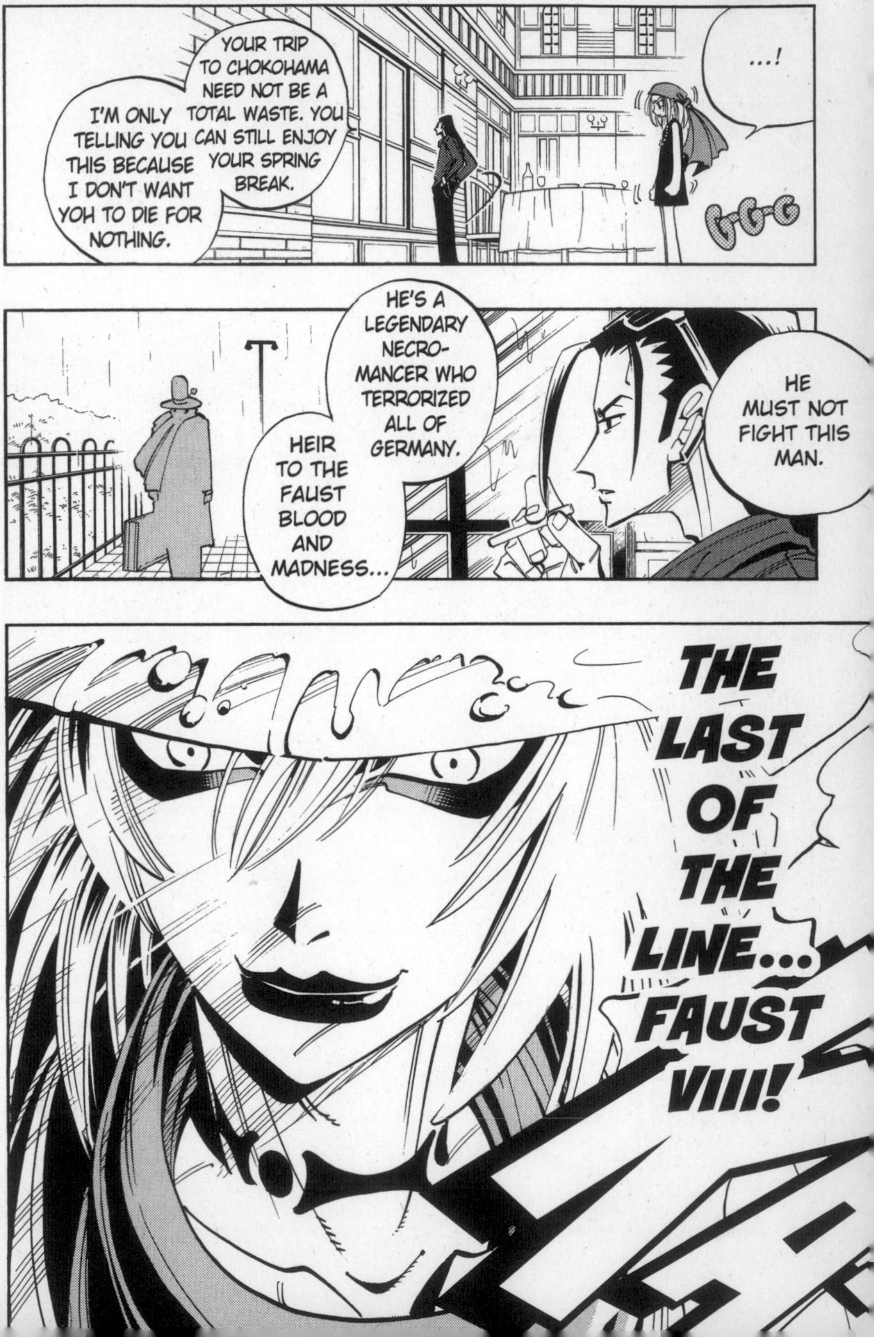

...!
YOUR TRIP TO CHOKOHAMA NEED NOT BE A TOTAL WASTE. YOU CAN STILL ENJOY YOUR SPRING BREAK.
I'M ONLY TELLING YOU THIS BECAUSE I DON'T WANT YOH TO DIE FOR NOTHING.
G-G-G
HE MUST NOT FIGHT THIS MAN.
HE'S A LEGENDARY NECRO-MANCER WHO TERRORIZED ALL OF GERMANY.
HEIR TO THE FAUST BLOOD AND MADNESS...
THE LAST OF THE LINE... FAUST VIII!

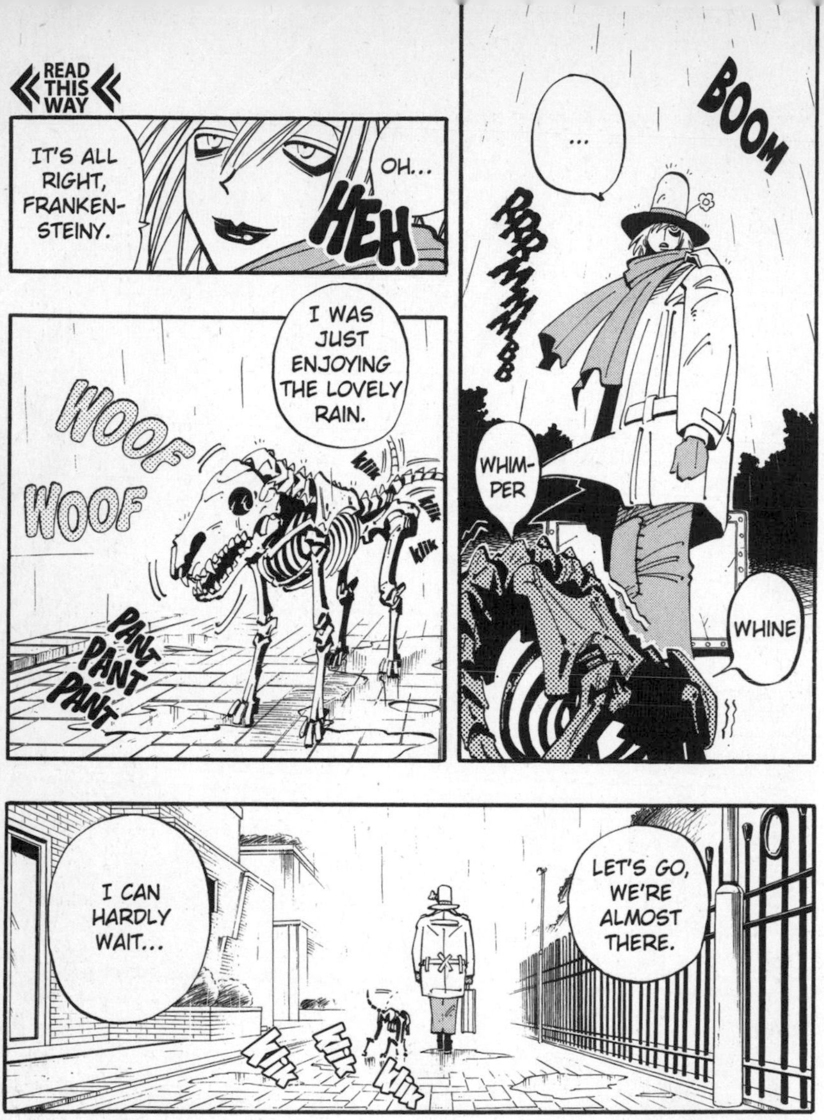
READ THIS WAY
BOOM
...
RRRMMMBB
WHIM-PER
WHINE
IT'S ALL RIGHT, FRANKEN-STEINY.
OH...
HEH
I WAS JUST ENJOYING THE LOVELY RAIN.
WOOF WOOF
KLIK KLIK KLIK
PANT PANT PANT
LET'S GO, WE'RE ALMOST THERE.
I CAN HARDLY WAIT...
KLIK KLIK KLIK
THE RAIN SOFTENS THE EARTH AND MAKES IT EASIER FOR *THEM* TO CRAWL OUT.
KSSSH

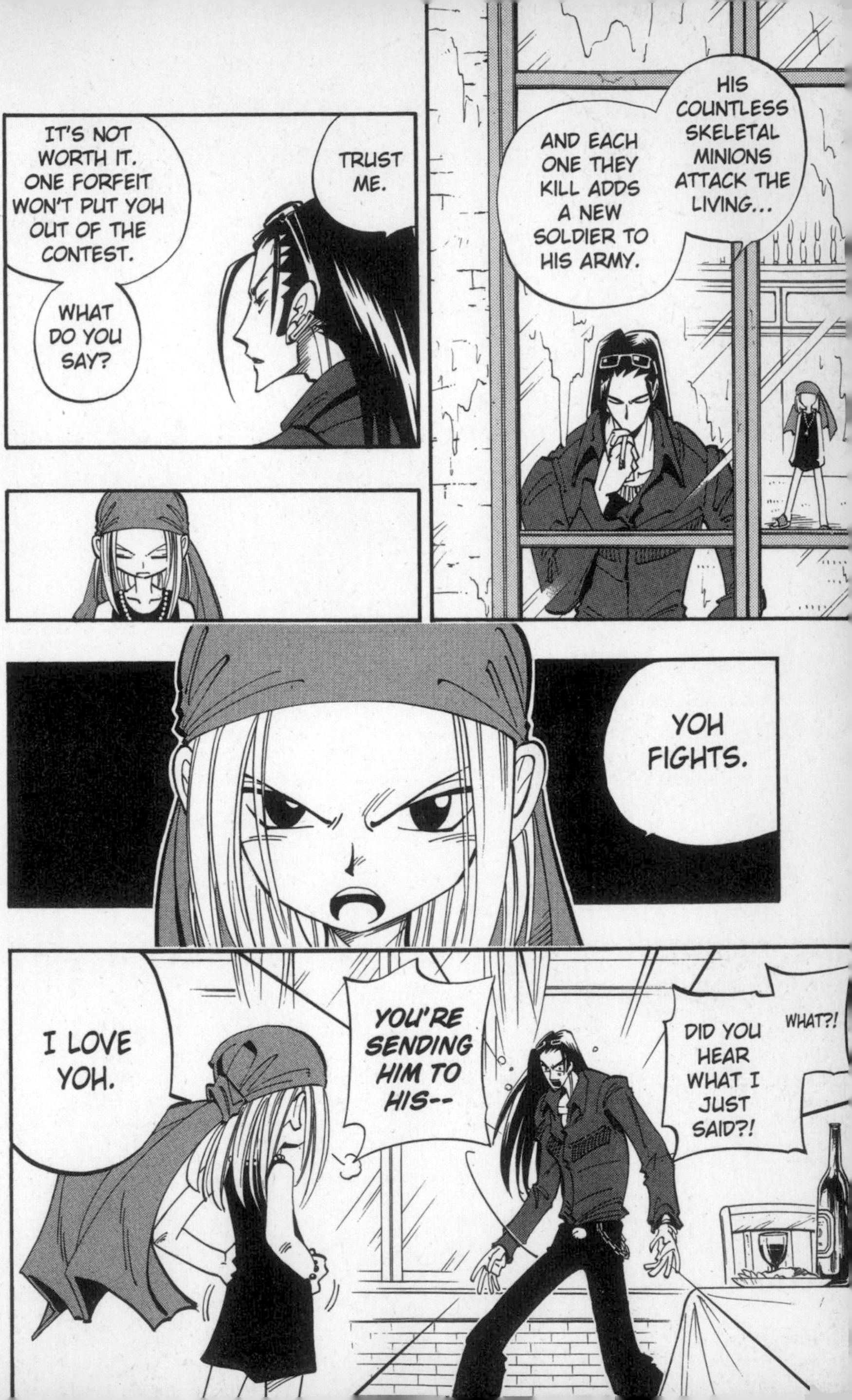
HIS COUNTLESS SKELETAL MINIONS ATTACK THE LIVING...
AND EACH ONE THEY KILL ADDS A NEW SOLDIER TO HIS ARMY.
TRUST ME.
IT'S NOT WORTH IT. ONE FORFEIT WON'T PUT YOH OUT OF THE CONTEST.
WHAT DO YOU SAY?
YOH FIGHTS.
WHAT?!
DID YOU HEAR WHAT I JUST SAID?!
YOU'RE SENDING HIM TO HIS--
I LOVE YOH.

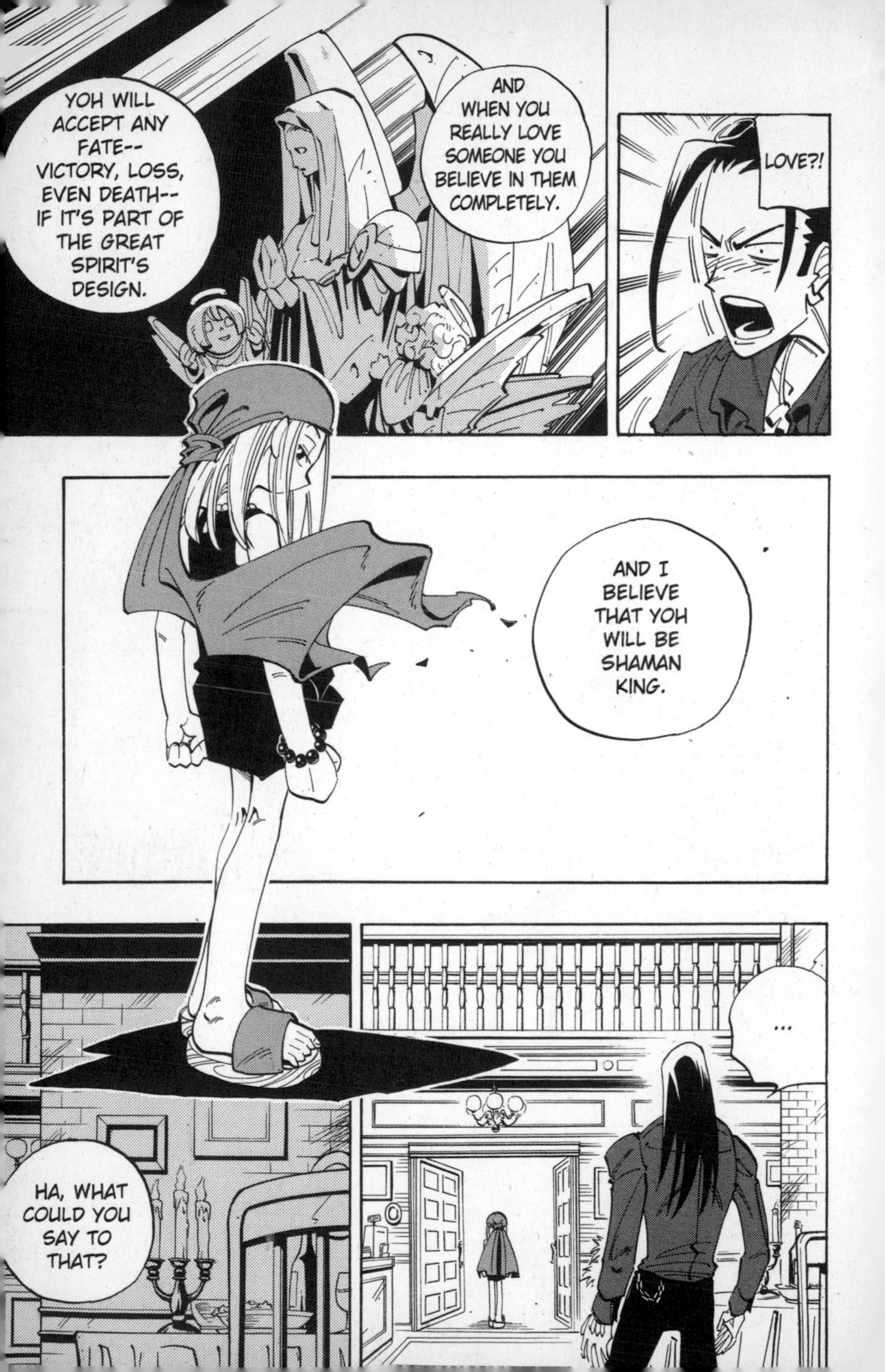
YOH WILL ACCEPT ANY FATE-- VICTORY, LOSS, EVEN DEATH-- IF IT'S PART OF THE GREAT SPIRIT'S DESIGN.
AND WHEN YOU REALLY LOVE SOMEONE YOU BELIEVE IN THEM COMPLETELY.
LOVE?!
AND I BELIEVE THAT YOH WILL BE SHAMAN KING.
HA, WHAT COULD YOU SAY TO THAT?
...

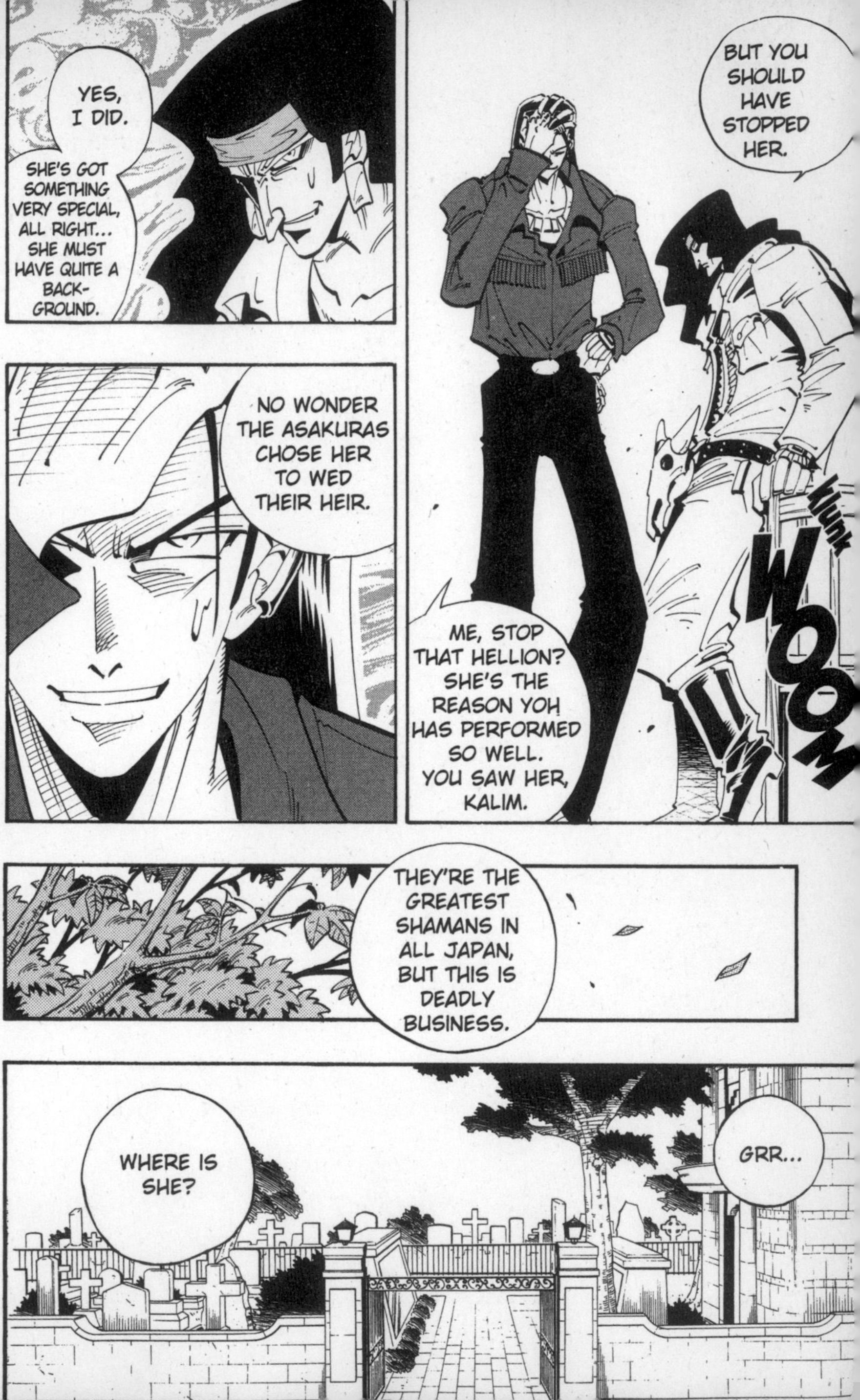
BUT YOU SHOULD HAVE STOPPED HER.
klunk
WOOM
ME, STOP THAT HELLION? SHE'S THE REASON YOH HAS PERFORMED SO WELL. YOU SAW HER, KALIM.
YES, I DID.
SHE'S GOT SOMETHING VERY SPECIAL, ALL RIGHT... SHE MUST HAVE QUITE A BACK-GROUND.
NO WONDER THE ASAKURAS CHOSE HER TO WED THEIR HEIR.
THEY'RE THE GREATEST SHAMANS IN ALL JAPAN, BUT THIS IS DEADLY BUSINESS.
GRR...
WHERE IS SHE?

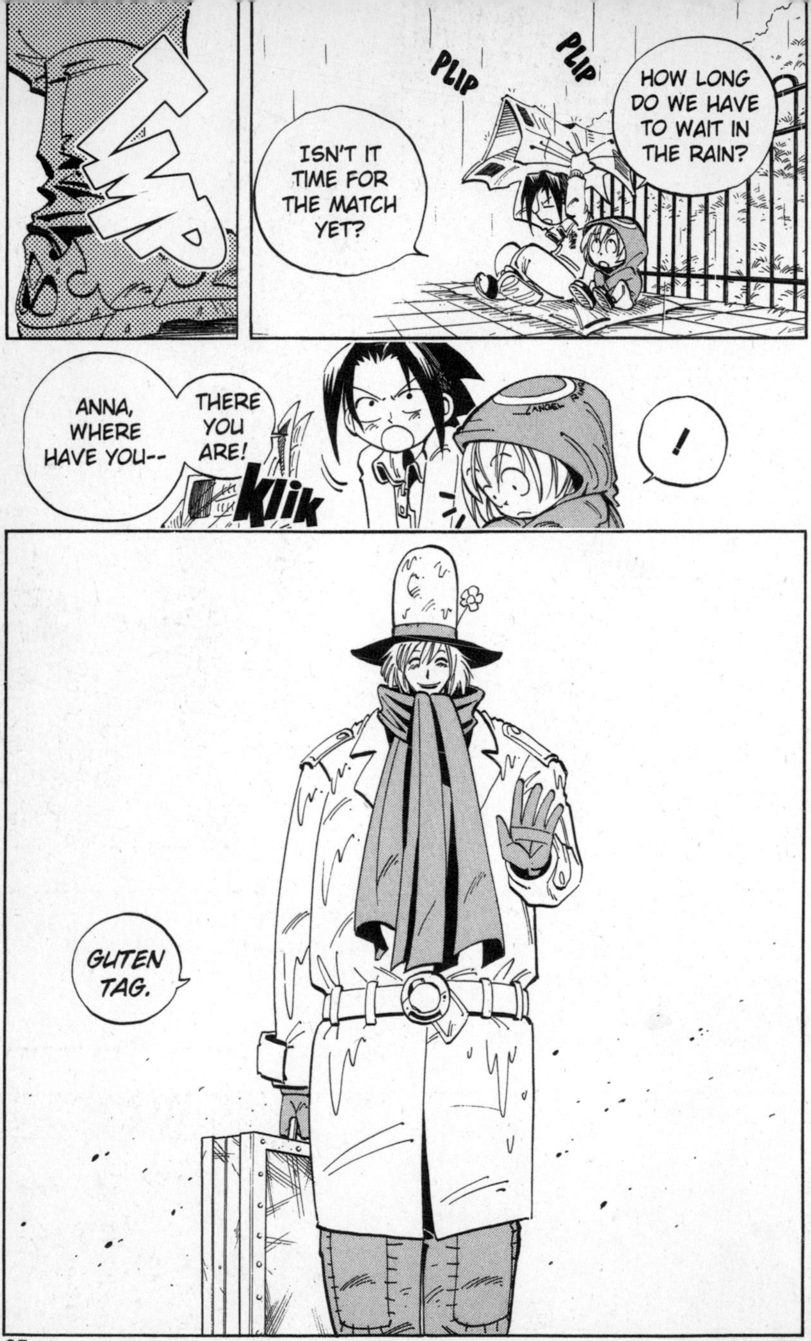
PLIP
HOW LONG DO WE HAVE TO WAIT IN THE RAIN?
PLIP
ISN'T IT TIME FOR THE MATCH YET?
TMP
!
THERE YOU ARE!
ANNA, WHERE HAVE YOU--
KLIK
GUTEN TAG.

SHAMAN
KING
5

BUTTERBUR

Reincarnation 40: Spill Your Guts

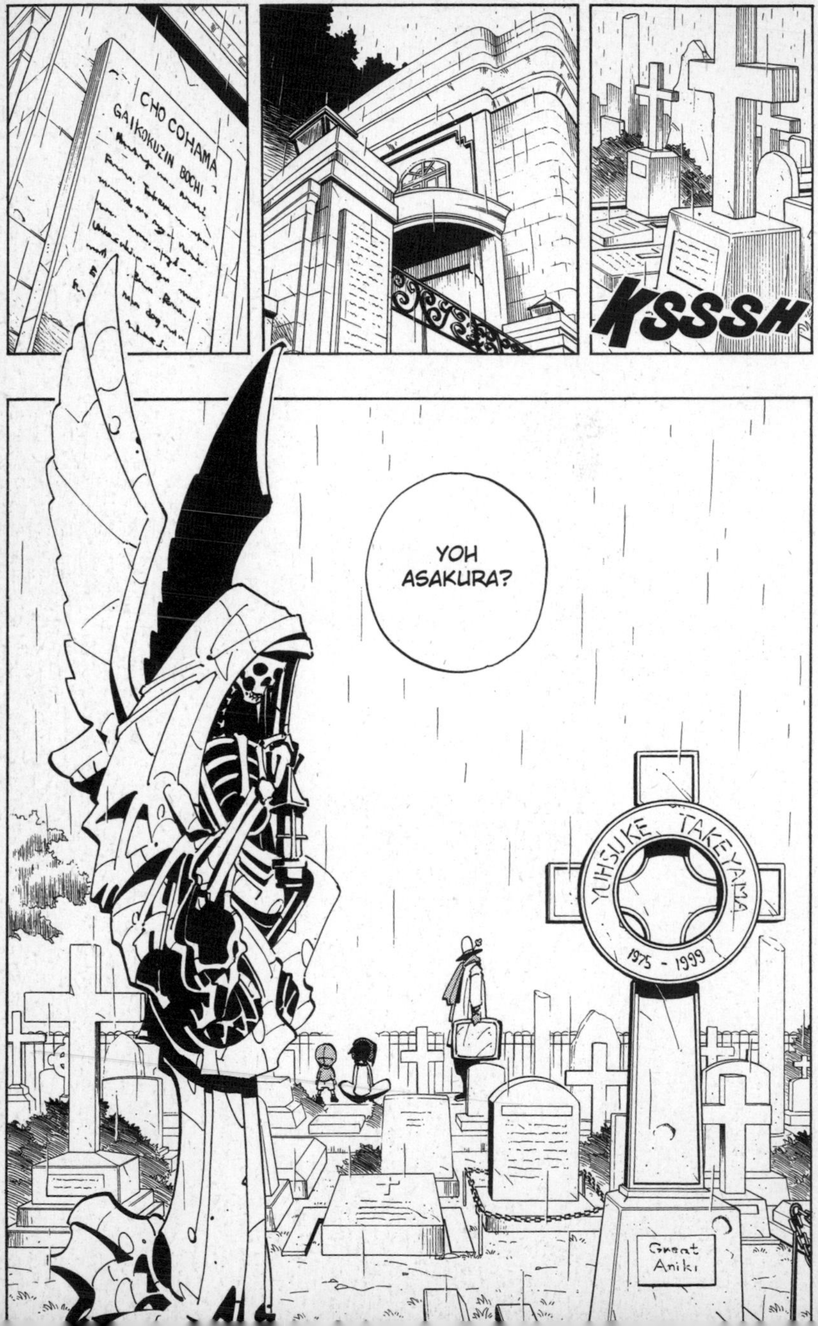
KSSSH
CHO COHAMA
GAIKOKUZIN BOCHI
YOH ASAKURA?
YUHSUKE TAKEYAMA
1975 - 1999
Great Aniki

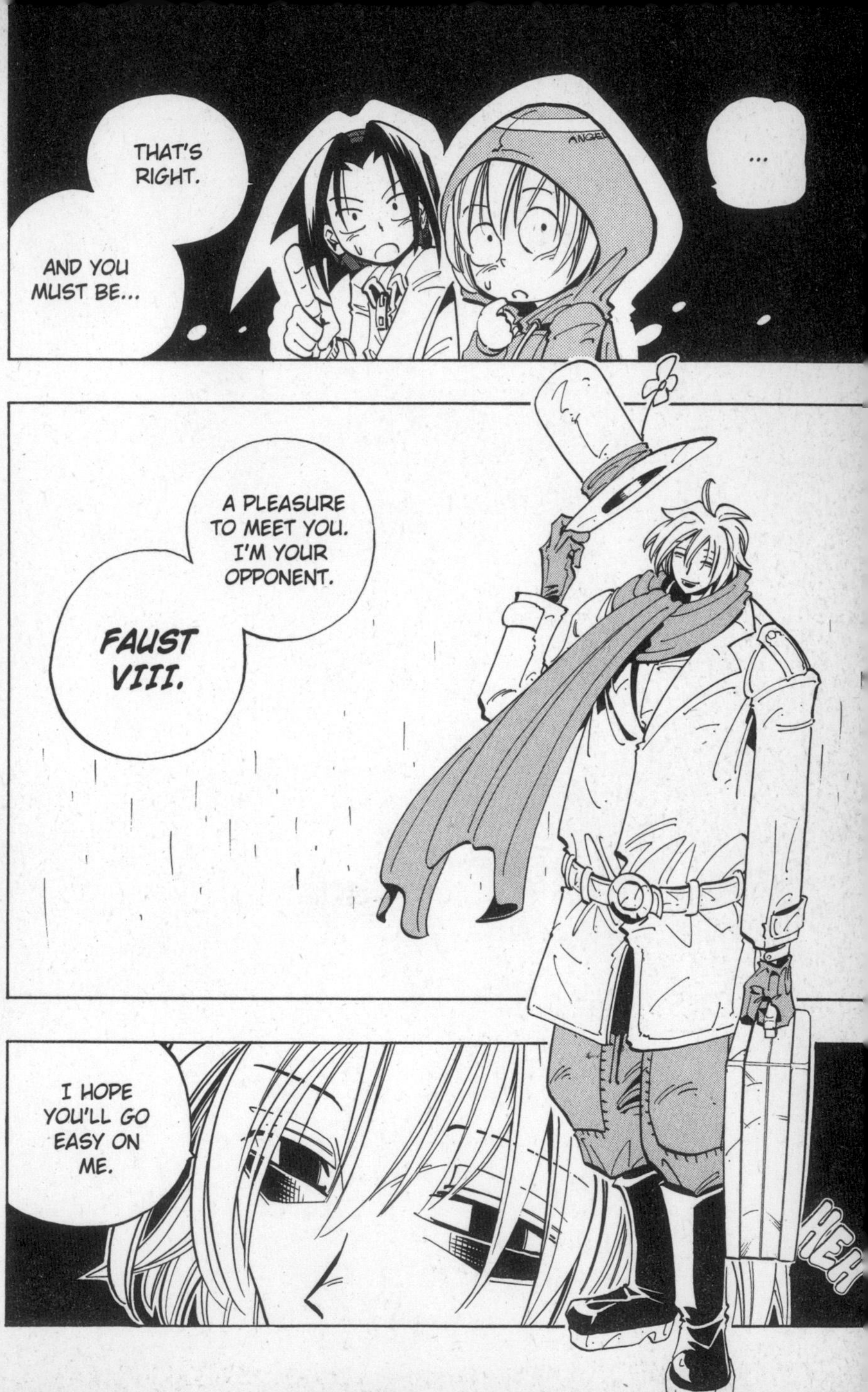
...
THAT'S RIGHT.
AND YOU MUST BE...
A PLEASURE TO MEET YOU. I'M YOUR OPPONENT.
FAUST VIII.
HEH
I HOPE YOU'LL GO EASY ON ME.

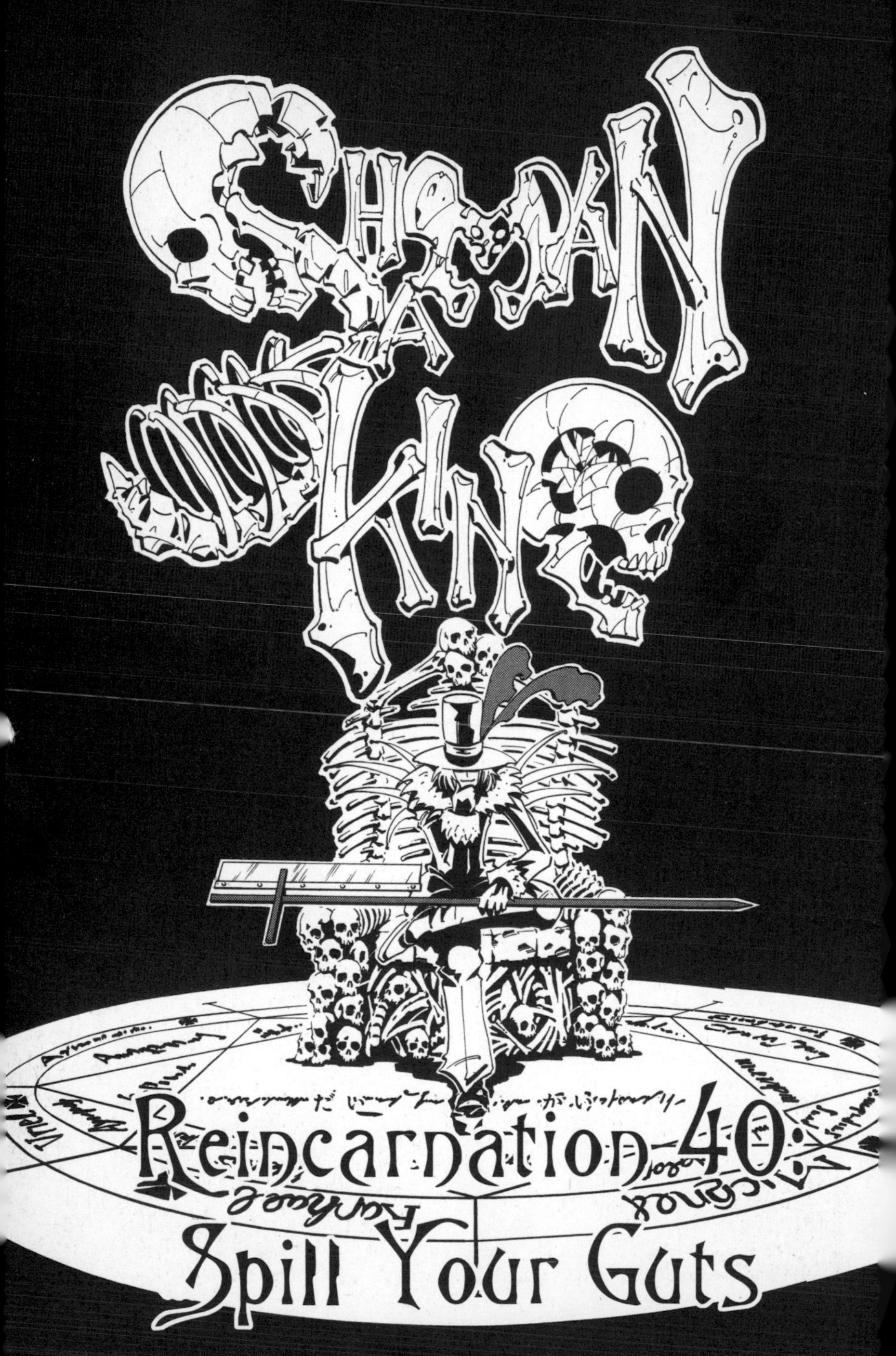
SHAMAN KING
Reincarnation 40:
Spill Your Guts

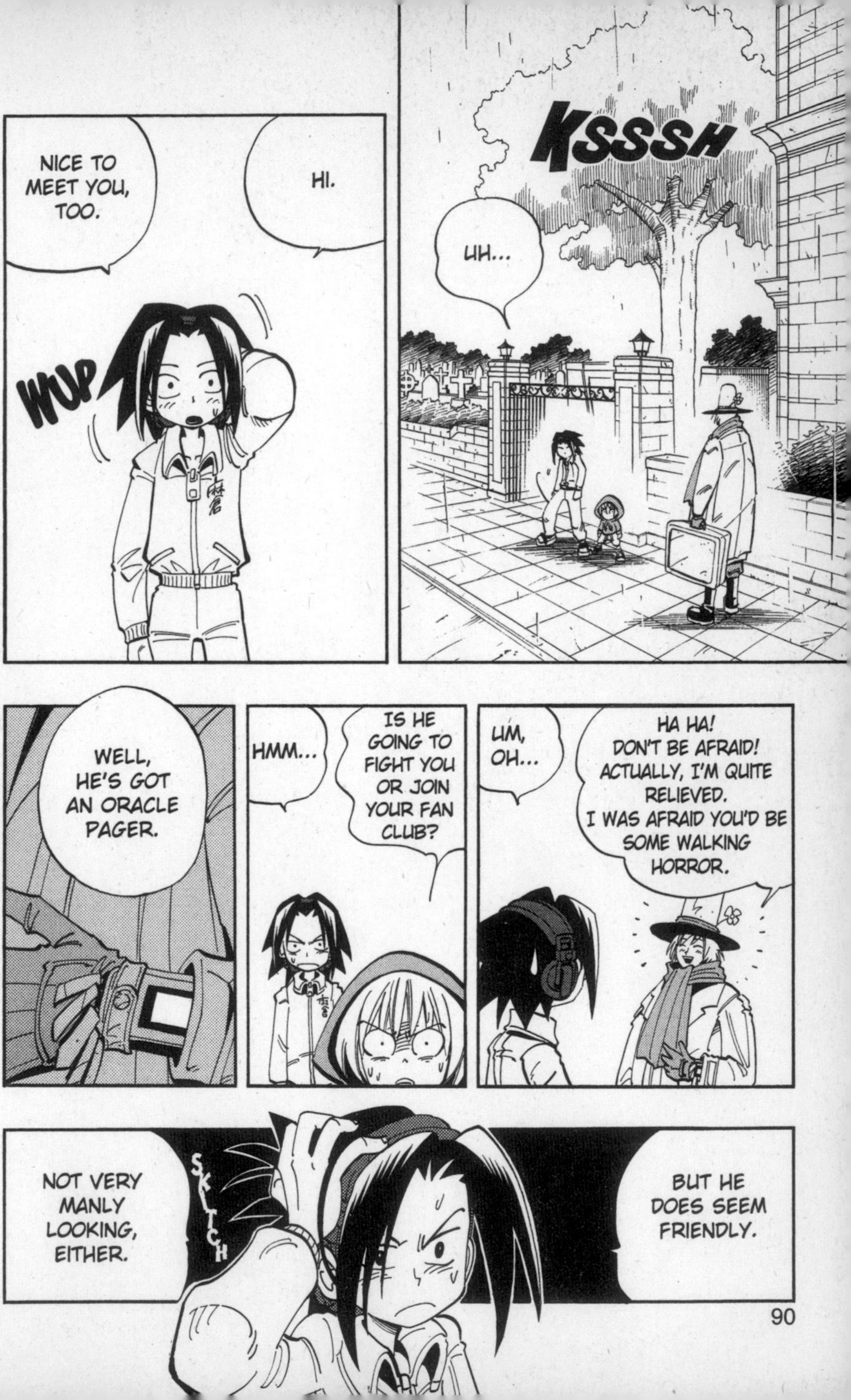
KSSSH
UH...
HI.
NICE TO MEET YOU, TOO.
WUP
HA HA! DON'T BE AFRAID! ACTUALLY, I'M QUITE RELIEVED. I WAS AFRAID YOU'D BE SOME WALKING HORROR.
UM, OH...
IS HE GOING TO FIGHT YOU OR JOIN YOUR FAN CLUB?
HMM...
WELL, HE'S GOT AN ORACLE PAGER.
BUT HE DOES SEEM FRIENDLY.
SKLTCH
NOT VERY MANLY LOOKING, EITHER.

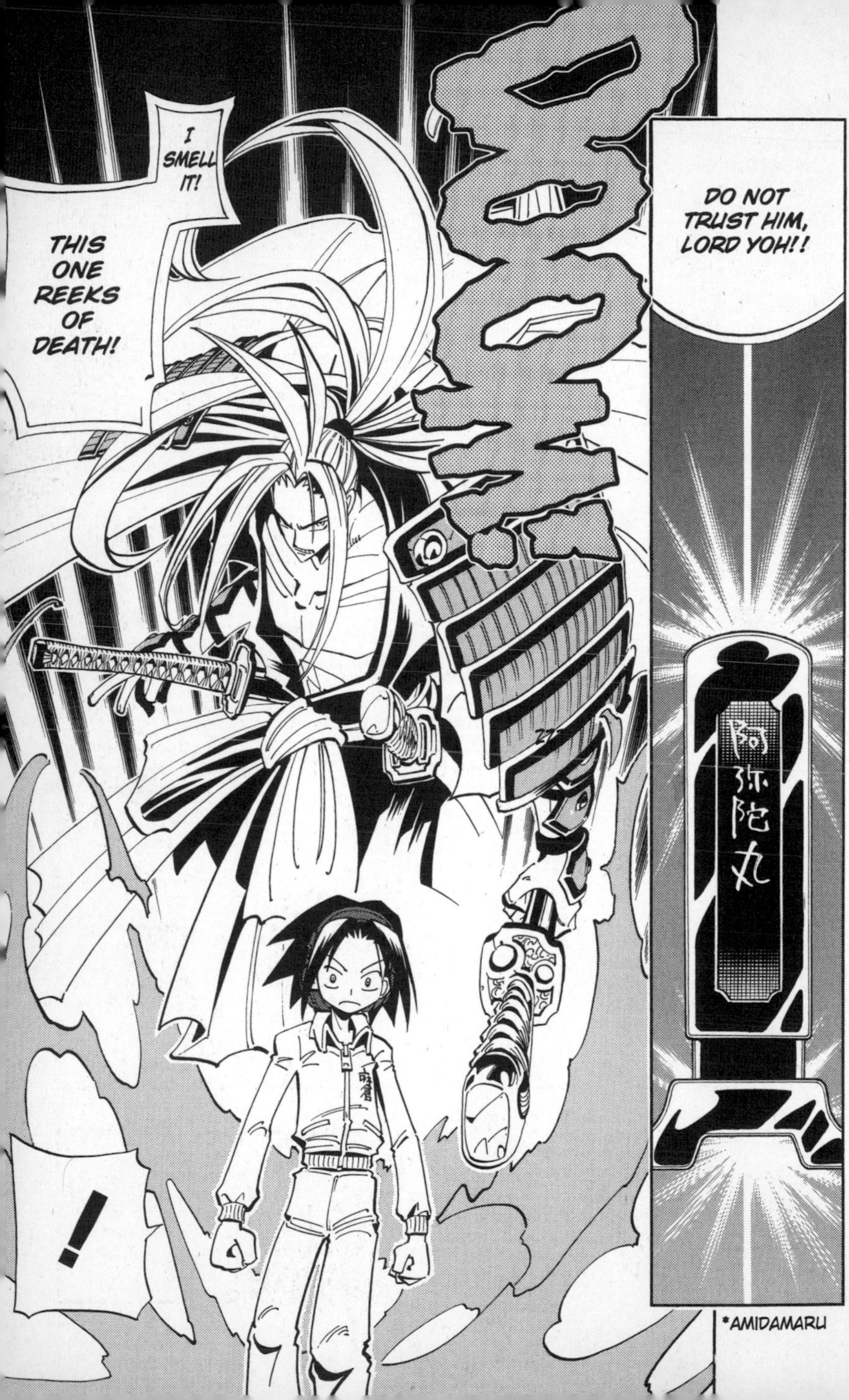
DO NOT TRUST HIM, LORD YOH!!
阿弥陀丸
I SMELL IT!
THIS ONE REEKS OF DEATH!
!

*AMIDAMARU

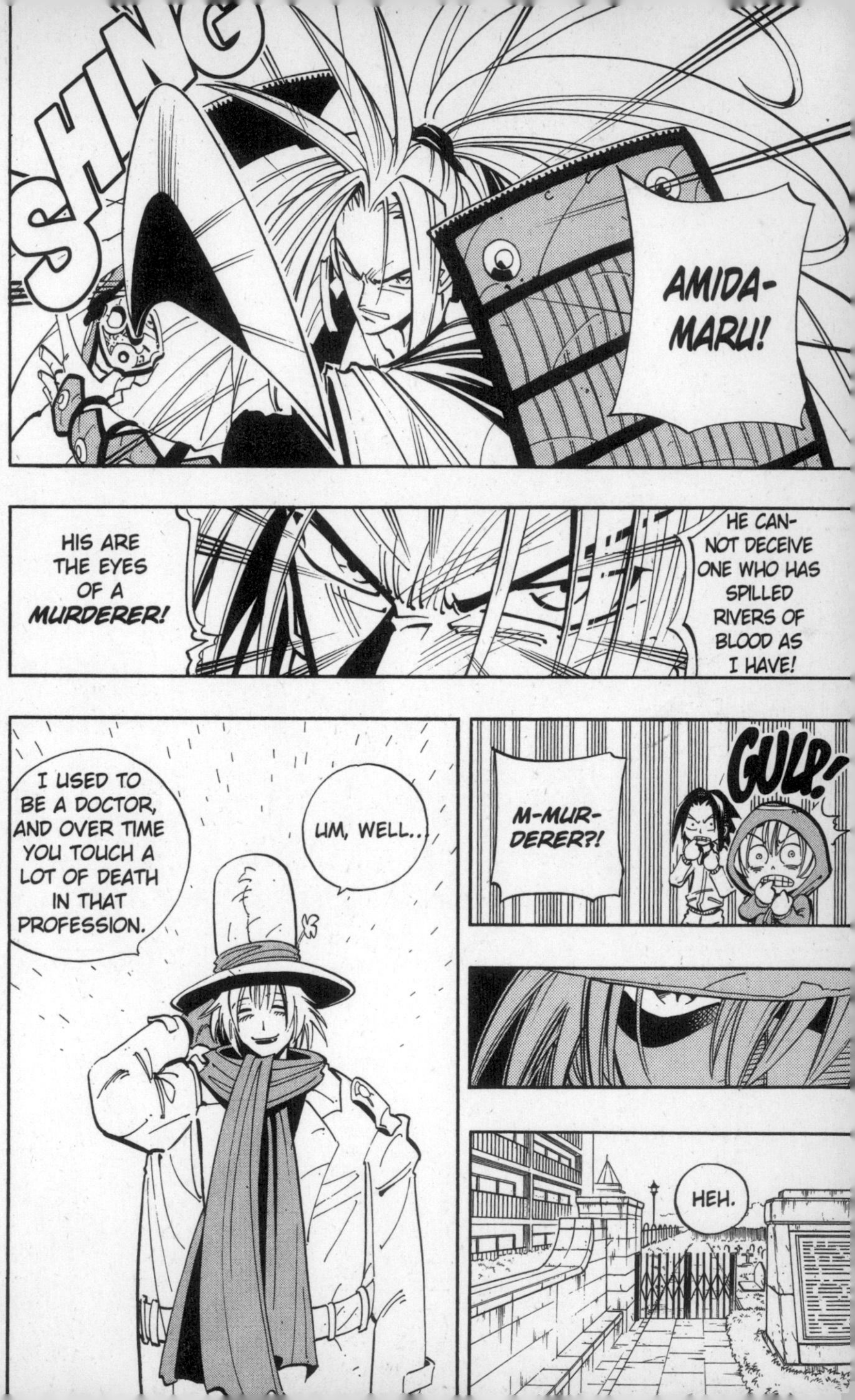
AMIDA-MARU!
SHING
HE CAN-NOT DECEIVE ONE WHO HAS SPILLED RIVERS OF BLOOD AS I HAVE!
HIS ARE THE EYES OF A MURDERER!
GULP!
M-MUR-DERER?!
HEH.
UM, WELL...
I USED TO BE A DOCTOR, AND OVER TIME YOU TOUCH A LOT OF DEATH IN THAT PROFESSION.

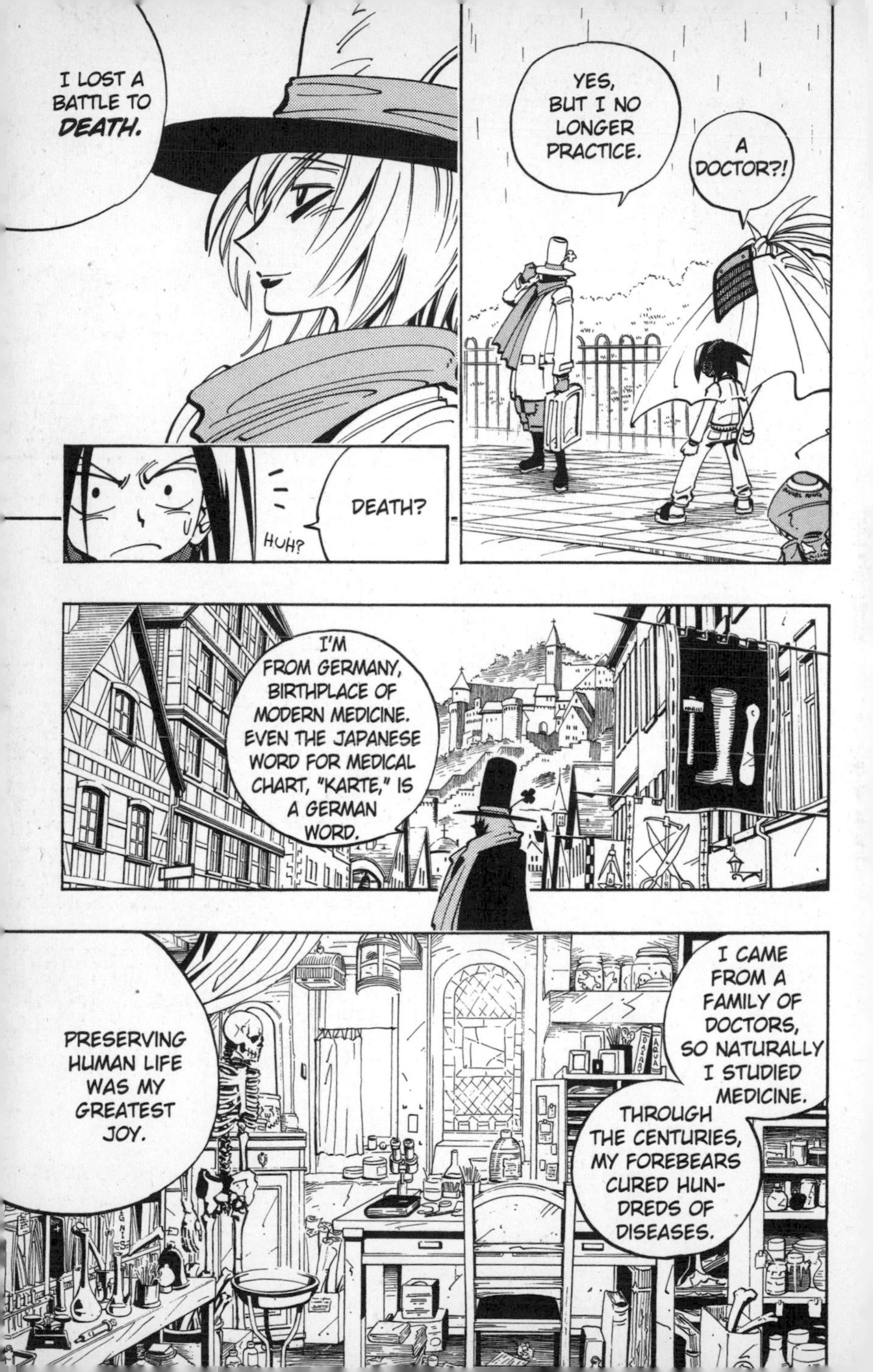
A DOCTOR?!
YES, BUT I NO LONGER PRACTICE.
I LOST A BATTLE TO *DEATH.*
DEATH?
HUH?
I'M FROM GERMANY, BIRTHPLACE OF MODERN MEDICINE. EVEN THE JAPANESE WORD FOR MEDICAL CHART, "KARTE," IS A GERMAN WORD.
I CAME FROM A FAMILY OF DOCTORS, SO NATURALLY I STUDIED MEDICINE.
THROUGH THE CENTURIES, MY FOREBEARS CURED HUN-DREDS OF DISEASES.
PRESERVING HUMAN LIFE WAS MY GREATEST JOY.

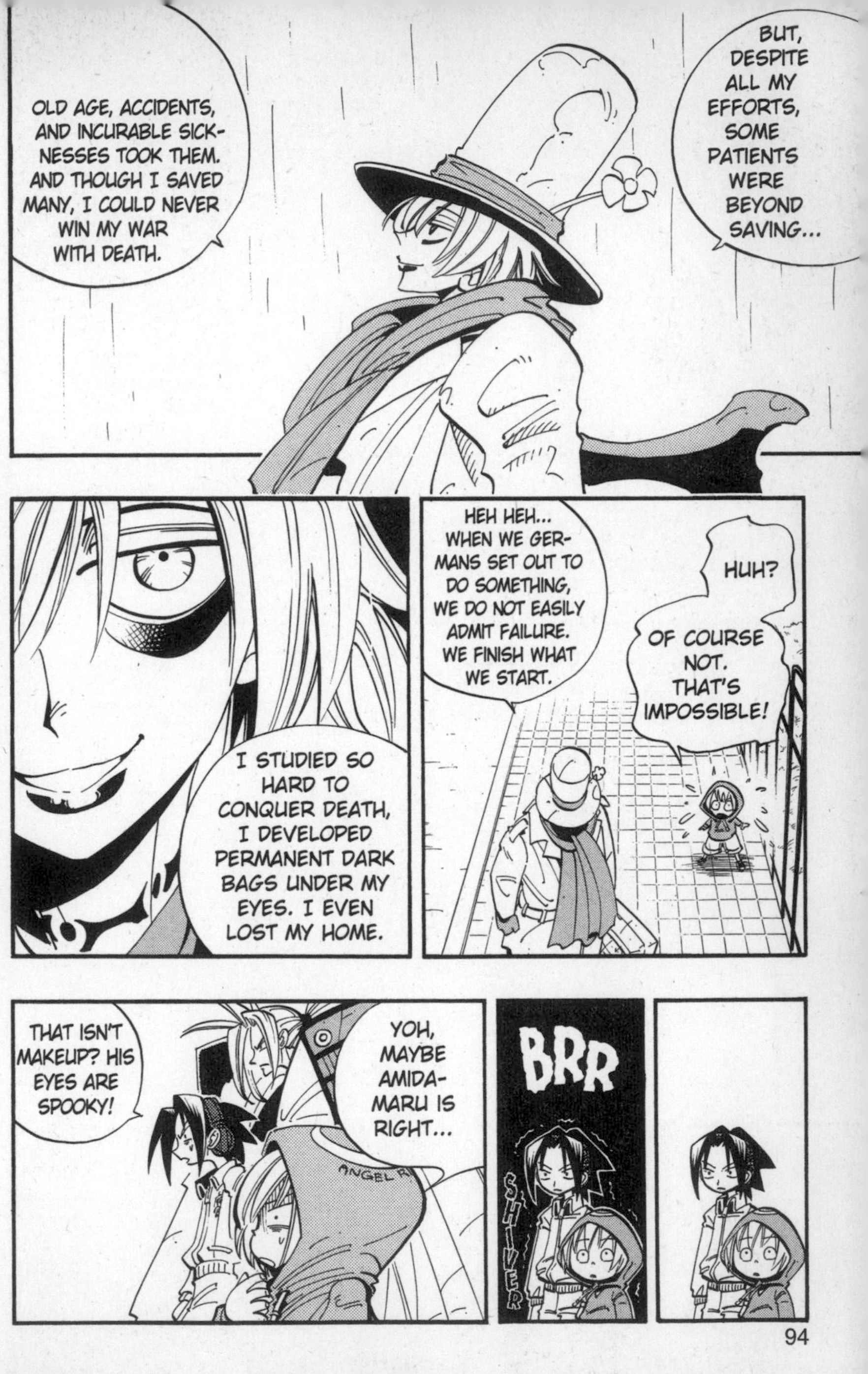
BUT, DESPITE ALL MY EFFORTS, SOME PATIENTS WERE BEYOND SAVING...
OLD AGE, ACCIDENTS, AND INCURABLE SICKNESSES TOOK THEM. AND THOUGH I SAVED MANY, I COULD NEVER WIN MY WAR WITH DEATH.
HUH?
OF COURSE NOT. THAT'S IMPOSSIBLE!
HEH HEH... WHEN WE GERMANS SET OUT TO DO SOMETHING, WE DO NOT EASILY ADMIT FAILURE. WE FINISH WHAT WE START.
I STUDIED SO HARD TO CONQUER DEATH, I DEVELOPED PERMANENT DARK BAGS UNDER MY EYES. I EVEN LOST MY HOME.
BRR
SHIVER
YOH, MAYBE AMIDAMARU IS RIGHT...
THAT ISN'T MAKEUP? HIS EYES ARE SPOOKY!
ANGEL R

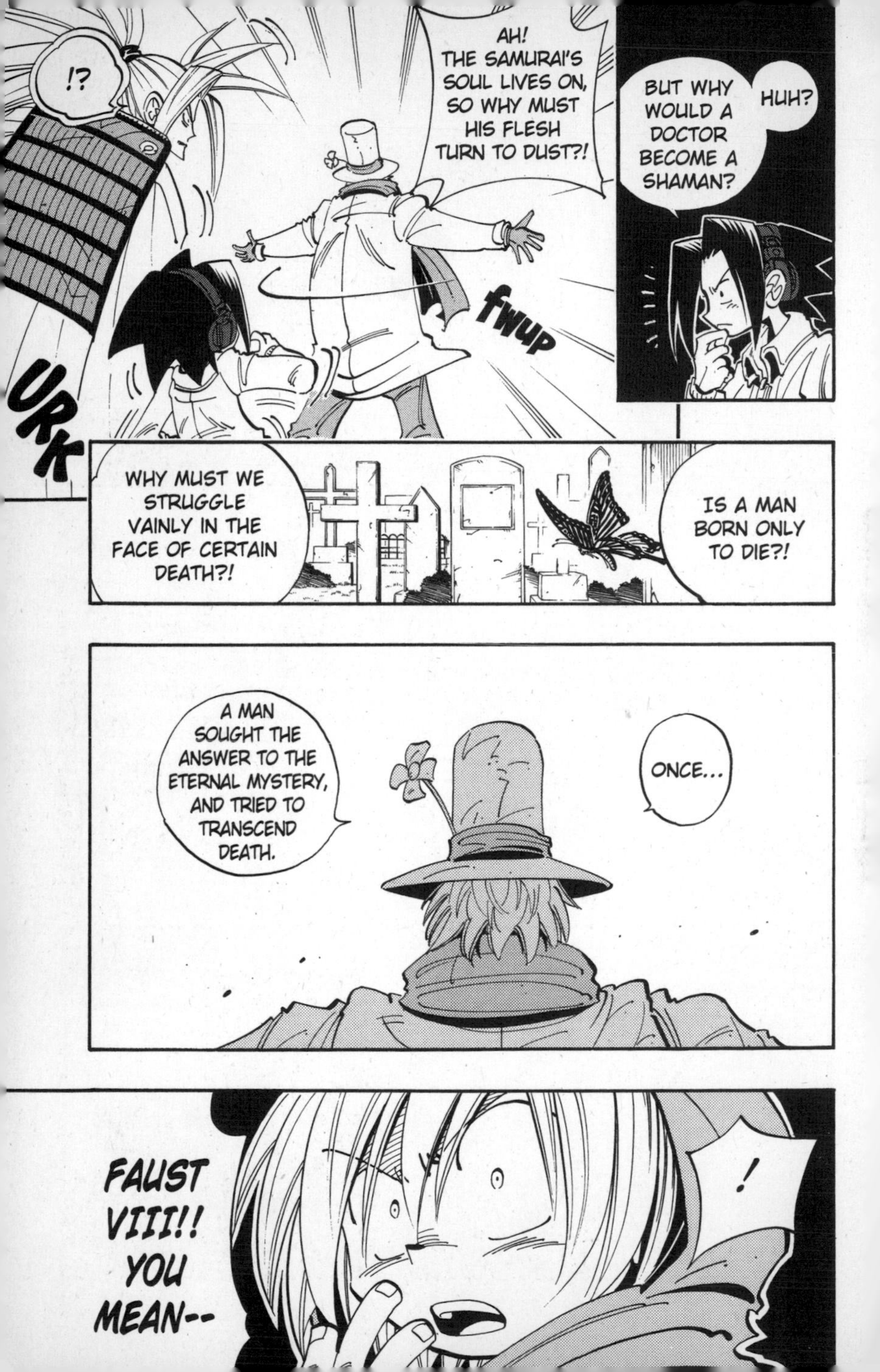
HUH?
BUT WHY WOULD A DOCTOR BECOME A SHAMAN?
AH! THE SAMURAI'S SOUL LIVES ON, SO WHY MUST HIS FLESH TURN TO DUST?!
fwup
!?
URK
IS A MAN BORN ONLY TO DIE?!
WHY MUST WE STRUGGLE VAINLY IN THE FACE OF CERTAIN DEATH?!
ONCE...
A MAN SOUGHT THE ANSWER TO THE ETERNAL MYSTERY, AND TRIED TO TRANSCEND DEATH.
!
FAUST VIII!! YOU MEAN--

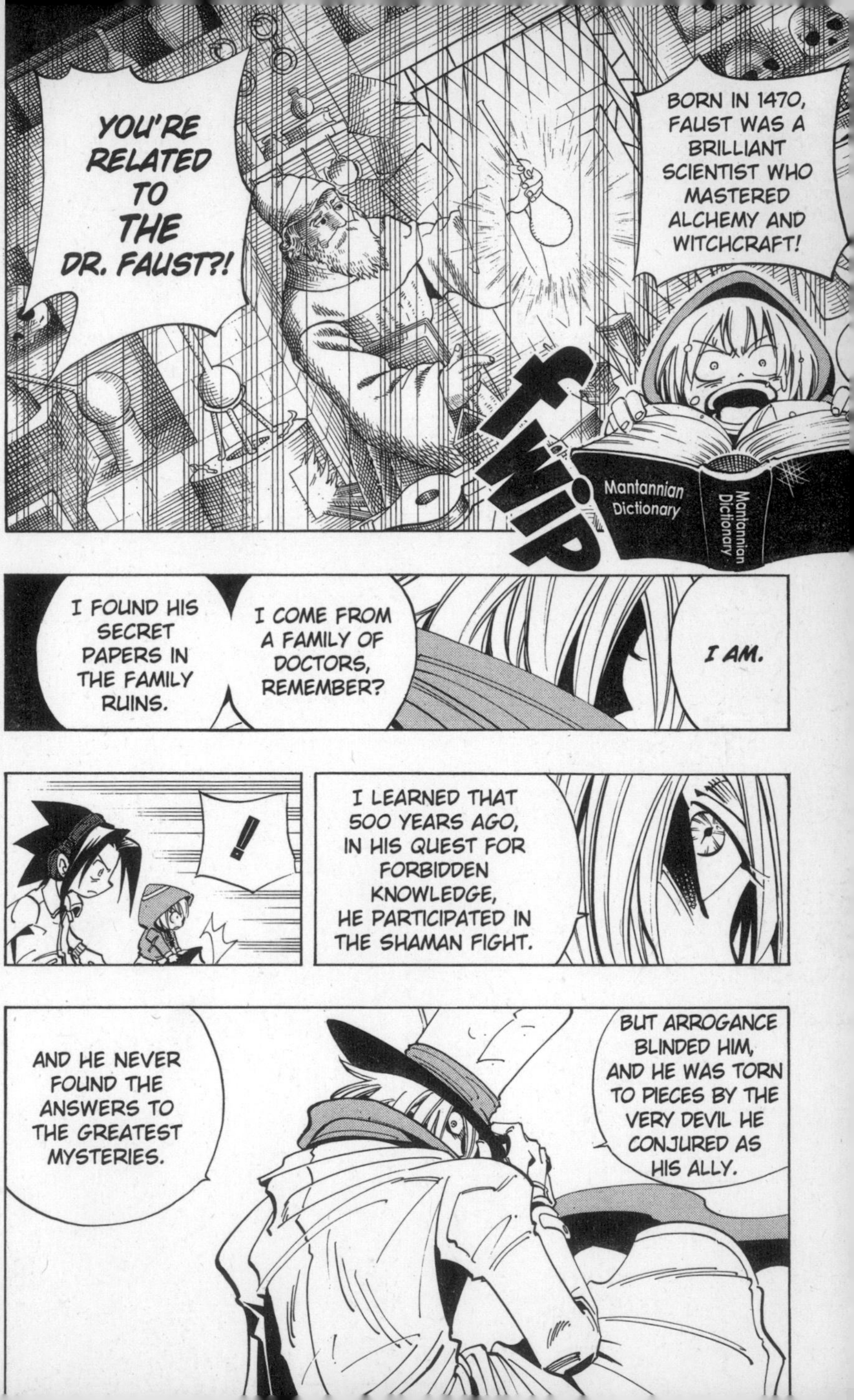
BORN IN 1470, FAUST WAS A BRILLIANT SCIENTIST WHO MASTERED ALCHEMY AND WITCHCRAFT!
YOU'RE RELATED TO THE DR. FAUST?!
FWIP
Mantannian Dictionary
Mantannian Dictionary
I AM.
I COME FROM A FAMILY OF DOCTORS, REMEMBER?
I FOUND HIS SECRET PAPERS IN THE FAMILY RUINS.
I LEARNED THAT 500 YEARS AGO, IN HIS QUEST FOR FORBIDDEN KNOWLEDGE, HE PARTICIPATED IN THE SHAMAN FIGHT.
!
BUT ARROGANCE BLINDED HIM, AND HE WAS TORN TO PIECES BY THE VERY DEVIL HE CONJURED AS HIS ALLY.
AND HE NEVER FOUND THE ANSWERS TO THE GREATEST MYSTERIES.

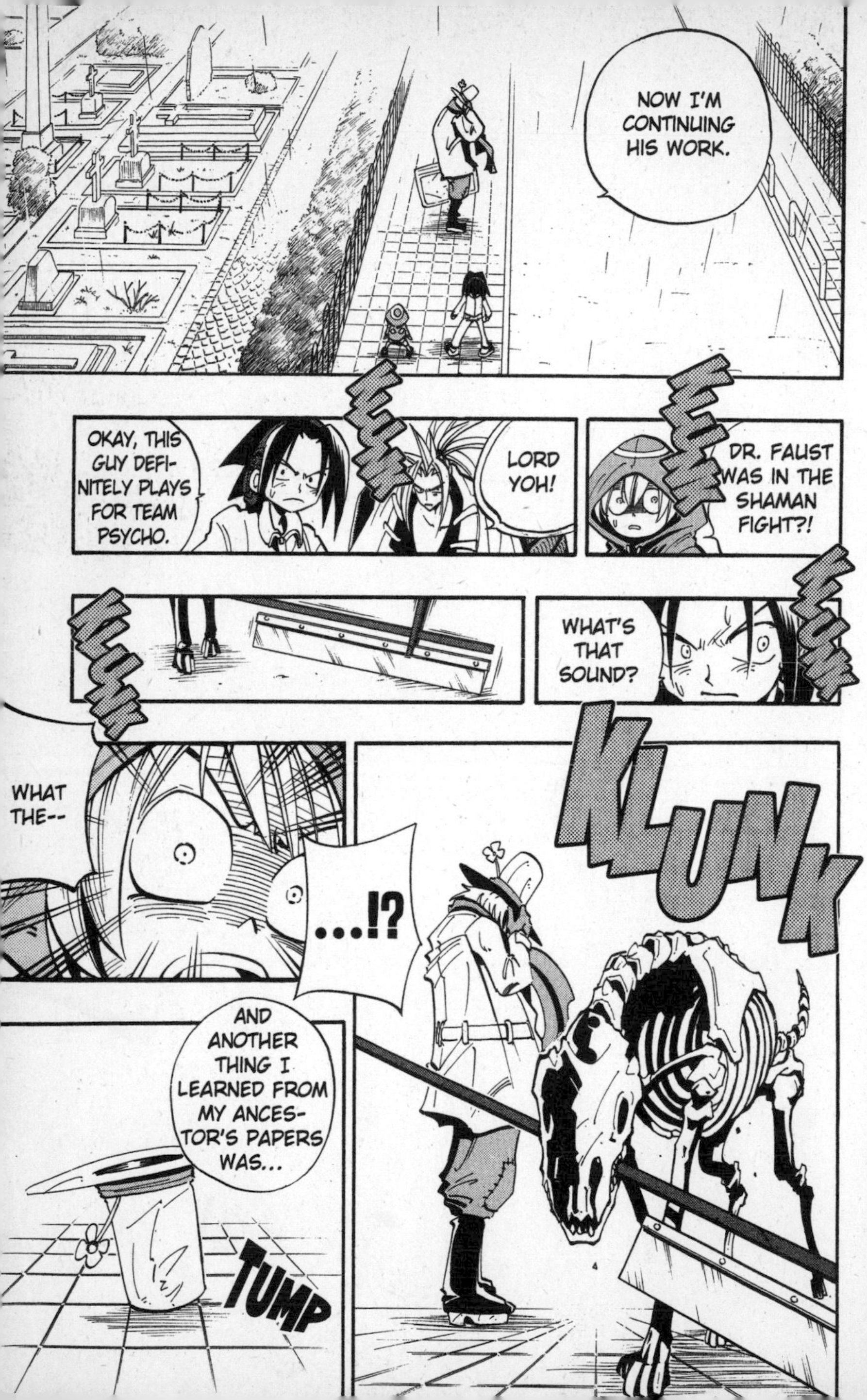
NOW I'M CONTINUING HIS WORK.
KLUNK
DR. FAUST WAS IN THE SHAMAN FIGHT?!
KLUNK
LORD YOH!
OKAY, THIS GUY DEFINITELY PLAYS FOR TEAM PSYCHO.
KLUNK
WHAT'S THAT SOUND?
KLUNK
KLUNK
...!?
WHAT THE--
AND ANOTHER THING I LEARNED FROM MY ANCESTOR'S PAPERS WAS...
TUMP

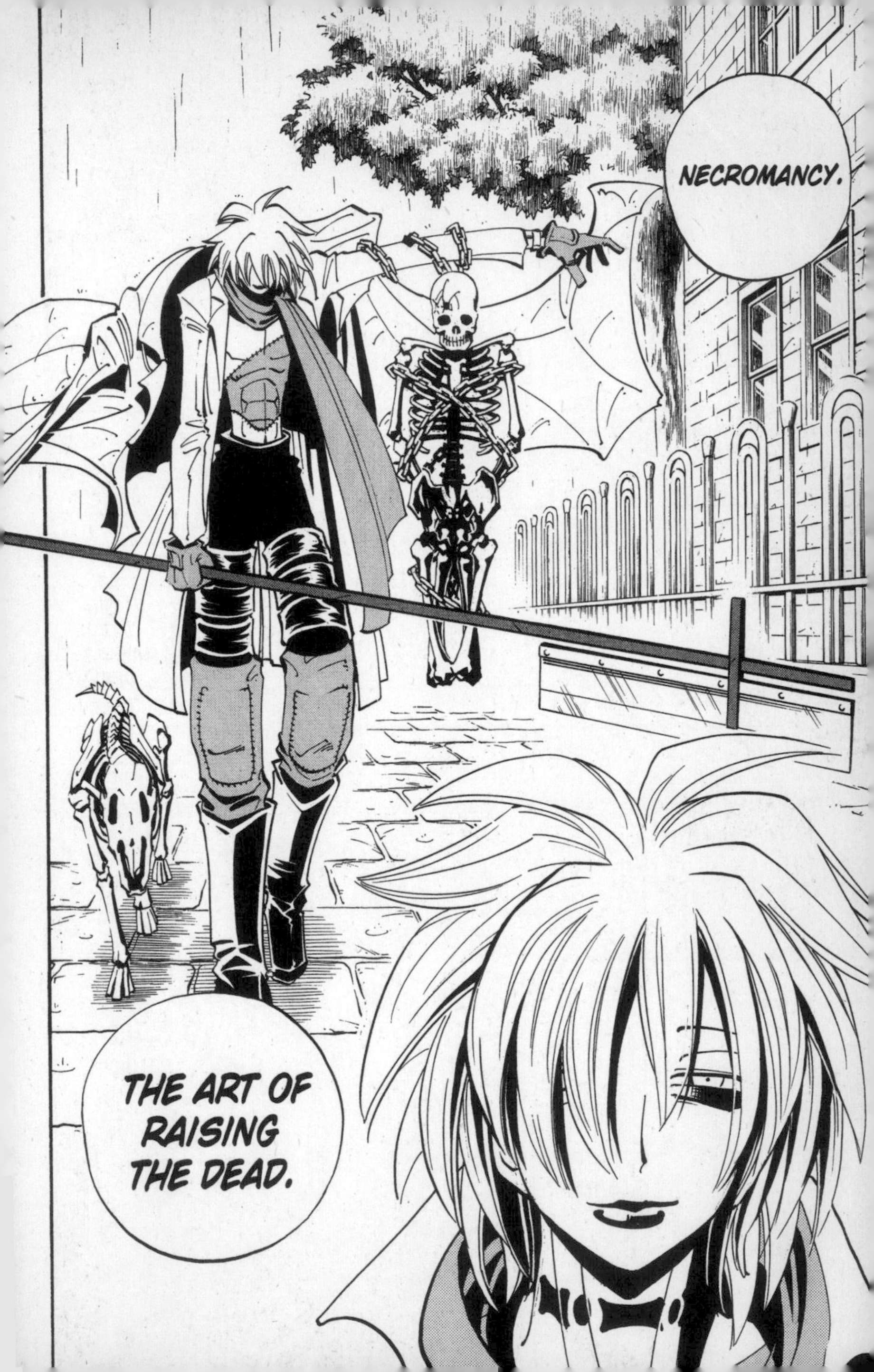
NECROMANCY.
THE ART OF RAISING THE DEAD.

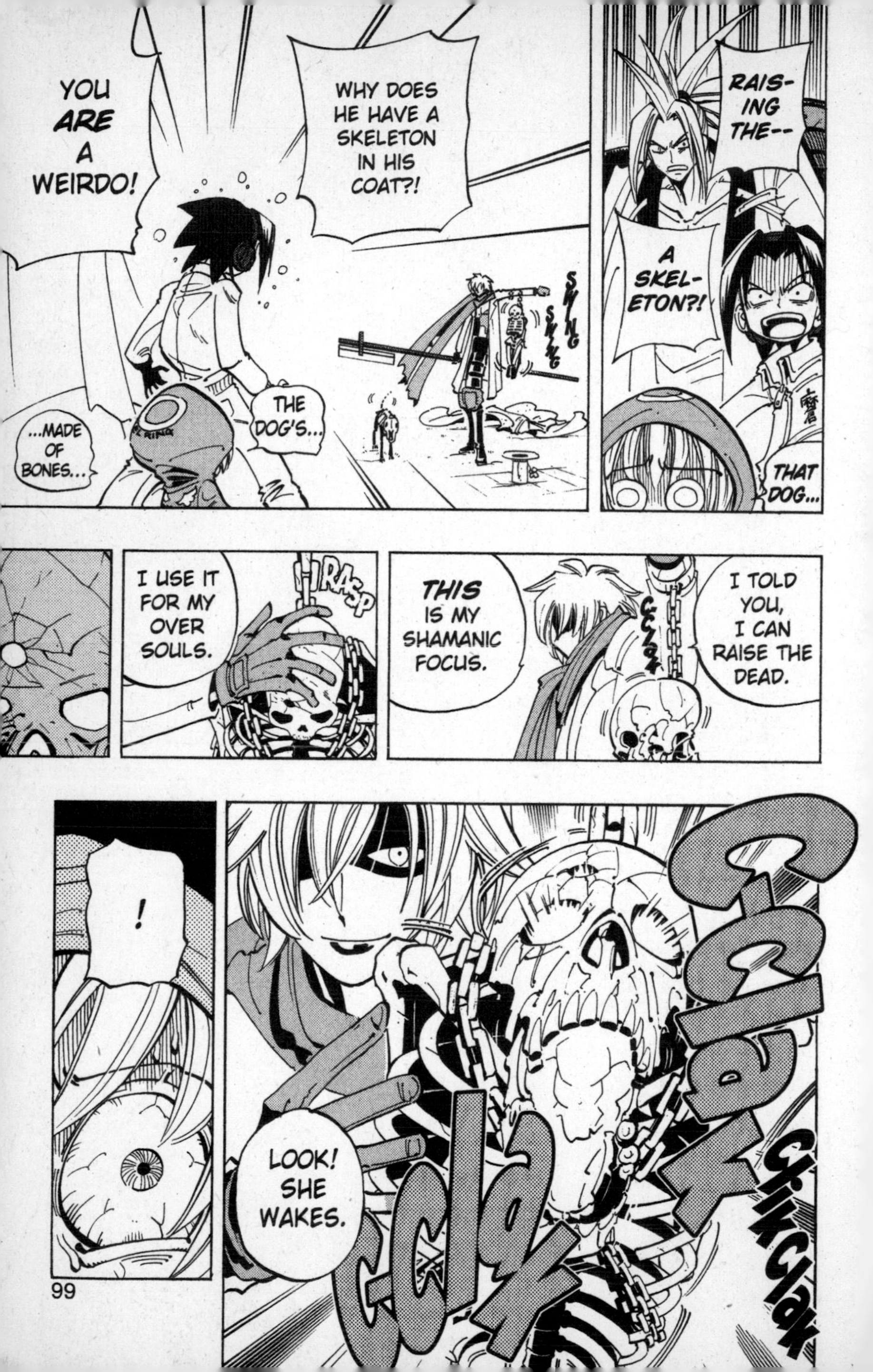
RAIS-ING THE--
A SKEL-ETON?!
THAT DOG...
WHY DOES HE HAVE A SKELETON IN HIS COAT?!
YOU ARE A WEIRDO!
SWING SWING
THE DOG'S...
...MADE OF BONES...
I TOLD YOU, I CAN RAISE THE DEAD.
CCLAK
THIS IS MY SHAMANIC FOCUS.
RASP
I USE IT FOR MY OVER SOULS.
CCLAK
CHIK CLAK
LOOK! SHE WAKES.
CCLAK
!

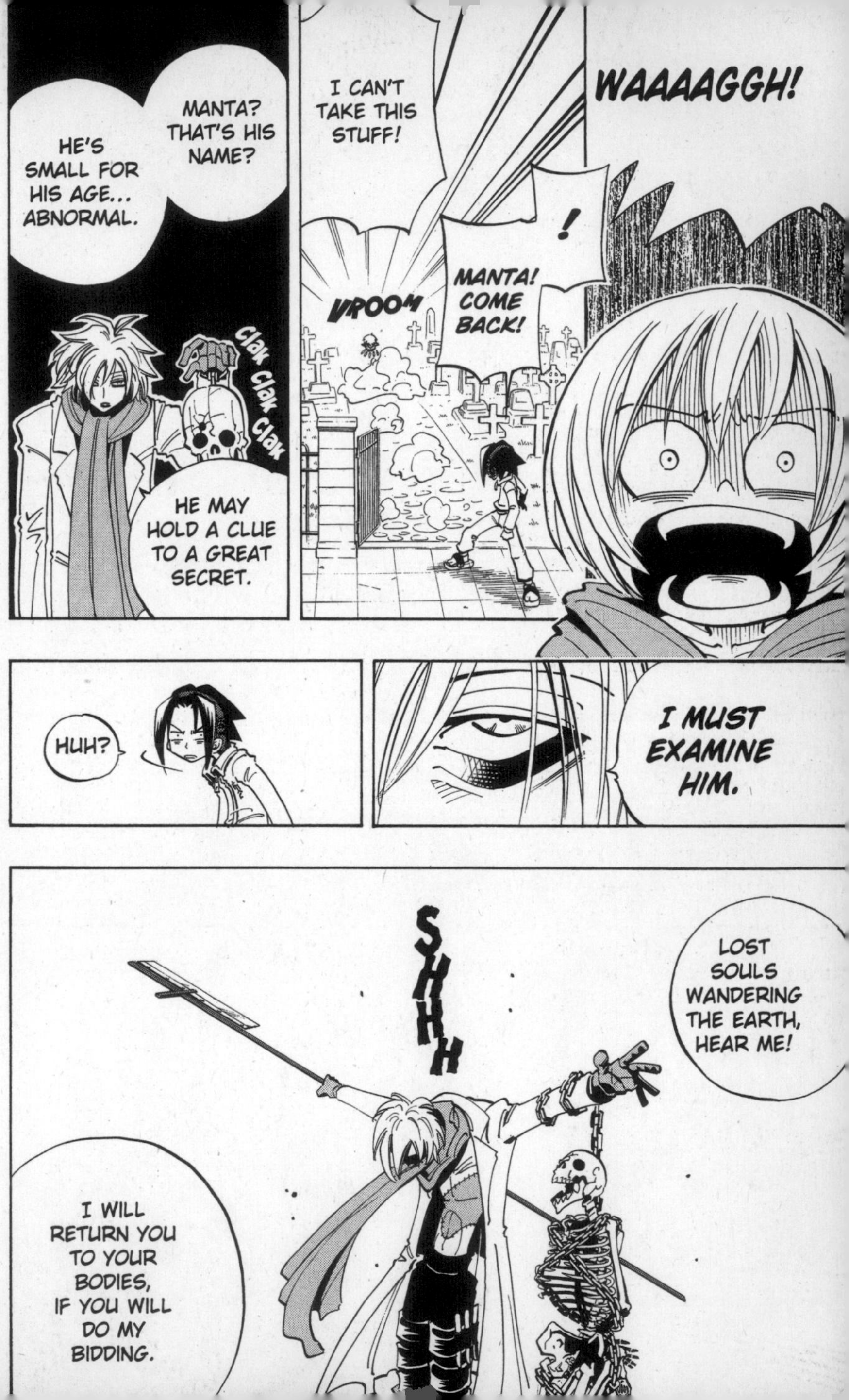
WAAAAGGH!
!
I CAN'T TAKE THIS STUFF!
VROOM
MANTA! COME BACK!
MANTA? THAT'S HIS NAME?
HE'S SMALL FOR HIS AGE... ABNORMAL.
Clak Clak Clak
HE MAY HOLD A CLUE TO A GREAT SECRET.
I MUST EXAMINE HIM.
HUH?
SHHHH
LOST SOULS WANDERING THE EARTH, HEAR ME!
I WILL RETURN YOU TO YOUR BODIES, IF YOU WILL DO MY BIDDING.

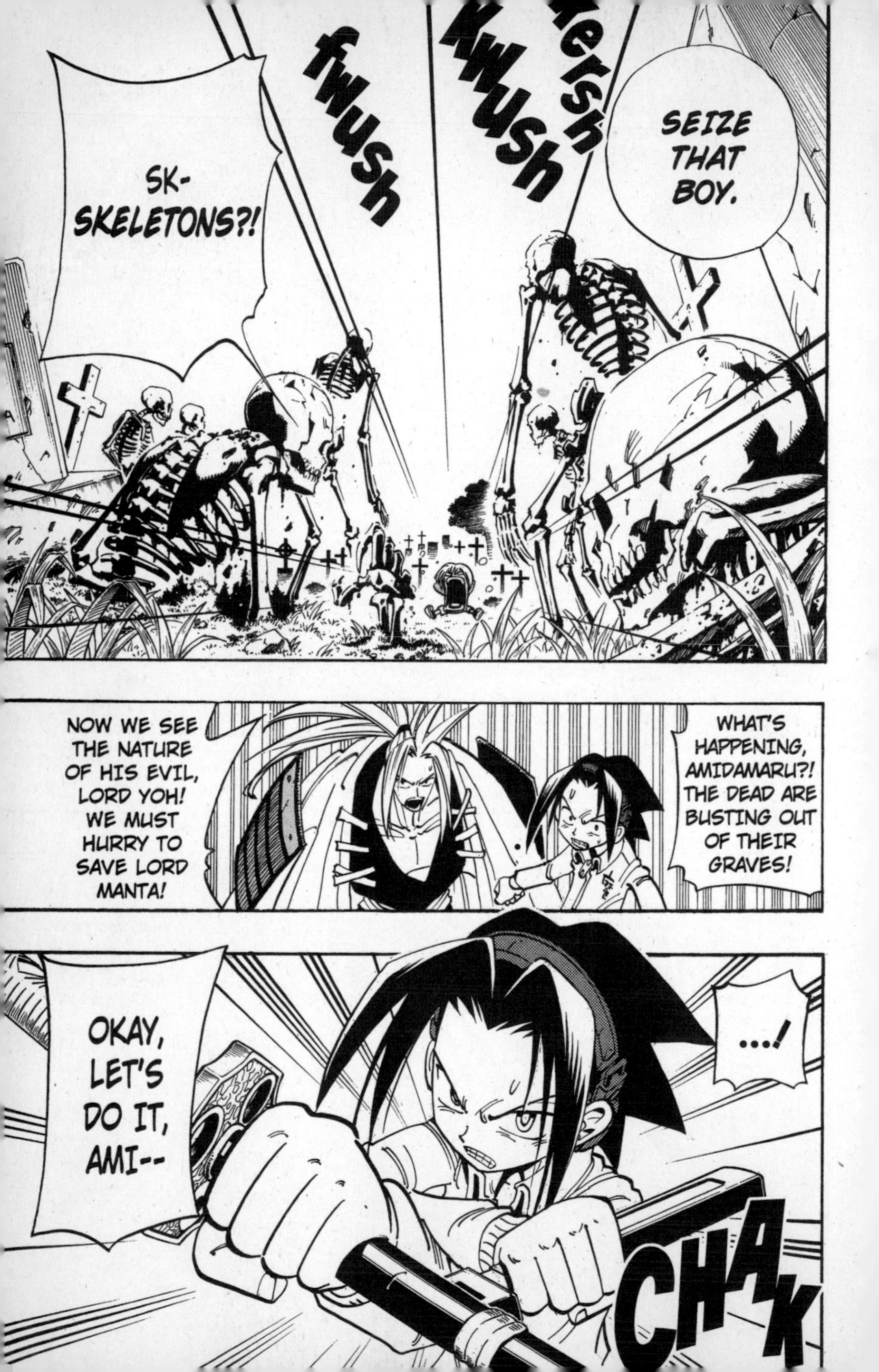
SEIZE THAT BOY.
ersh
kwush
fwush
SK- SKELETONS?!
WHAT'S HAPPENING, AMIDAMARU?! THE DEAD ARE BUSTING OUT OF THEIR GRAVES!
NOW WE SEE THE NATURE OF HIS EVIL, LORD YOH! WE MUST HURRY TO SAVE LORD MANTA!
...!
CHAK
OKAY, LET'S DO IT, AMI--

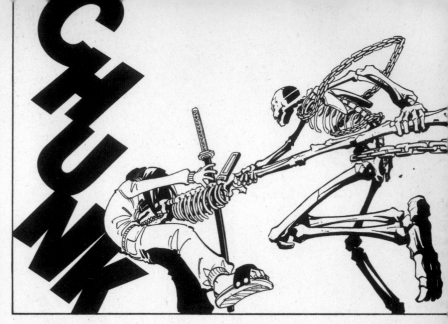

CHUNK
GGH...?!
...
AS I SAID, WE GERMANS LIKE TO FINISH WHAT WE START.
MEET MY LOVELY ASSISTANT, ELIZA.
SHE'S MY REGISTERED SPIRIT ALLY FOR THE SHAMAN FIGHT.
...!
I HAVE BEEN CHECKING MY ORACLE PAGER AND OUR BATTLE HASN'T BEGUN YET, YES? IF YOU WISH TO LIVE TO FIGHT ME, DO NOT IMPEDE MY RESEARCH.

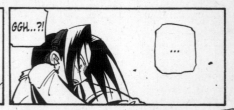

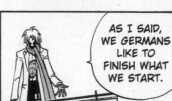

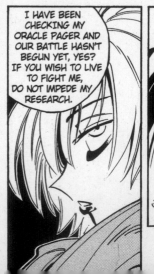

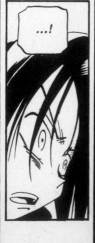

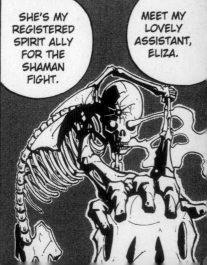

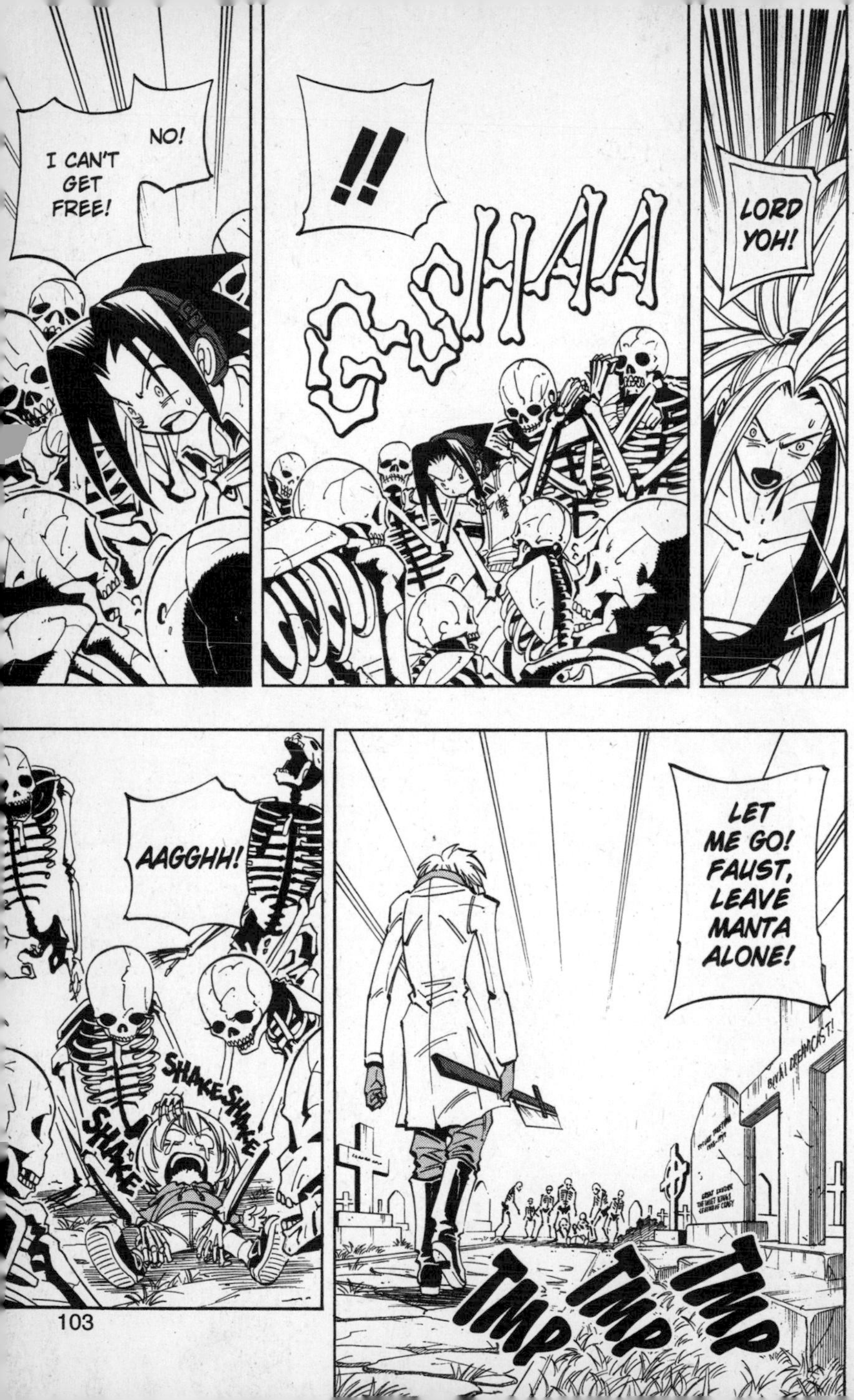
LORD YOH!
!!
G-SHAA
NO! I CAN'T GET FREE!
LET ME GO! FAUST, LEAVE MANTA ALONE!
TMP TMP TMP
AAGGHH!
SHAKE SHAKE
SHAKE
SHAKE

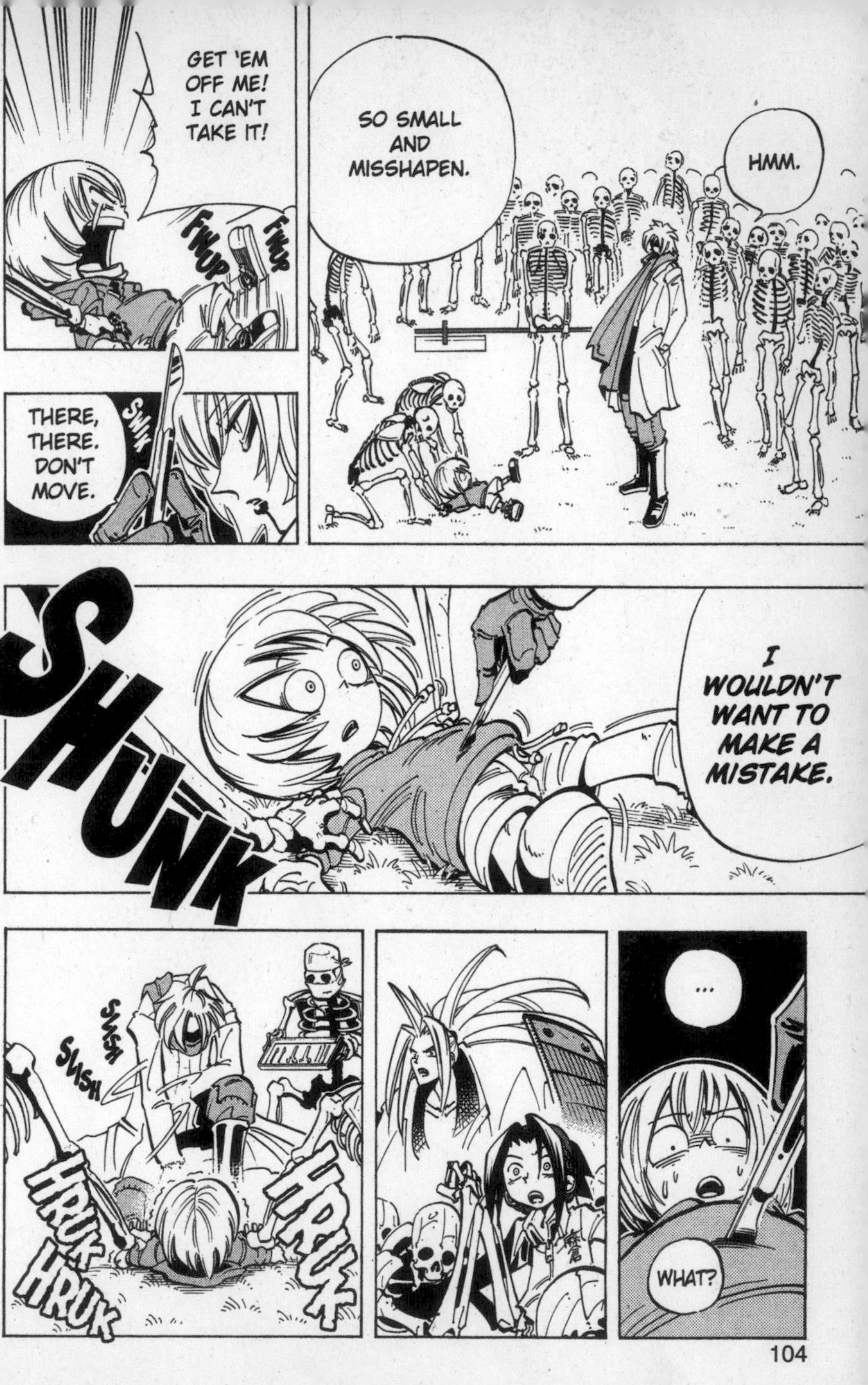
HMM.
SO SMALL AND MISSHAPEN.
GET 'EM OFF ME! I CAN'T TAKE IT!
FWUP
FWUP
SWIK
THERE, THERE. DON'T MOVE.
I WOULDN'T WANT TO MAKE A MISTAKE.
SHUNK
...
WHAT?
SWISH
SWISH
HRUK
HRUK
HRUK

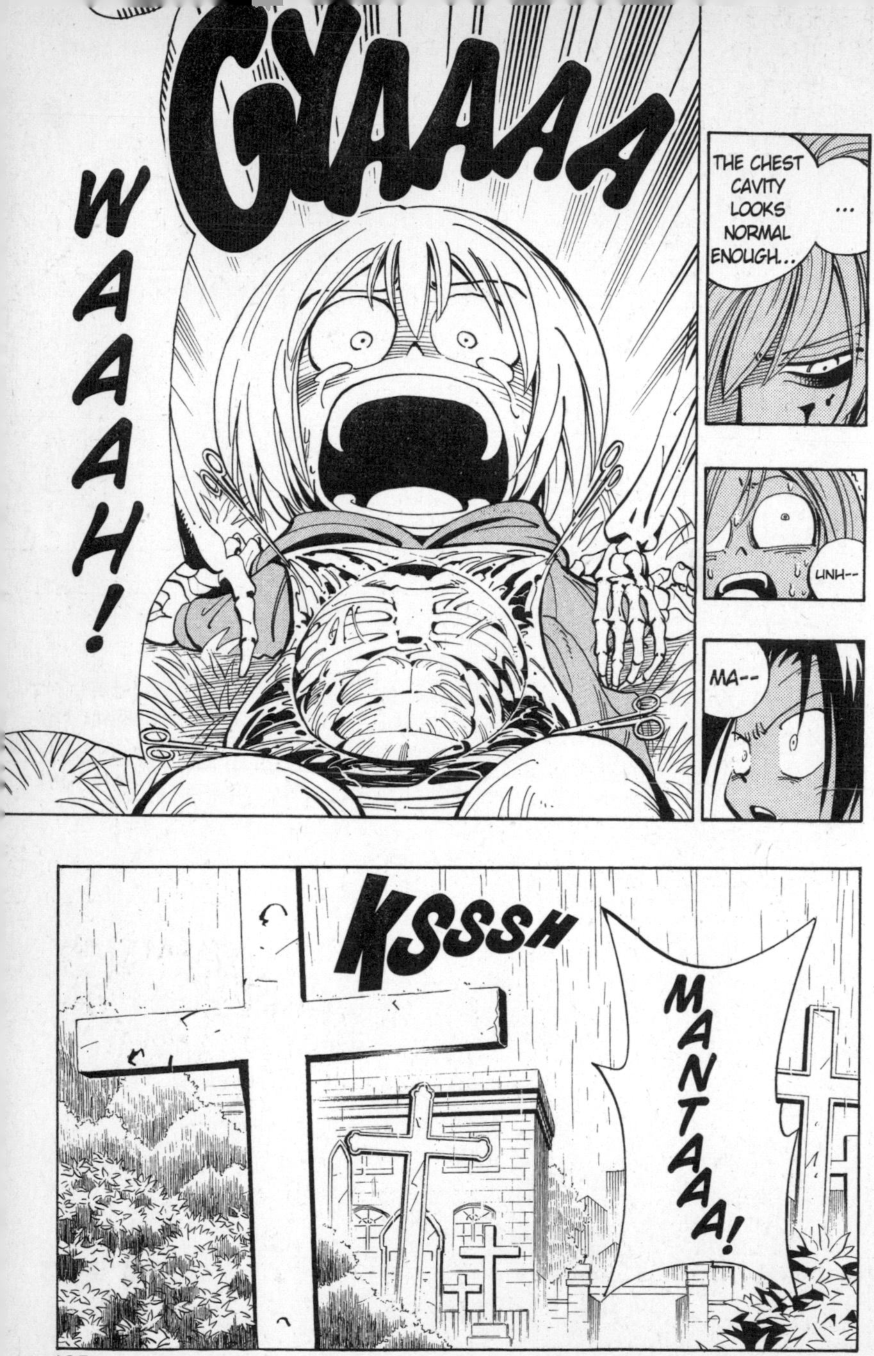
THE CHEST CAVITY LOOKS NORMAL ENOUGH...
...
UNH--
MA--
GYAAAA
WAAAAH!
KSSSH
MANTAAAA!

SHAMAN KING CHARACTER FILE No.22

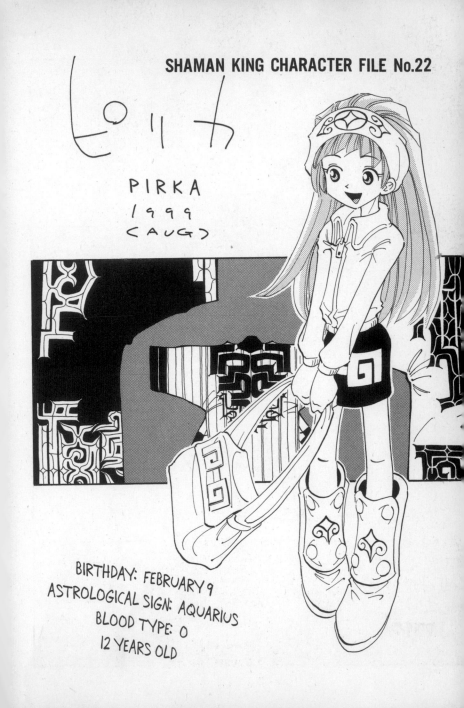

ピリカ

PIRKA

1999

(AUG)

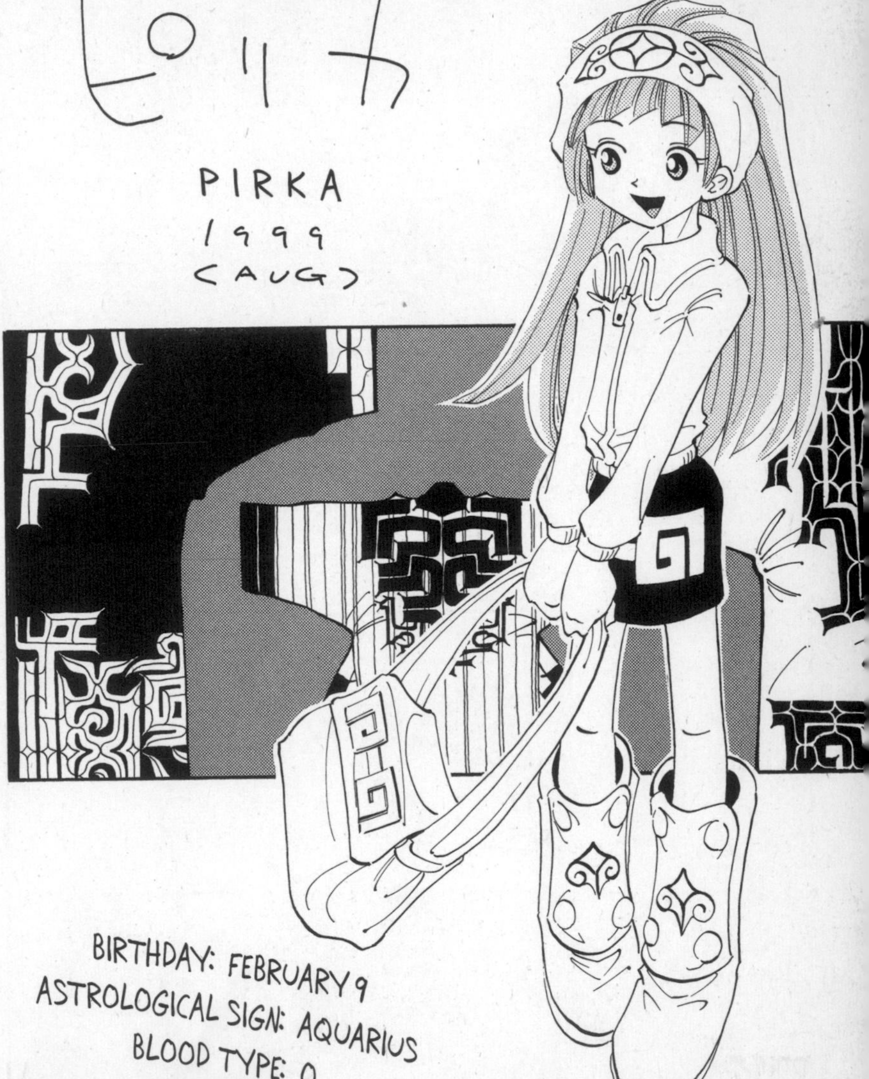

BIRTHDAY: FEBRUARY 9

ASTROLOGICAL SIGN: AQUARIUS

BLOOD TYPE: O

12 YEARS OLD

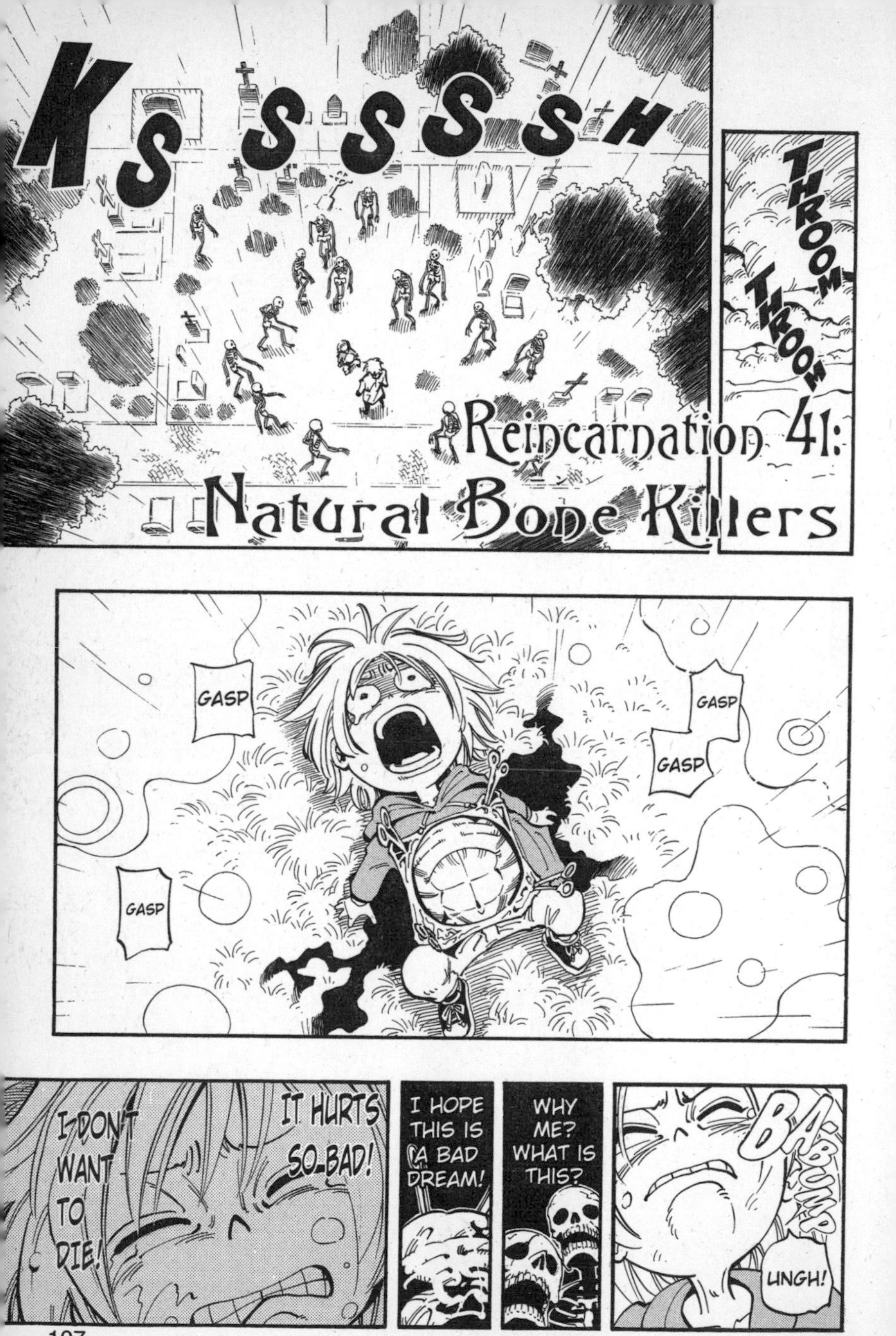
THROOM THROOM
KSSSSSH
Reincarnation 41:
Natural Bone Killers
GASP
GASP
GASP
GASP
BA-BUMP
UNGH!
WHY ME? WHAT IS THIS?
I HOPE THIS IS A BAD DREAM!
IT HURTS SO BAD!
I DON'T WANT TO DIE!

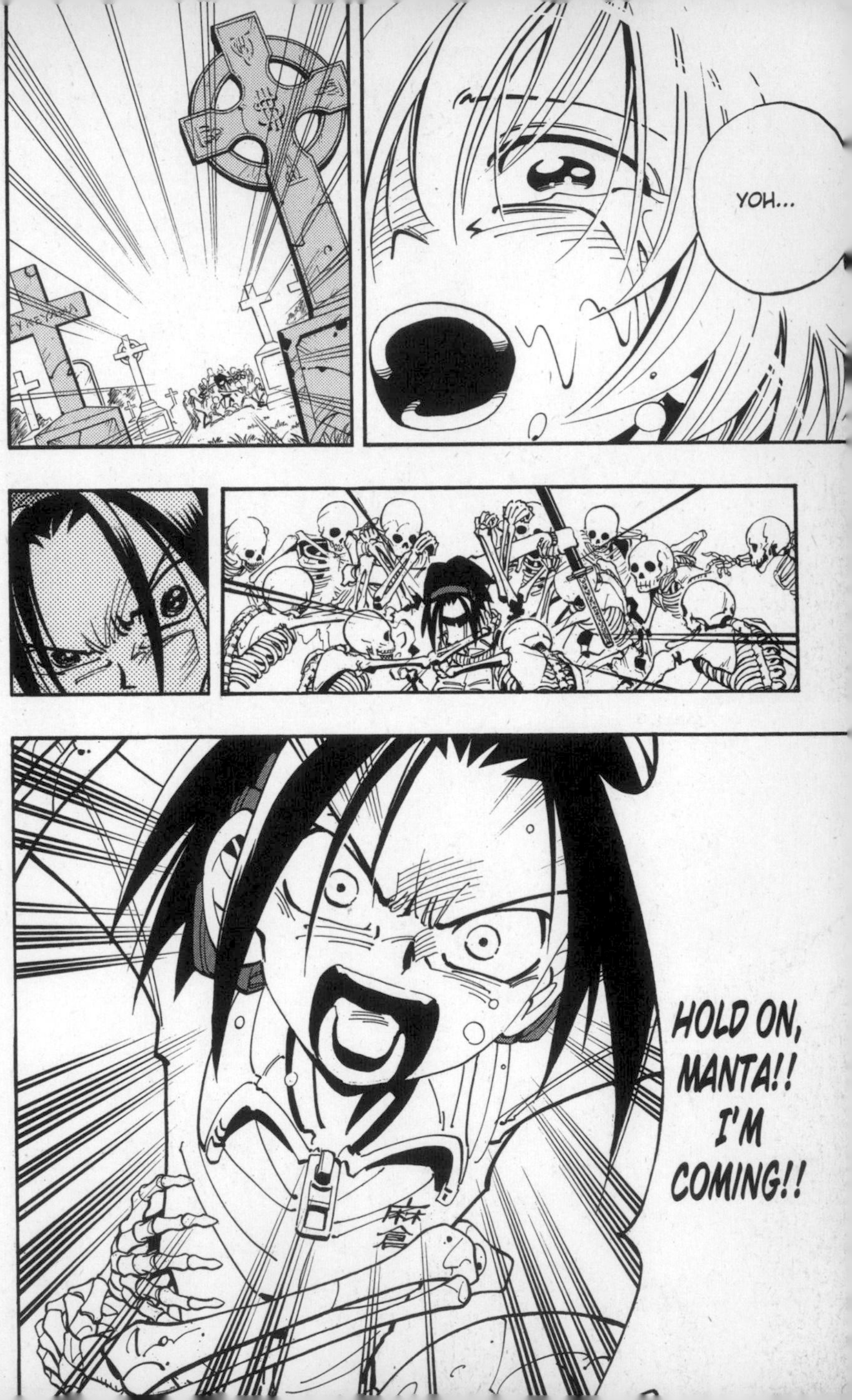
YOH...
HOLD ON, MANTA!! I'M COMING!!

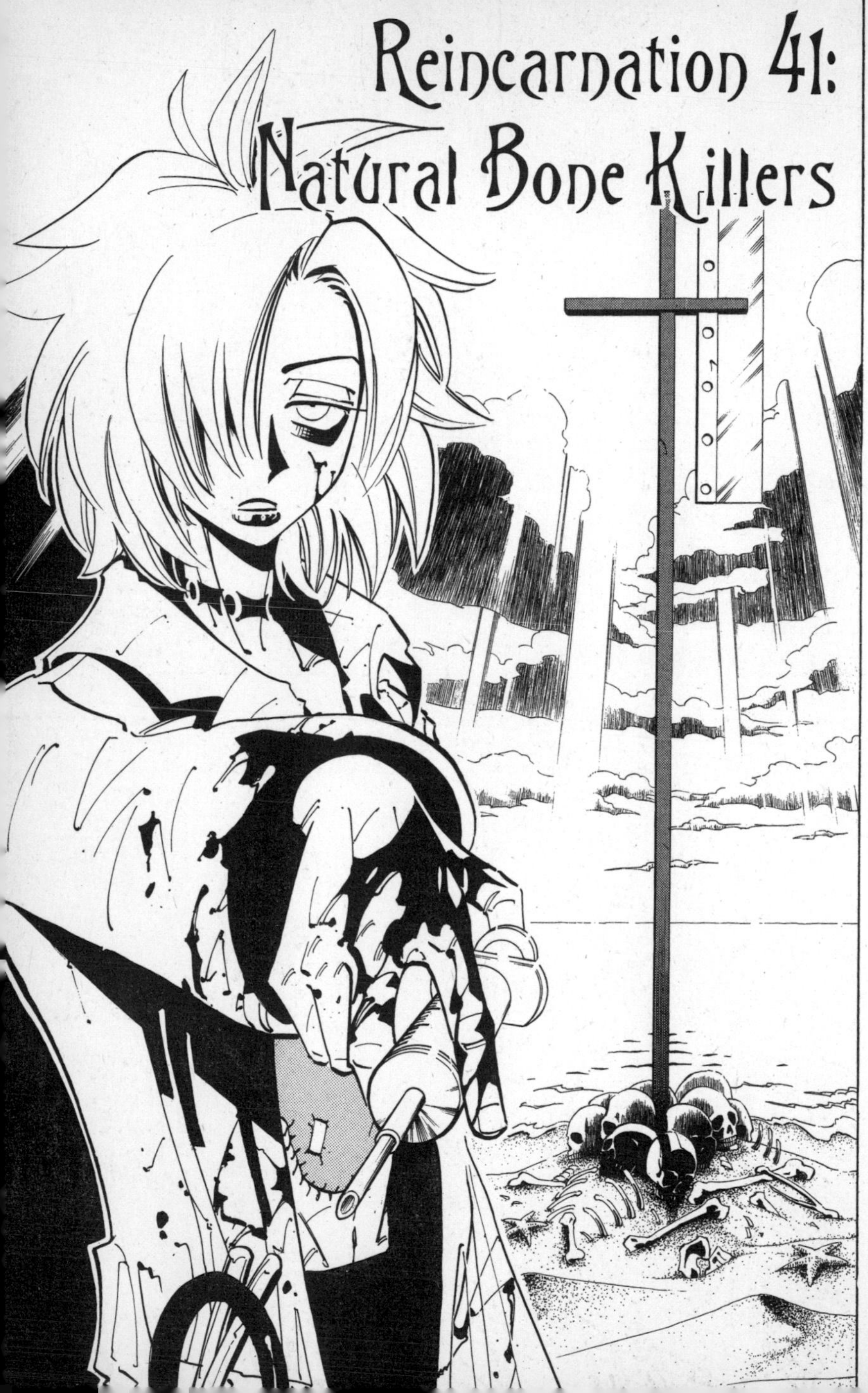
Reincarnation 41:
Natural Bone Killers

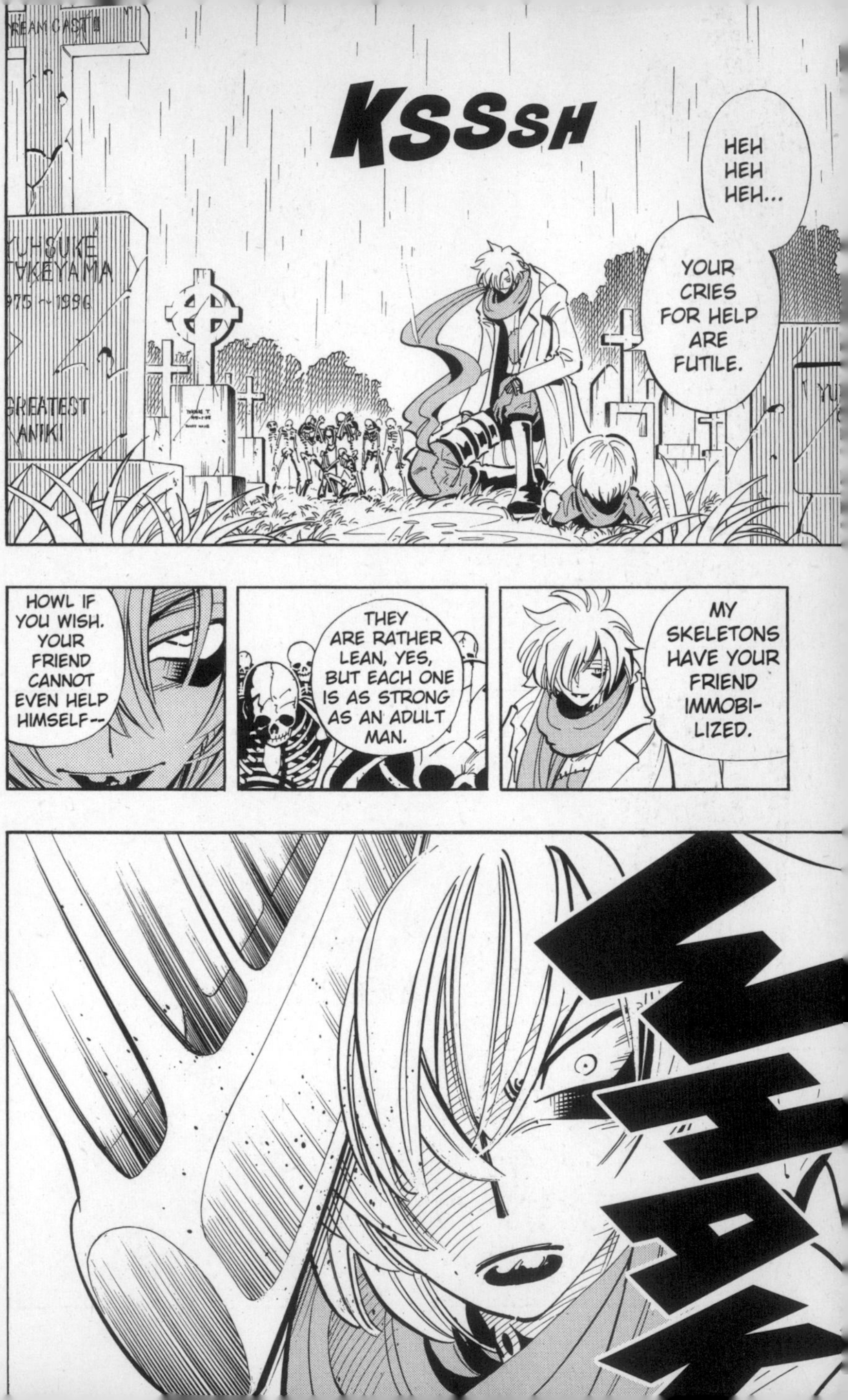
KSSSH
HEH HEH HEH...
YOUR CRIES FOR HELP ARE FUTILE.
GREATEST ANIKI
MY SKELETONS HAVE YOUR FRIEND IMMOBI-LIZED.
THEY ARE RATHER LEAN, YES, BUT EACH ONE IS AS STRONG AS AN ADULT MAN.
HOWL IF YOU WISH. YOUR FRIEND CANNOT EVEN HELP HIMSELF--

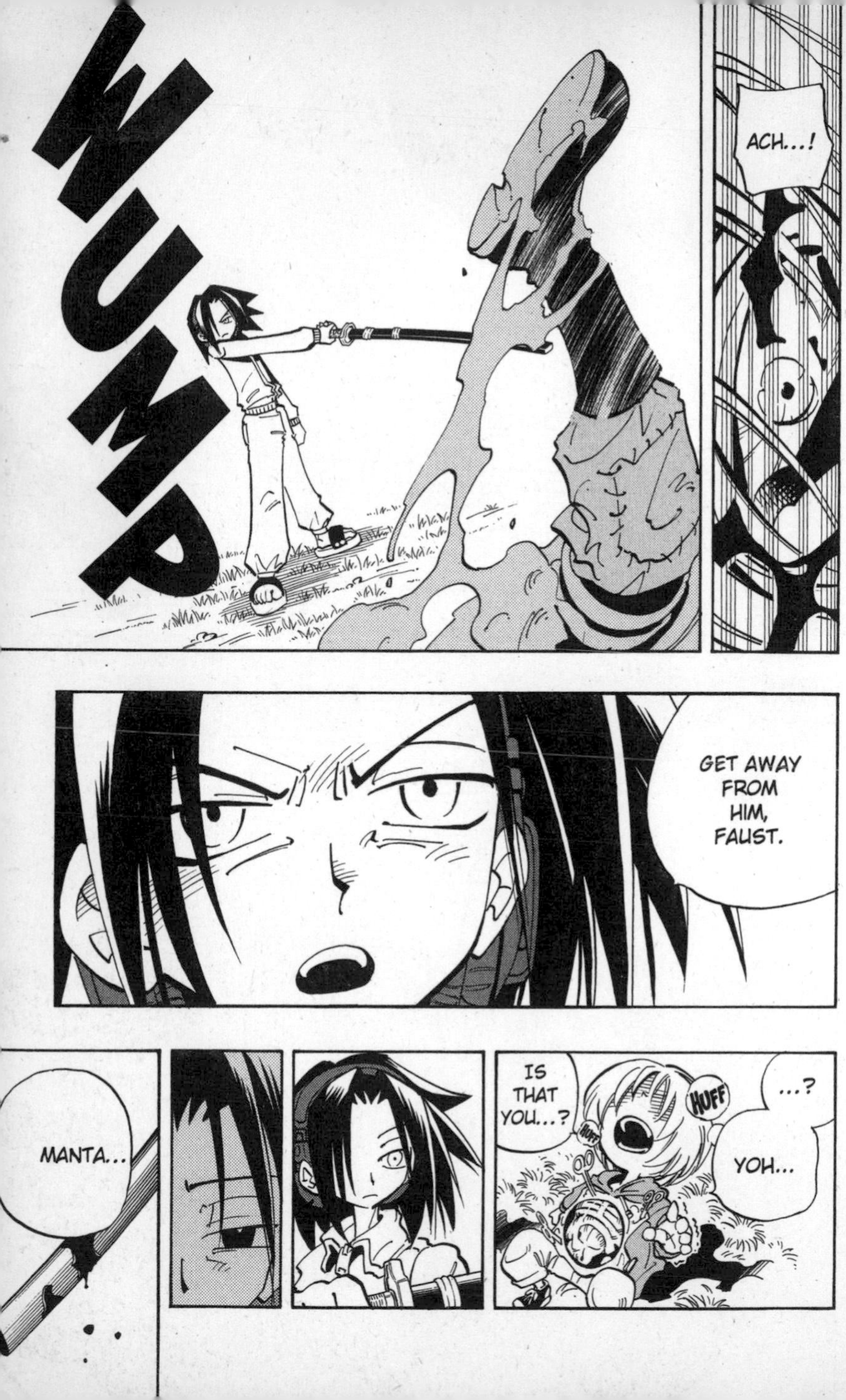
ACH...!
WUMP
GET AWAY FROM HIM, FAUST.
...?
HUFF
YOH...
HUFF
IS THAT YOU...?
MANTA...

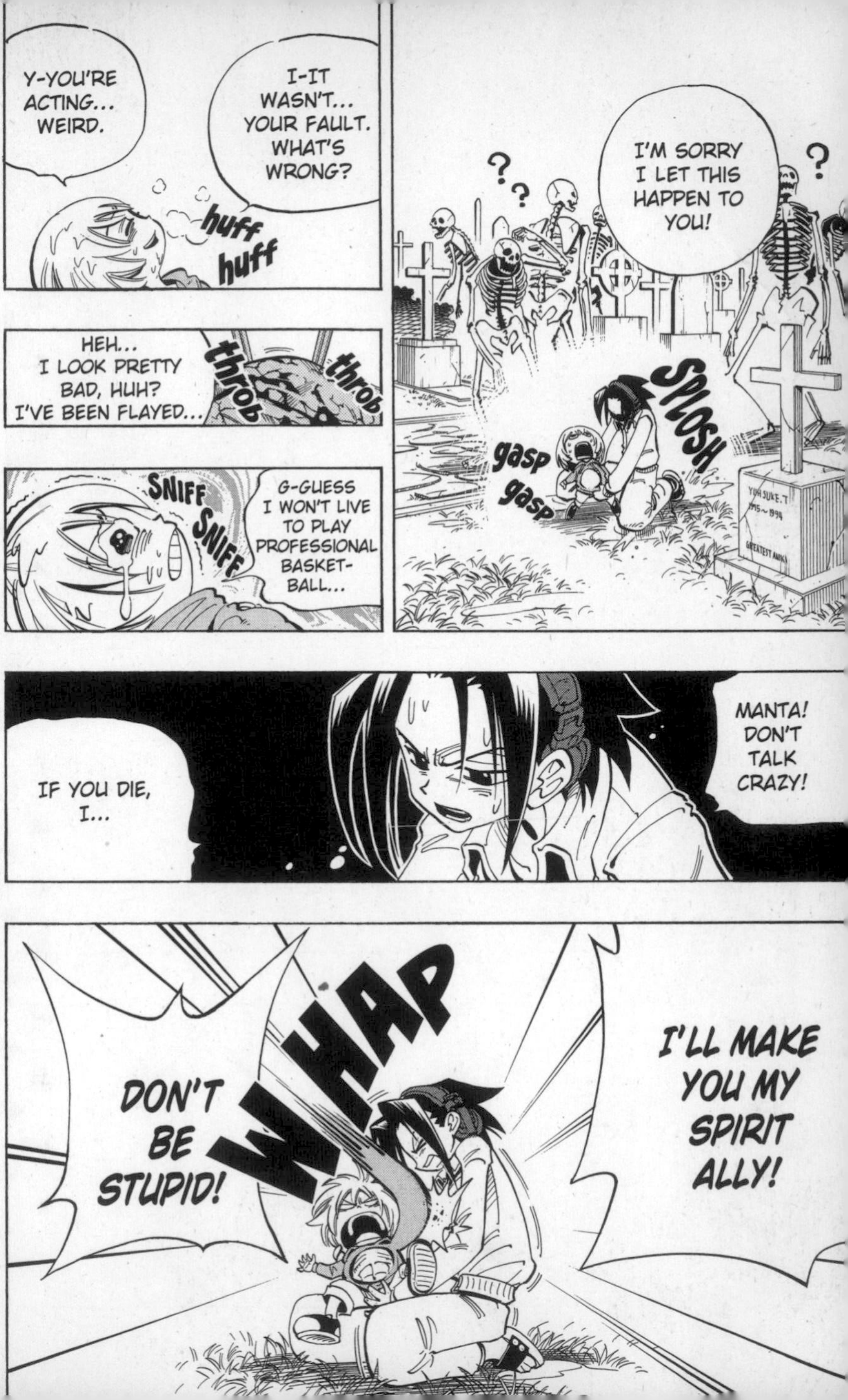
I'M SORRY I LET THIS HAPPEN TO YOU!
SPLOSH
gasp gasp
I-IT WASN'T... YOUR FAULT. WHAT'S WRONG?
Y-YOU'RE ACTING... WEIRD.
huff huff
HEH... I LOOK PRETTY BAD, HUH? I'VE BEEN FLAYED...
throb throb
G-GUESS I WON'T LIVE TO PLAY PROFESSIONAL BASKET-BALL...
SNIFF SNIFF
MANTA! DON'T TALK CRAZY!
IF YOU DIE, I...
I'LL MAKE YOU MY SPIRIT ALLY!
WHAP
DON'T BE STUPID!

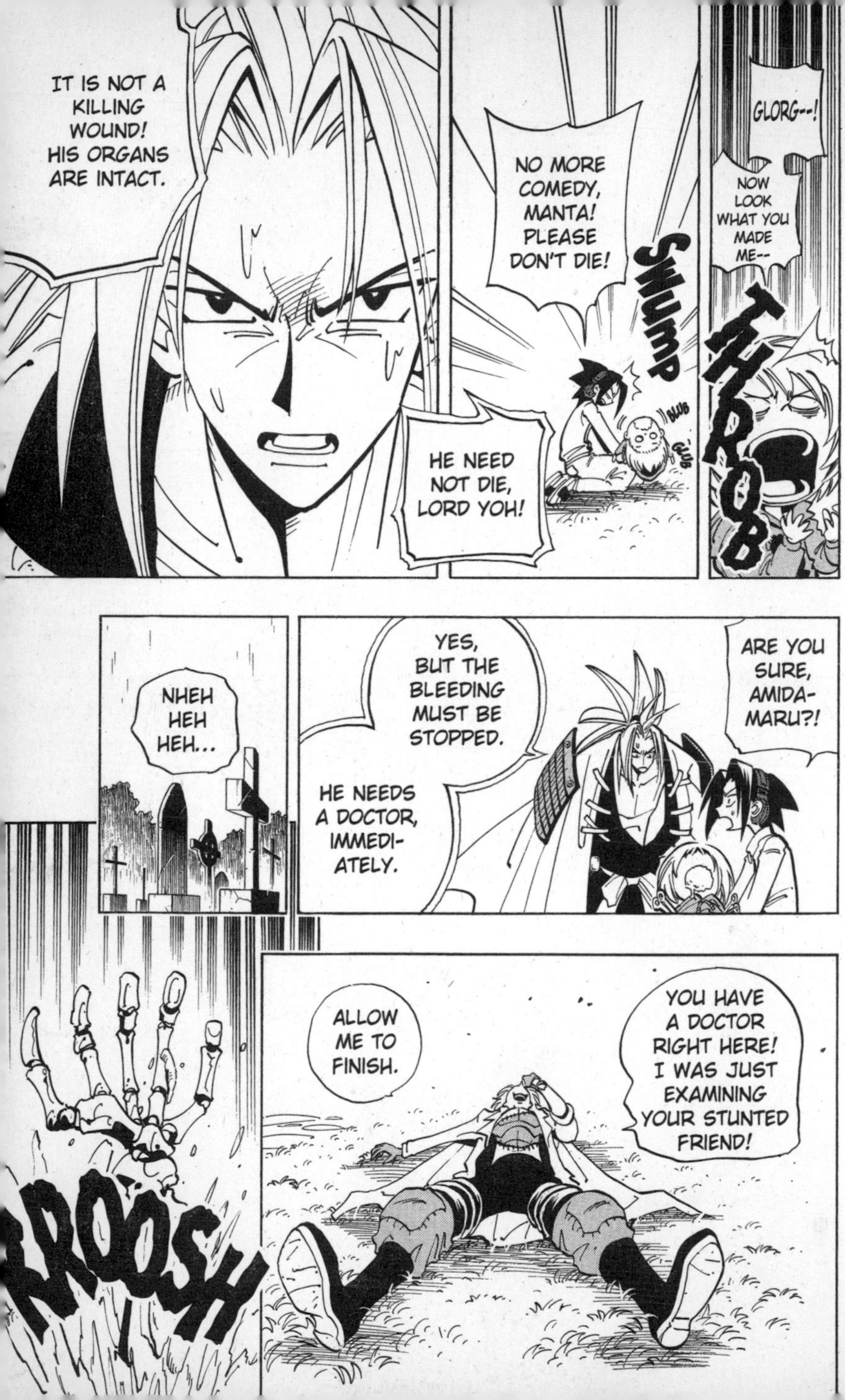
GLORG--!
NOW LOOK WHAT YOU MADE ME--
THROB
NO MORE COMEDY, MANTA! PLEASE DON'T DIE!
SHUMP
BLUB
GLUB
HE NEED NOT DIE, LORD YOH!
IT IS NOT A KILLING WOUND! HIS ORGANS ARE INTACT.
ARE YOU SURE, AMIDA-MARU?!
YES, BUT THE BLEEDING MUST BE STOPPED.
HE NEEDS A DOCTOR, IMMEDIATELY.
NHEH HEH HEH...
YOU HAVE A DOCTOR RIGHT HERE! I WAS JUST EXAMINING YOUR STUNTED FRIEND!
ALLOW ME TO FINISH.
FROOSH

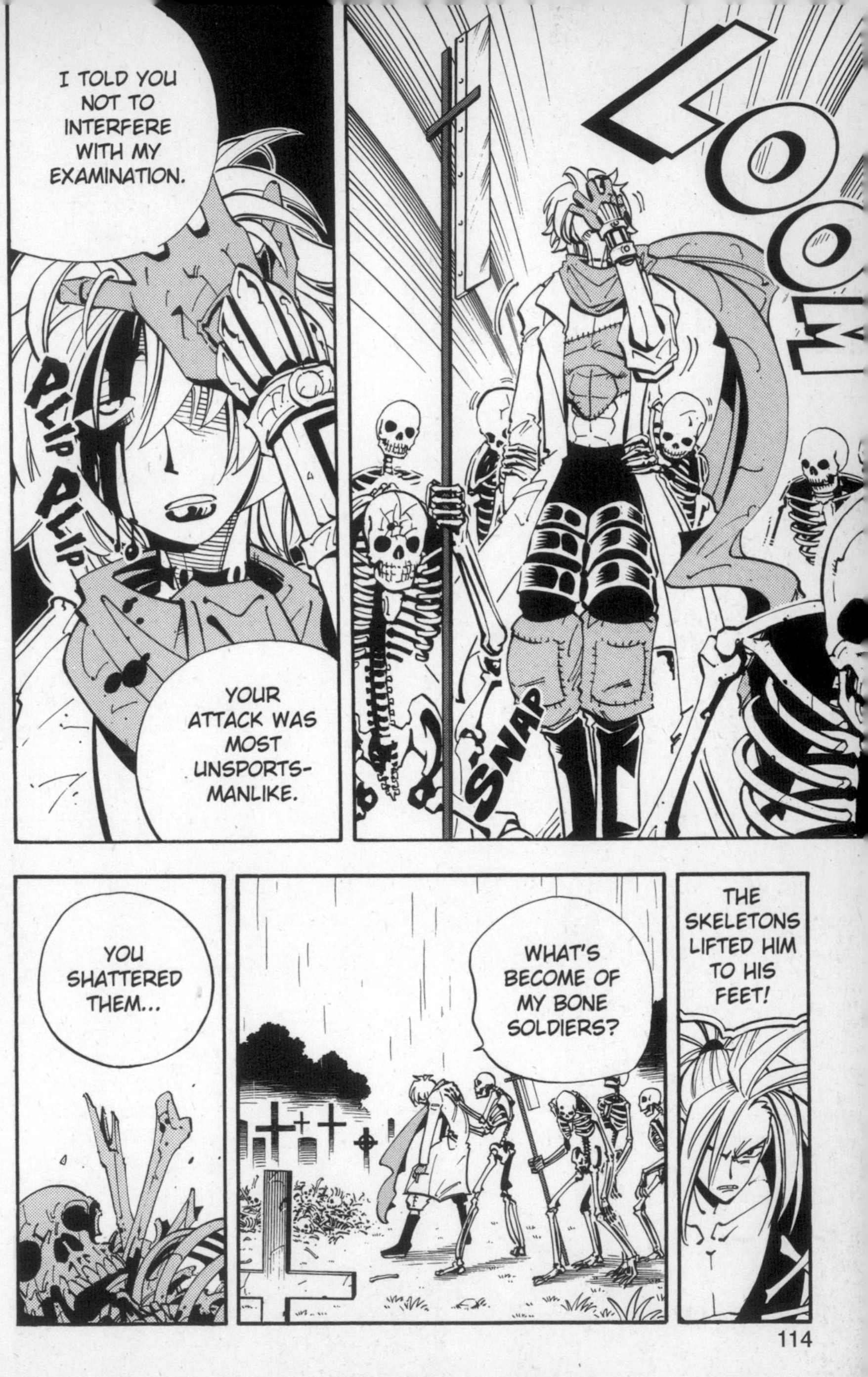
LOOM
SNAP
I TOLD YOU NOT TO INTERFERE WITH MY EXAMINATION.
PLIP PLIP PLIP
YOUR ATTACK WAS MOST UNSPORTS-MANLIKE.
THE SKELETONS LIFTED HIM TO HIS FEET!
WHAT'S BECOME OF MY BONE SOLDIERS?
YOU SHATTERED THEM...

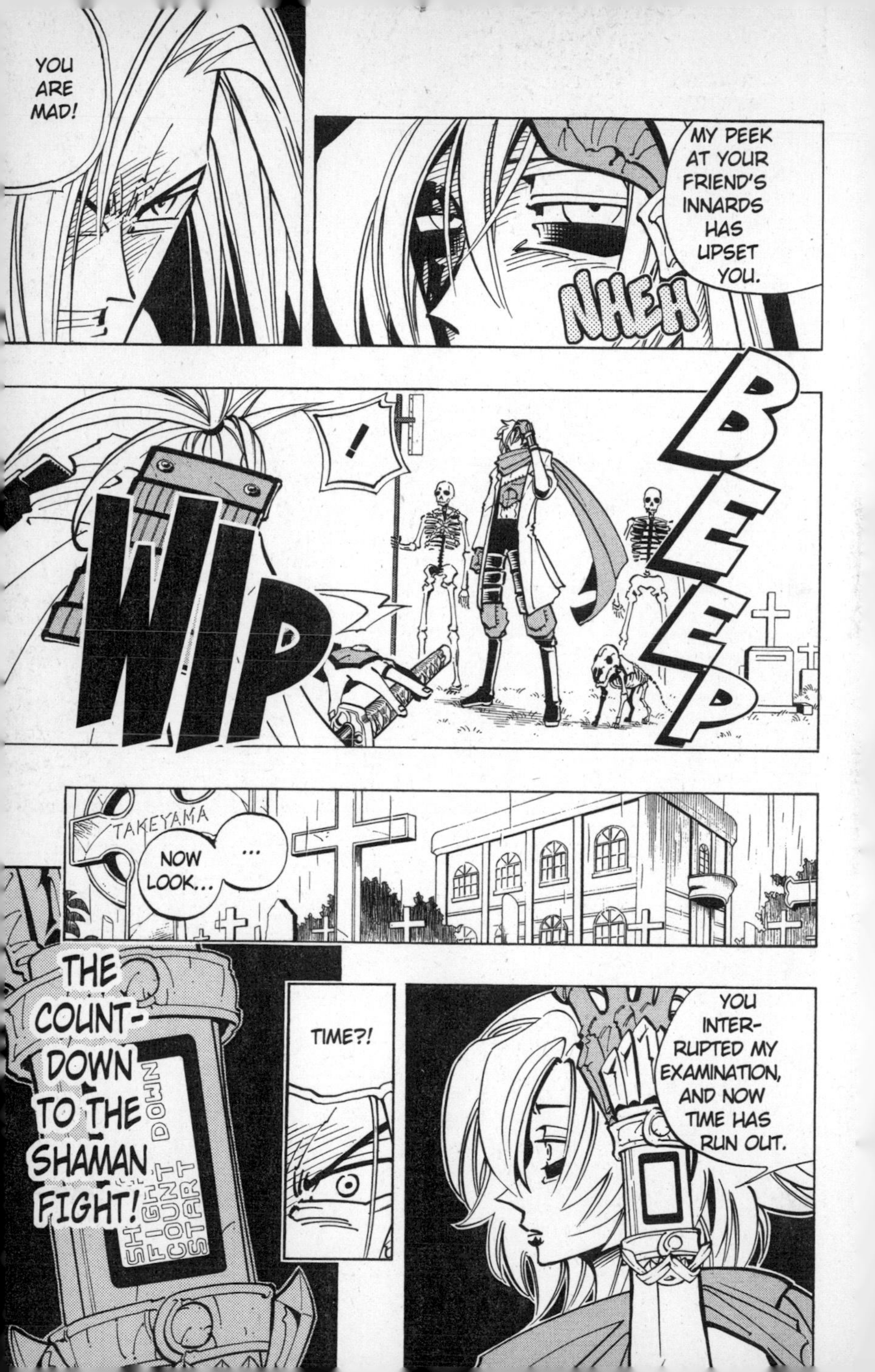
MY PEEK AT YOUR FRIEND'S INNARDS HAS UPSET YOU.
NHEH
YOU ARE MAD!
BEEP
!
WIP
...
TAKEYAMA
NOW LOOK...
YOU INTERRUPTED MY EXAMINATION, AND NOW TIME HAS RUN OUT.
TIME?!
THE COUNT-DOWN TO THE SHAMAN FIGHT!

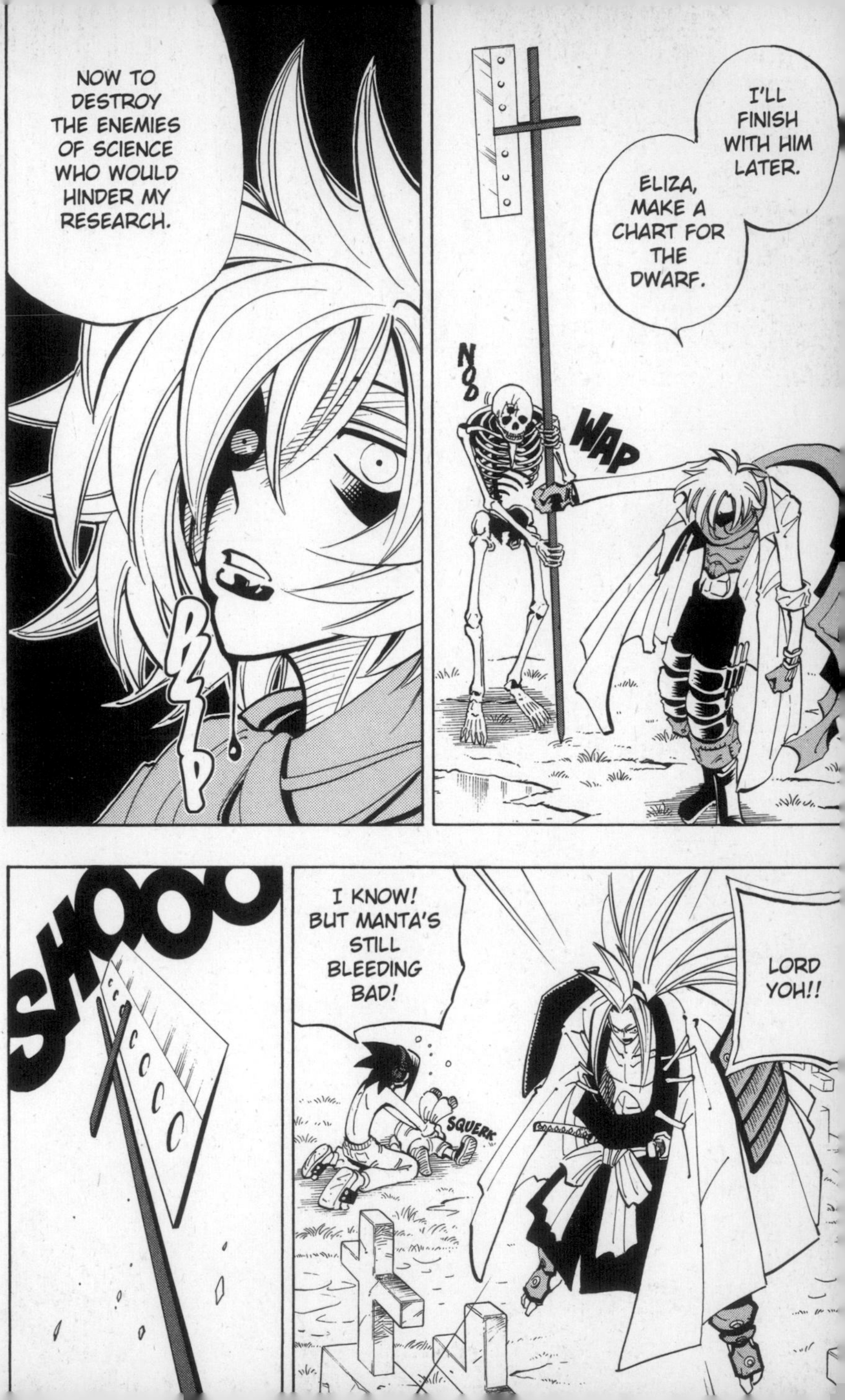
I'LL FINISH WITH HIM LATER.
ELIZA, MAKE A CHART FOR THE DWARF.
NOD
WAP
NOW TO DESTROY THE ENEMIES OF SCIENCE WHO WOULD HINDER MY RESEARCH.
LORD YOH!!
I KNOW! BUT MANTA'S STILL BLEEDING BAD!
SQUERK
SHOOO

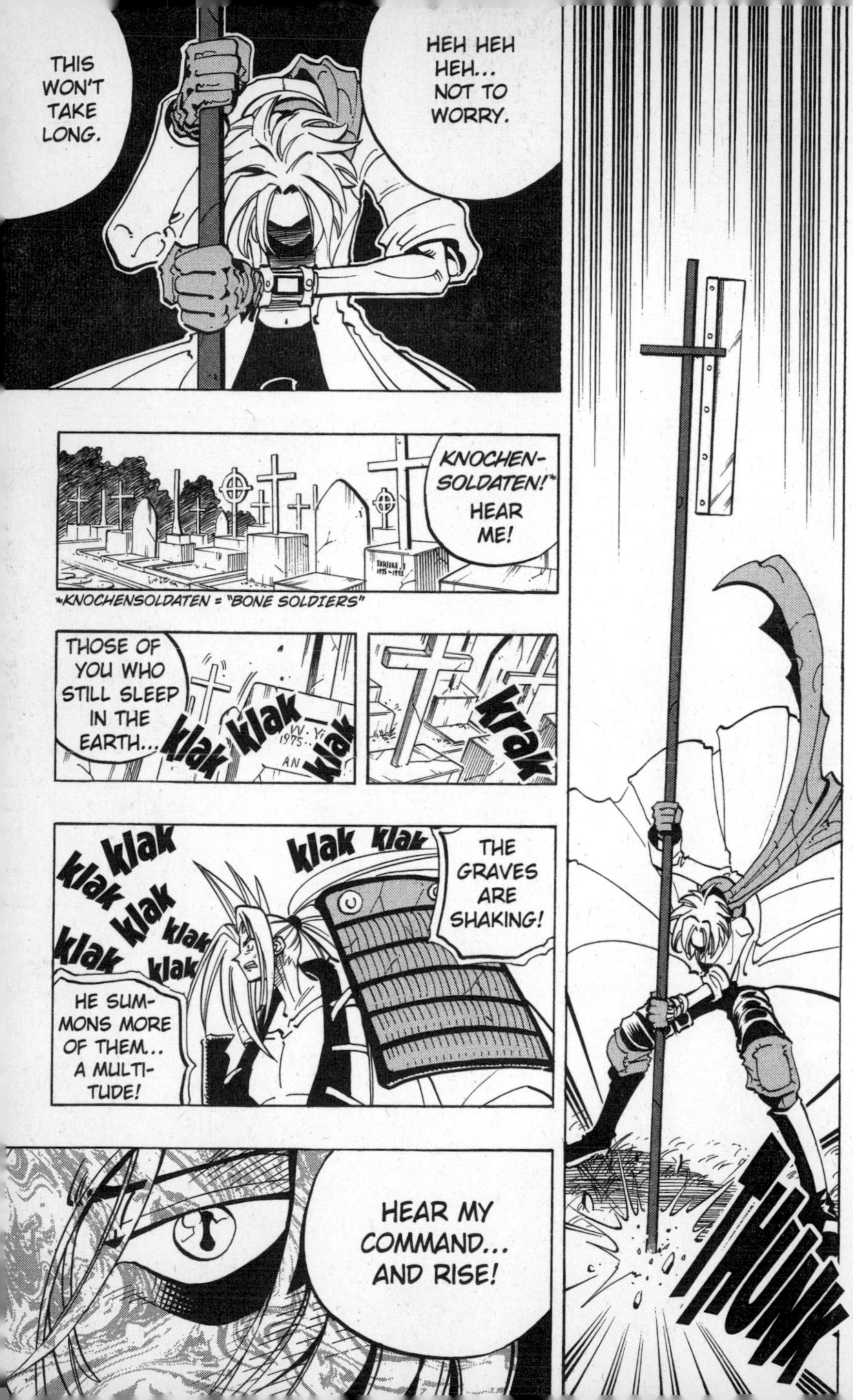
THUNK
HEH HEH HEH... NOT TO WORRY.
THIS WON'T TAKE LONG.
KNOCHEN-SOLDATEN!* HEAR ME!
*KNOCHENSOLDATEN = "BONE SOLDIERS"
krak
THOSE OF YOU WHO STILL SLEEP IN THE EARTH...
klak klak klak
klak klak
THE GRAVES ARE SHAKING!
klak klak klak klak klak klak
HE SUM-MONS MORE OF THEM... A MULTI-TUDE!
HEAR MY COMMAND... AND RISE!

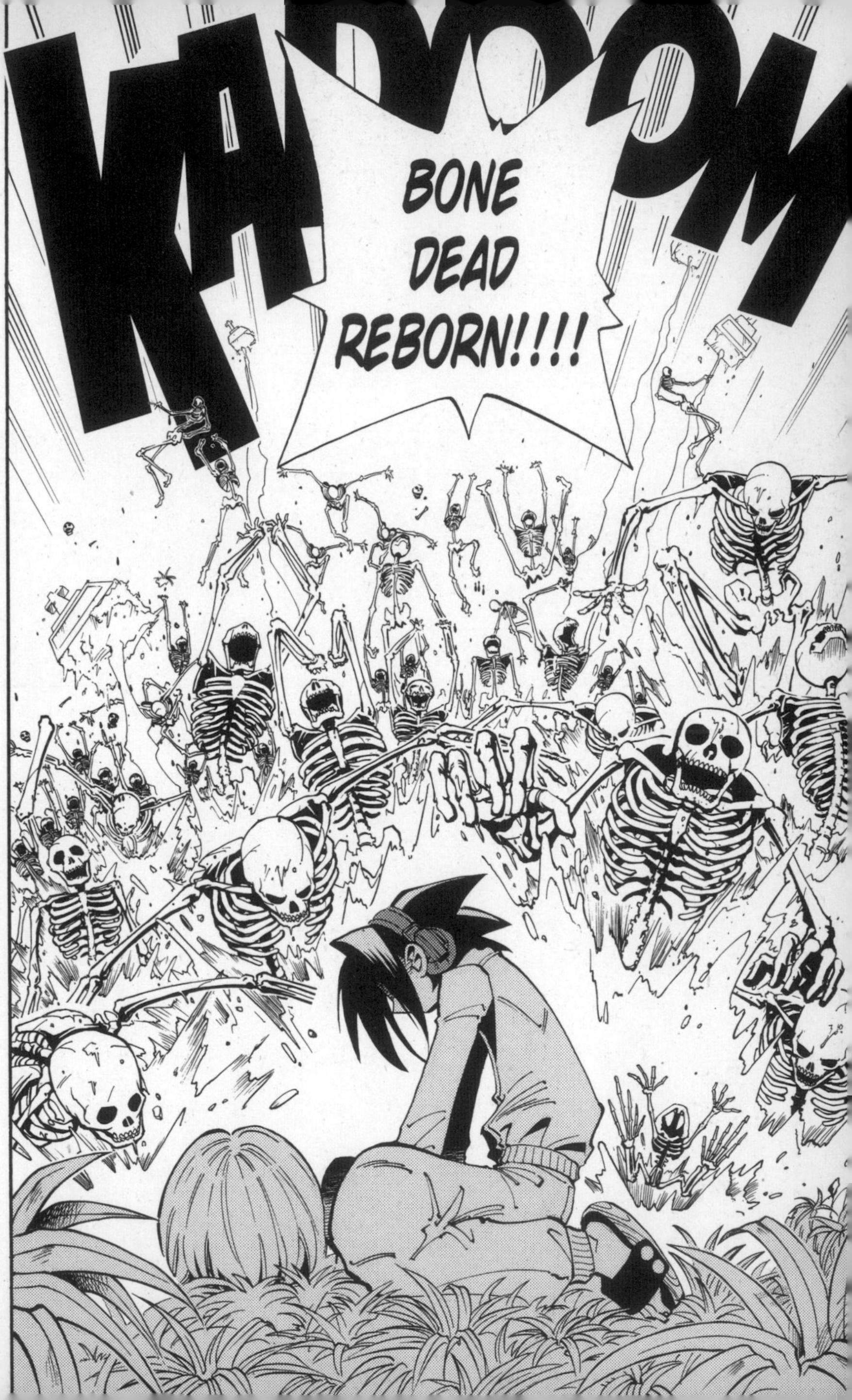
BONE DEAD REBORN!!!!

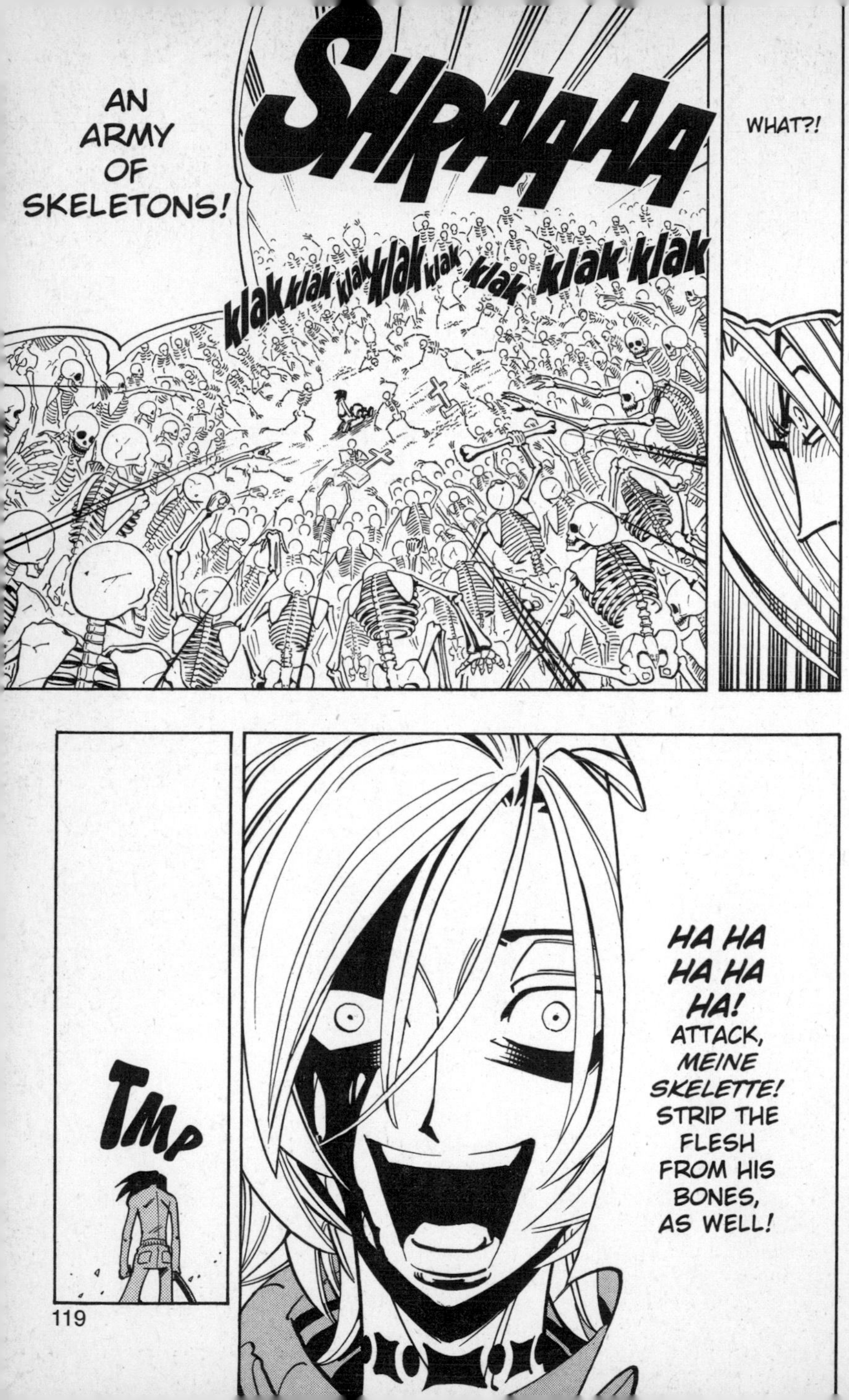
WHAT?!
SHRAAAA
AN ARMY OF SKELETONS!
klak klak klak klak klak klak klak klak
HA HA HA HA HA! ATTACK, MEINE SKELETTE! STRIP THE FLESH FROM HIS BONES, AS WELL!
TMP

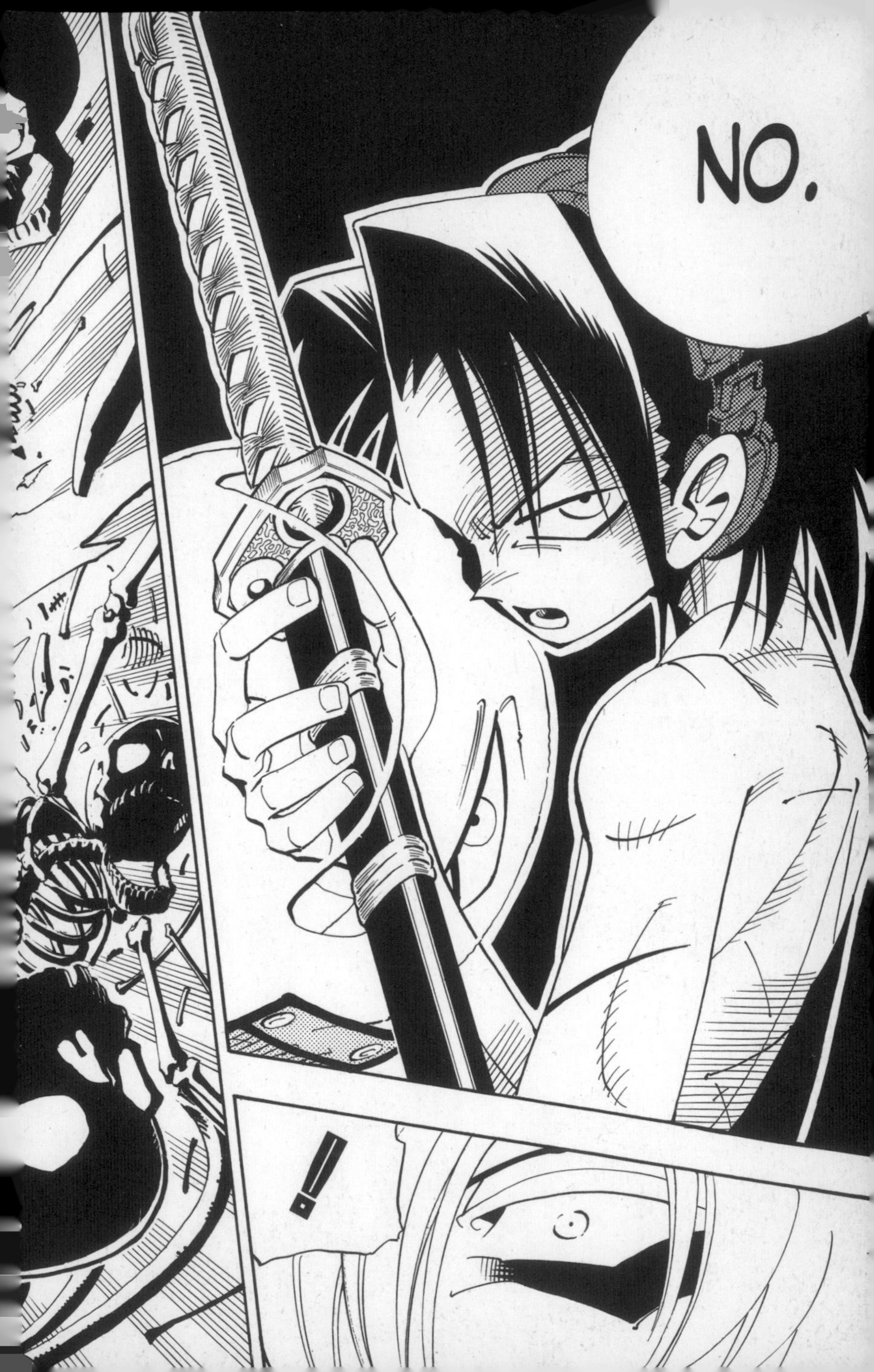
NO.
!

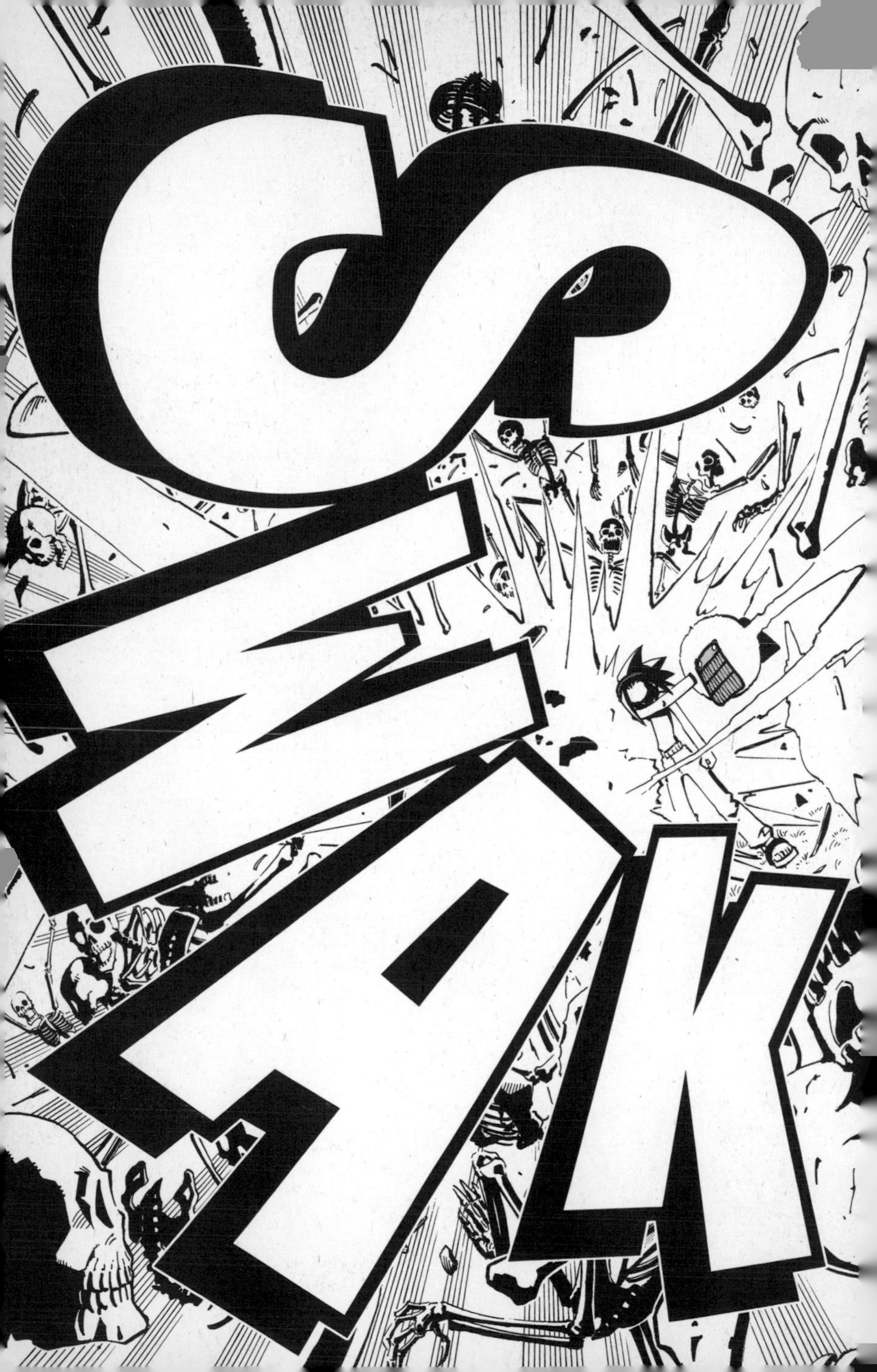

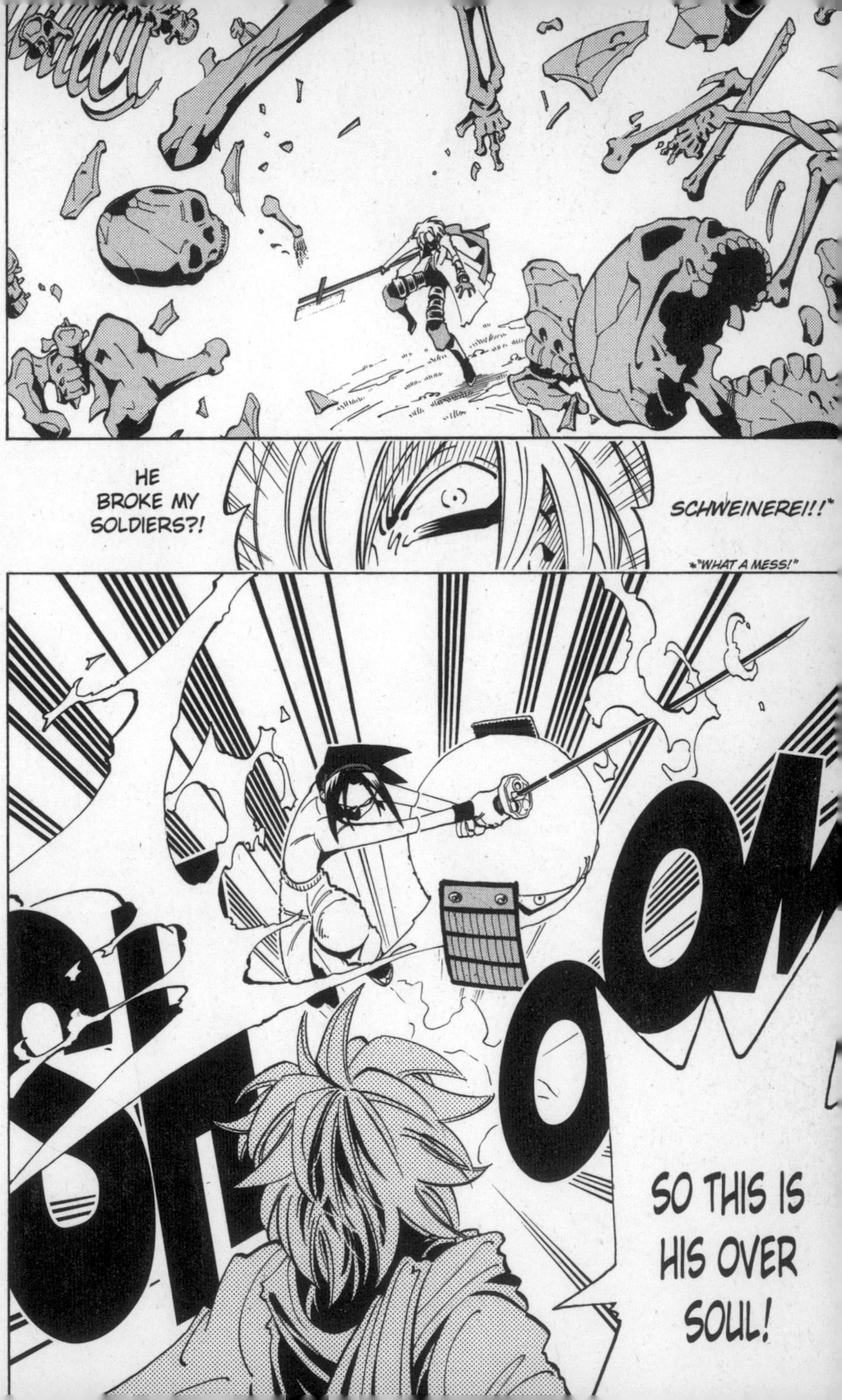
SCHWEINEREI!!*
HE BROKE MY SOLDIERS?!
*"WHAT A MESS!"
SO THIS IS HIS OVER SOUL!

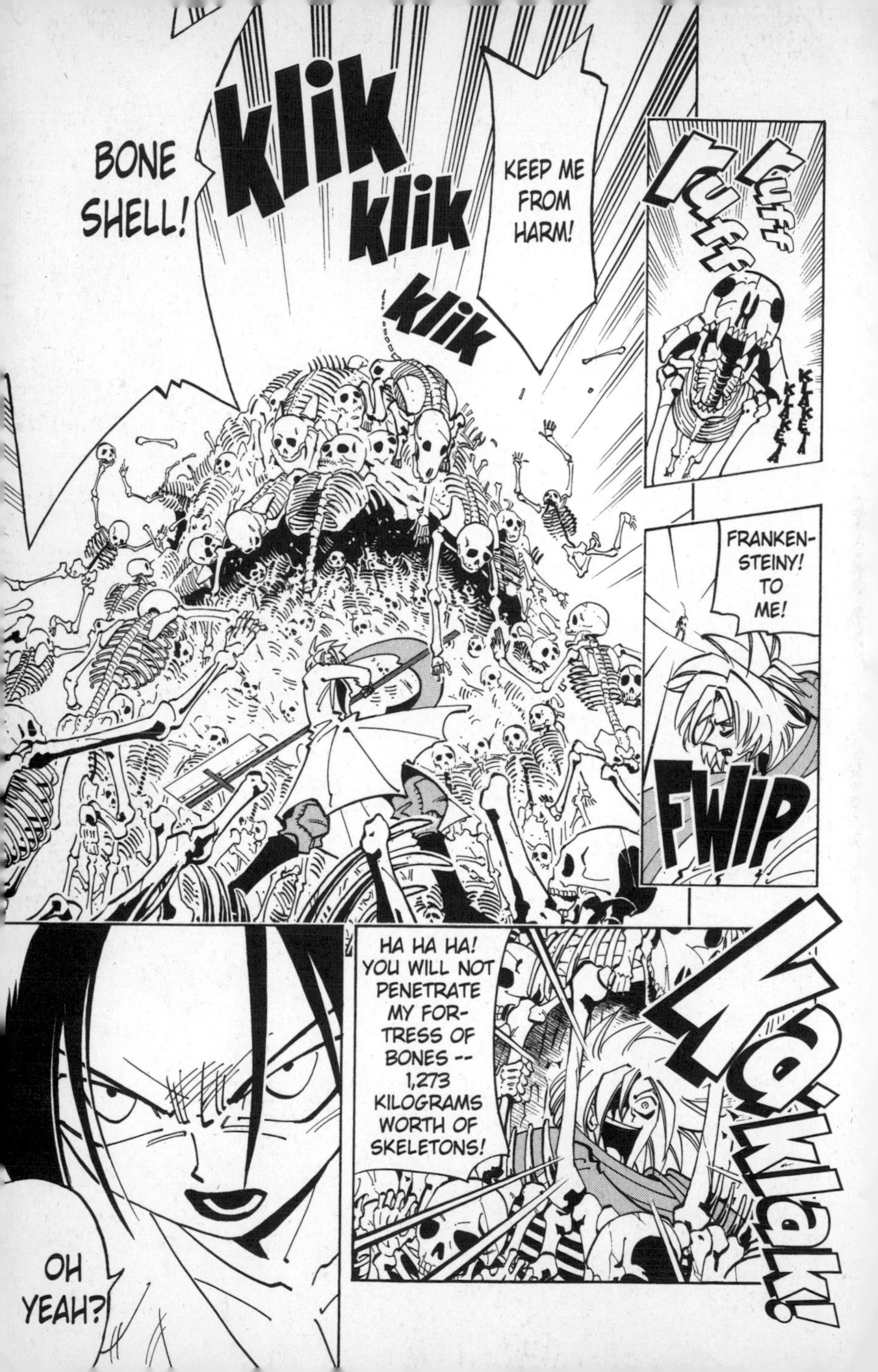
ruff
ruff
KLAKETA
KLAKETA
FRANKEN-STEINY! TO ME!
FWIP
KEEP ME FROM HARM!
klik
klik
BONE SHELL!
klik
HA HA HA! YOU WILL NOT PENETRATE MY FOR-TRESS OF BONES -- 1,273 KILOGRAMS WORTH OF SKELETONS!
OH YEAH?

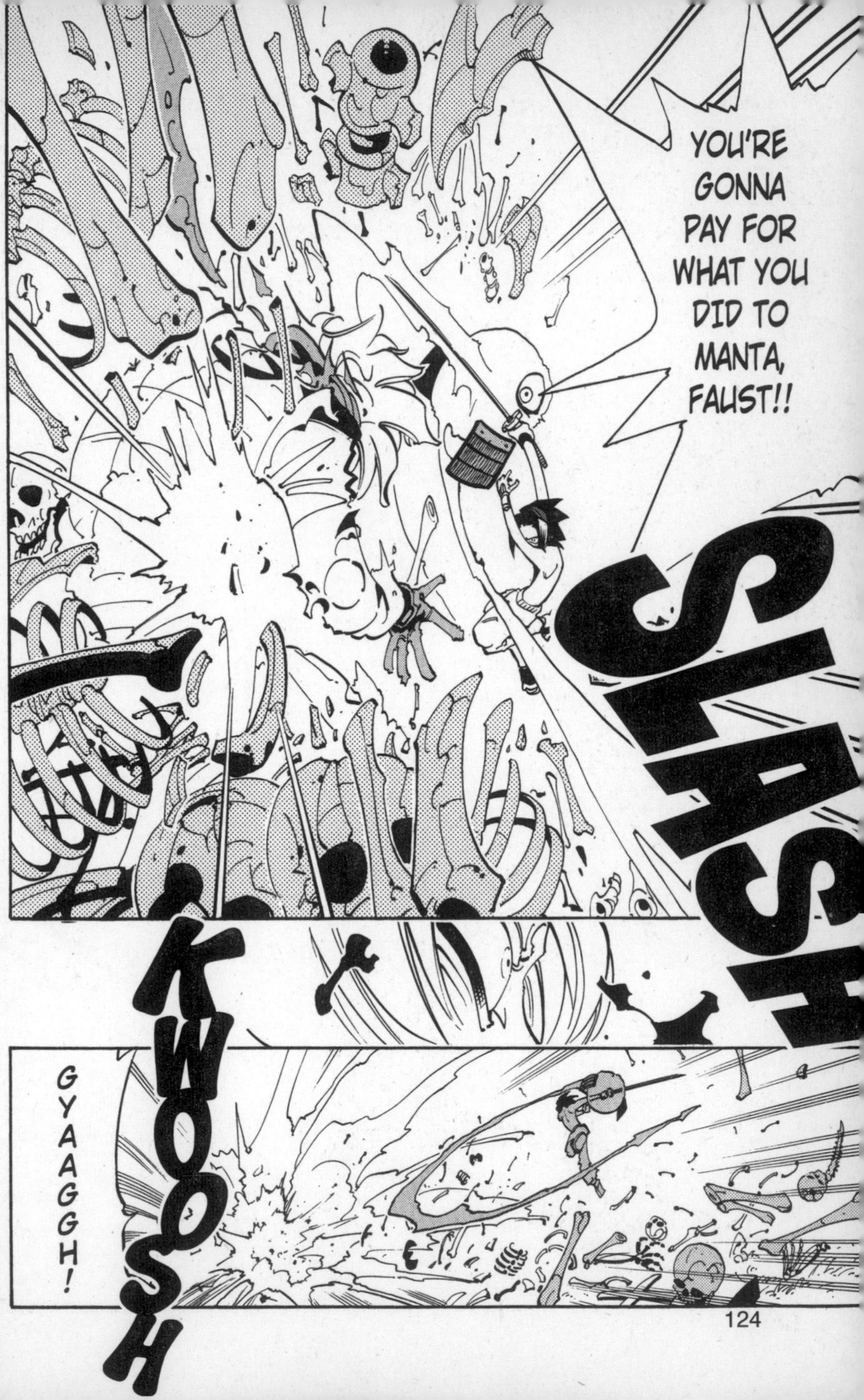
YOU'RE GONNA PAY FOR WHAT YOU DID TO MANTA, FAUST!!
SLASH
KWOOSH
GYAAAGGH!

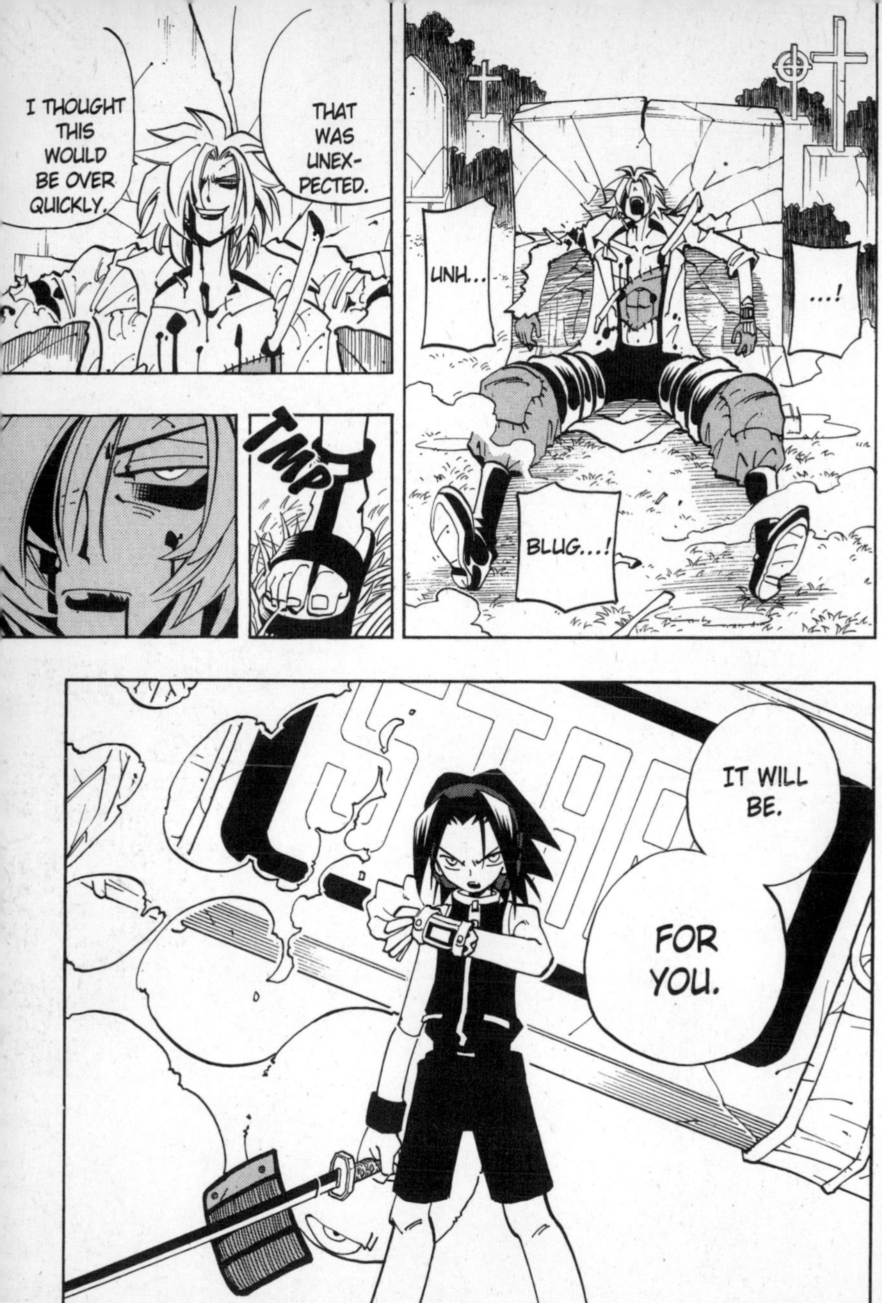
...!
UNH...
BLUG...!
THAT WAS UNEXPECTED.
I THOUGHT THIS WOULD BE OVER QUICKLY.
TMP
IT WILL BE.
FOR YOU.

SHAMAN
KING
5

THE
SUN-SUNSHINE
BUILDING

Reincarnation 42: The Atrocity Exhibition

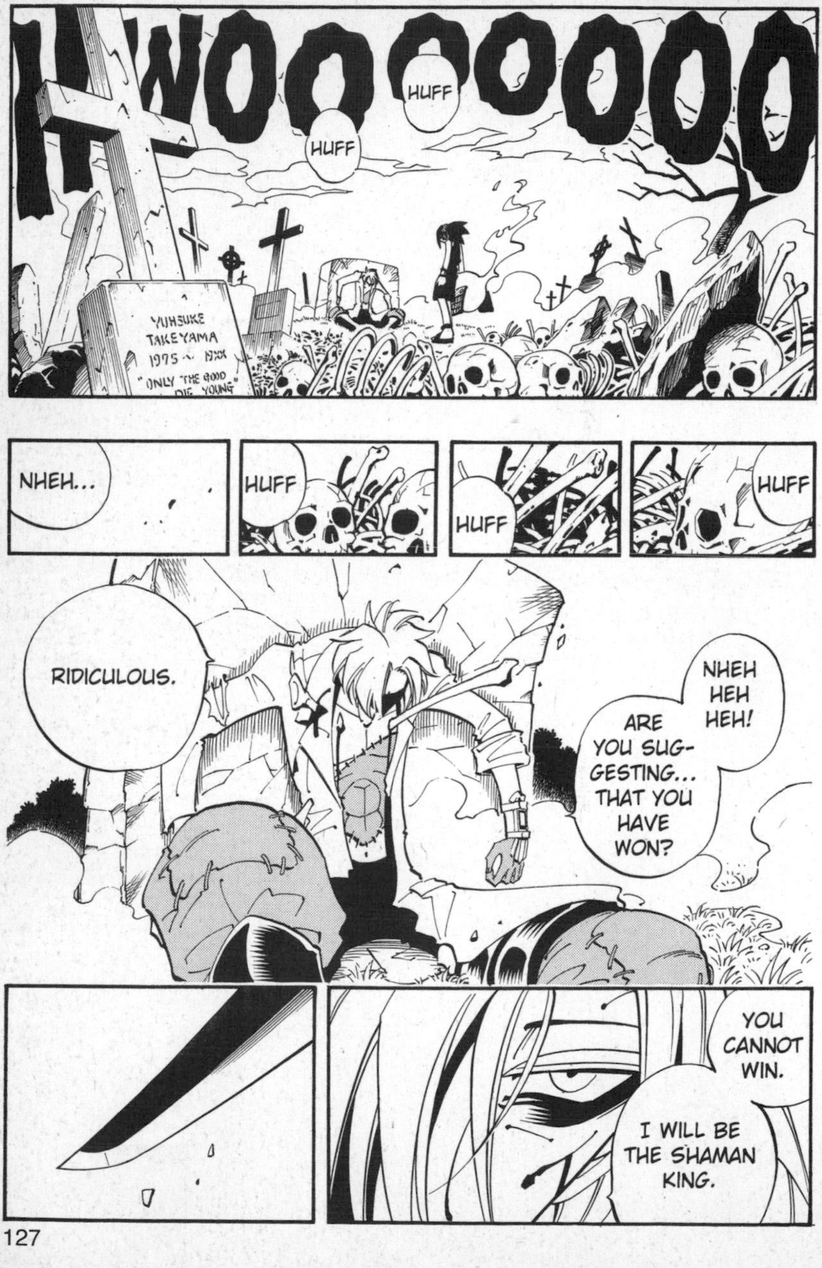
HWOOOOOOO
HUFF
HUFF
YUHSUKE TAKEYAMA 1975 ~ 19XX "ONLY THE GOOD DIE YOUNG"
HUFF
HUFF
HUFF
NHEH...
NHEH HEH HEH!
ARE YOU SUG-GESTING... THAT YOU HAVE WON?
RIDICULOUS.
YOU CANNOT WIN.
I WILL BE THE SHAMAN KING.

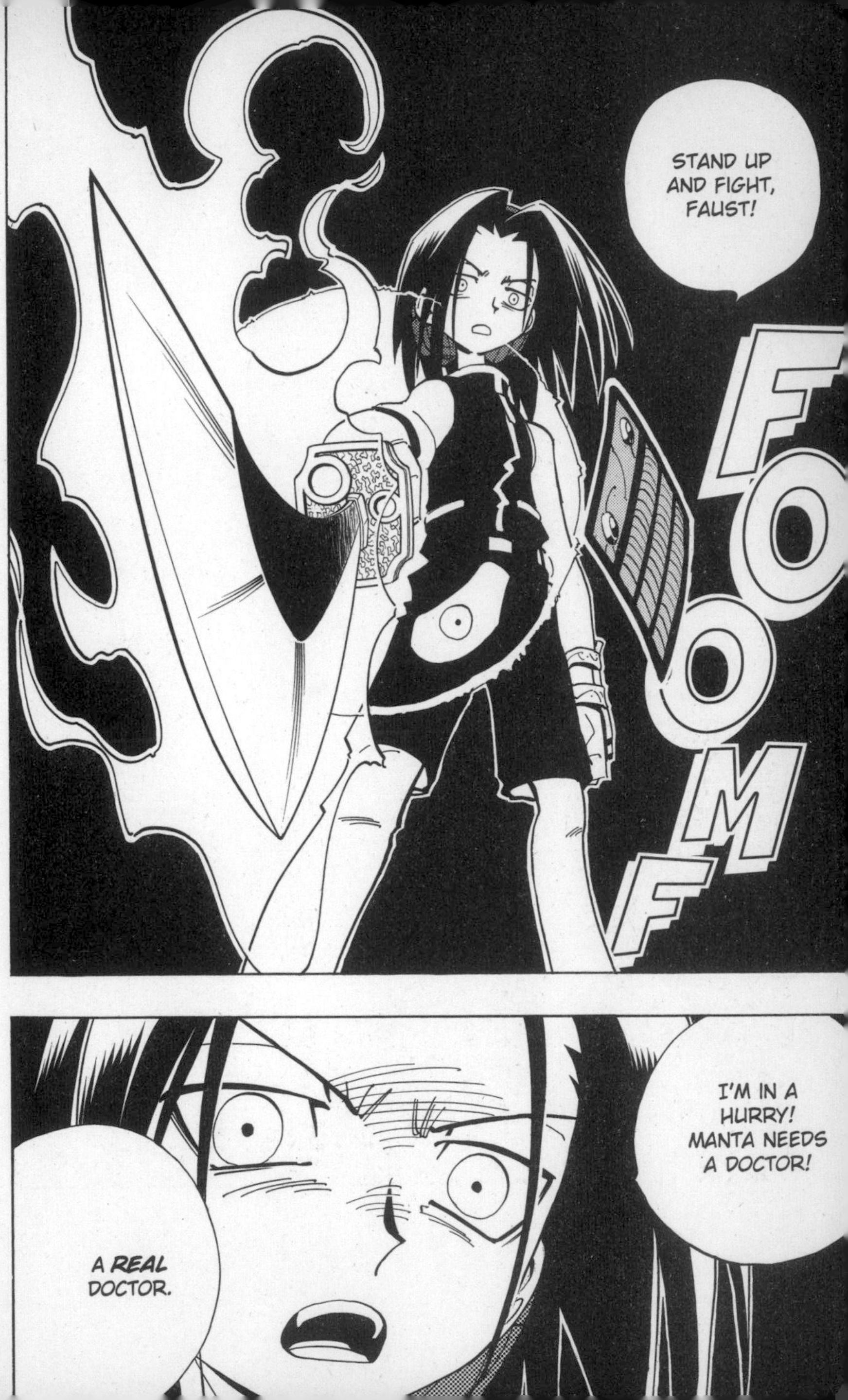
STAND UP AND FIGHT, FAUST!
FOOMF
I'M IN A HURRY! MANTA NEEDS A DOCTOR!
A *REAL* DOCTOR.

Reincarnation 42:

The Atrocity Exhibition

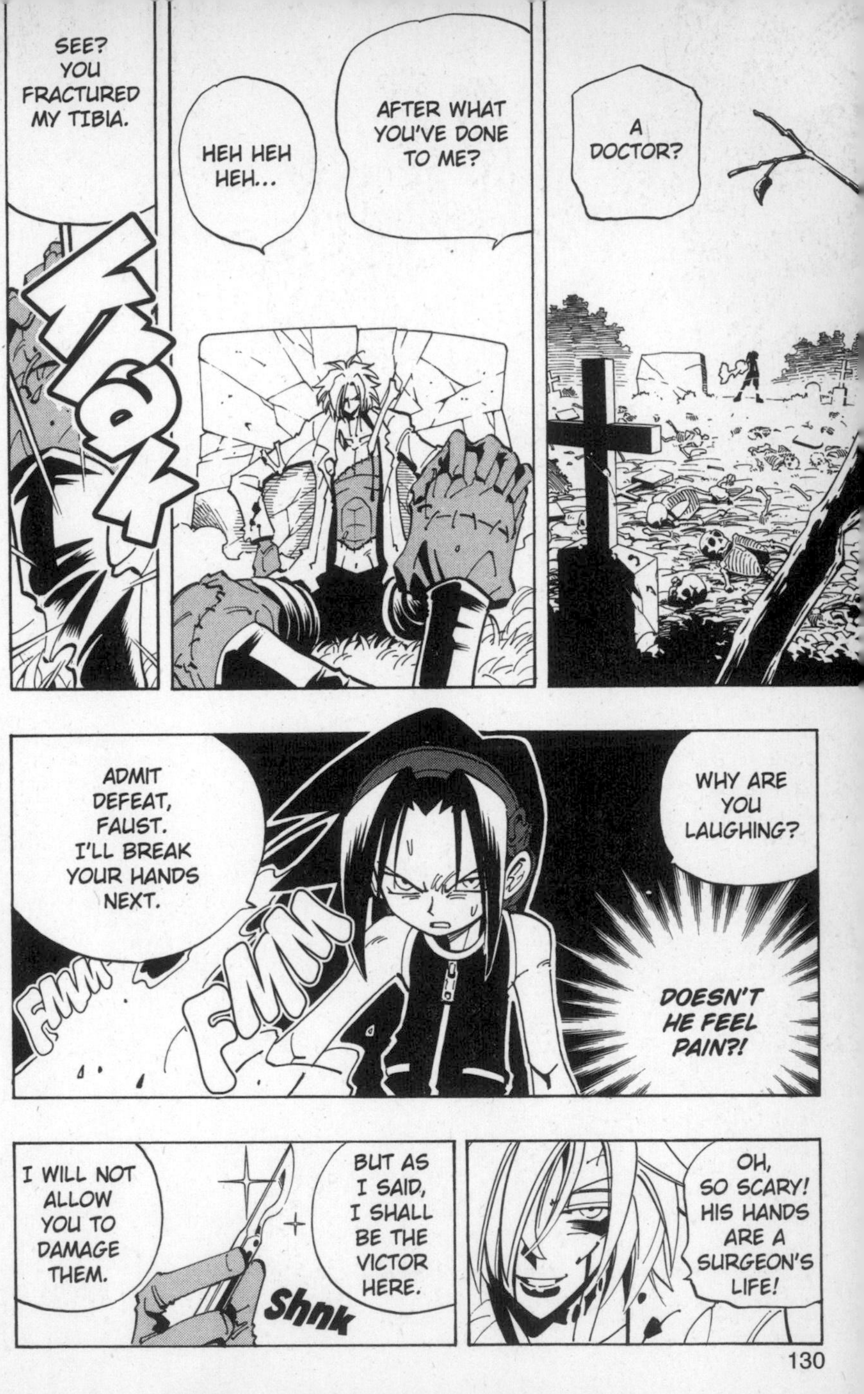
A DOCTOR?
AFTER WHAT YOU'VE DONE TO ME?
HEH HEH HEH...
SEE? YOU FRACTURED MY TIBIA.
WHY ARE YOU LAUGHING?
DOESN'T HE FEEL PAIN?!
ADMIT DEFEAT, FAUST. I'LL BREAK YOUR HANDS NEXT.
FMMM
OH, SO SCARY! HIS HANDS ARE A SURGEON'S LIFE!
BUT AS I SAID, I SHALL BE THE VICTOR HERE.
I WILL NOT ALLOW YOU TO DAMAGE THEM.
Shnk

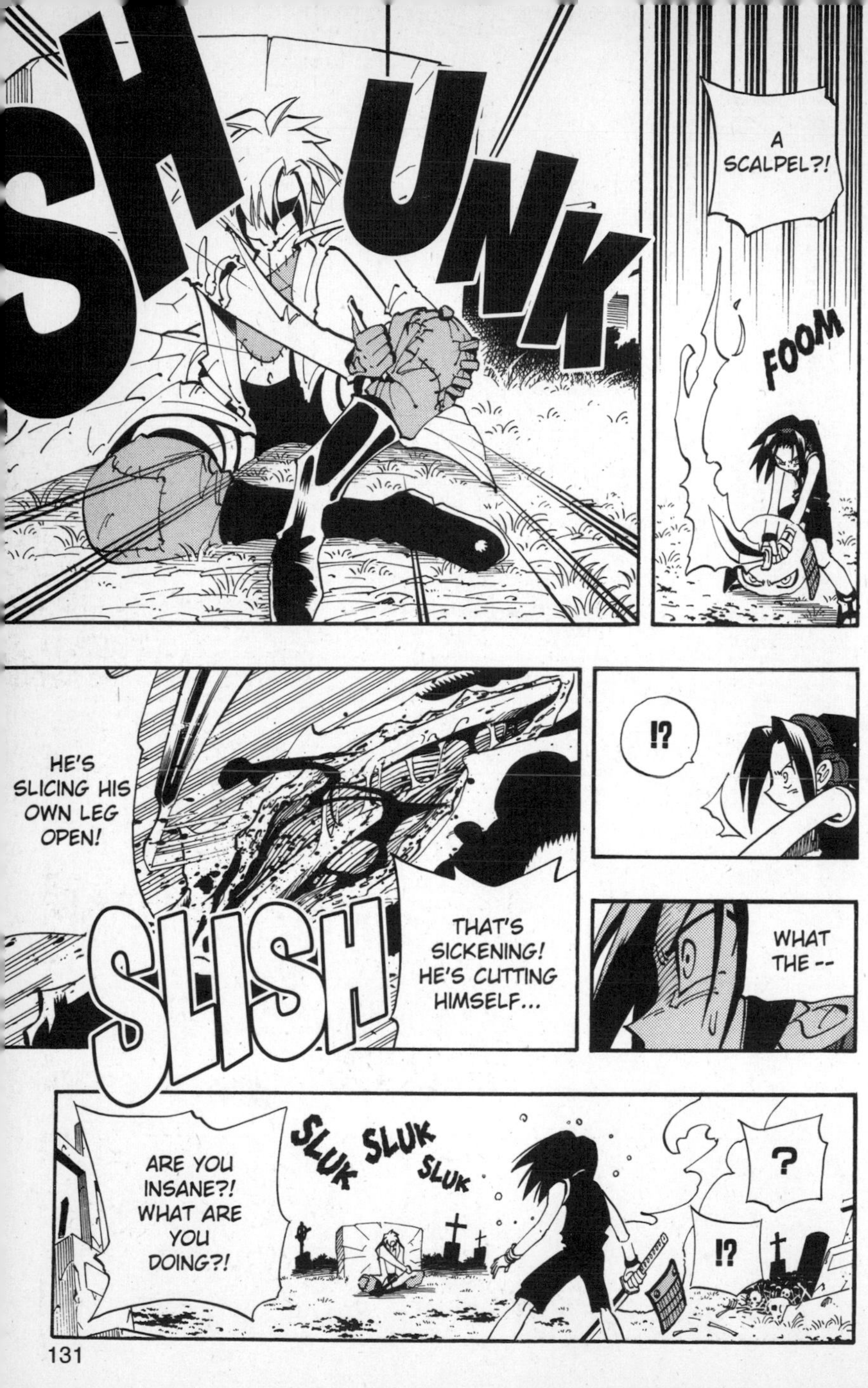
A SCALPEL?!
FOOM
SHUNK
!?
WHAT THE --
HE'S SLICING HIS OWN LEG OPEN!
THAT'S SICKENING! HE'S CUTTING HIMSELF...
SLISH
?
!?
SLUK
SLUK
SLUK
SLUK
ARE YOU INSANE?! WHAT ARE YOU DOING?!

READ THIS WAY

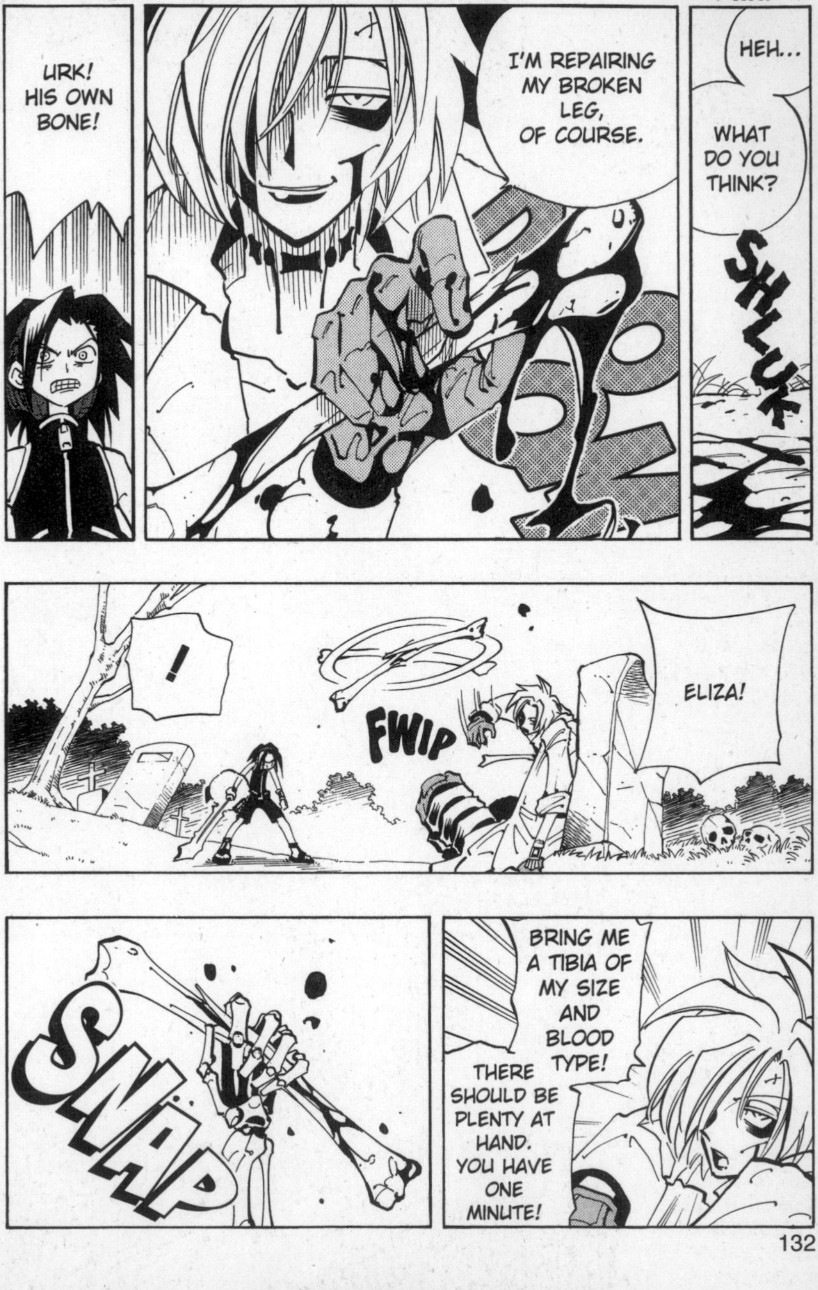
HEH...
WHAT DO YOU THINK?
SHLUK
I'M REPAIRING MY BROKEN LEG, OF COURSE.
URK! HIS OWN BONE!
ELIZA!
!
FWIP
BRING ME A TIBIA OF MY SIZE AND BLOOD TYPE!
THERE SHOULD BE PLENTY AT HAND. YOU HAVE ONE MINUTE!
SNAP

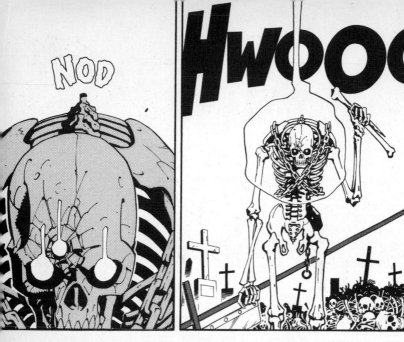

HWOOO
NOD
...
NHEH HEH. SURPRISED? AMAZED? SHOCKED?
HUFF
HUFF
...
IT'S VERY SIMPLE. I'M TRANS-PLANTING THE WHOLE TIBIA.
IT'S ILLEGAL, BUT IT HEALS FASTER THIS WAY.
IT TAKES 8-10 WEEKS FOR A FRACTURED ADULT TIBIA TO MEND, BUT A MERE 2-3 WEEKS FOR THE MUSCLES TO ATTACH TO BONE.
I'LL JUST SUTURE THE LIGAMENTS AND MY LEG WILL BE AS GOOD AS NEW IN SHORT ORDER.

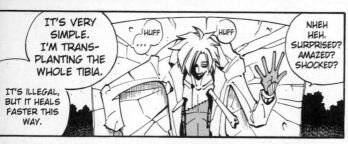

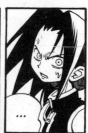

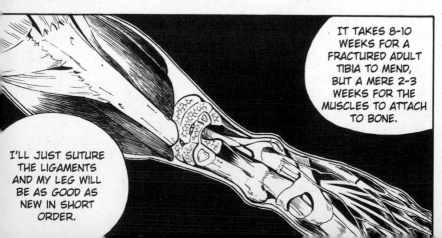

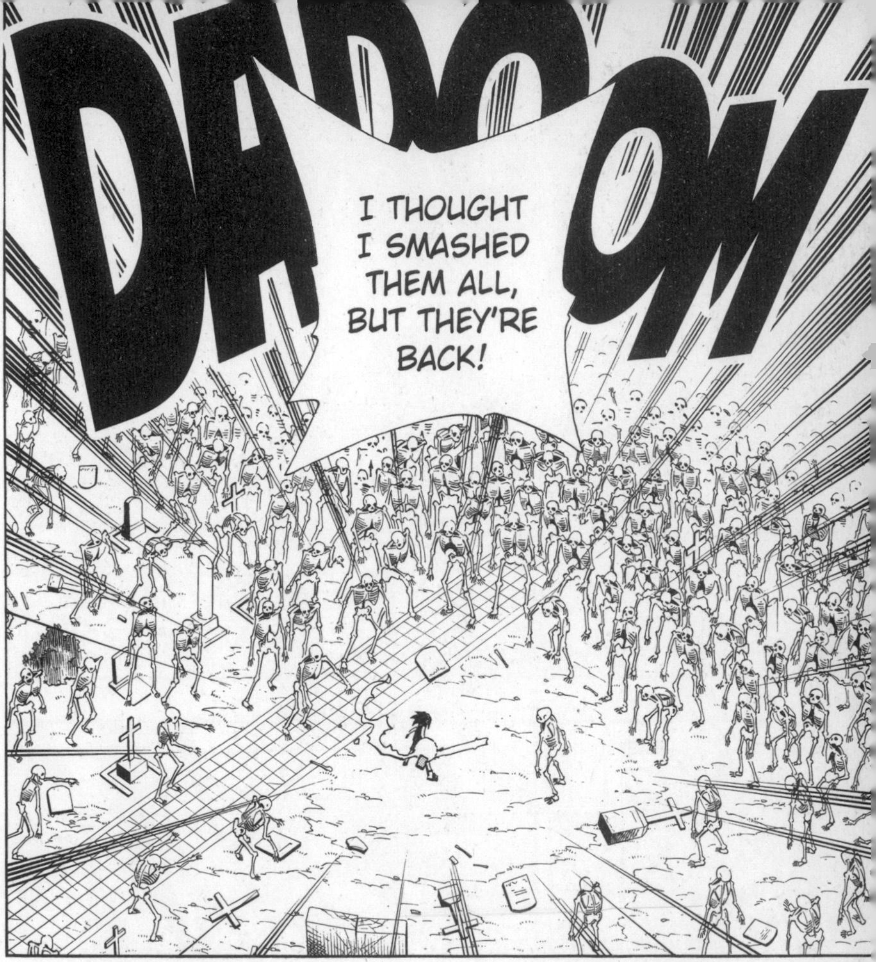
DADOOM
I THOUGHT I SMASHED THEM ALL, BUT THEY'RE BACK!

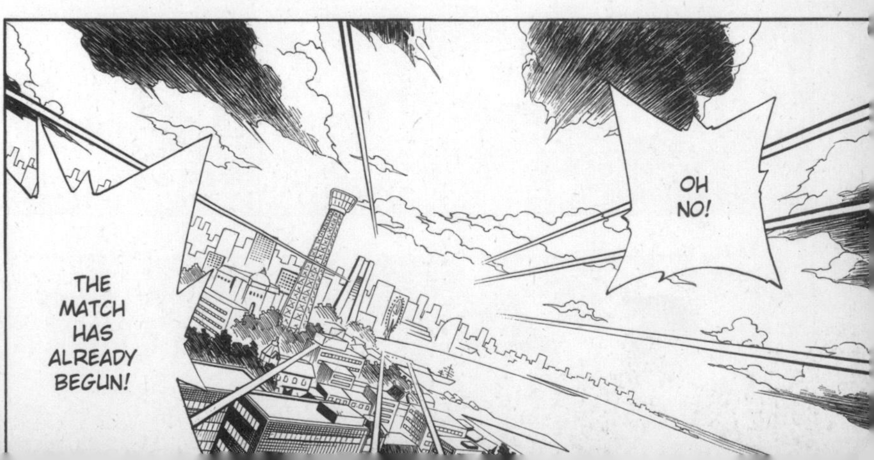
OH NO!
THE MATCH HAS ALREADY BEGUN!

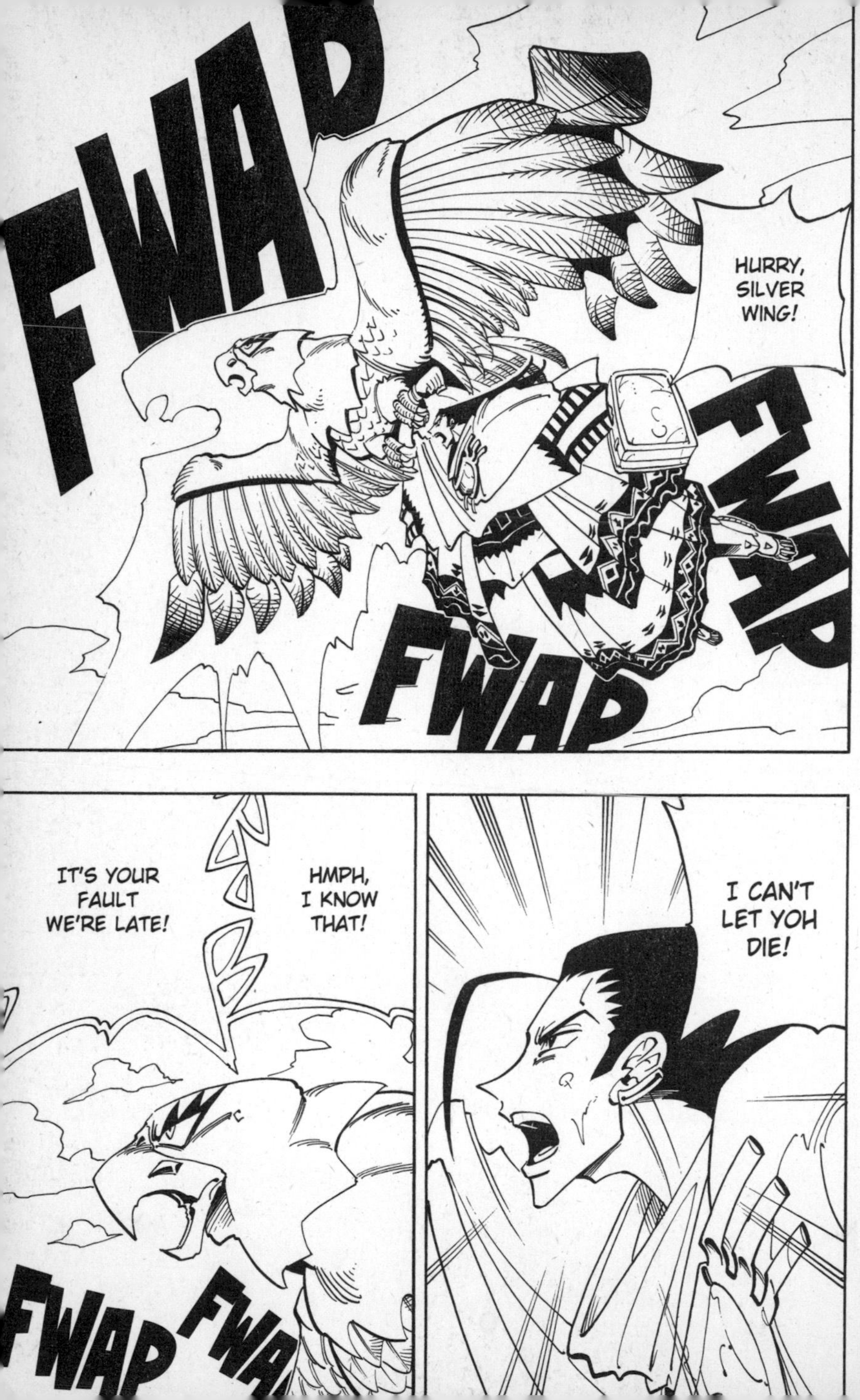
HURRY, SILVER WING!
FWAP
FWAP
FWAP
I CAN'T LET YOH DIE!
HMPH, I KNOW THAT!
IT'S YOUR FAULT WE'RE LATE!
FWA
FWAP

READ THIS WAY

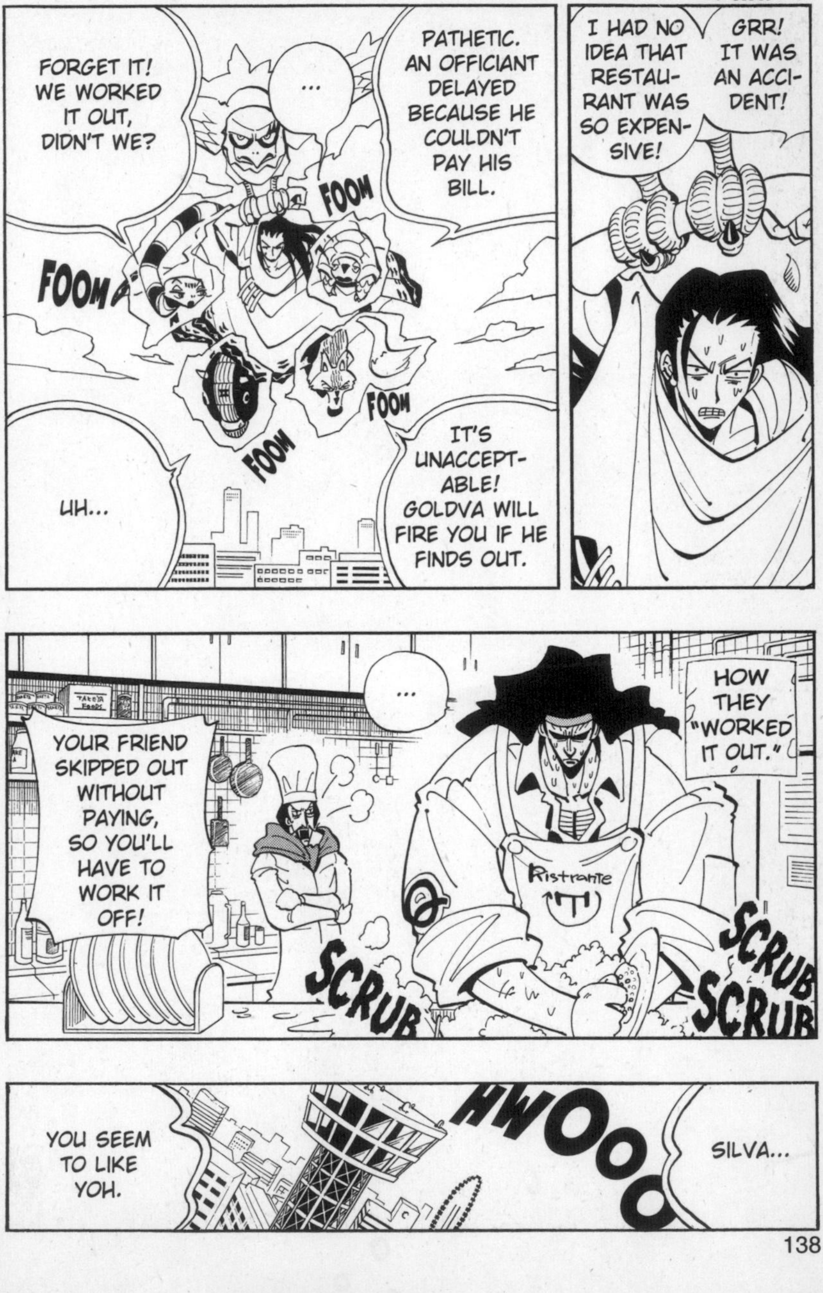
GRR! IT WAS AN ACCIDENT!
I HAD NO IDEA THAT RESTAURANT WAS SO EXPENSIVE!
PATHETIC. AN OFFICIANT DELAYED BECAUSE HE COULDN'T PAY HIS BILL.
...
FORGET IT! WE WORKED IT OUT, DIDN'T WE?
FOOM
FOOM
IT'S UNACCEPTABLE! GOLDVA WILL FIRE YOU IF HE FINDS OUT.
FOOM
FOOM
UH...
HOW THEY "WORKED IT OUT."
...
YOUR FRIEND SKIPPED OUT WITHOUT PAYING, SO YOU'LL HAVE TO WORK IT OFF!
Ristrante
SCRUB SCRUB
SCRUB
SILVA...
HWOOO
YOU SEEM TO LIKE YOH.

READ THIS WAY

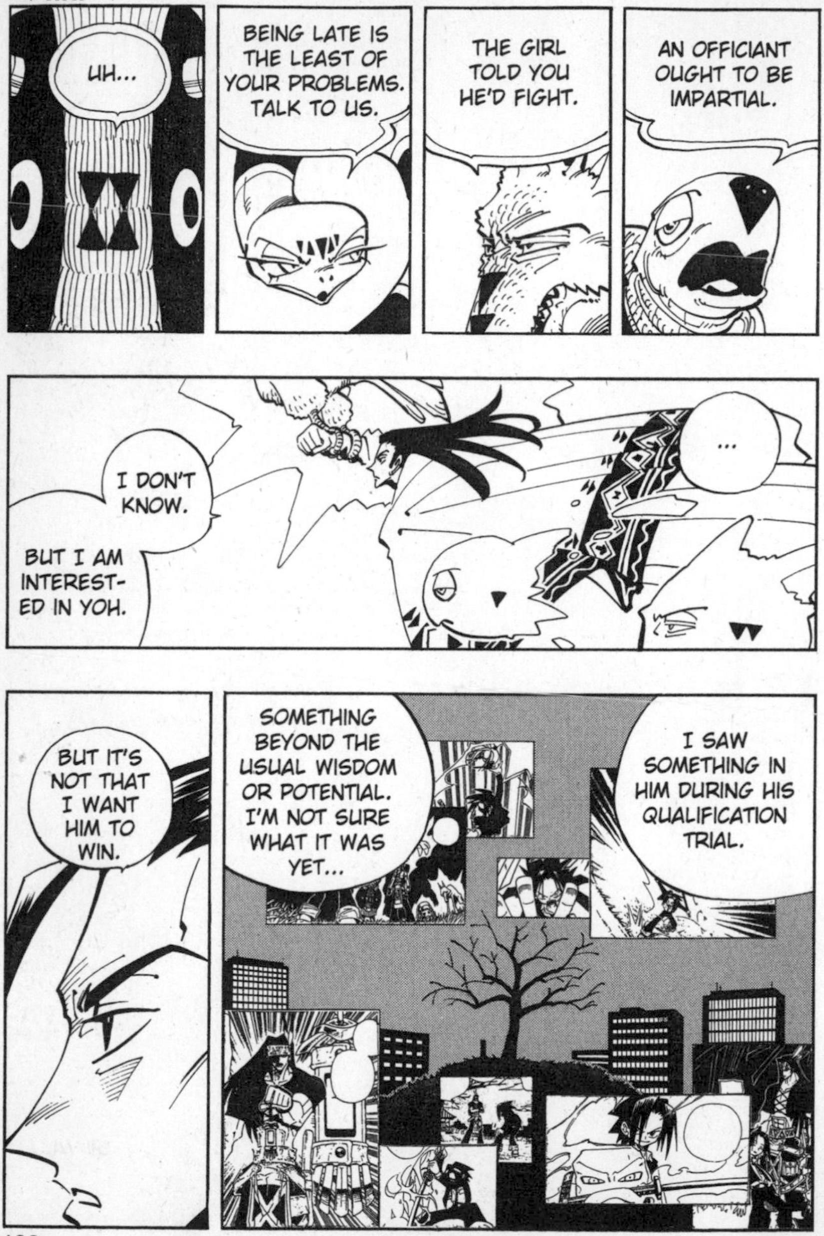

AN OFFICIANT OUGHT TO BE IMPARTIAL.
THE GIRL TOLD YOU HE'D FIGHT.
BEING LATE IS THE LEAST OF YOUR PROBLEMS. TALK TO US.
UH...
...
I DON'T KNOW.
BUT I AM INTEREST-ED IN YOH.
I SAW SOMETHING IN HIM DURING HIS QUALIFICATION TRIAL.
SOMETHING BEYOND THE USUAL WISDOM OR POTENTIAL. I'M NOT SURE WHAT IT WAS YET...
BUT IT'S NOT THAT I WANT HIM TO WIN.

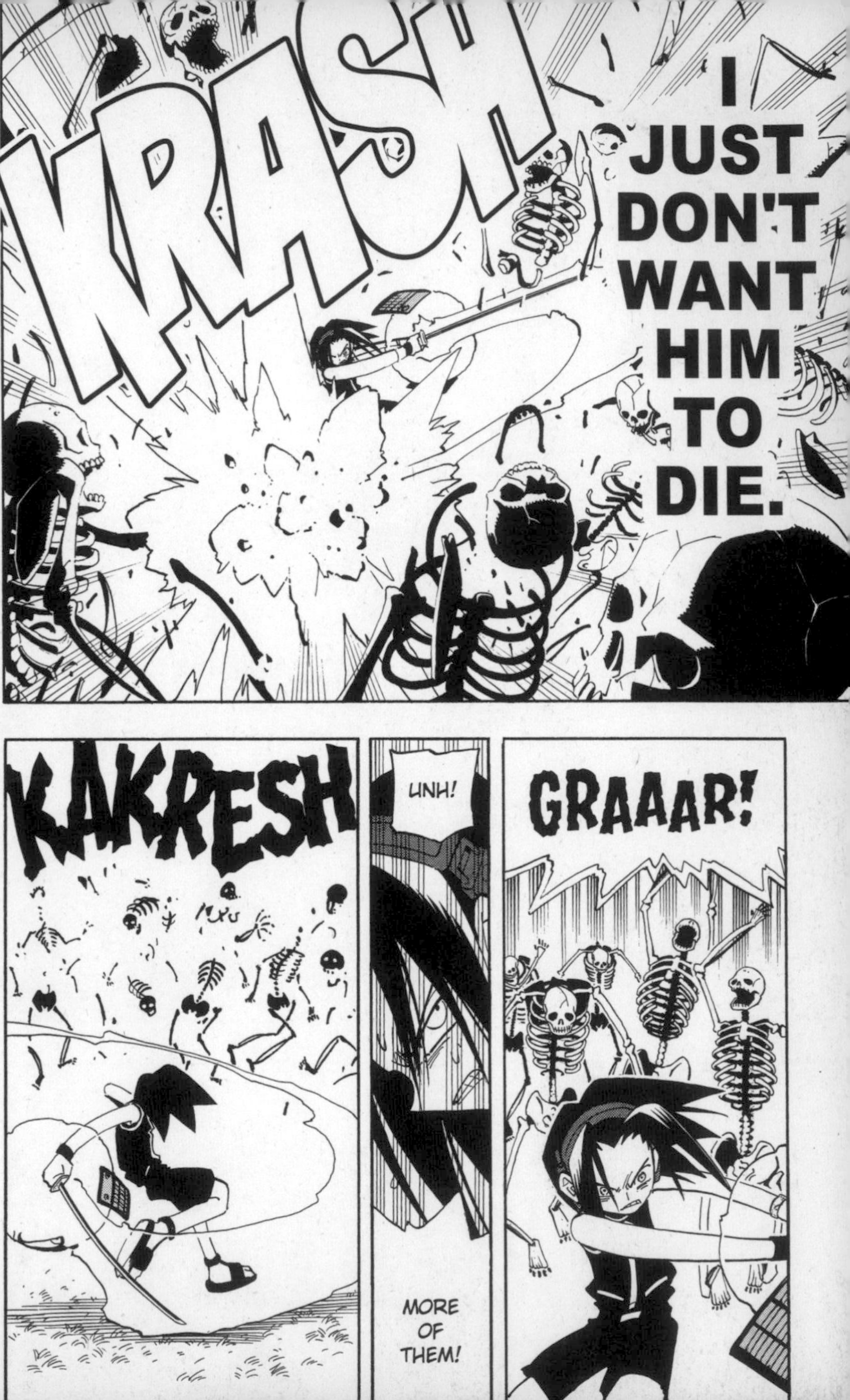
KRASH
I JUST DON'T WANT HIM TO DIE.
GRAAAR!
UNH!
MORE OF THEM!
KAKRESH

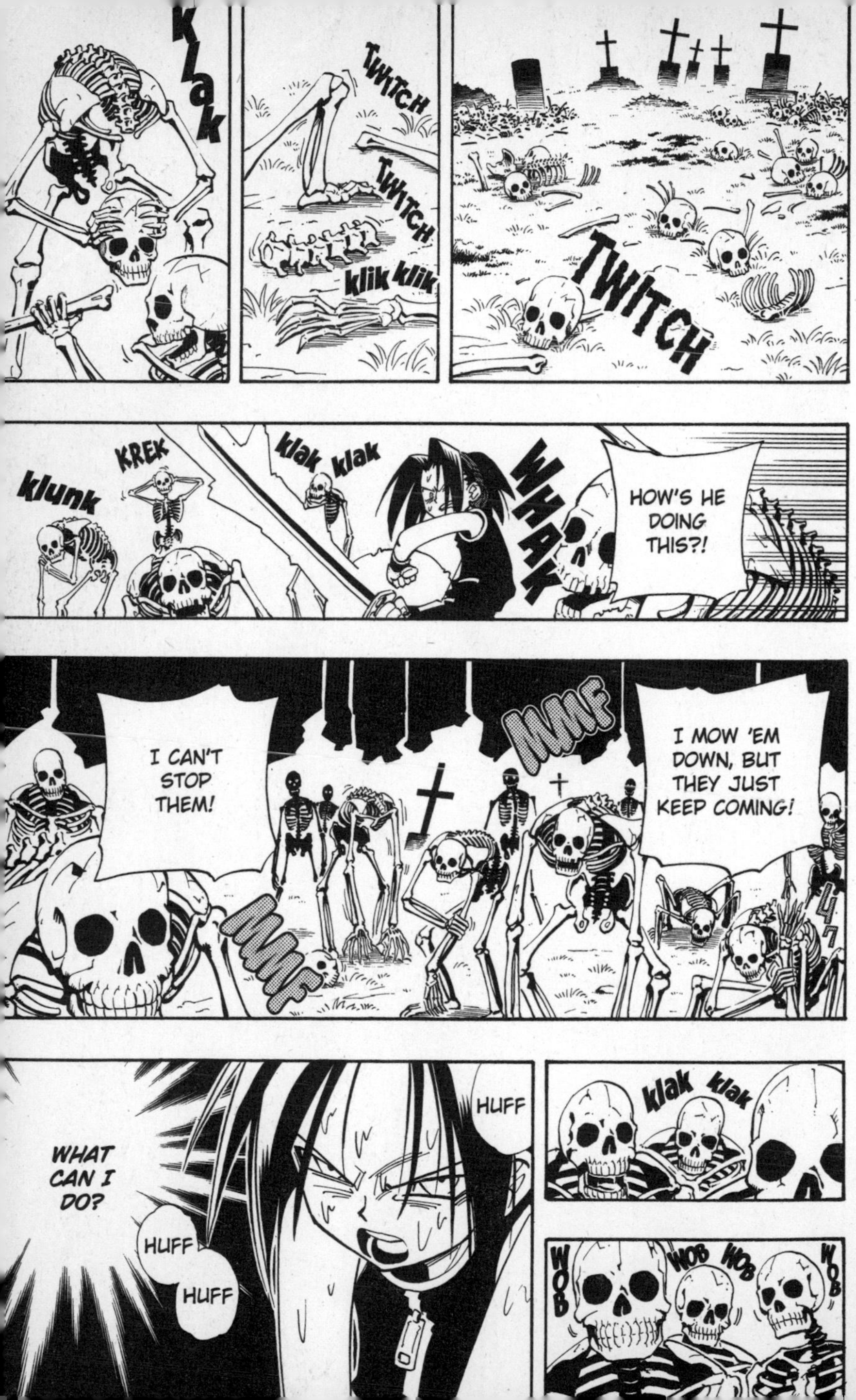
TWITCH
TWITCH
TWITCH
klik klik
KLAK
HOW'S HE DOING THIS?!
WHAK
klak klak
KREK
klunk
I MOW 'EM DOWN, BUT THEY JUST KEEP COMING!
MMF
I CAN'T STOP THEM!
MMF
klak klak
WOB WOB WOB WOB
HUFF
WHAT CAN I DO?
HUFF
HUFF

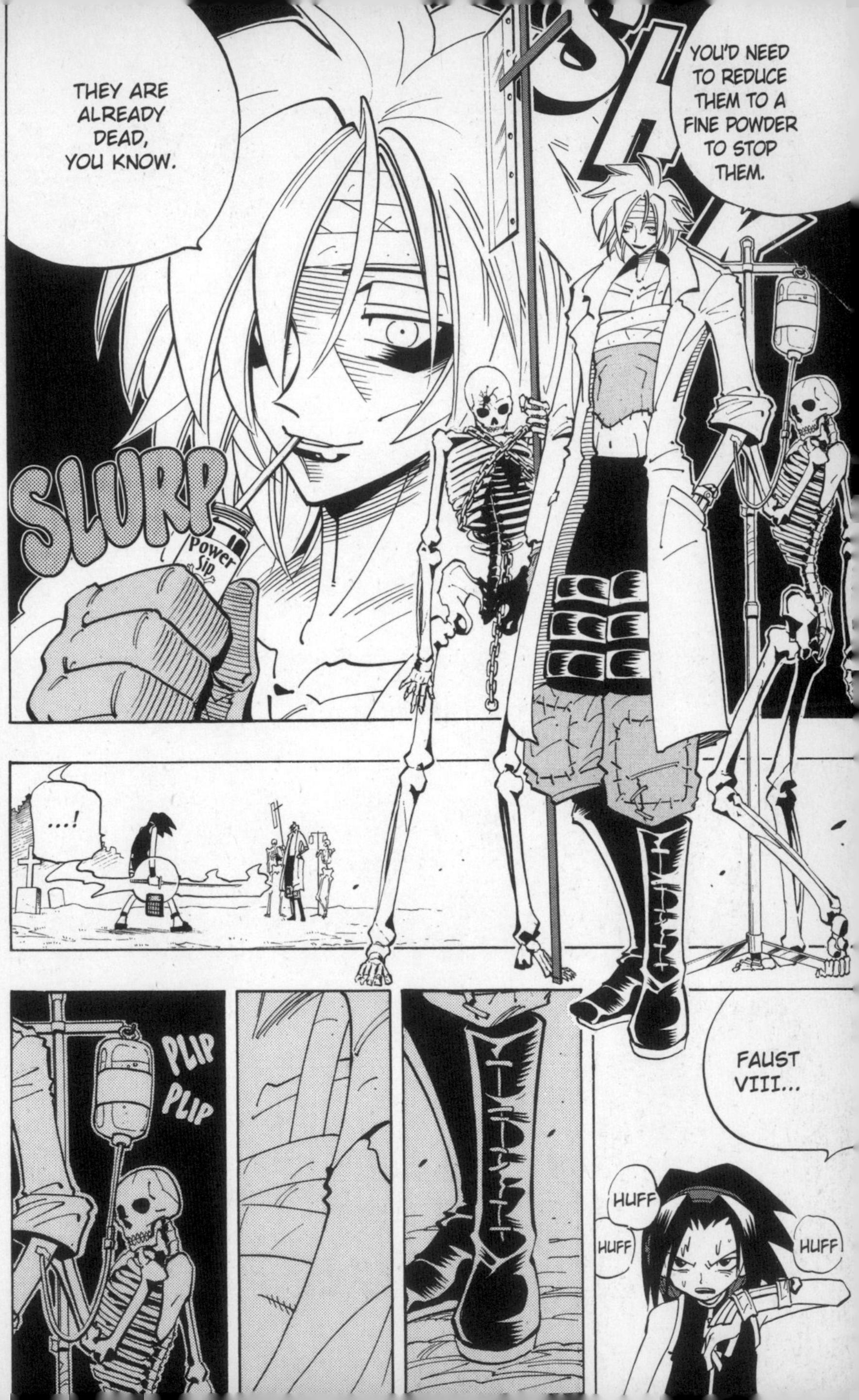
YOU'D NEED TO REDUCE THEM TO A FINE POWDER TO STOP THEM.
THEY ARE ALREADY DEAD, YOU KNOW.
SLURP
Power Sip
...!
FAUST VIII...
HUFF
HUFF
HUFF
PLIP
PLIP

READ THIS WAY

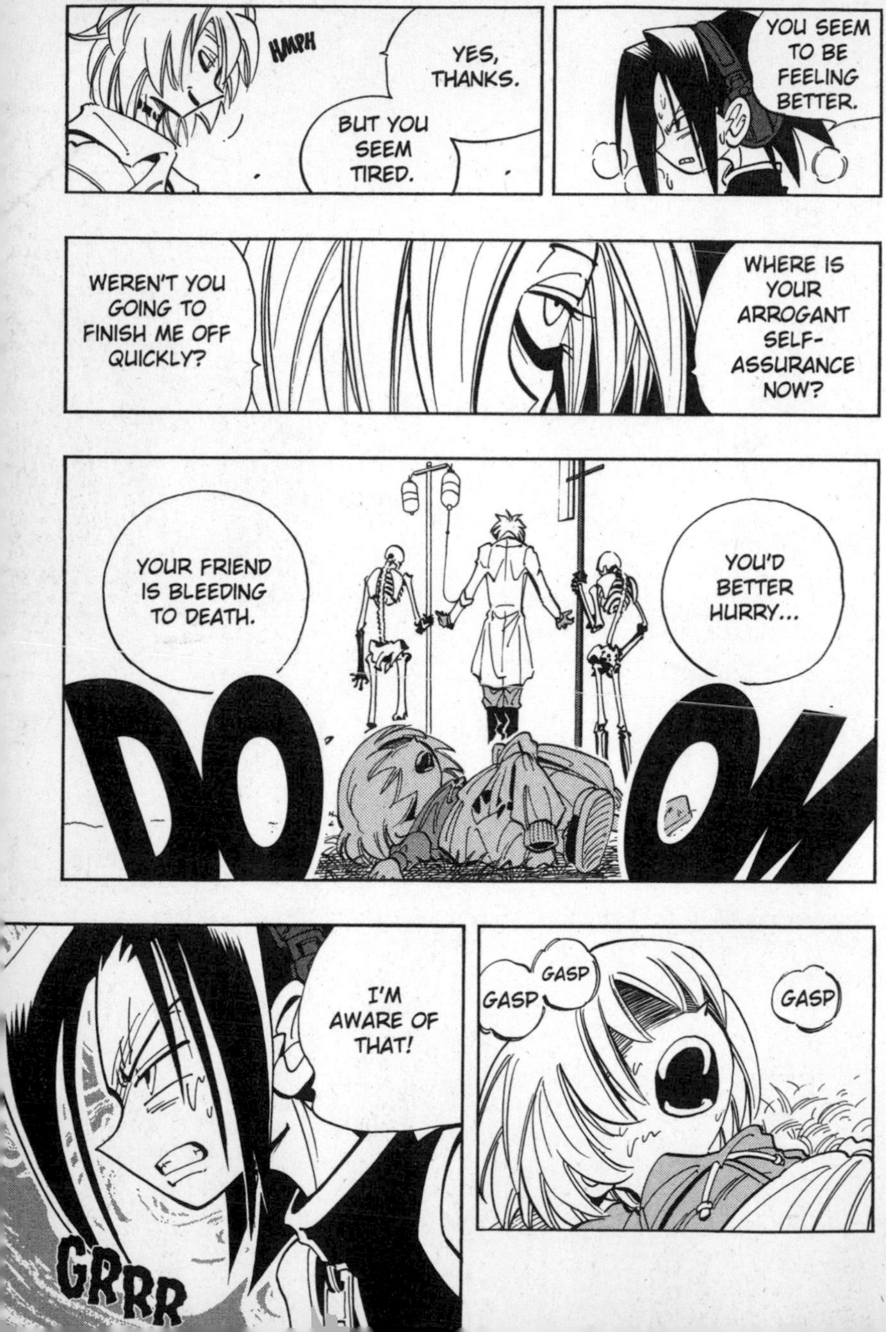
YOU SEEM TO BE FEELING BETTER.
HMPH
YES, THANKS.
BUT YOU SEEM TIRED.
WHERE IS YOUR ARROGANT SELF-ASSURANCE NOW?
WEREN'T YOU GOING TO FINISH ME OFF QUICKLY?
YOUR FRIEND IS BLEEDING TO DEATH.
YOU'D BETTER HURRY...
DOOM
GASP
GASP
GASP
I'M AWARE OF THAT!
GRRR

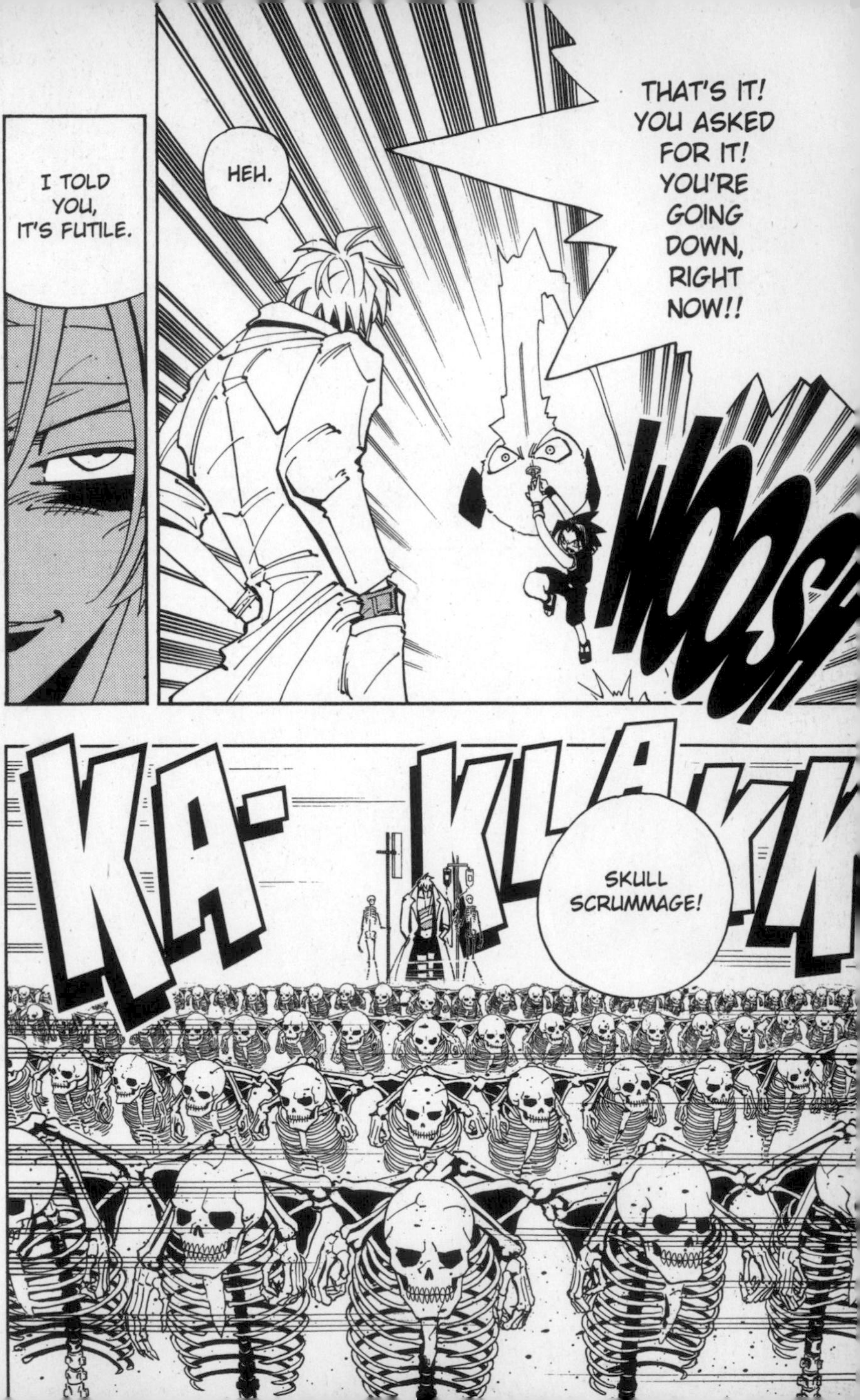
THAT'S IT! YOU ASKED FOR IT! YOU'RE GOING DOWN, RIGHT NOW!!
HEH.
WOOSH
I TOLD YOU, IT'S FUTILE.
KA-KLA
SKULL SCRUMMAGE!

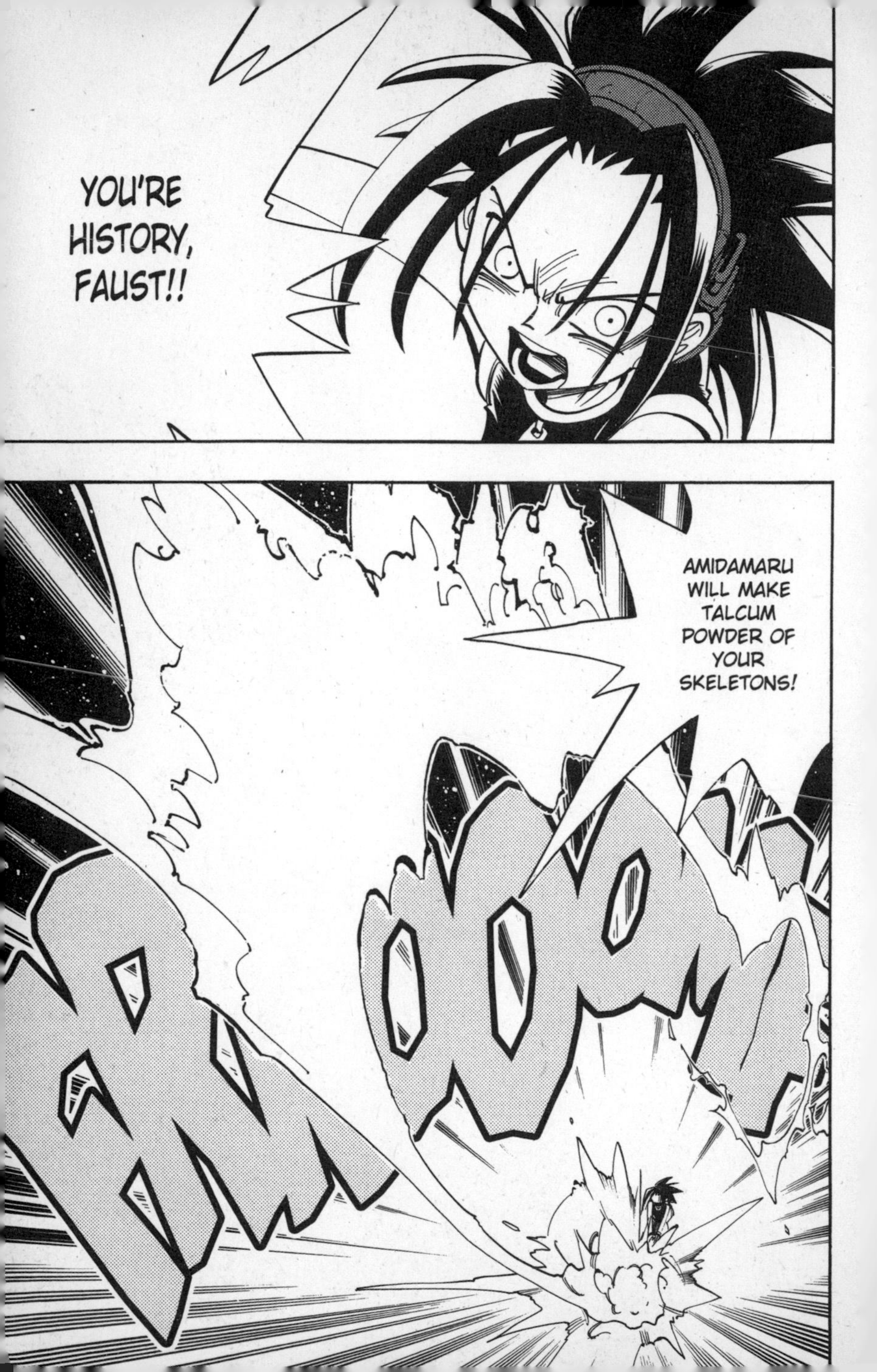
YOU'RE HISTORY, FAUST!!
AMIDAMARU WILL MAKE TALCUM POWDER OF YOUR SKELETONS!
BOOM

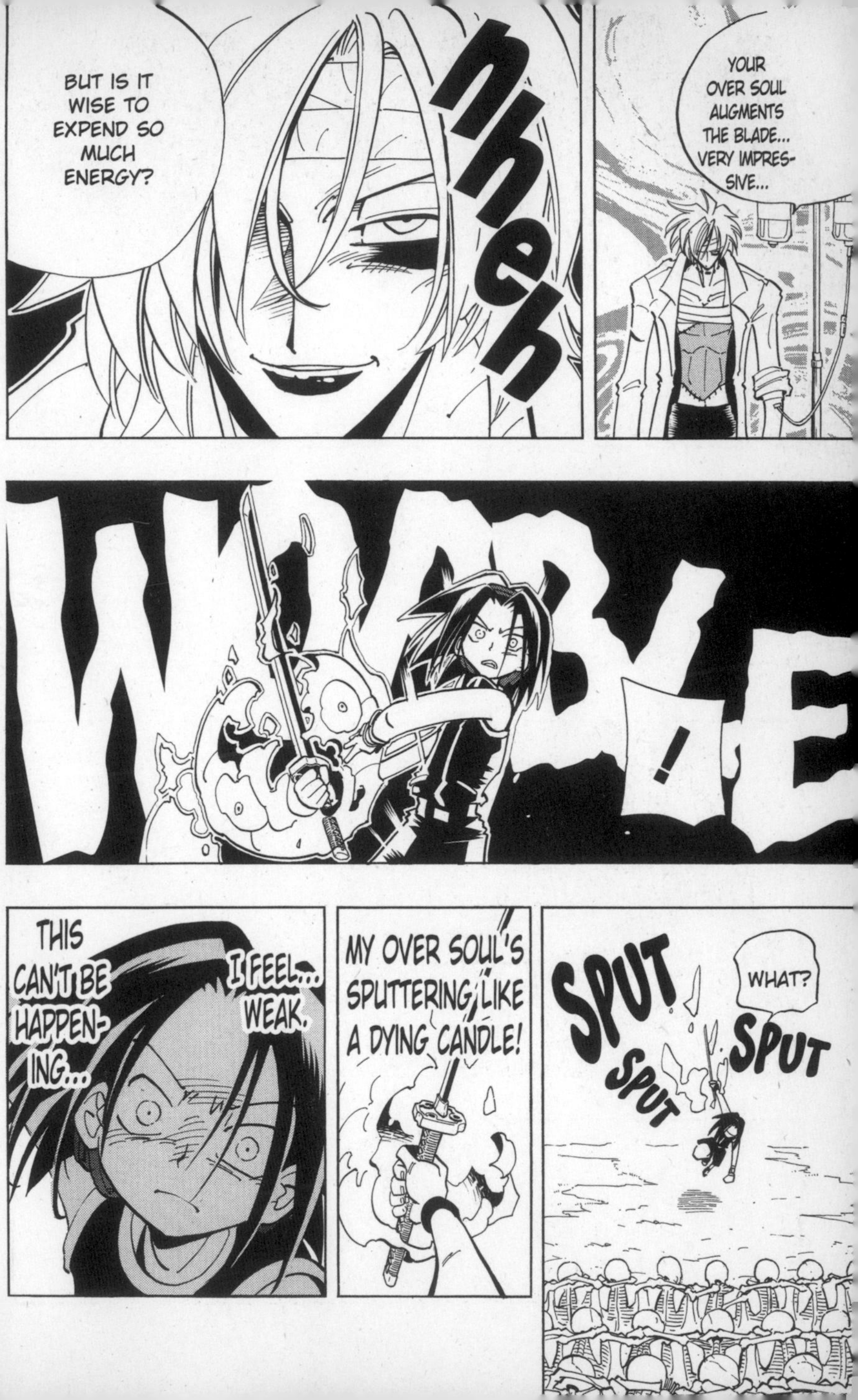
YOUR OVER SOUL AUGMENTS THE BLADE... VERY IMPRES-SIVE...
nheh
BUT IS IT WISE TO EXPEND SO MUCH ENERGY?
!
SPUT
WHAT?
SPUT
SPUT
MY OVER SOUL'S SPUTTERING LIKE A DYING CANDLE!
THIS CAN'T BE HAPPEN-ING...
I FEEL... WEAK.

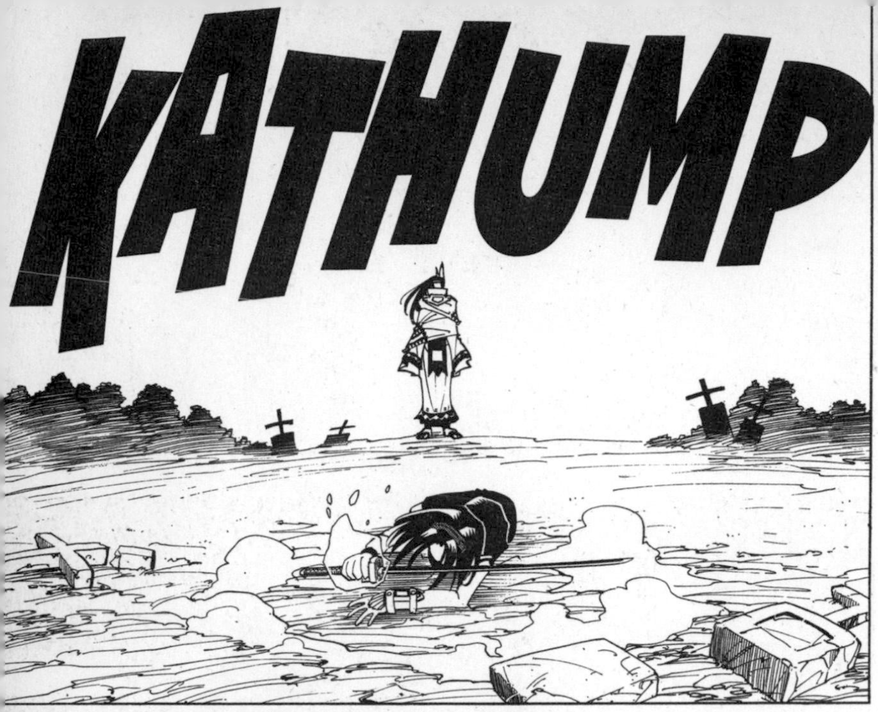
KATHUMP

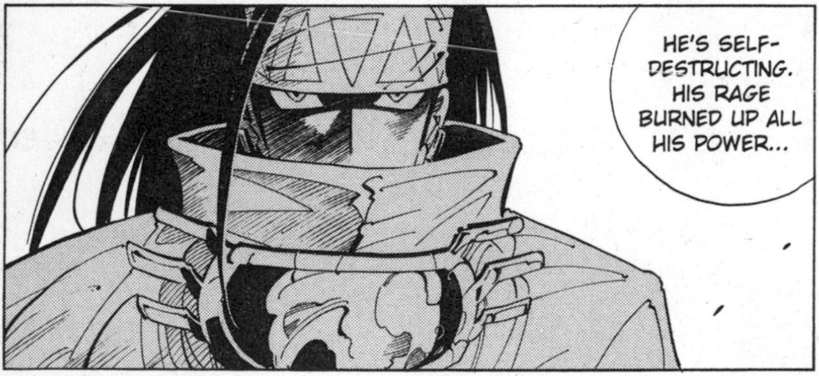
HE'S SELF-DESTRUCTING. HIS RAGE BURNED UP ALL HIS POWER...

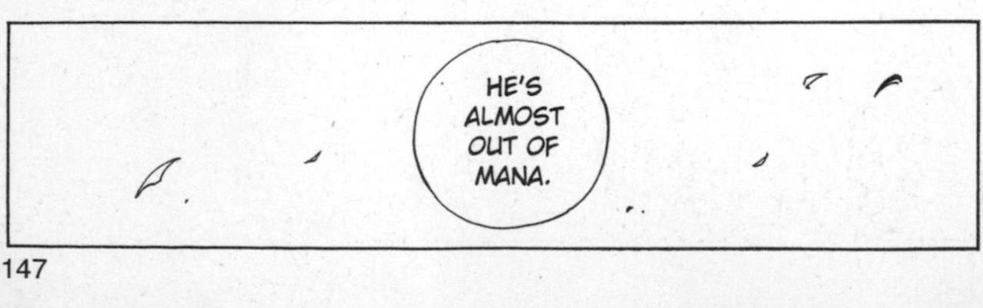
HE'S ALMOST OUT OF MANA.

SHAMAN KING CHARACTER FILE No.23

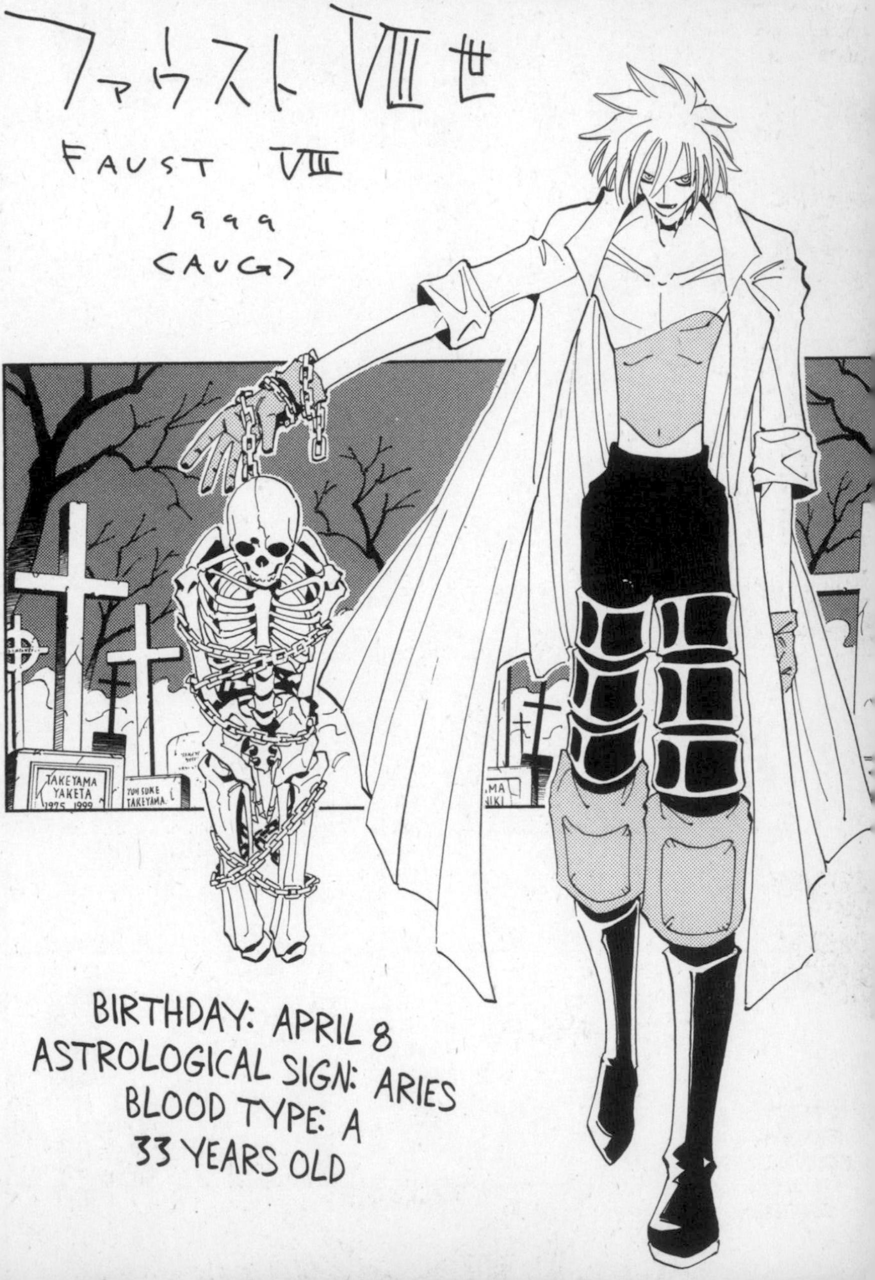
ファウストVIII世
FAUST VIII
1999
<AUG>
TAKEYAMA YAKETA 1975-1999
YUH SUKE TAKEYAMA

BIRTHDAY: APRIL 8
ASTROLOGICAL SIGN: ARIES
BLOOD TYPE: A
33 YEARS OLD

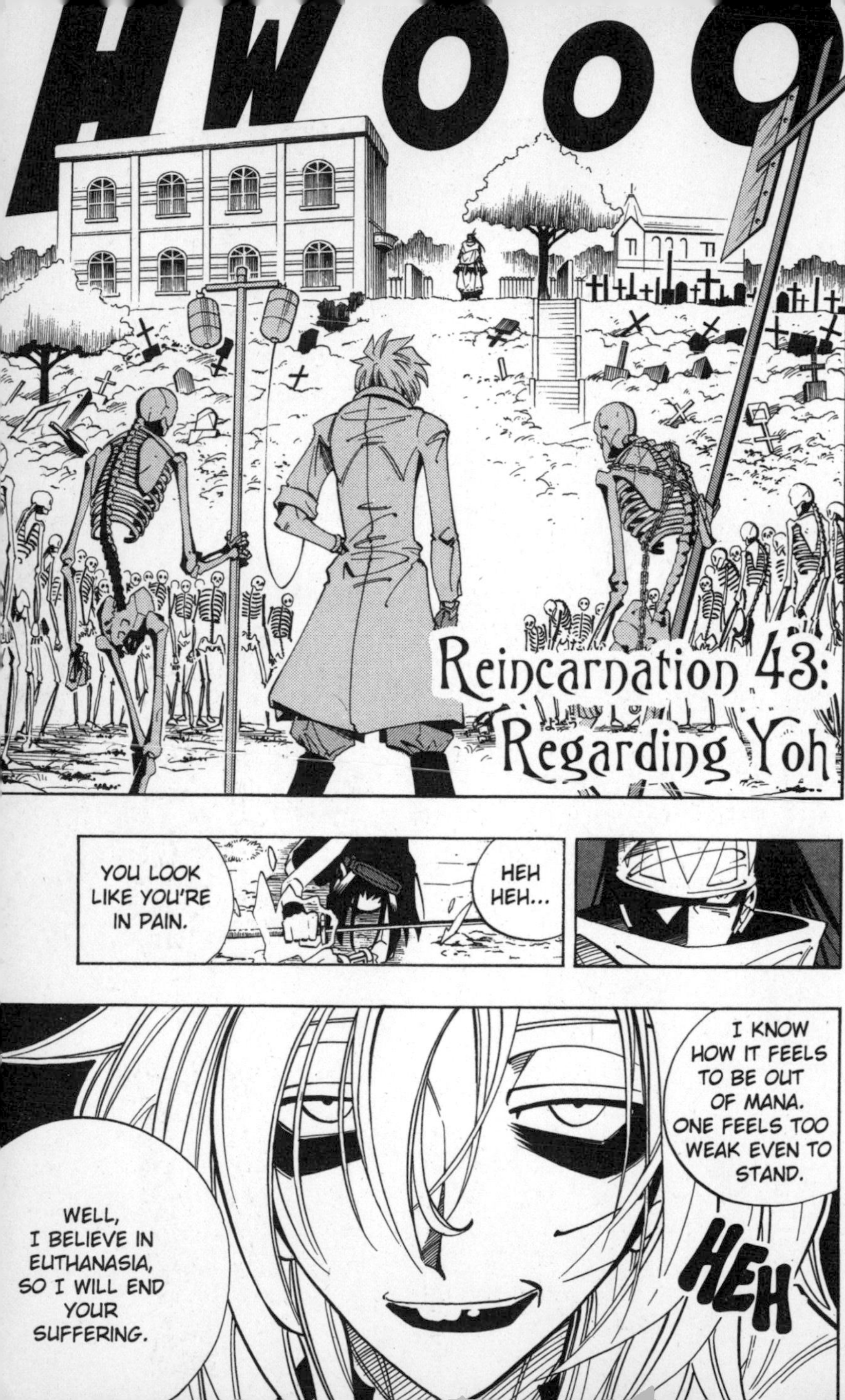
HWOOO
Reincarnation 43: Regarding Yoh
HEH HEH...
YOU LOOK LIKE YOU'RE IN PAIN.
I KNOW HOW IT FEELS TO BE OUT OF MANA. ONE FEELS TOO WEAK EVEN TO STAND.
HEH
WELL, I BELIEVE IN EUTHANASIA, SO I WILL END YOUR SUFFERING.

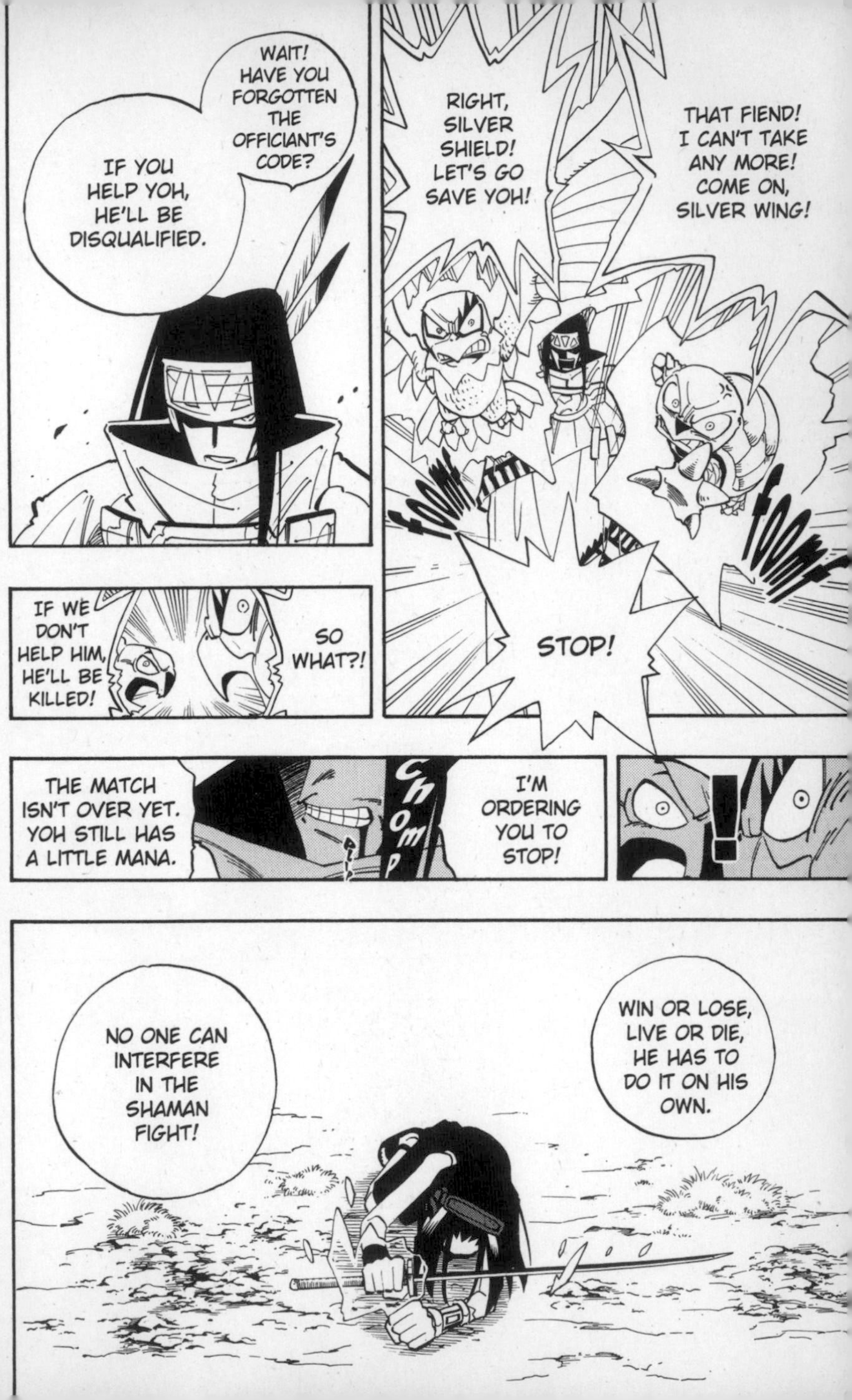
THAT FIEND! I CAN'T TAKE ANY MORE! COME ON, SILVER WING!
RIGHT, SILVER SHIELD! LET'S GO SAVE YOH!
FOOM
FOOM
STOP!
WAIT! HAVE YOU FORGOTTEN THE OFFICIANT'S CODE?
IF YOU HELP YOH, HE'LL BE DISQUALIFIED.
IF WE DON'T HELP HIM, HE'LL BE KILLED!
SO WHAT?!
!
I'M ORDERING YOU TO STOP!
CHOMP
THE MATCH ISN'T OVER YET. YOH STILL HAS A LITTLE MANA.
WIN OR LOSE, LIVE OR DIE, HE HAS TO DO IT ON HIS OWN.
NO ONE CAN INTERFERE IN THE SHAMAN FIGHT!

Reincarnation 43: Regarding Yoh

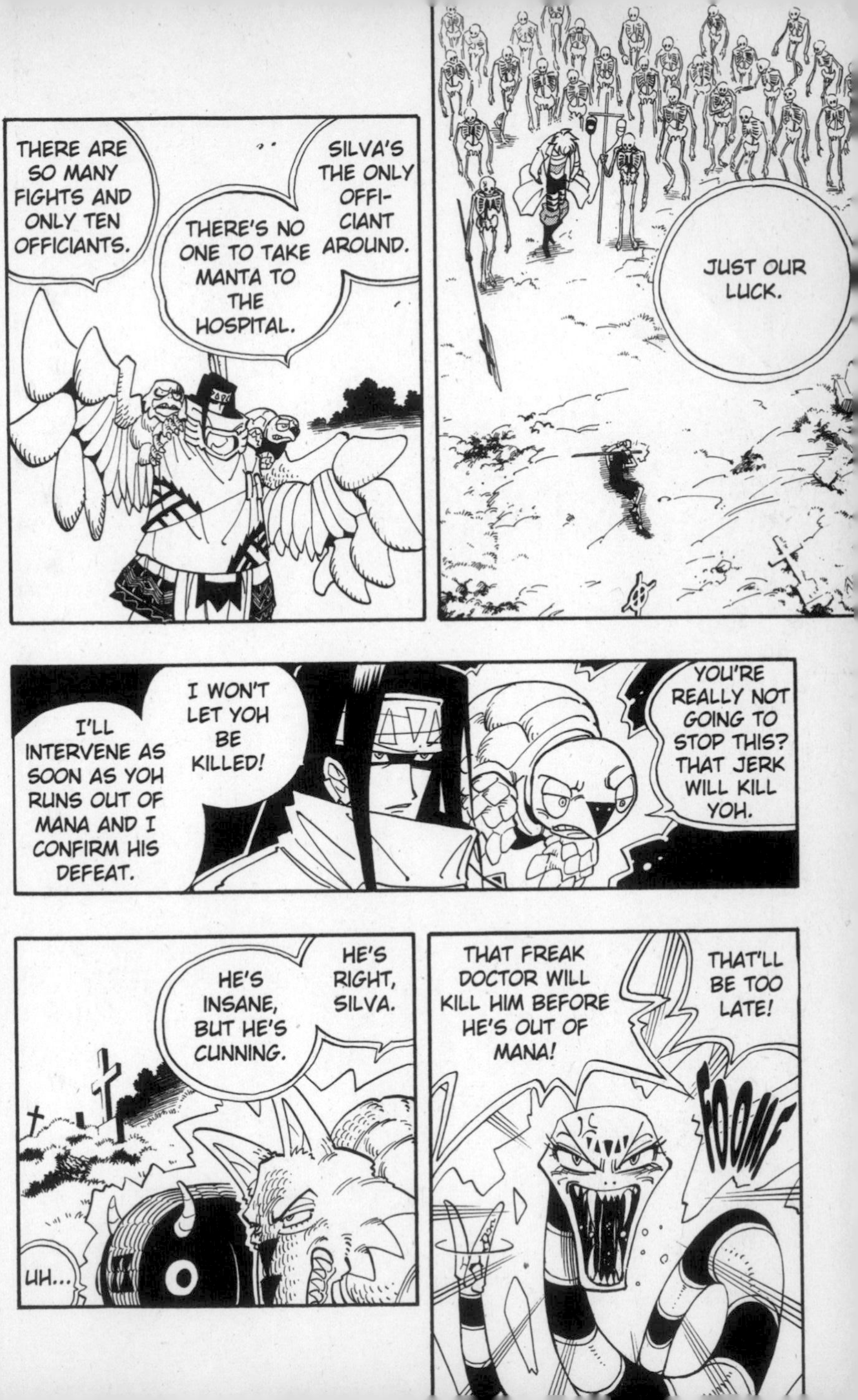

JUST OUR LUCK.
SILVA'S THE ONLY OFFICIANT AROUND.
THERE'S NO ONE TO TAKE MANTA TO THE HOSPITAL.
THERE ARE SO MANY FIGHTS AND ONLY TEN OFFICIANTS.
YOU'RE REALLY NOT GOING TO STOP THIS? THAT JERK WILL KILL YOH.
I WON'T LET YOH BE KILLED!
I'LL INTERVENE AS SOON AS YOH RUNS OUT OF MANA AND I CONFIRM HIS DEFEAT.
THAT'LL BE TOO LATE!
THAT FREAK DOCTOR WILL KILL HIM BEFORE HE'S OUT OF MANA!
FOOMF
HE'S RIGHT, SILVA.
HE'S INSANE, BUT HE'S CUNNING.
UH...

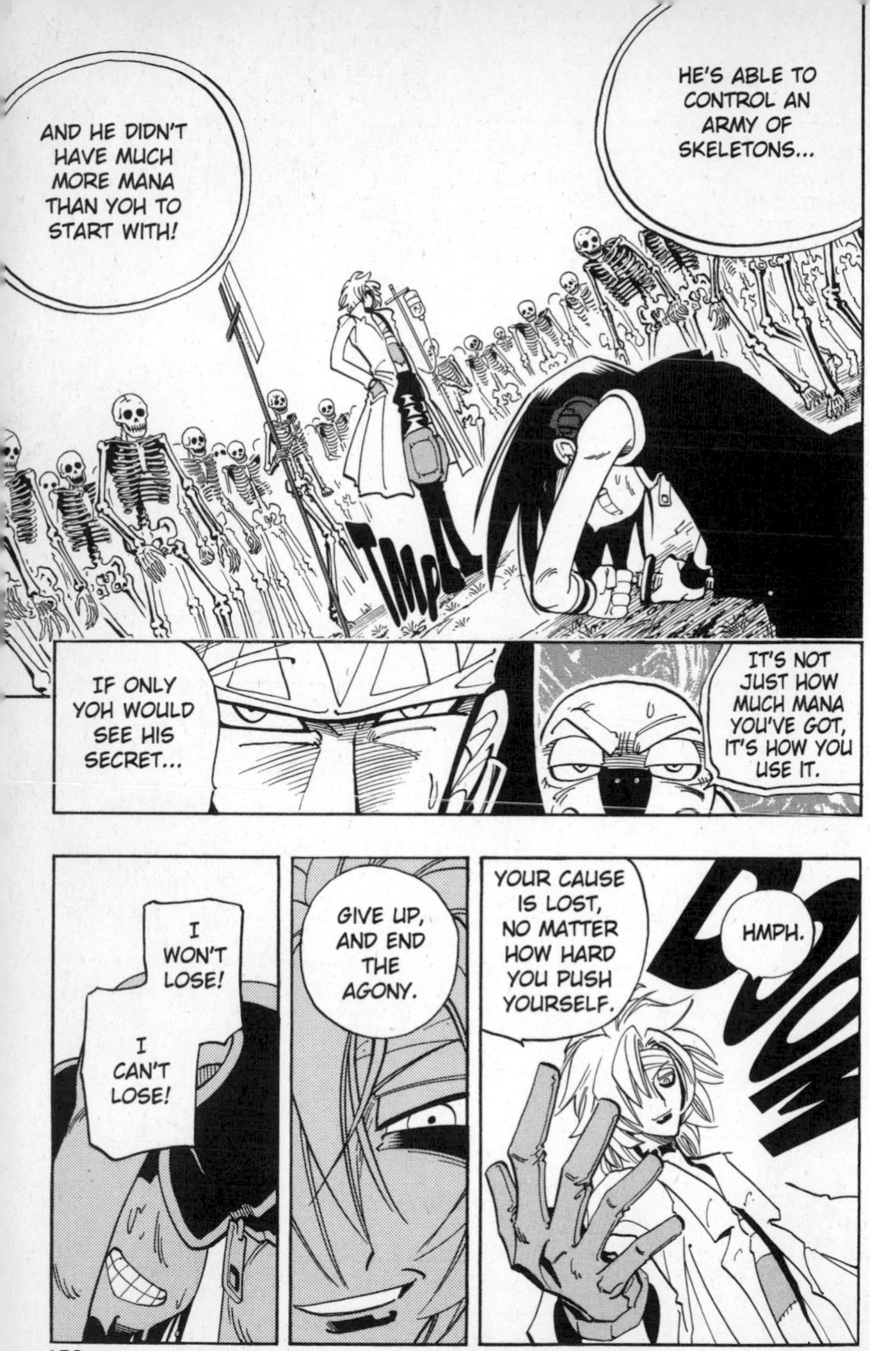
HE'S ABLE TO CONTROL AN ARMY OF SKELETONS...
AND HE DIDN'T HAVE MUCH MORE MANA THAN YOH TO START WITH!
TMP
IT'S NOT JUST HOW MUCH MANA YOU'VE GOT, IT'S HOW YOU USE IT.
IF ONLY YOH WOULD SEE HIS SECRET...
YOUR CAUSE IS LOST, NO MATTER HOW HARD YOU PUSH YOURSELF.
HMPH.
GIVE UP, AND END THE AGONY.
I WON'T LOSE!
I CAN'T LOSE!

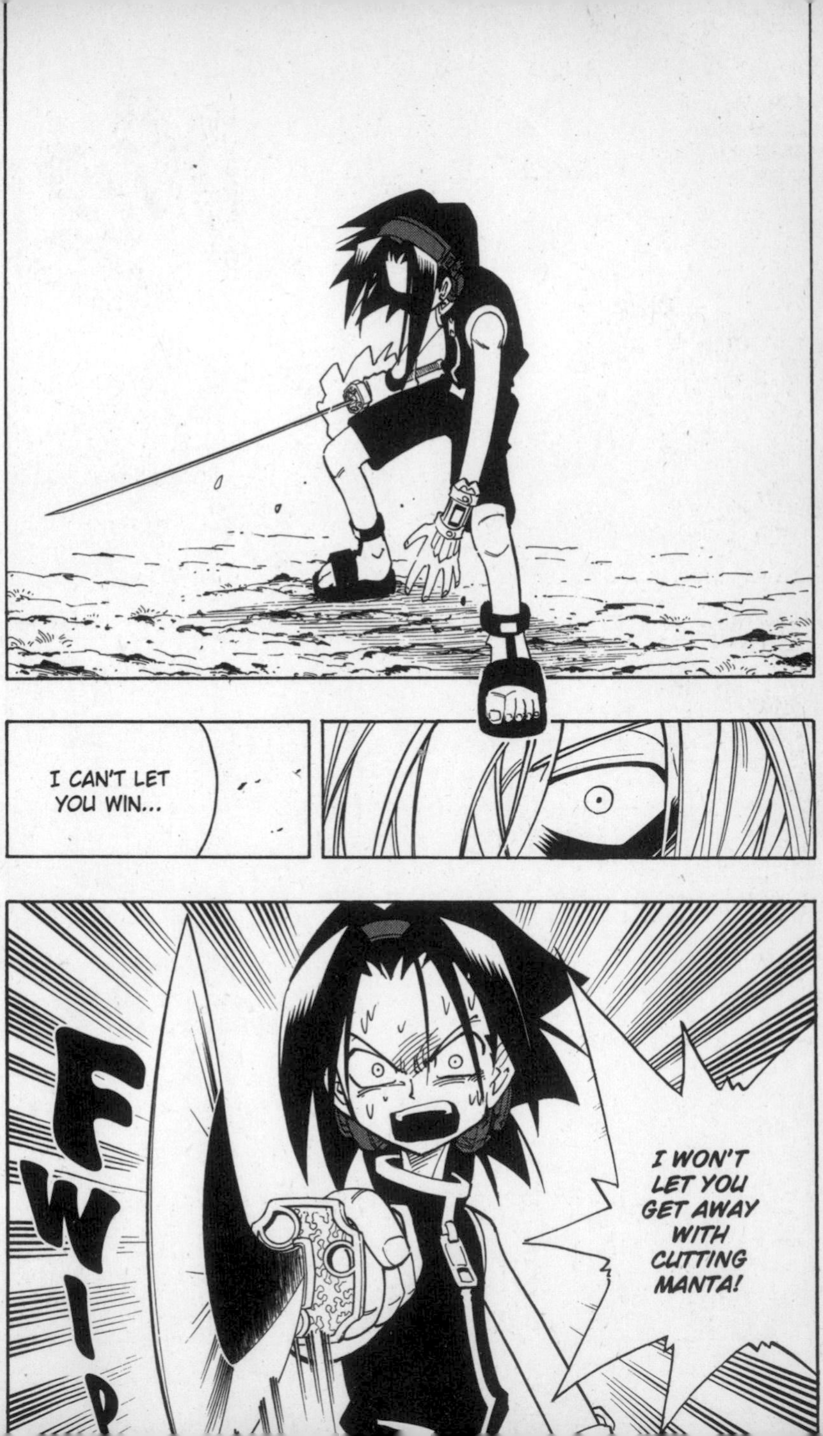
I CAN'T LET YOU WIN...
I WON'T LET YOU GET AWAY WITH CUTTING MANTA!
FWIP

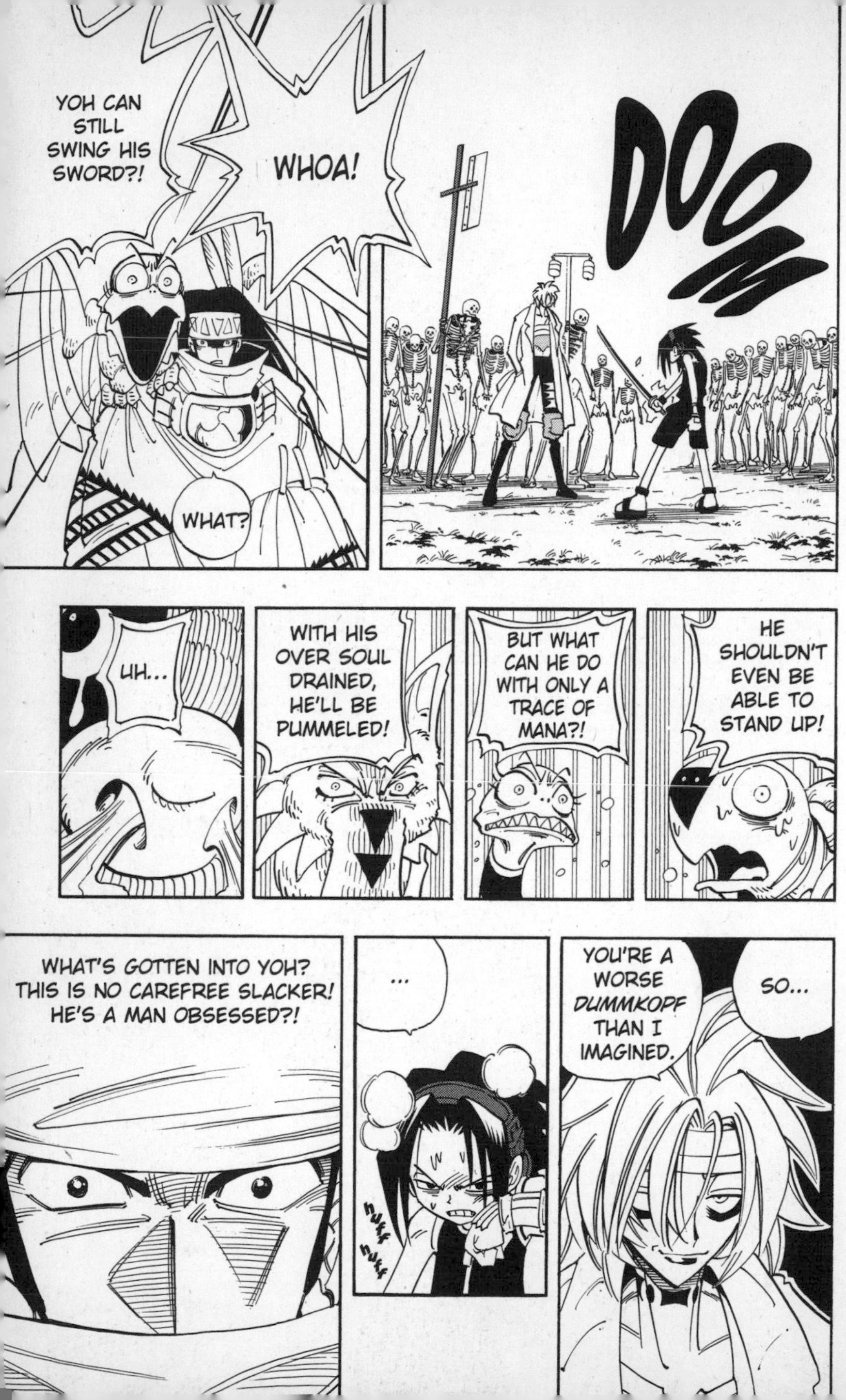
DOOM
WHOA!
YOH CAN STILL SWING HIS SWORD?!
WHAT?
HE SHOULDN'T EVEN BE ABLE TO STAND UP!
BUT WHAT CAN HE DO WITH ONLY A TRACE OF MANA?!
WITH HIS OVER SOUL DRAINED, HE'LL BE PUMMELED!
UH...
SO...
YOU'RE A WORSE *DUMMKOPF* THAN I IMAGINED.
...
huff huff
WHAT'S GOTTEN INTO YOH? THIS IS NO CAREFREE SLACKER! HE'S A MAN OBSESSED?!

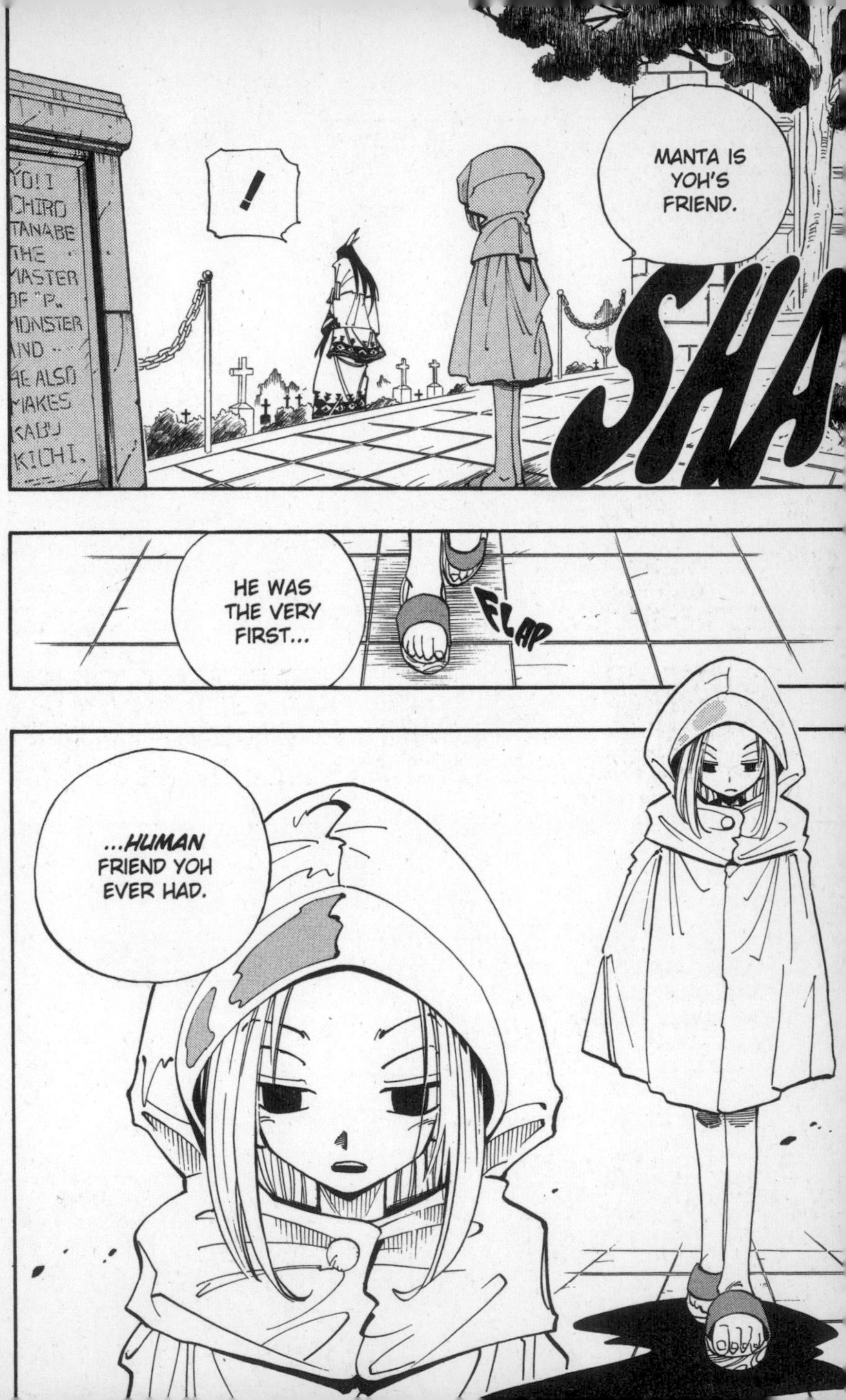
MANTA IS YOH'S FRIEND.
SHA
!
YO!ICHIRO TANABE THE MASTER OF "P. MONSTER AND -- HE ALSO MAKES KABU KICHI.
HE WAS THE VERY FIRST...
FLAP
...HUMAN FRIEND YOH EVER HAD.

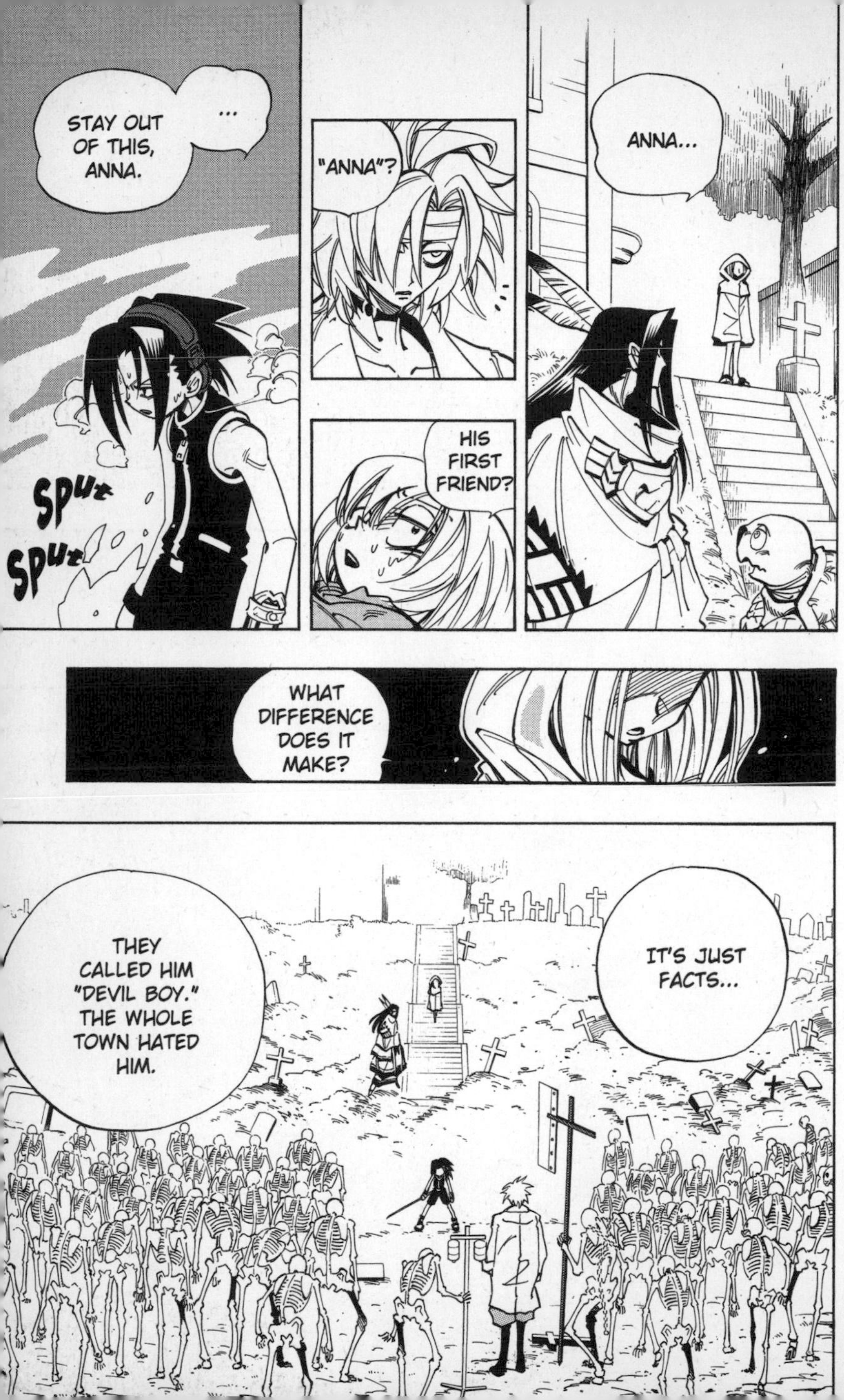
ANNA...
"ANNA"?
HIS FIRST FRIEND?
...
STAY OUT OF THIS, ANNA.
SPUT
SPUT
WHAT DIFFERENCE DOES IT MAKE?
IT'S JUST FACTS...
THEY CALLED HIM "DEVIL BOY." THE WHOLE TOWN HATED HIM.

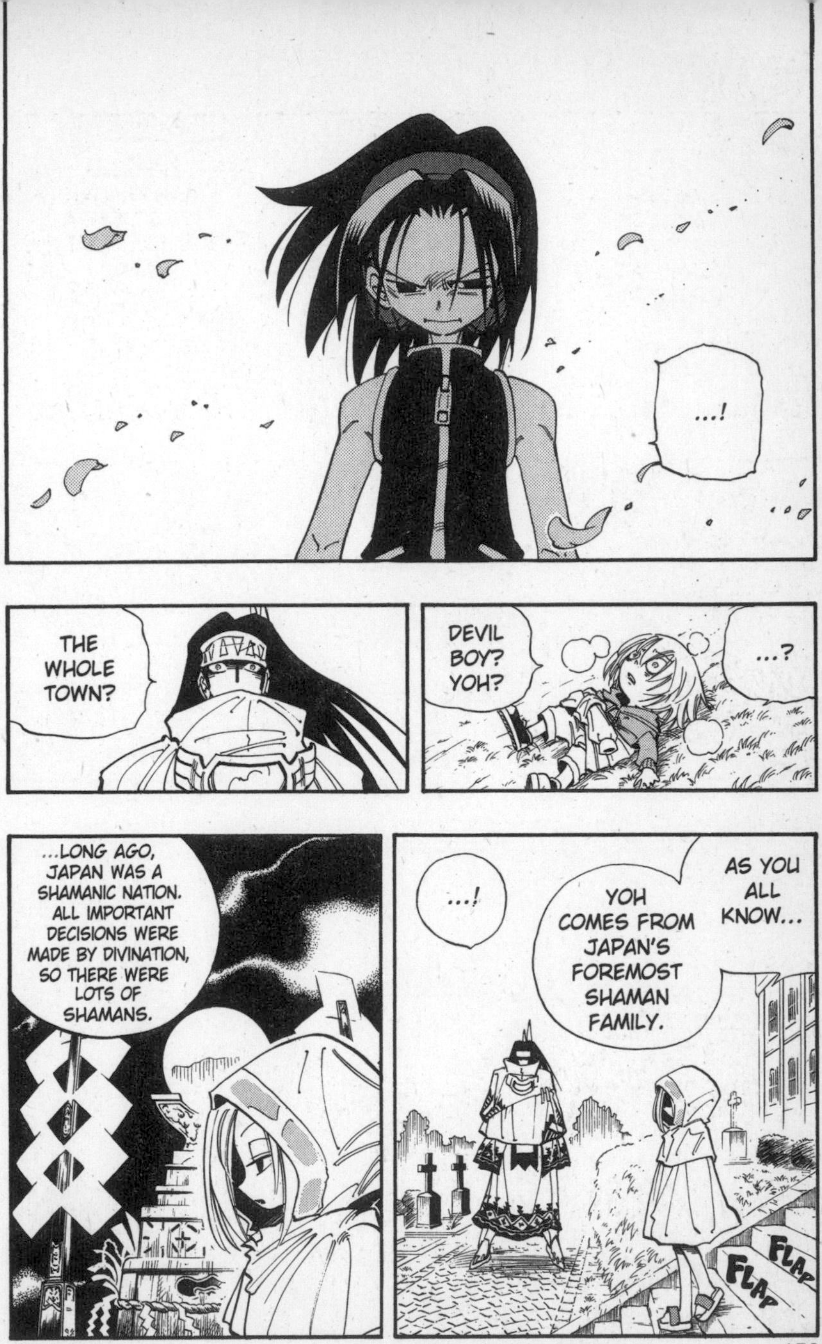
...!
...?
DEVIL BOY? YOH?
THE WHOLE TOWN?
AS YOU ALL KNOW...
YOH COMES FROM JAPAN'S FOREMOST SHAMAN FAMILY.
...!
FLAP
FLAP
...LONG AGO, JAPAN WAS A SHAMANIC NATION. ALL IMPORTANT DECISIONS WERE MADE BY DIVINATION, SO THERE WERE LOTS OF SHAMANS.

READ THIS WAY

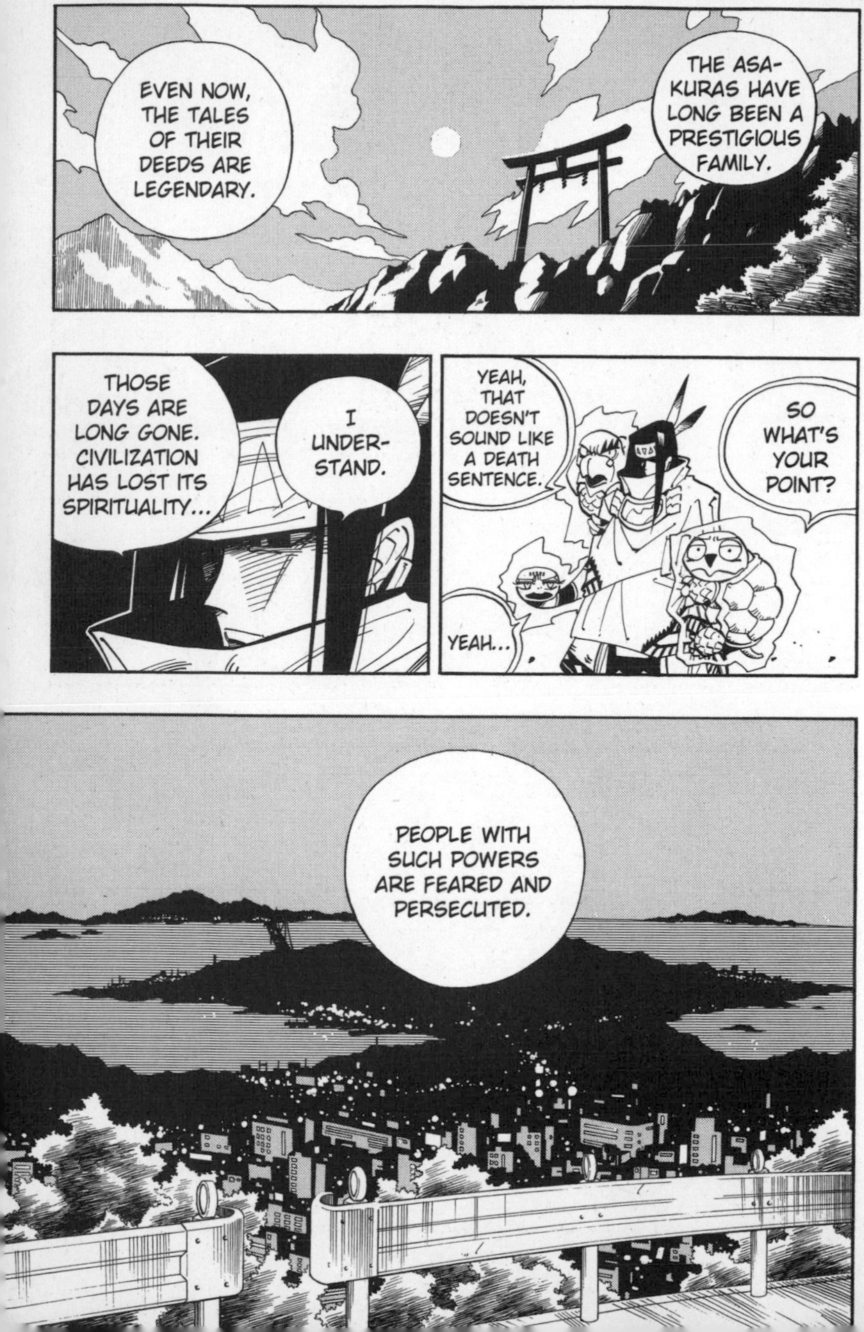
THE ASA-KURAS HAVE LONG BEEN A PRESTIGIOUS FAMILY.
EVEN NOW, THE TALES OF THEIR DEEDS ARE LEGENDARY.
SO WHAT'S YOUR POINT?
YEAH, THAT DOESN'T SOUND LIKE A DEATH SENTENCE.
YEAH...
I UNDER-STAND.
THOSE DAYS ARE LONG GONE. CIVILIZATION HAS LOST ITS SPIRITUALITY...
PEOPLE WITH SUCH POWERS ARE FEARED AND PERSECUTED.

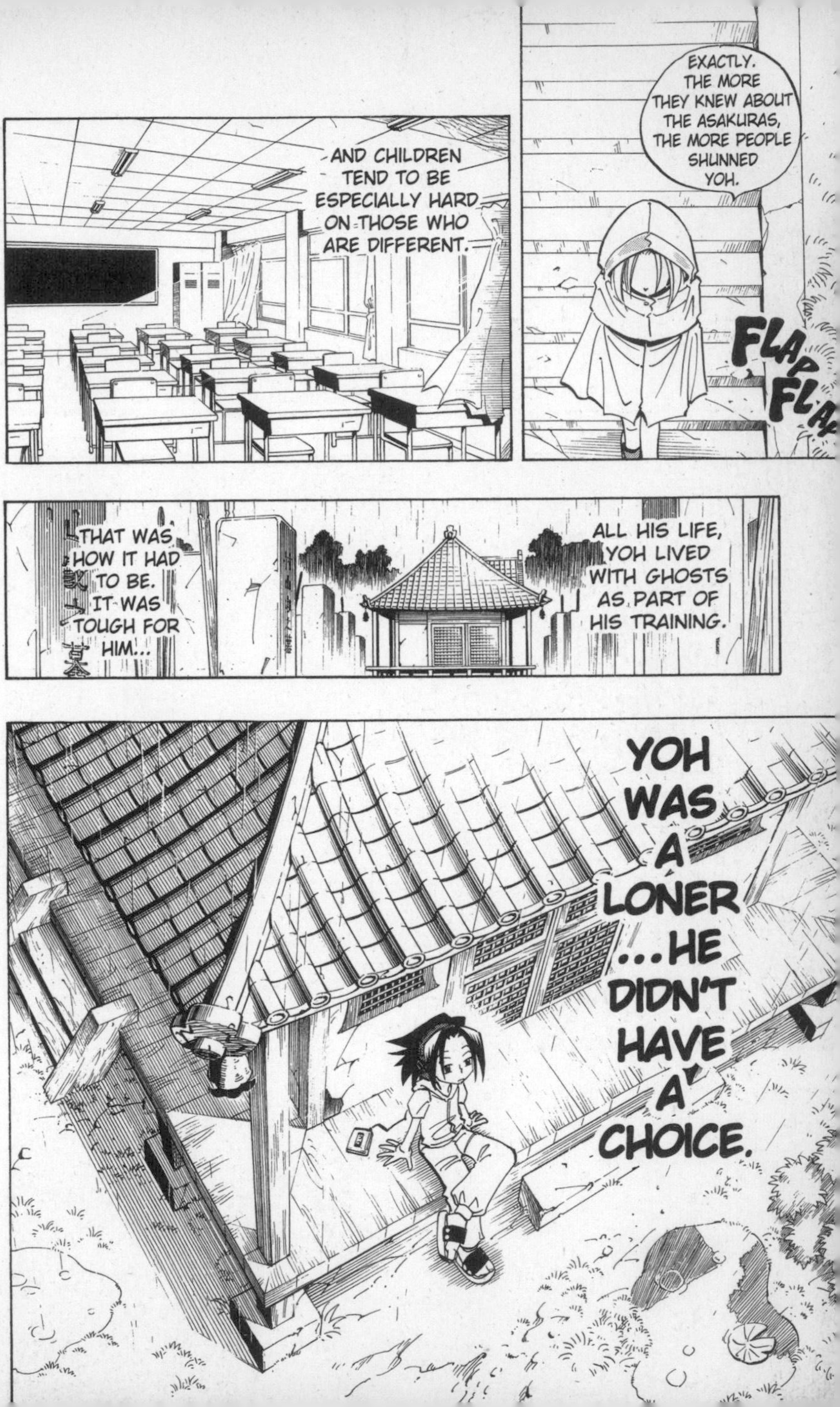
EXACTLY. THE MORE THEY KNEW ABOUT THE ASAKURAS, THE MORE PEOPLE SHUNNED YOH.
FLAP FLAP
AND CHILDREN TEND TO BE ESPECIALLY HARD ON THOSE WHO ARE DIFFERENT.
ALL HIS LIFE, YOH LIVED WITH GHOSTS AS PART OF HIS TRAINING.
THAT WAS HOW IT HAD TO BE. IT WAS TOUGH FOR HIM...
YOH WAS A LONER ...HE DIDN'T HAVE A CHOICE.

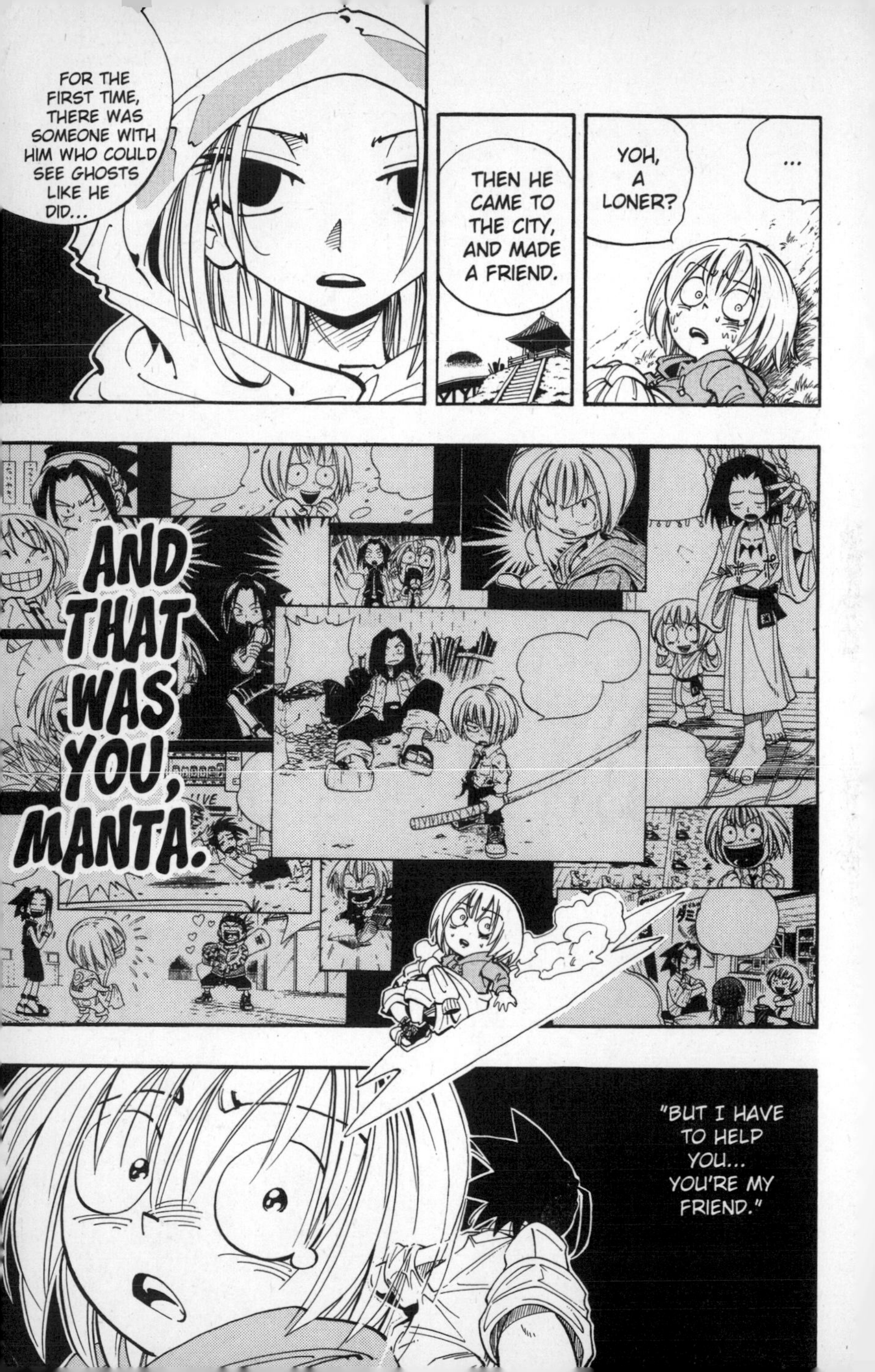
...
YOH, A LONER?
THEN HE CAME TO THE CITY, AND MADE A FRIEND.
FOR THE FIRST TIME, THERE WAS SOMEONE WITH HIM WHO COULD SEE GHOSTS LIKE HE DID...
AND THAT WAS YOU, MANTA.
"BUT I HAVE TO HELP YOU... YOU'RE MY FRIEND."

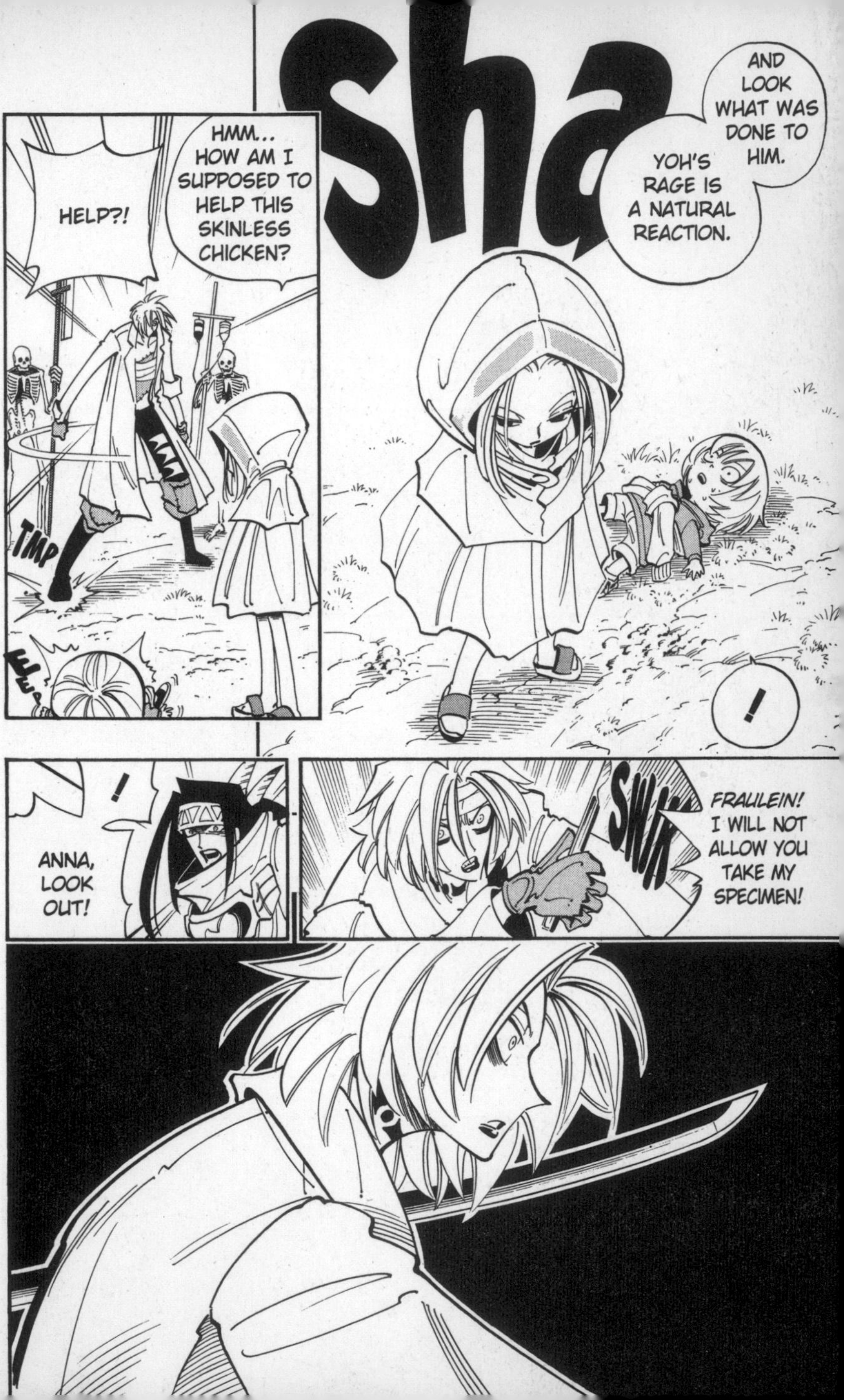
Sha
YOH'S RAGE IS A NATURAL REACTION.
AND LOOK WHAT WAS DONE TO HIM.
!
HELP?!
HMM... HOW AM I SUPPOSED TO HELP THIS SKINLESS CHICKEN?
TMP
SWK
FRAULEIN! I WILL NOT ALLOW YOU TAKE MY SPECIMEN!
!
ANNA, LOOK OUT!

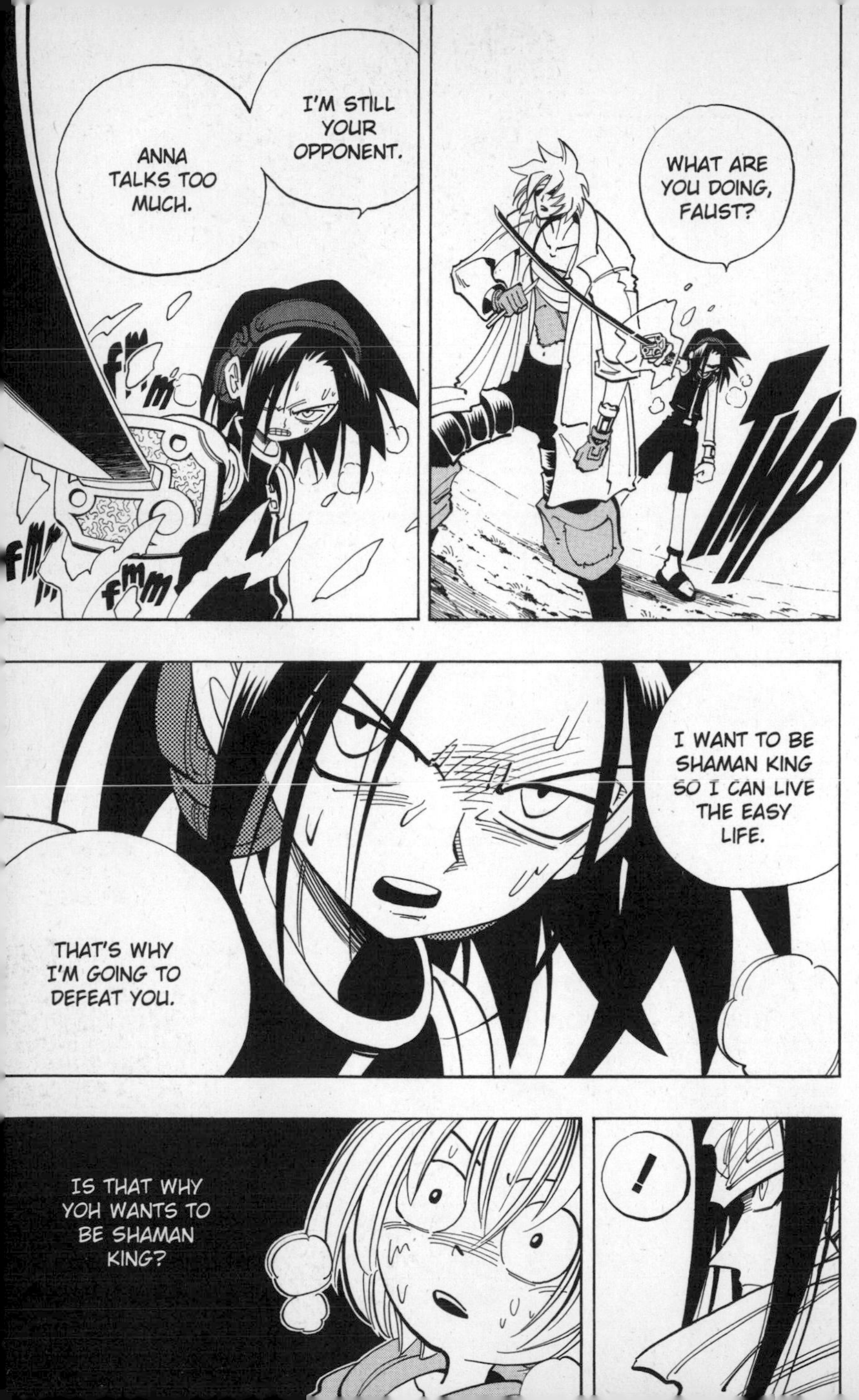
WHAT ARE YOU DOING, FAUST?
TMP
I'M STILL YOUR OPPONENT.
ANNA TALKS TOO MUCH.
fmm
fmm
fmm
I WANT TO BE SHAMAN KING SO I CAN LIVE THE EASY LIFE.
THAT'S WHY I'M GOING TO DEFEAT YOU.
!
IS THAT WHY YOH WANTS TO BE SHAMAN KING?

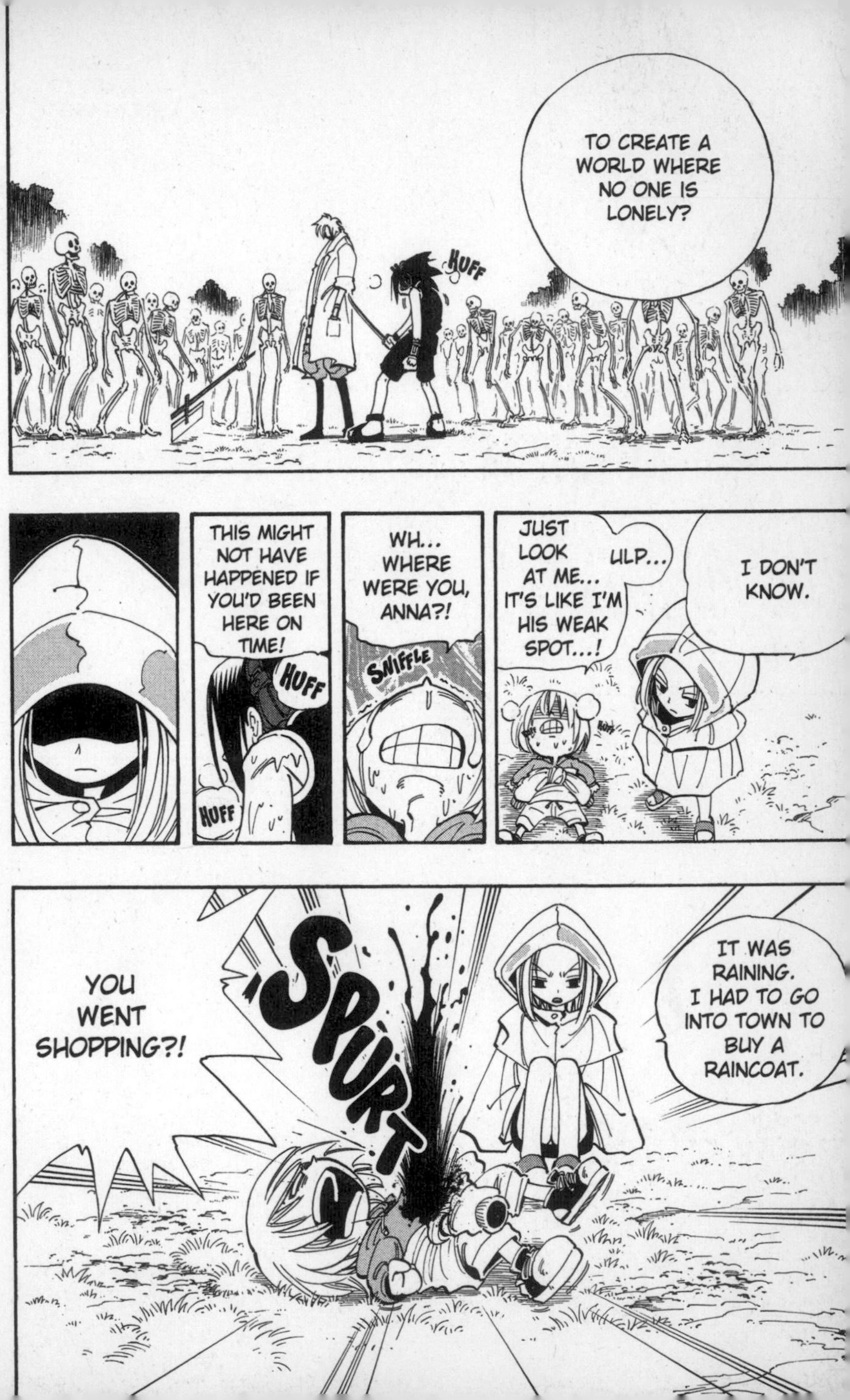
TO CREATE A WORLD WHERE NO ONE IS LONELY?
HUFF
I DON'T KNOW.
ULP...
JUST LOOK AT ME... IT'S LIKE I'M HIS WEAK SPOT...!
WH... WHERE WERE YOU, ANNA?!
SNIFFLE
THIS MIGHT NOT HAVE HAPPENED IF YOU'D BEEN HERE ON TIME!
HUFF
HUFF
IT WAS RAINING. I HAD TO GO INTO TOWN TO BUY A RAINCOAT.
SPURT
YOU WENT SHOPPING?!

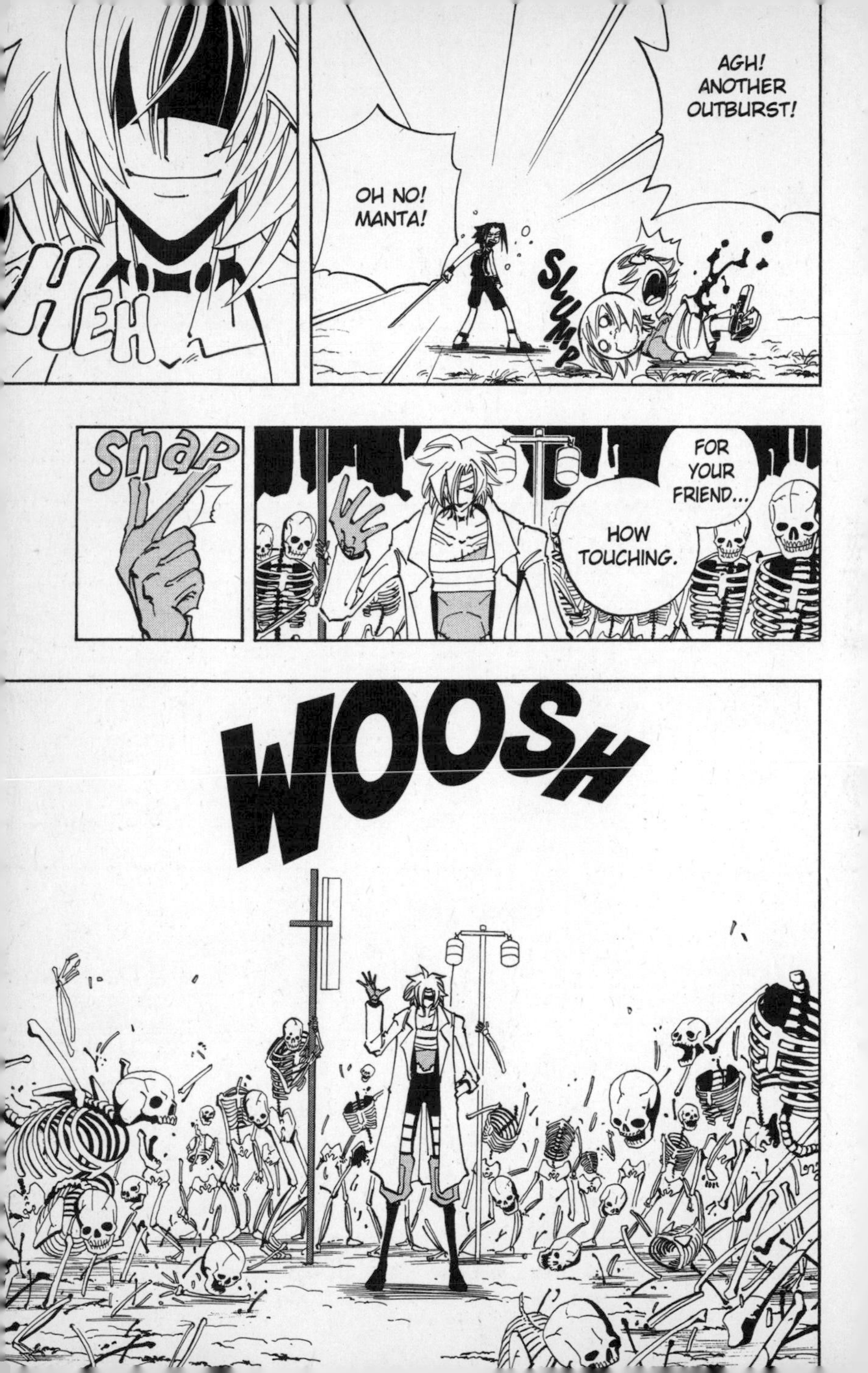
AGH! ANOTHER OUTBURST!
OH NO! MANTA!
SLUMP
HEH
FOR YOUR FRIEND...
HOW TOUCHING.
SNAP
WOOSH

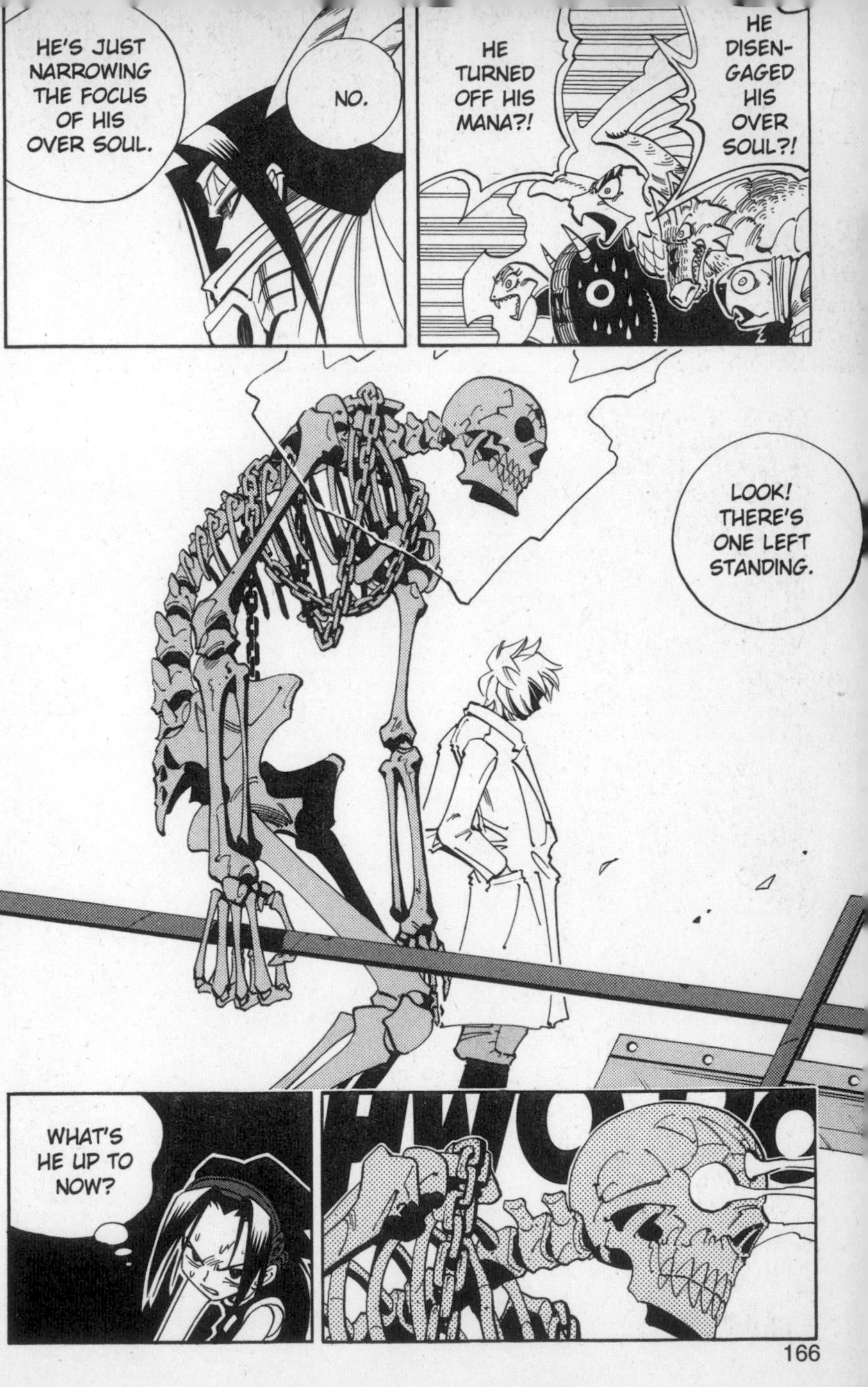
HE DISEN-GAGED HIS OVER SOUL?!
HE TURNED OFF HIS MANA?!
NO.
HE'S JUST NARROWING THE FOCUS OF HIS OVER SOUL.
LOOK! THERE'S ONE LEFT STANDING.
WHAT'S HE UP TO NOW?

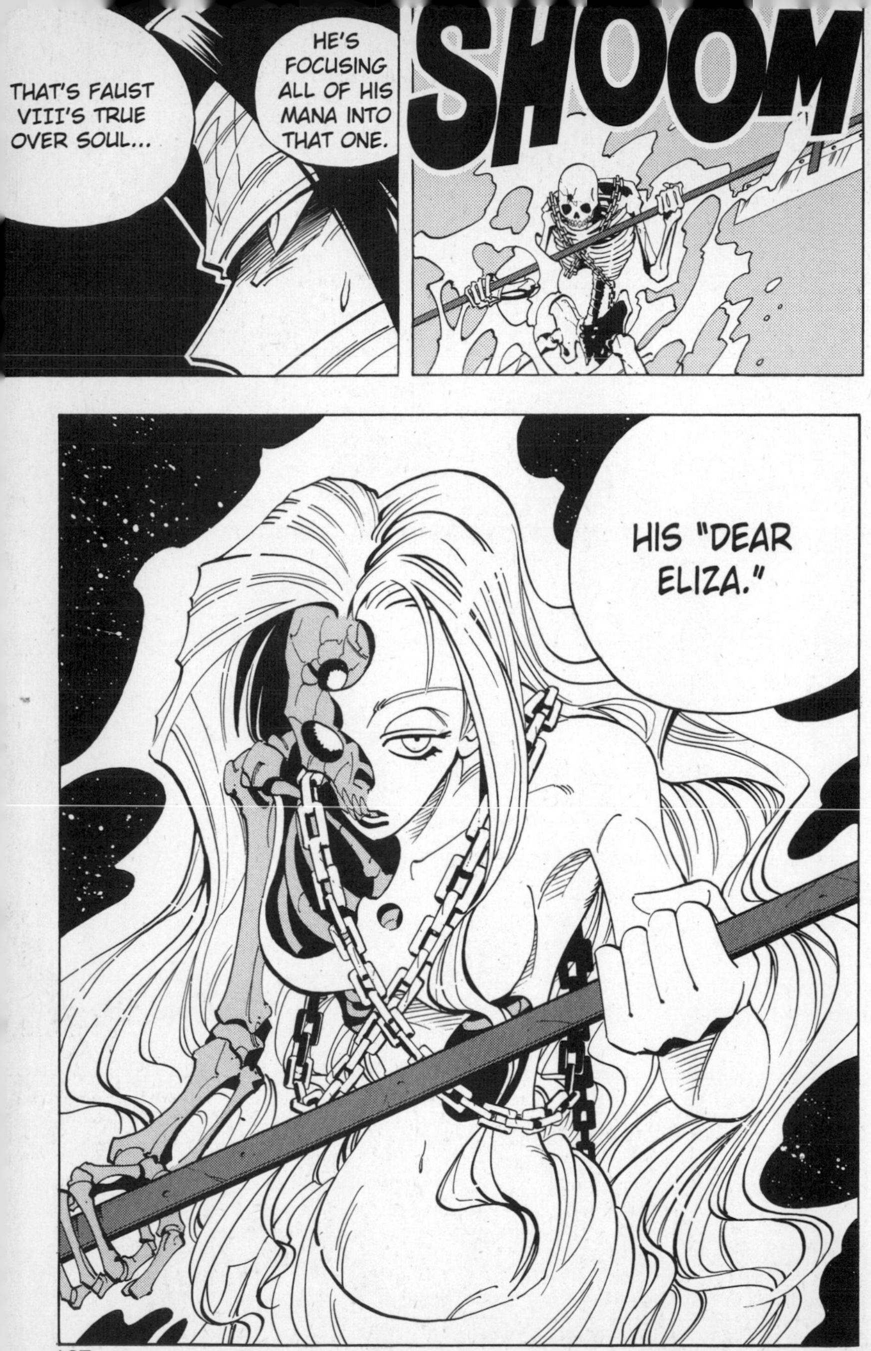
SHOOM
HE'S FOCUSING ALL OF HIS MANA INTO THAT ONE.
THAT'S FAUST VIII'S TRUE OVER SOUL...
HIS "DEAR ELIZA."

SHAMAN
KING
5

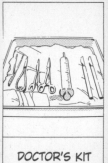

DOCTOR'S KIT

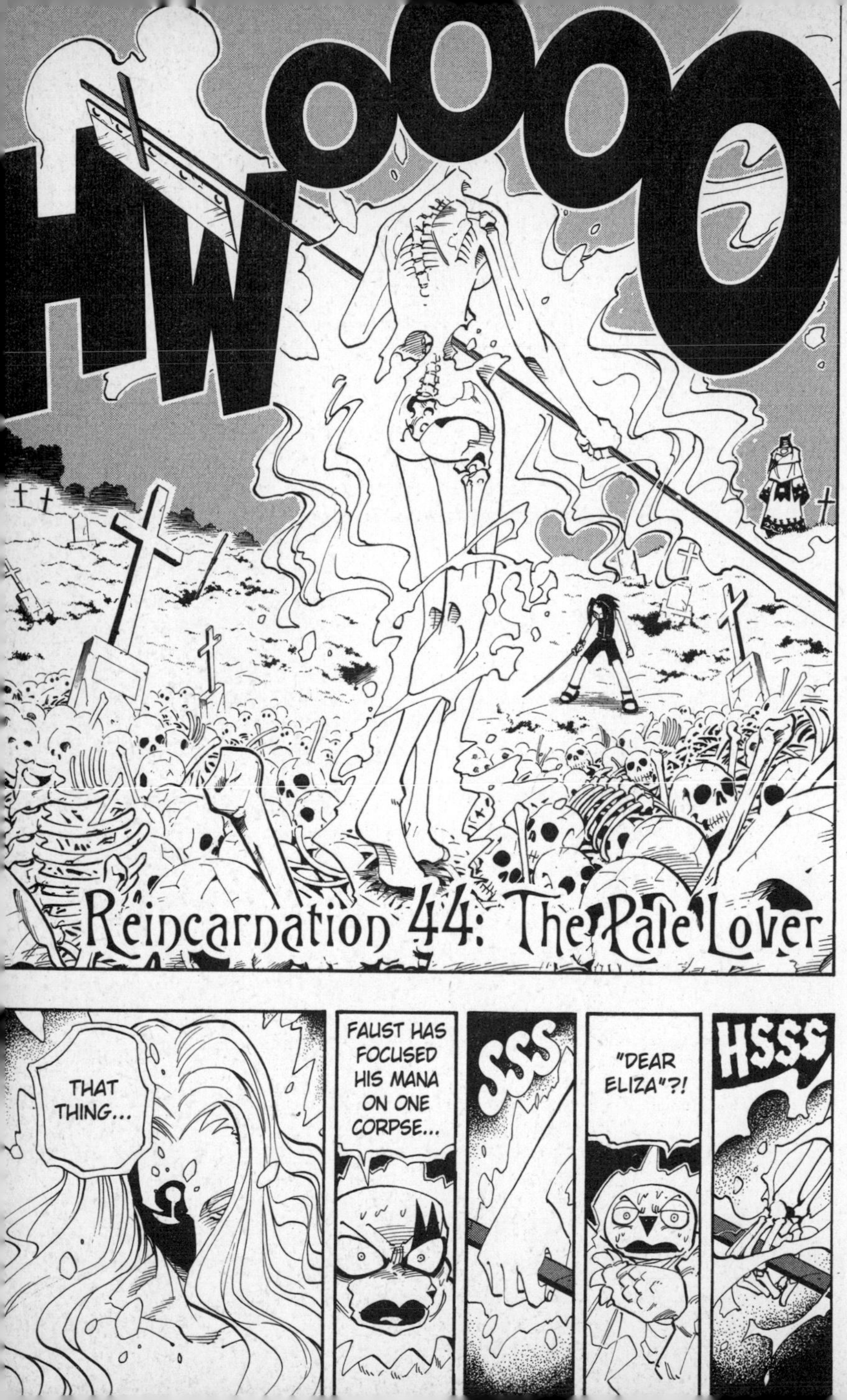
HWOOOO
Reincarnation 44: The Pale Lover
HSSS
"DEAR ELIZA"?!
SSS
FAUST HAS FOCUSED HIS MANA ON ONE CORPSE...
THAT THING...

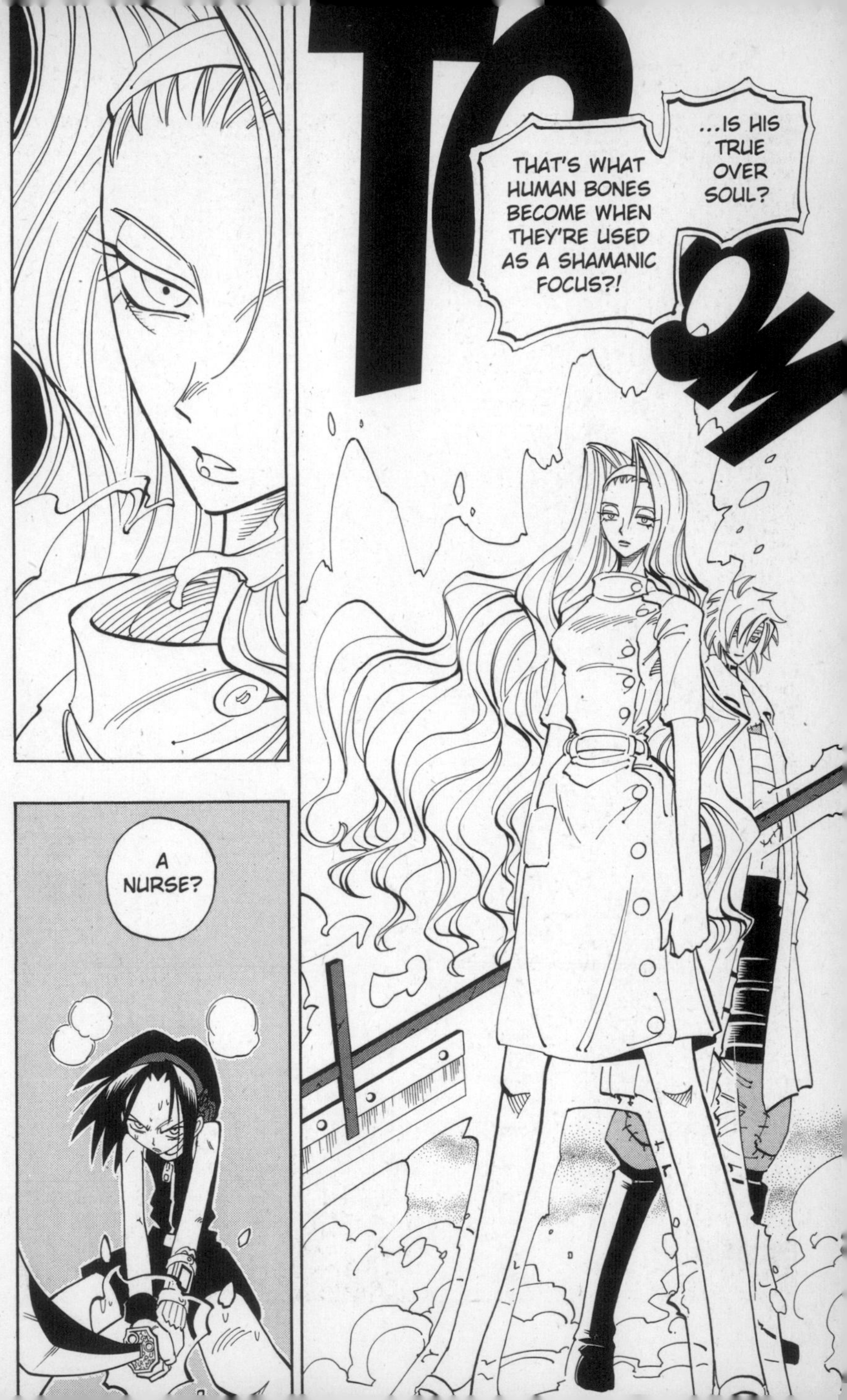
TOOM
...IS HIS TRUE OVER SOUL?
THAT'S WHAT HUMAN BONES BECOME WHEN THEY'RE USED AS A SHAMANIC FOCUS?!
A NURSE?

Reincarnation 44: The Pale Lover

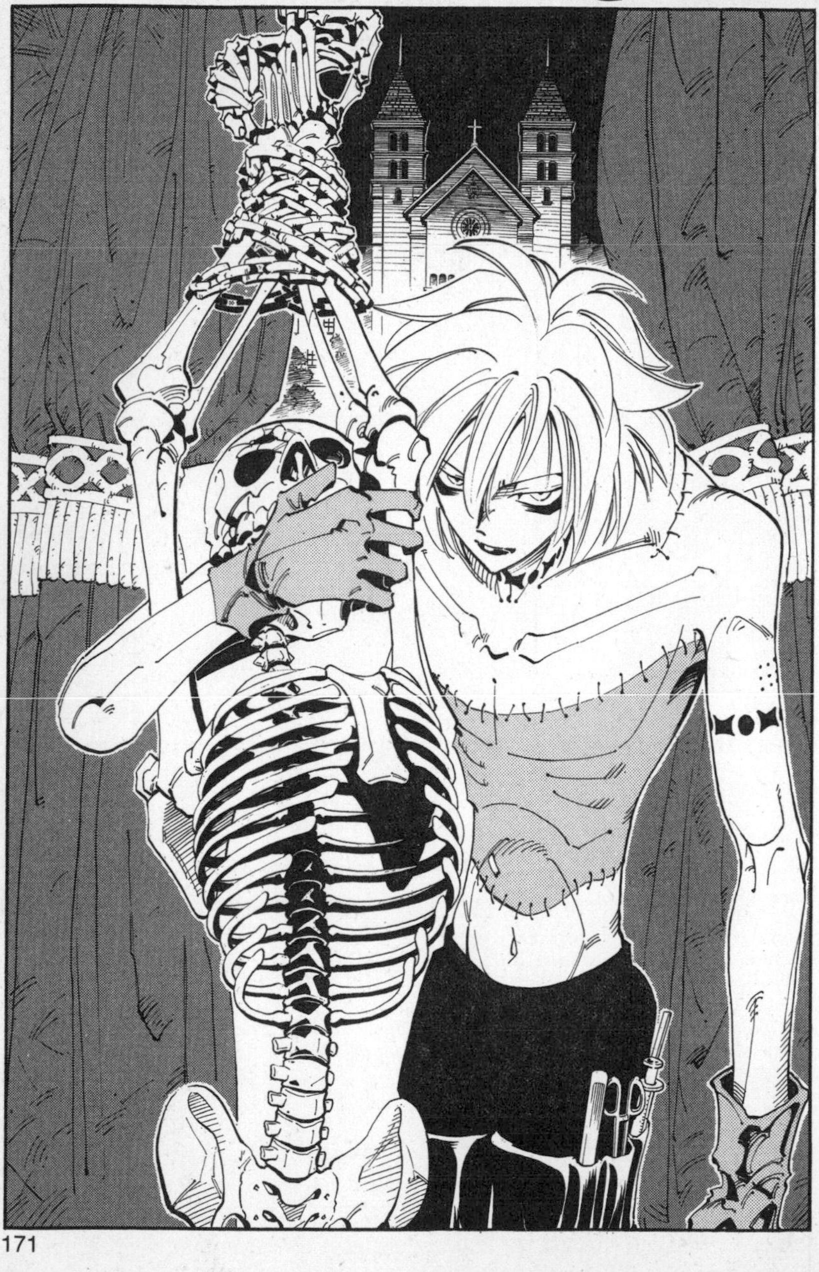

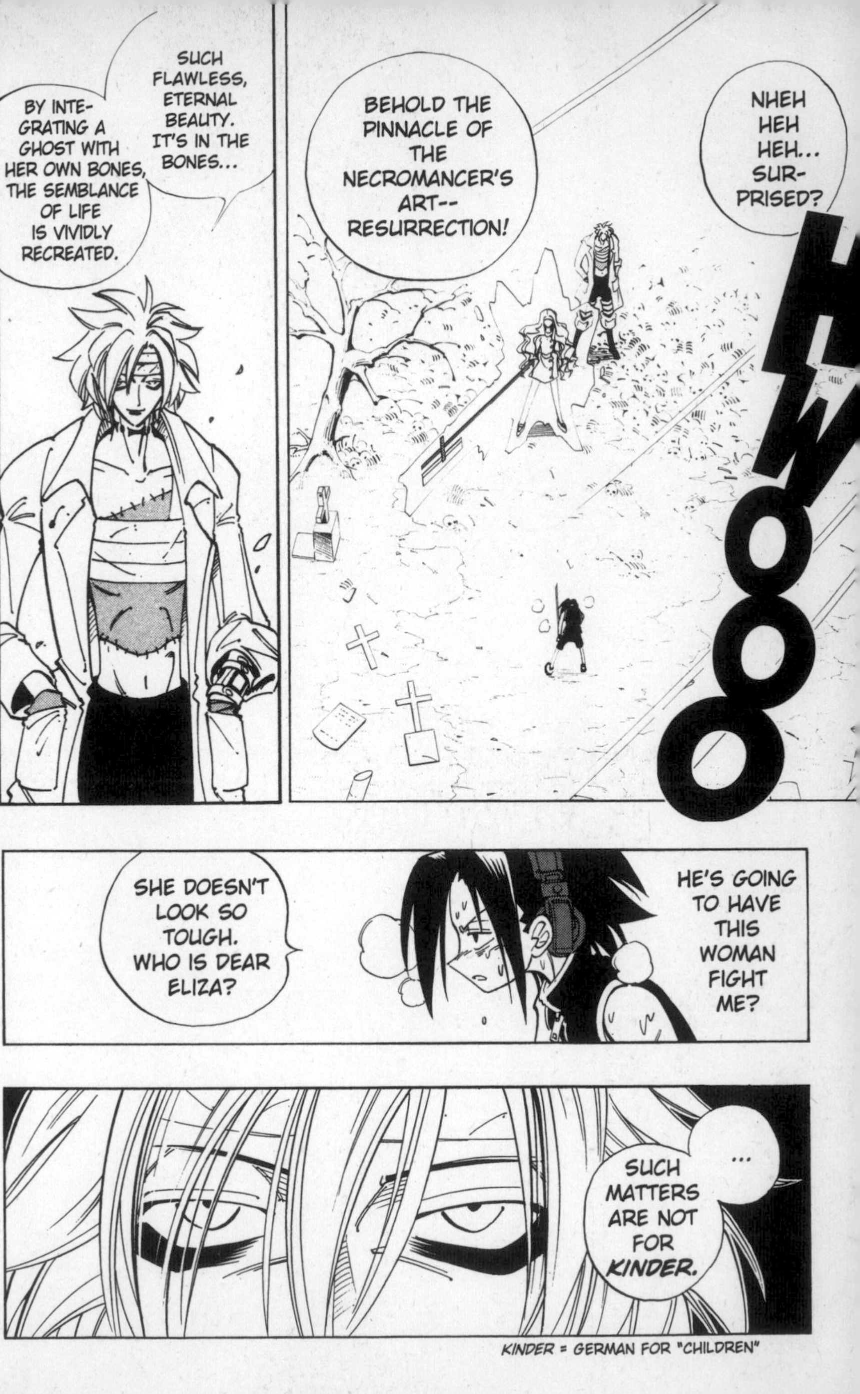
NHEH HEH HEH... SUR-PRISED?
BEHOLD THE PINNACLE OF THE NECROMANCER'S ART--RESURRECTION!
HWOOO
SUCH FLAWLESS, ETERNAL BEAUTY. IT'S IN THE BONES...
BY INTE-GRATING A GHOST WITH HER OWN BONES, THE SEMBLANCE OF LIFE IS VIVIDLY RECREATED.
HE'S GOING TO HAVE THIS WOMAN FIGHT ME?
SHE DOESN'T LOOK SO TOUGH. WHO IS DEAR ELIZA?
...
SUCH MATTERS ARE NOT FOR *KINDER.*

KINDER = GERMAN FOR "CHILDREN"

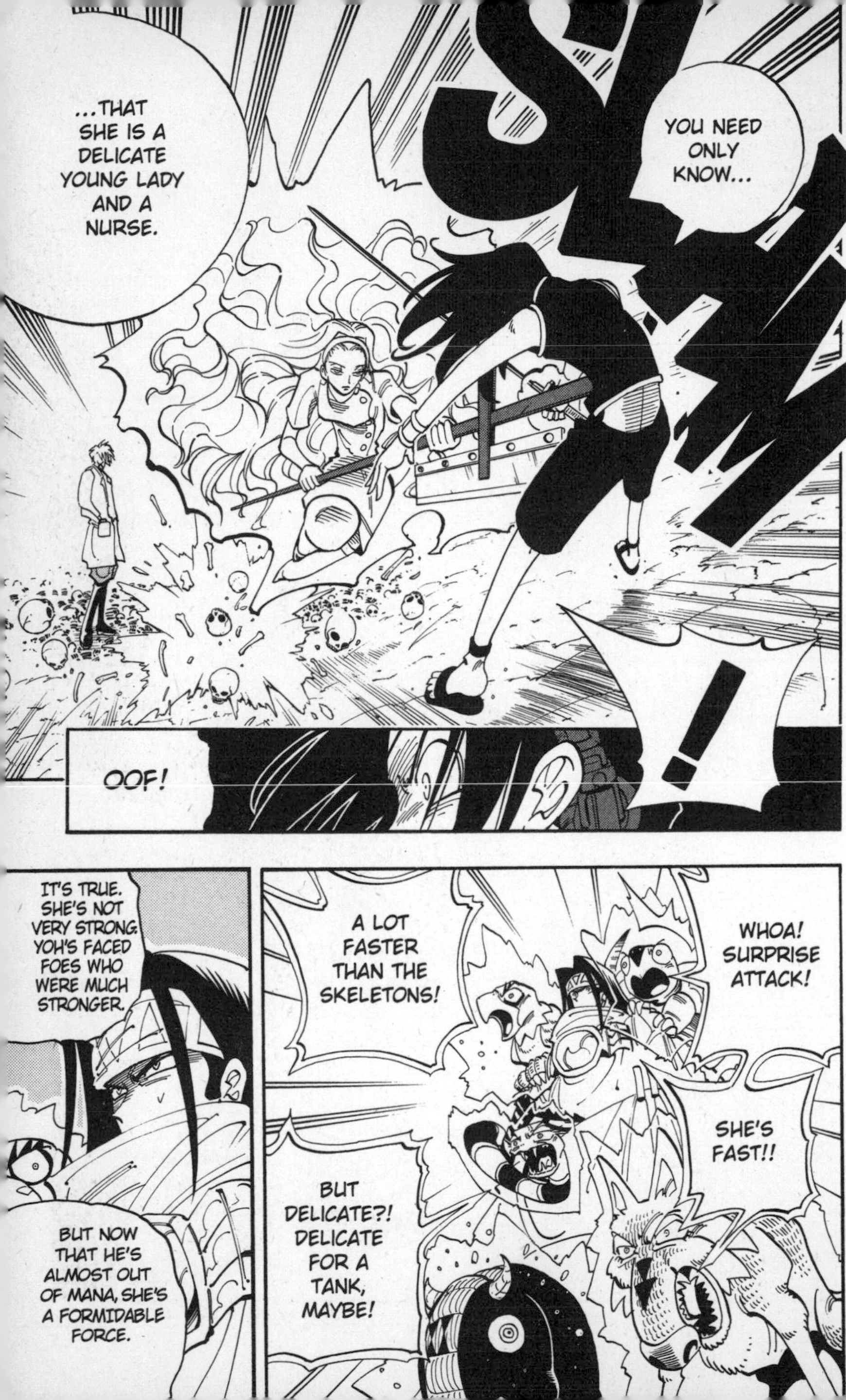
YOU NEED ONLY KNOW...
...THAT SHE IS A DELICATE YOUNG LADY AND A NURSE.
!
OOF!
WHOA! SURPRISE ATTACK!
A LOT FASTER THAN THE SKELETONS!
SHE'S FAST!!
BUT DELICATE?! DELICATE FOR A TANK, MAYBE!
IT'S TRUE. SHE'S NOT VERY STRONG. YOH'S FACED FOES WHO WERE MUCH STRONGER.
BUT NOW THAT HE'S ALMOST OUT OF MANA, SHE'S A FORMIDABLE FORCE.

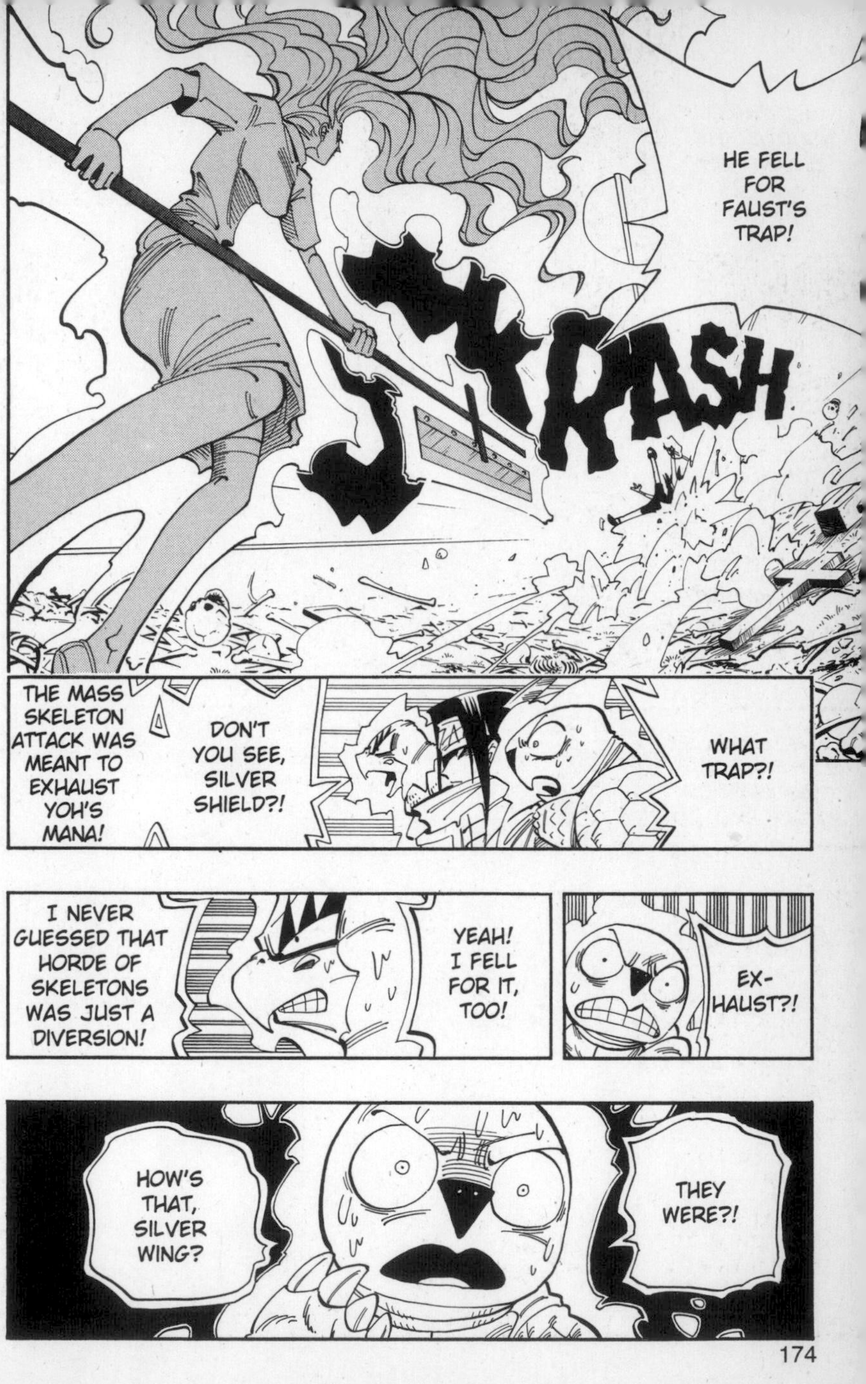
HE FELL FOR FAUST'S TRAP!
KRASH
WHAT TRAP?!
DON'T YOU SEE, SILVER SHIELD?!
THE MASS SKELETON ATTACK WAS MEANT TO EXHAUST YOH'S MANA!
EX-HAUST?!
YEAH! I FELL FOR IT, TOO!
I NEVER GUESSED THAT HORDE OF SKELETONS WAS JUST A DIVERSION!
THEY WERE?!
HOW'S THAT, SILVER WING?

NO SHAMAN'S SUPPLY OF MANA IS TRULY INEX-HAUSTIBLE.
SILVER TAIL?
TMP
THEY STARTED WITH ABOUT EQUAL MANA.
YET FAUST WAS ABLE TO CONTROL AN ARMY OF BONES!
HERE'S HIS TRICK!
FAUST EXPENDED LESS THAN 1% OF HIS MANA ON EACH SKELETON!
A SHAMAN'S OVER SOUL ALLOWS HIM TO USE HIS MANA AND HIS SPIRIT ALLY TO AFFECT THE MATERIAL WORLD.
MY SOUL (SPIRIT ALLY)
WOLF'S TAIL (FOCUS)
OVER SOUL (ME)
AMIDAMARU'S SOUL
INTEGRATION
HARUSAME (FOCUS)
OVER SOUL (AMIDAMARU)
I INTEGRATE WITH A WOLF'S TAIL, AND AMIDAMARU INTEGRATES WITH HIS SWORD, TO FORM OVER SOULS!
THE EXACT APPEARANCE DEPENDS ON THE SHAMAN--BUT LOOK AT FAUST'S OVER SOUL!

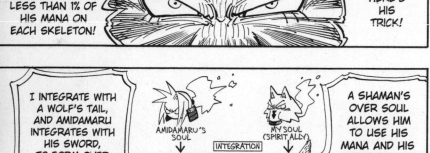

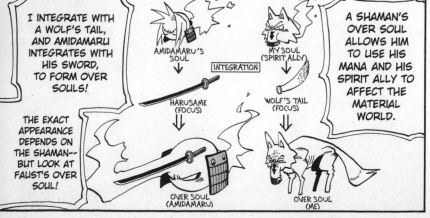

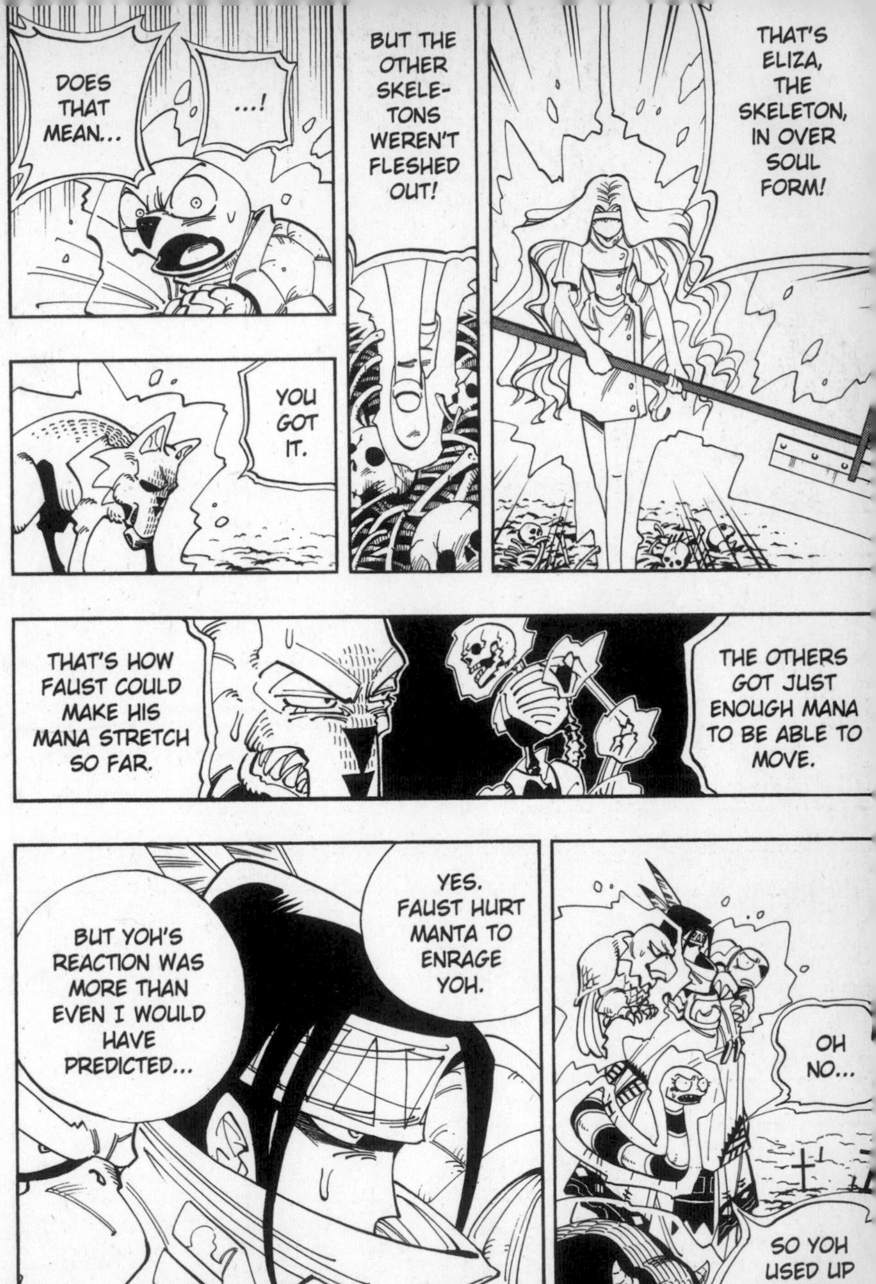
THAT'S ELIZA, THE SKELETON, IN OVER SOUL FORM!
BUT THE OTHER SKELE- TONS WEREN'T FLESHED OUT!
...!
DOES THAT MEAN...
YOU GOT IT.
THE OTHERS GOT JUST ENOUGH MANA TO BE ABLE TO MOVE.
THAT'S HOW FAUST COULD MAKE HIS MANA STRETCH SO FAR.
OH NO...
SO YOH USED UP HIS MANA SWATTING DECOYS!
YES. FAUST HURT MANTA TO ENRAGE YOH.
BUT YOH'S REACTION WAS MORE THAN EVEN I WOULD HAVE PREDICTED...

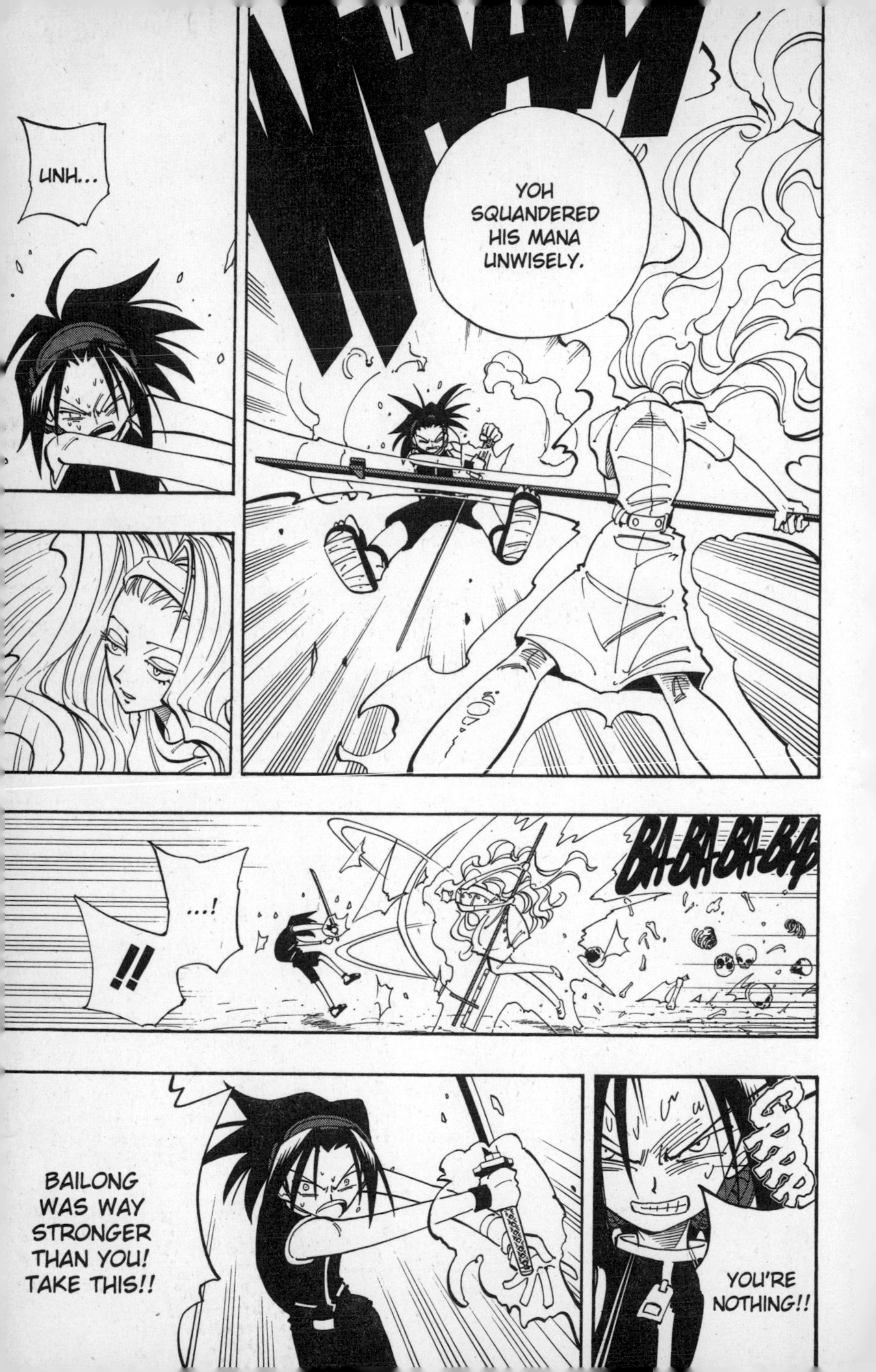
YOH SQUANDERED HIS MANA UNWISELY.
UNH...
BA-BA-BA-BA
...!
!!
YOU'RE NOTHING!!
BAILONG WAS WAY STRONGER THAN YOU! TAKE THIS!!

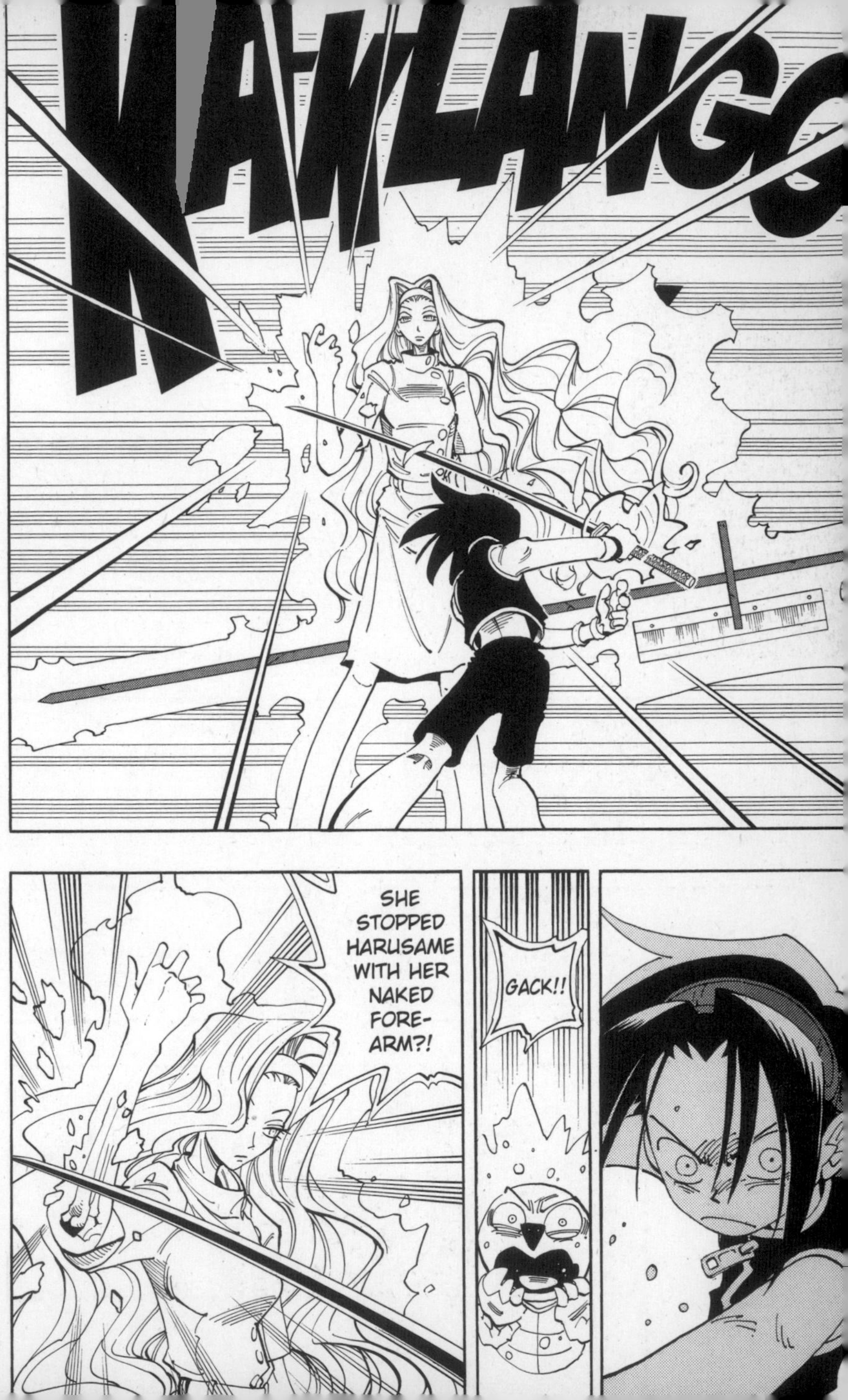
KA-KLANG
GACK!!
SHE STOPPED HARUSAME WITH HER NAKED FORE-ARM?!

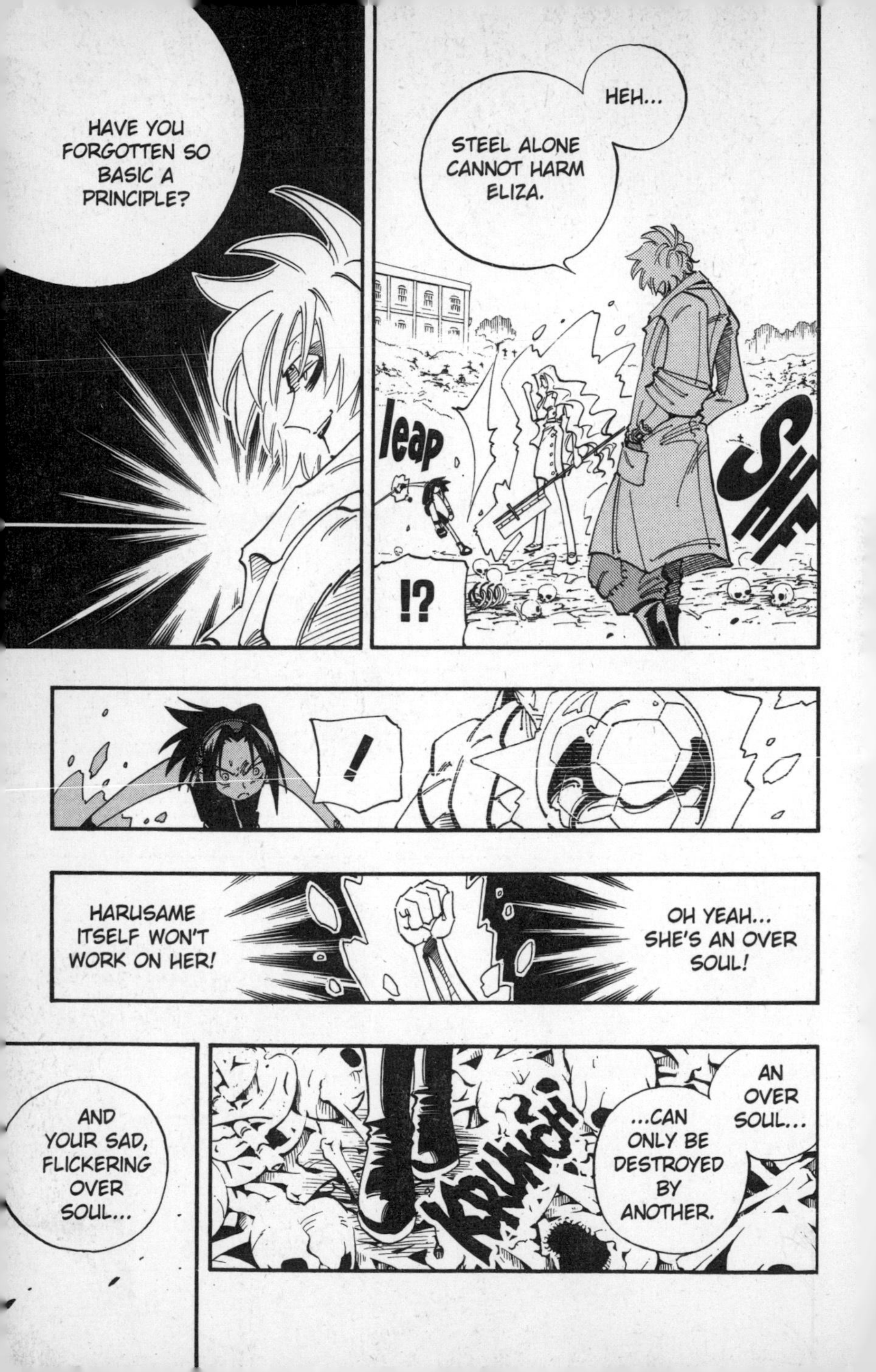
HEH...
STEEL ALONE CANNOT HARM ELIZA.
SHF
leap
!?
HAVE YOU FORGOTTEN SO BASIC A PRINCIPLE?
!
OH YEAH... SHE'S AN OVER SOUL!
HARUSAME ITSELF WON'T WORK ON HER!
AN OVER SOUL...
...CAN ONLY BE DESTROYED BY ANOTHER.
KRUNCH
AND YOUR SAD, FLICKERING OVER SOUL...

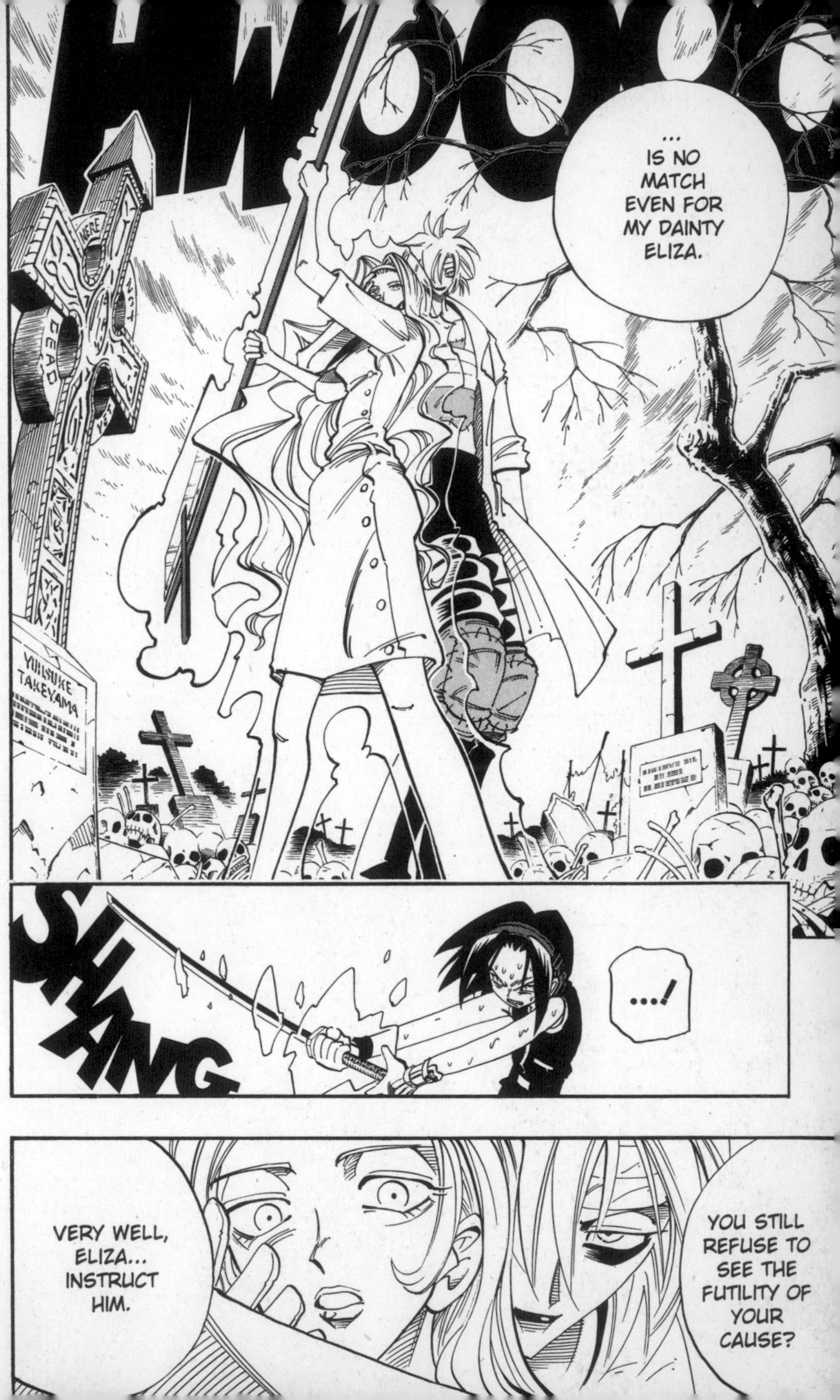
HWOOO
...
IS NO MATCH EVEN FOR MY DAINTY ELIZA.
WERE NOT DEAD YET
YUUSUKE TAKEYAMA
...!
SHANG
YOU STILL REFUSE TO SEE THE FUTILITY OF YOUR CAUSE?
VERY WELL, ELIZA... INSTRUCT HIM.

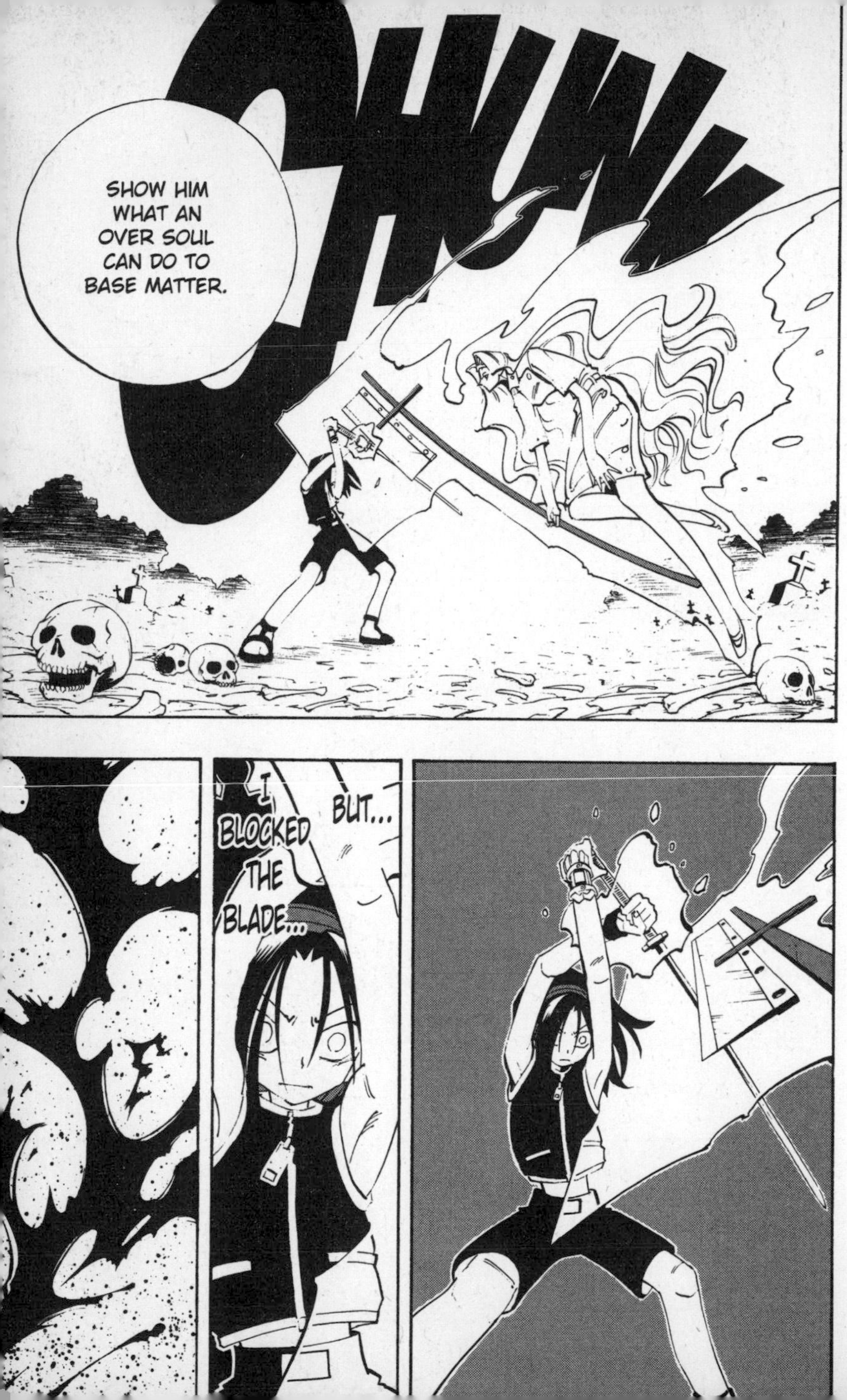
CHUNK
SHOW HIM WHAT AN OVER SOUL CAN DO TO BASE MATTER.
I BLOCKED THE BLADE...
BUT...

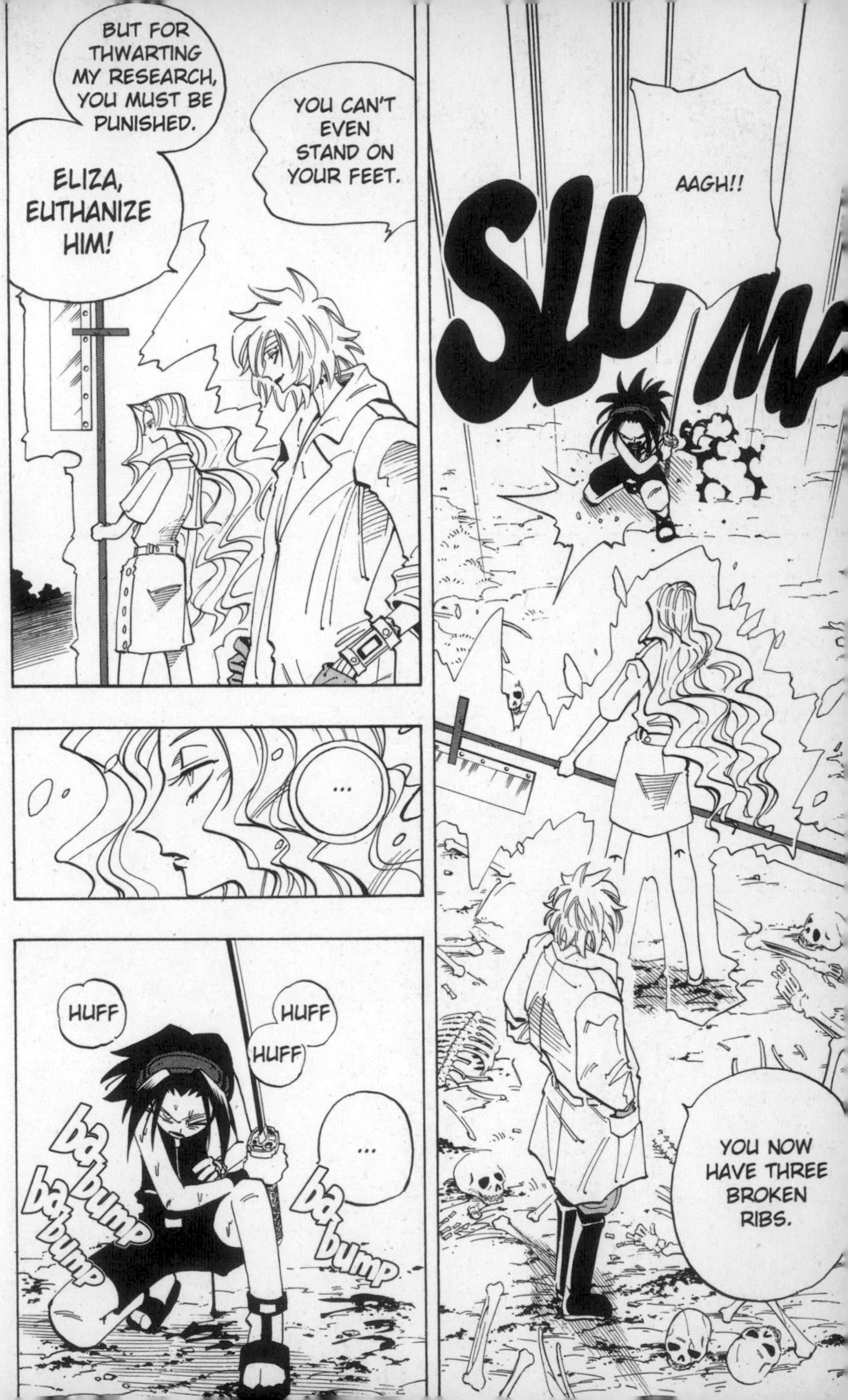
AAGH!!
YOU NOW HAVE THREE BROKEN RIBS.
YOU CAN'T EVEN STAND ON YOUR FEET.
BUT FOR THWARTING MY RESEARCH, YOU MUST BE PUNISHED.
ELIZA, EUTHANIZE HIM!
...
HUFF
HUFF
HUFF
...
ba bump
ba bump
ba bump

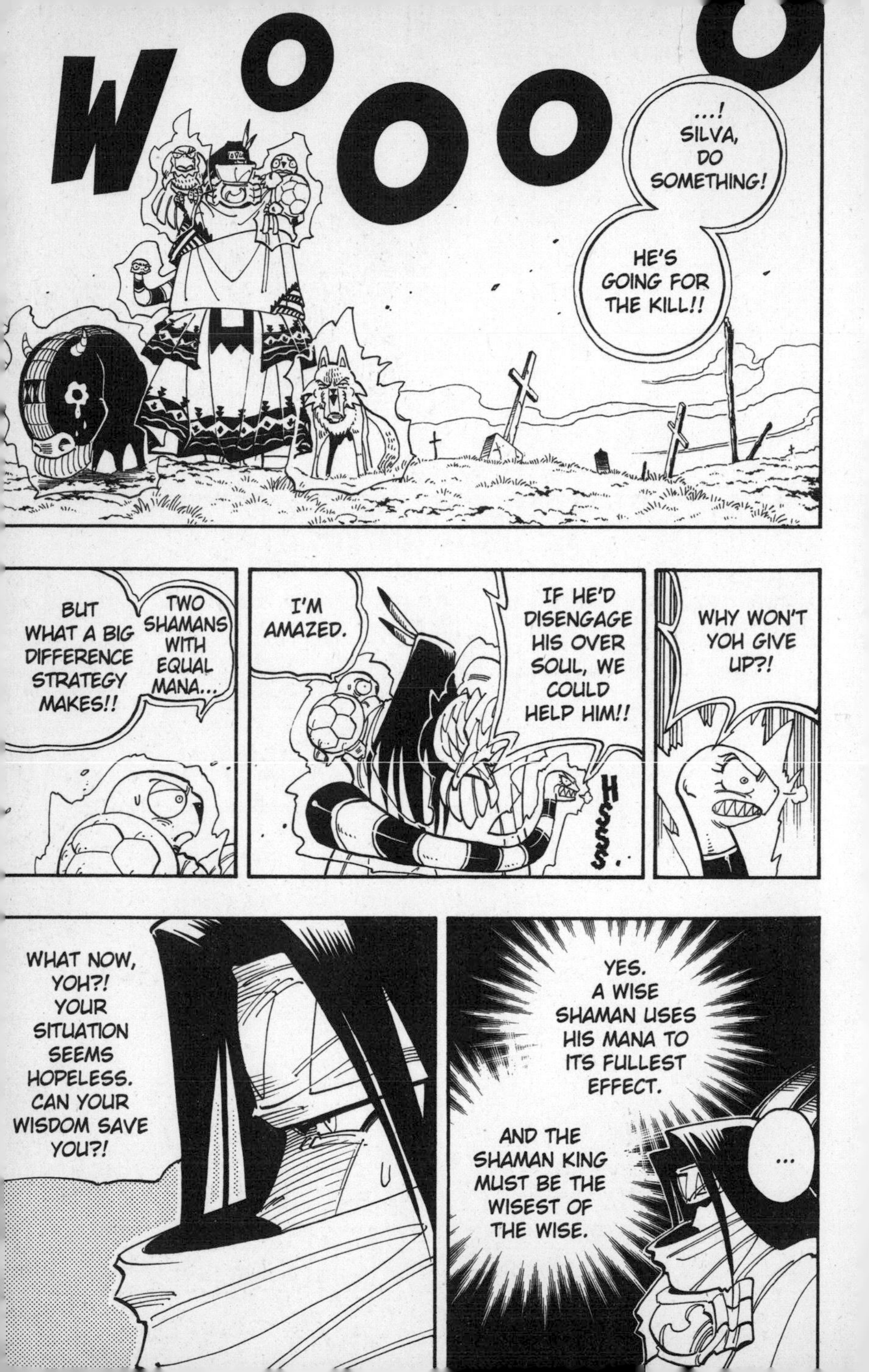
WOOOOO
...! SILVA, DO SOMETHING!
HE'S GOING FOR THE KILL!!
WHY WON'T YOH GIVE UP?!
IF HE'D DISENGAGE HIS OVER SOUL, WE COULD HELP HIM!!
I'M AMAZED.
HSSSS
TWO SHAMANS WITH EQUAL MANA...
BUT WHAT A BIG DIFFERENCE STRATEGY MAKES!!
YES. A WISE SHAMAN USES HIS MANA TO ITS FULLEST EFFECT.
AND THE SHAMAN KING MUST BE THE WISEST OF THE WISE.
...
WHAT NOW, YOH?! YOUR SITUATION SEEMS HOPELESS. CAN YOUR WISDOM SAVE YOU?!

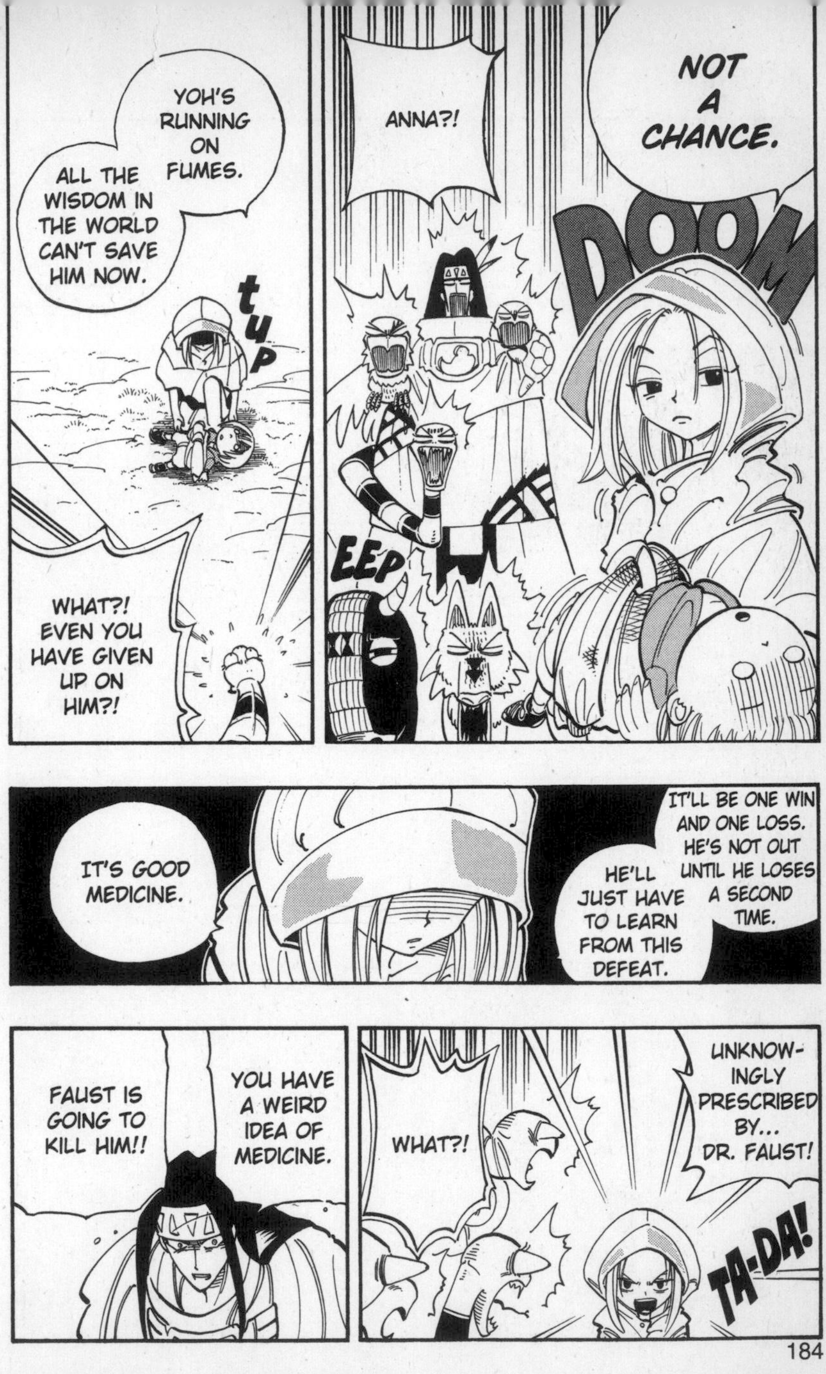
NOT A CHANCE.
DOOM
ANNA?!
EEP
YOH'S RUNNING ON FUMES.
ALL THE WISDOM IN THE WORLD CAN'T SAVE HIM NOW.
TUP
WHAT?! EVEN YOU HAVE GIVEN UP ON HIM?!
IT'LL BE ONE WIN AND ONE LOSS. HE'S NOT OUT UNTIL HE LOSES A SECOND TIME.
HE'LL JUST HAVE TO LEARN FROM THIS DEFEAT.
IT'S GOOD MEDICINE.
UNKNOW-INGLY PRESCRIBED BY... DR. FAUST!
TA-DA!
WHAT?!
YOU HAVE A WEIRD IDEA OF MEDICINE.
FAUST IS GOING TO KILL HIM!!

READ THIS WAY

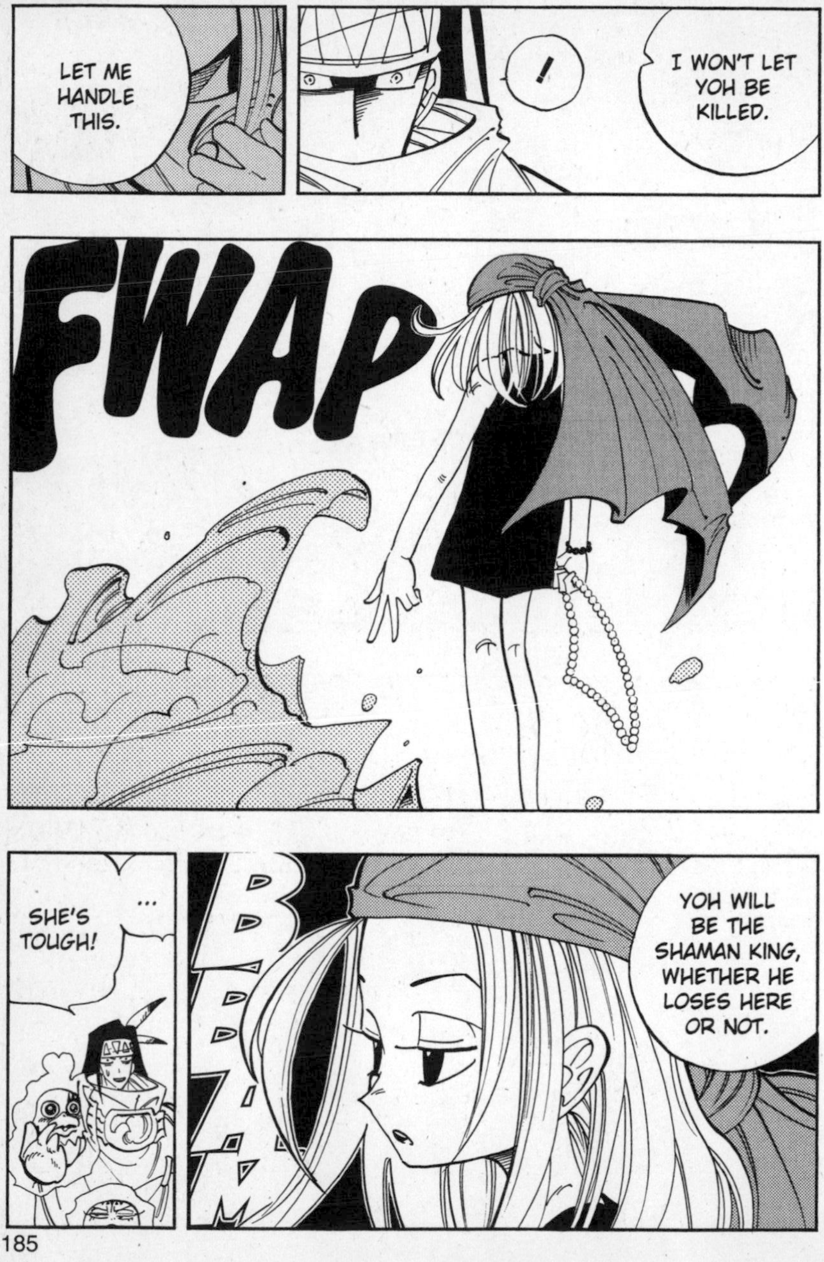

I WON'T LET YOH BE KILLED.
!
LET ME HANDLE THIS.
FWAP
YOH WILL BE THE SHAMAN KING, WHETHER HE LOSES HERE OR NOT.
...
SHE'S TOUGH!

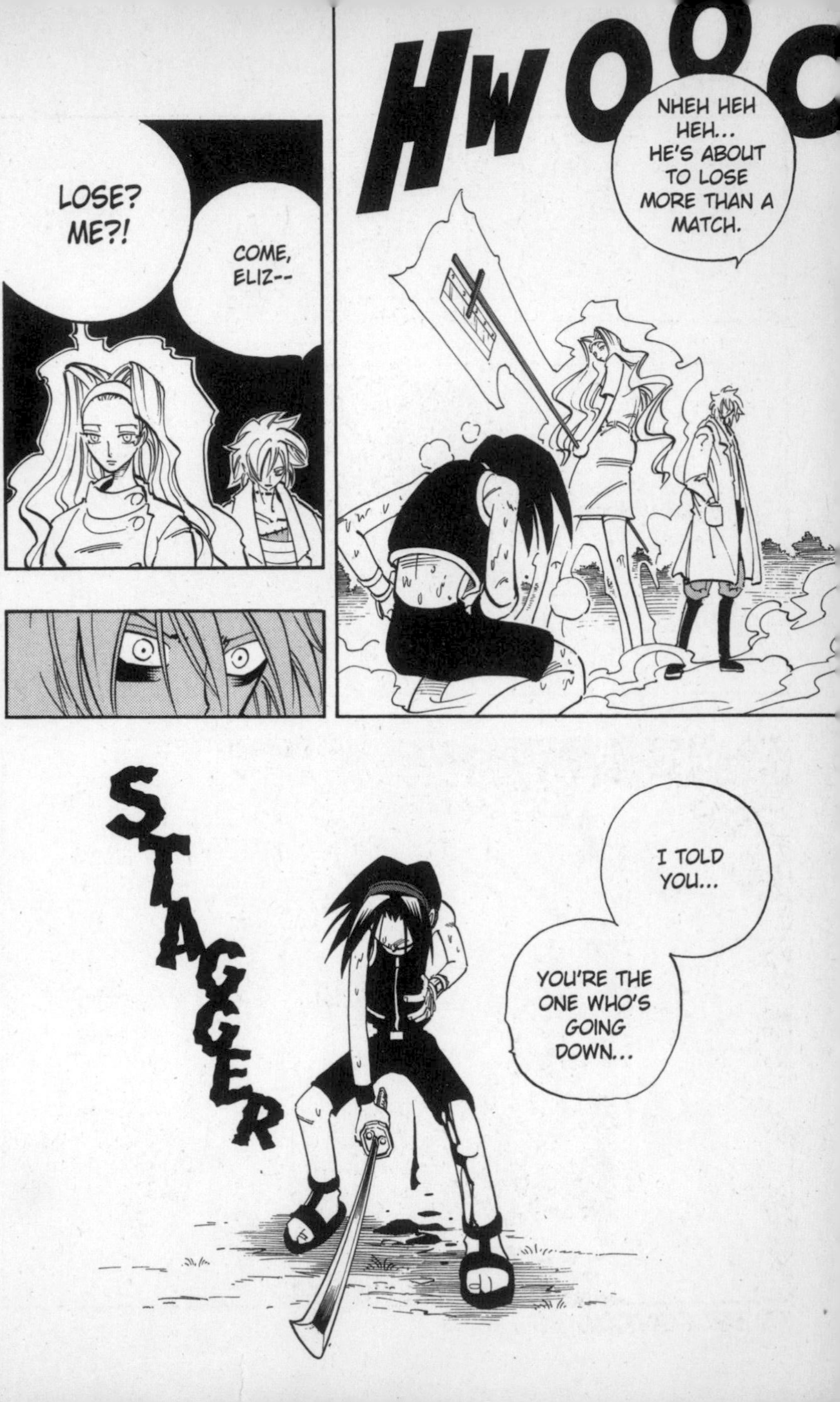
HWOO
NHEH HEH HEH... HE'S ABOUT TO LOSE MORE THAN A MATCH.
COME, ELIZ--
LOSE? ME?!
STAGER
I TOLD YOU...
YOU'RE THE ONE WHO'S GOING DOWN...

READ THIS WAY

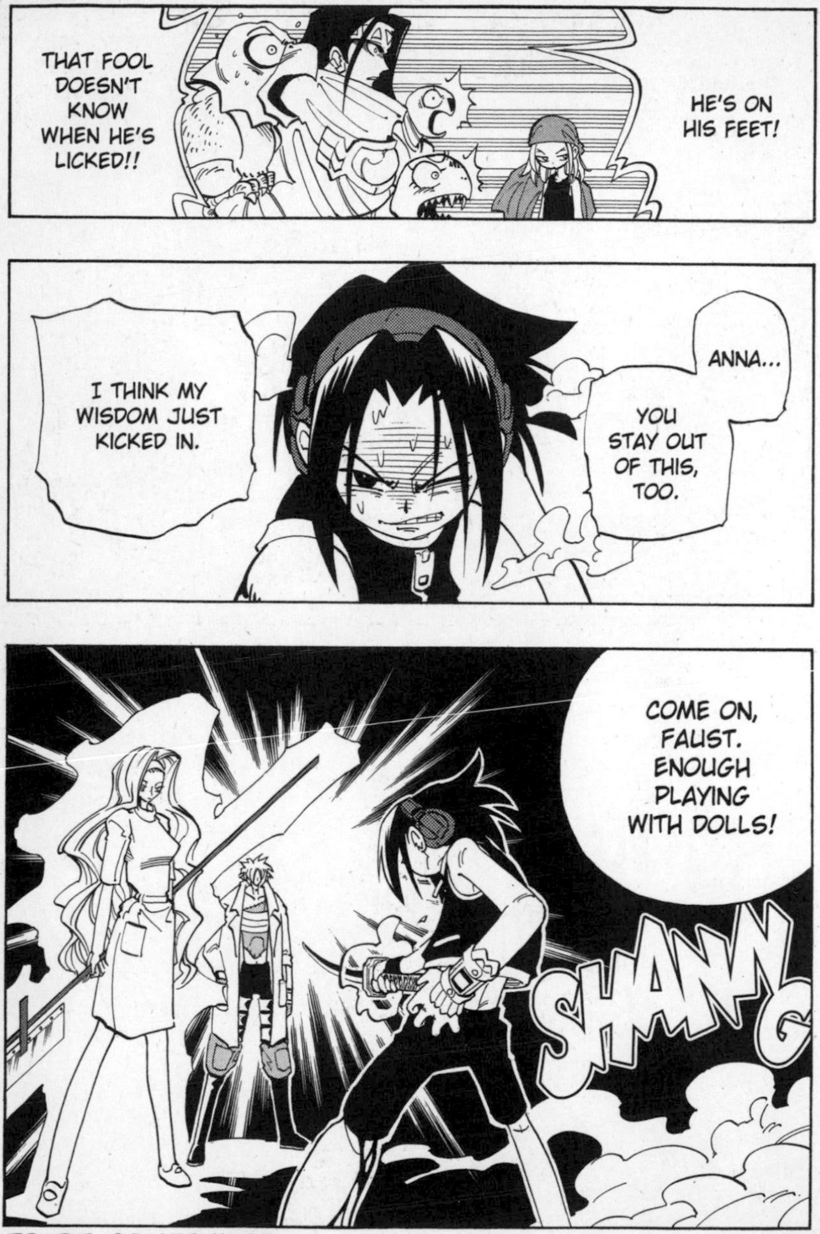
HE'S ON HIS FEET!
THAT FOOL DOESN'T KNOW WHEN HE'S LICKED!!
ANNA...
YOU STAY OUT OF THIS, TOO.
I THINK MY WISDOM JUST KICKED IN.
COME ON, FAUST. ENOUGH PLAYING WITH DOLLS!
SHANNG

TO BE CONTINUED...

READ THIS WAY

TALES OF FUNBARI HILL
HIROYUKI TAKEI
YOH?
WHAT, ANNA?
GO BUY FOOD FOR DINNER.
Sproing
WHAT!? ME, AGAIN!?
throb throb
YOU GO DO THE SHOP-PING!!
I WISH I COULD SAY THAT TO HER FACE.
IT'S NOT FAIR. AND SHE HOLDS ALL OUR MONEY, TOO.
HMPH
AOKI RECORDS
BOB
Soul BOB
BōZ

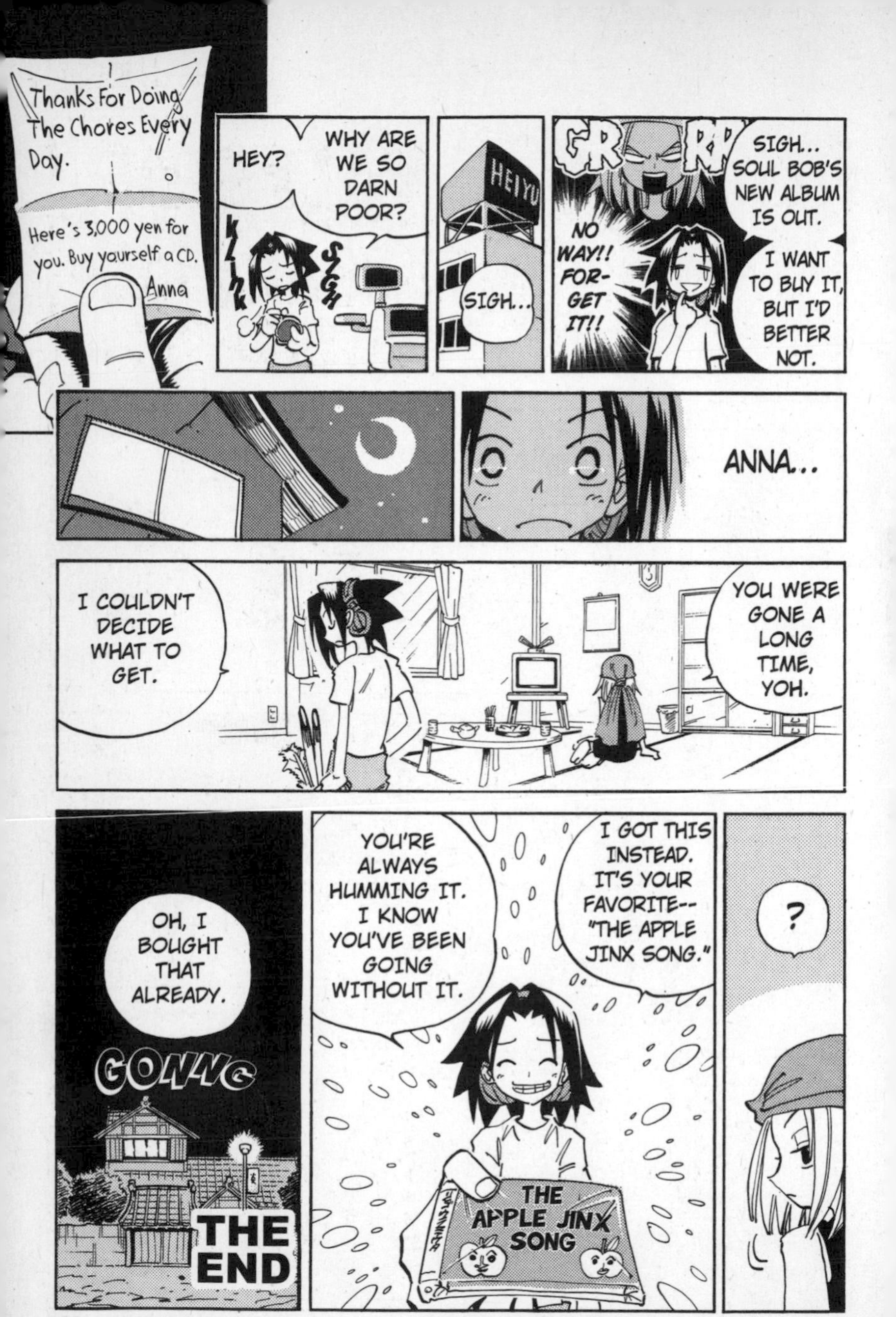

SIGH... SOUL BOB'S NEW ALBUM IS OUT.
I WANT TO BUY IT, BUT I'D BETTER NOT.
GRRR
NO WAY!! FORGET IT!!
HEIYU
SIGH...
WHY ARE WE SO DARN POOR?
HEY?
SIGH
Thanks For Doing The Chores Every Day.
Here's 3,000 yen for you. Buy yourself a CD.
Anna
ANNA...
YOU WERE GONE A LONG TIME, YOH.
I COULDN'T DECIDE WHAT TO GET.
?
I GOT THIS INSTEAD. IT'S YOUR FAVORITE-- "THE APPLE JINX SONG."
YOU'RE ALWAYS HUMMING IT. I KNOW YOU'VE BEEN GOING WITHOUT IT.
THE APPLE JINX SONG
OH, I BOUGHT THAT ALREADY.
GONNG
THE END

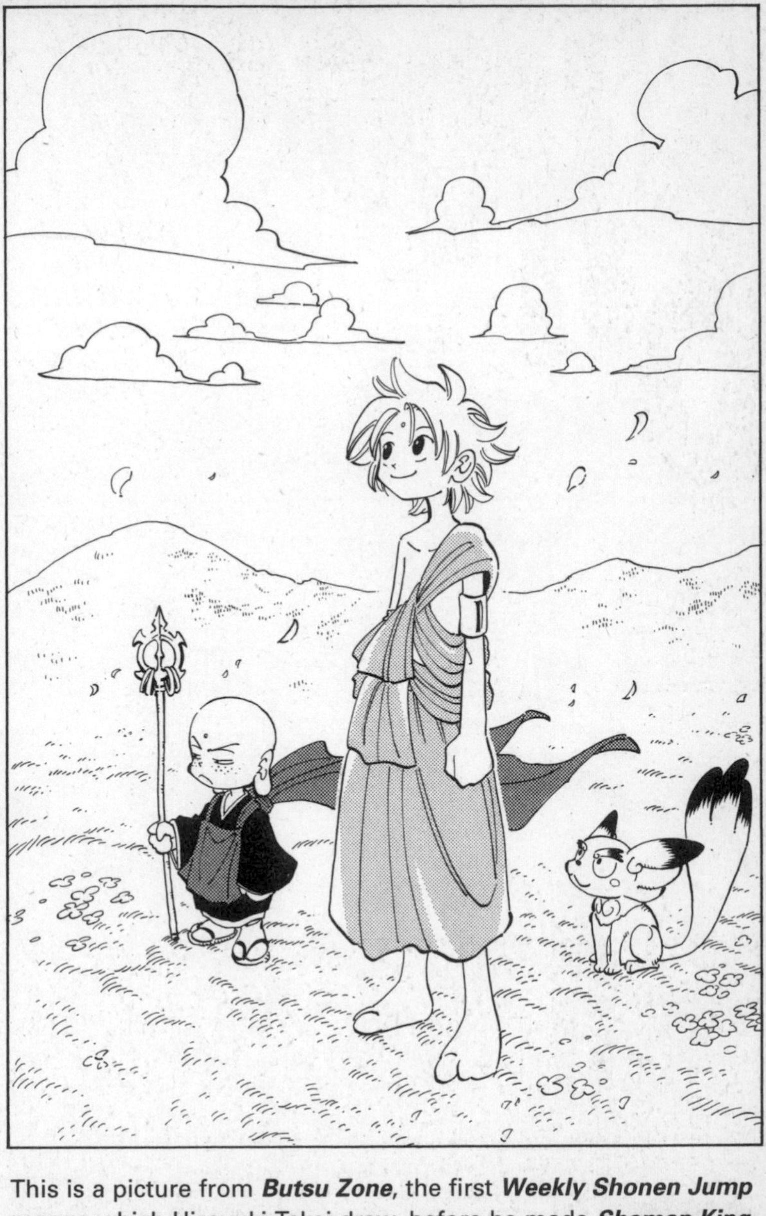

This is a picture from ***Butsu Zone***, the first ***Weekly Shonen Jump*** manga which Hiroyuki Takei drew, before he made ***Shaman King***.

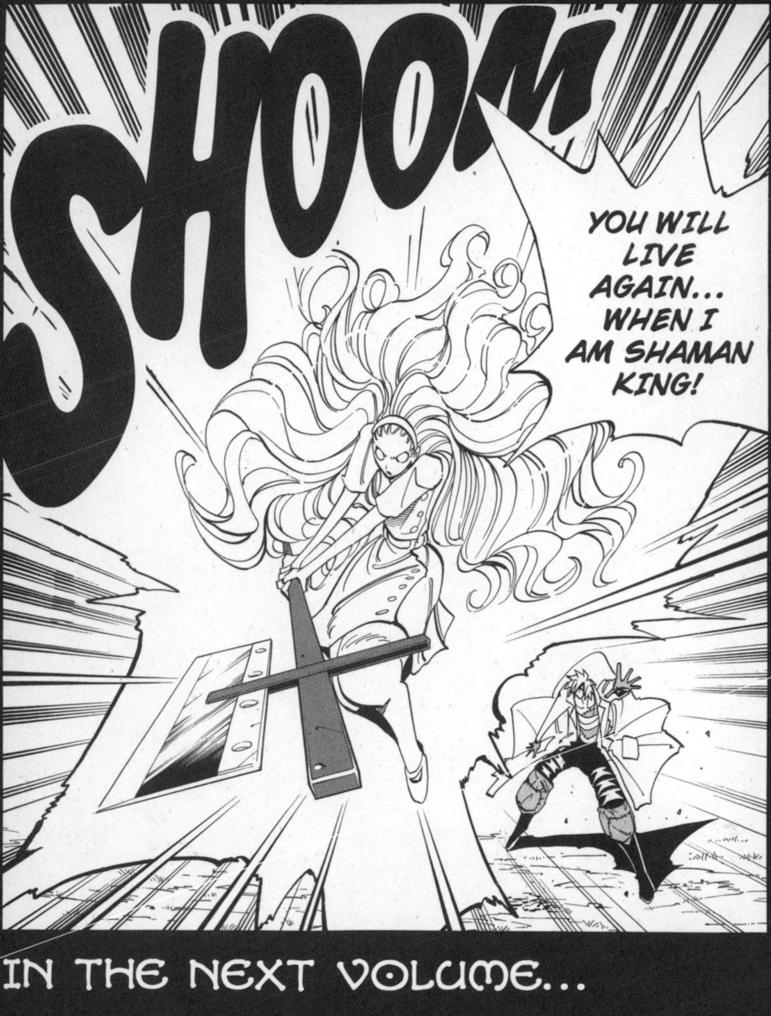
SHOOM
YOU WILL LIVE AGAIN... WHEN I AM SHAMAN KING!

IN THE NEXT VOLUME...

Infuriated by Yoh's mocking, Faust reveals the secret of Eliza, and what horrible deed drove him to become a shaman in the first place! Can Yoh's Japanese shamanism defeat Faust's necromancy with almost no mana? Then, Manta sets out in search of Yoh's ancestral home...while our hero descends into the netherworld to undergo his most bizarre ordeal yet!

AVAILABLE NOW!

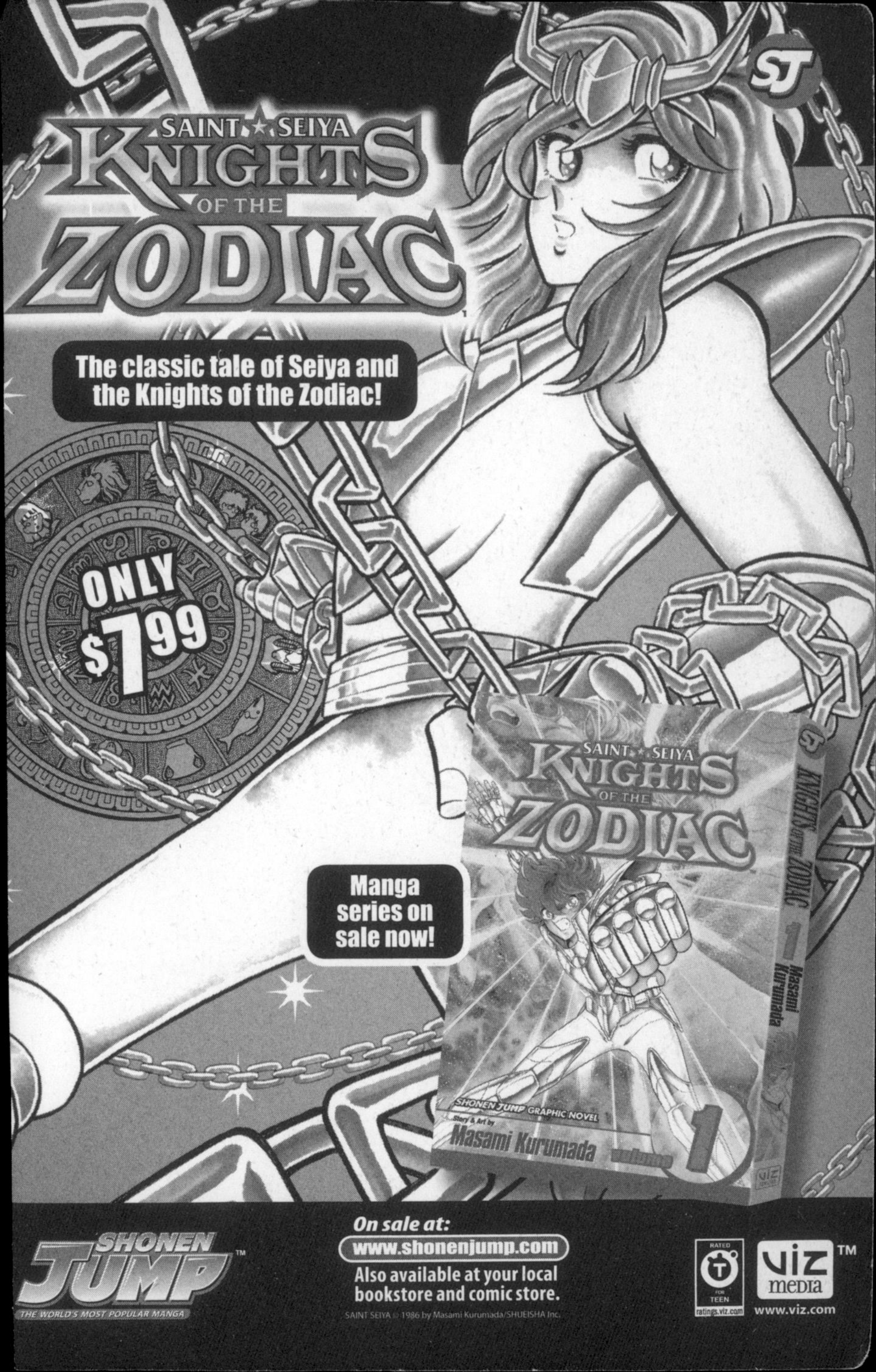

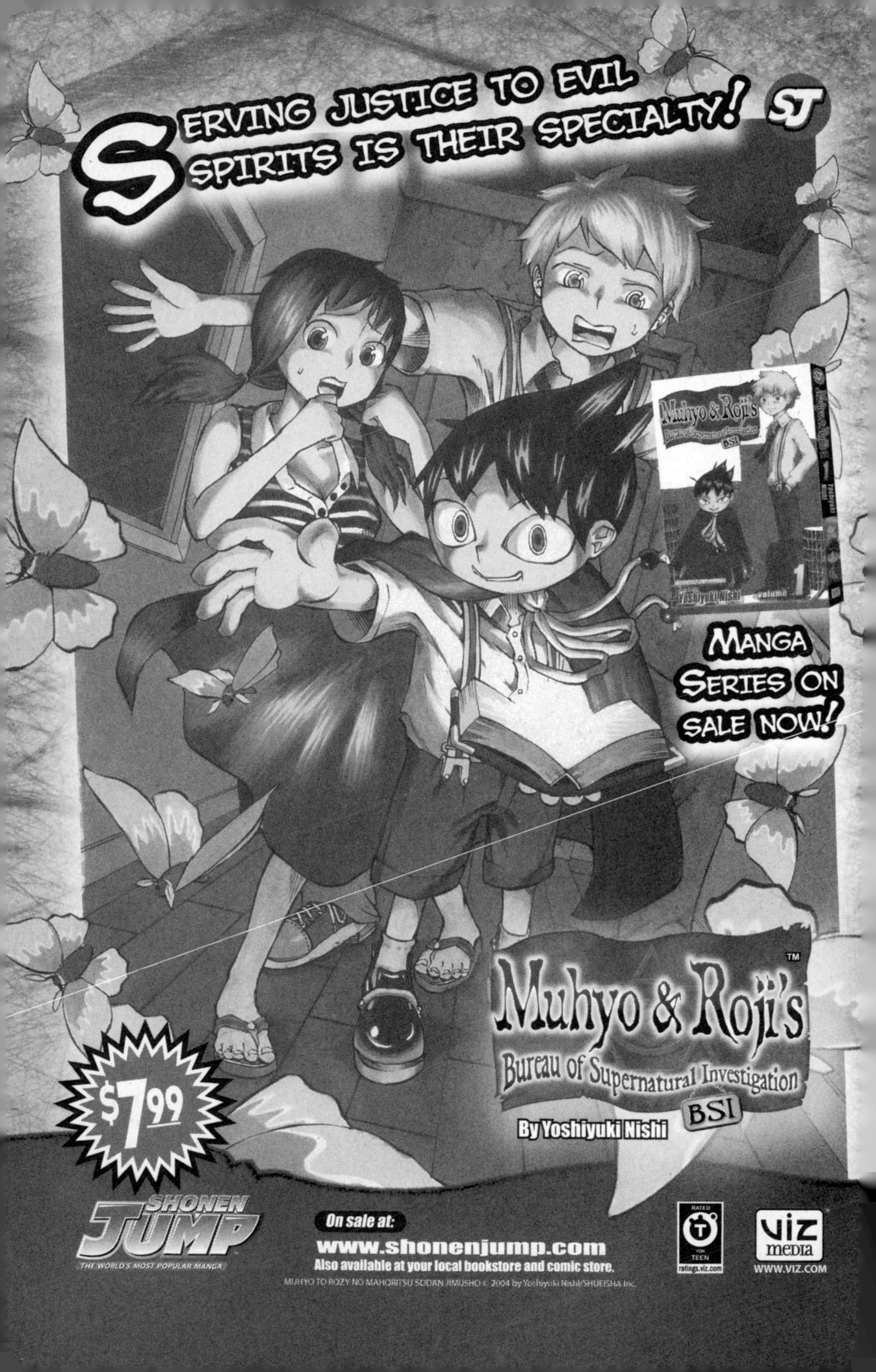
SERVING JUSTICE TO EVIL SPIRITS IS THEIR SPECIALTY!
SJ
MANGA SERIES ON SALE NOW!
Muhyo & Roji's™
Bureau of Supernatural Investigation
BSI
By Yoshiyuki Nishi
$7.99
SHONEN JUMP
THE WORLD'S MOST POPULAR MANGA
On sale at:
www.shonenjump.com
Also available at your local bookstore and comic store.
MUHYO TO ROZY NO MAHORITSU SODAN JIMUSHO © 2004 by Yoshiyuki Nishi/SHUEISHA Inc.
RATED T FOR TEEN
ratings.viz.com
viz media
WWW.VIZ.COM

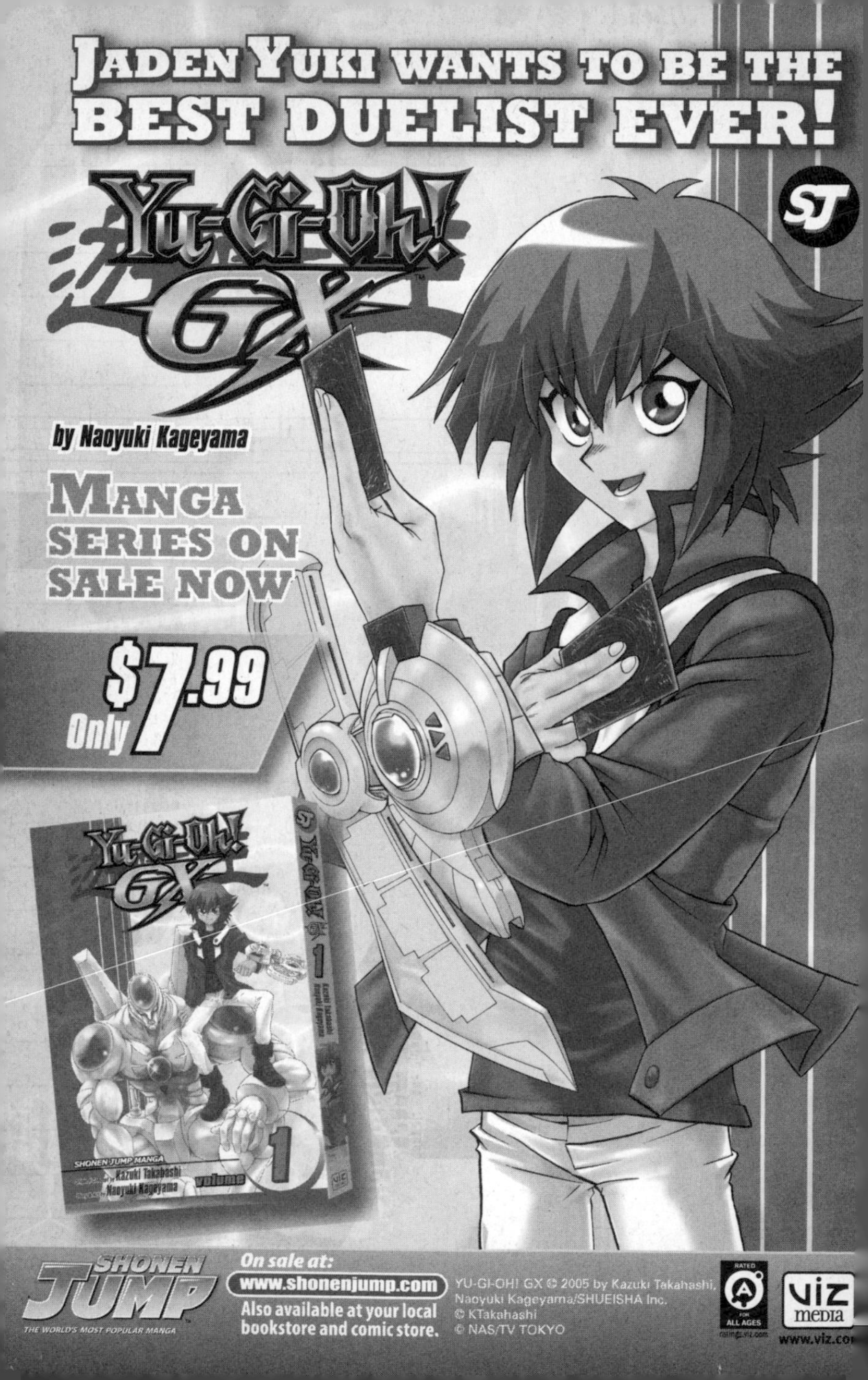
JADEN YUKI WANTS TO BE THE BEST DUELIST EVER!
SJ
YU-GI-OH! GX™
by Naoyuki Kageyama
MANGA SERIES ON SALE NOW
Only $7.99
YU-GI-OH! GX
SJ
1
SHONEN JUMP MANGA
Kazuki Takahashi
Naoyuki Kageyama
volume 1
SHONEN JUMP
THE WORLD'S MOST POPULAR MANGA
On sale at:
www.shonenjump.com
Also available at your local bookstore and comic store.
YU-GI-OH! GX © 2005 by Kazuki Takahashi, Naoyuki Kageyama/SHUEISHA Inc.
© KTakahashi
© NAS/TV TOKYO
RATED A FOR ALL AGES
viz media
www.viz.co

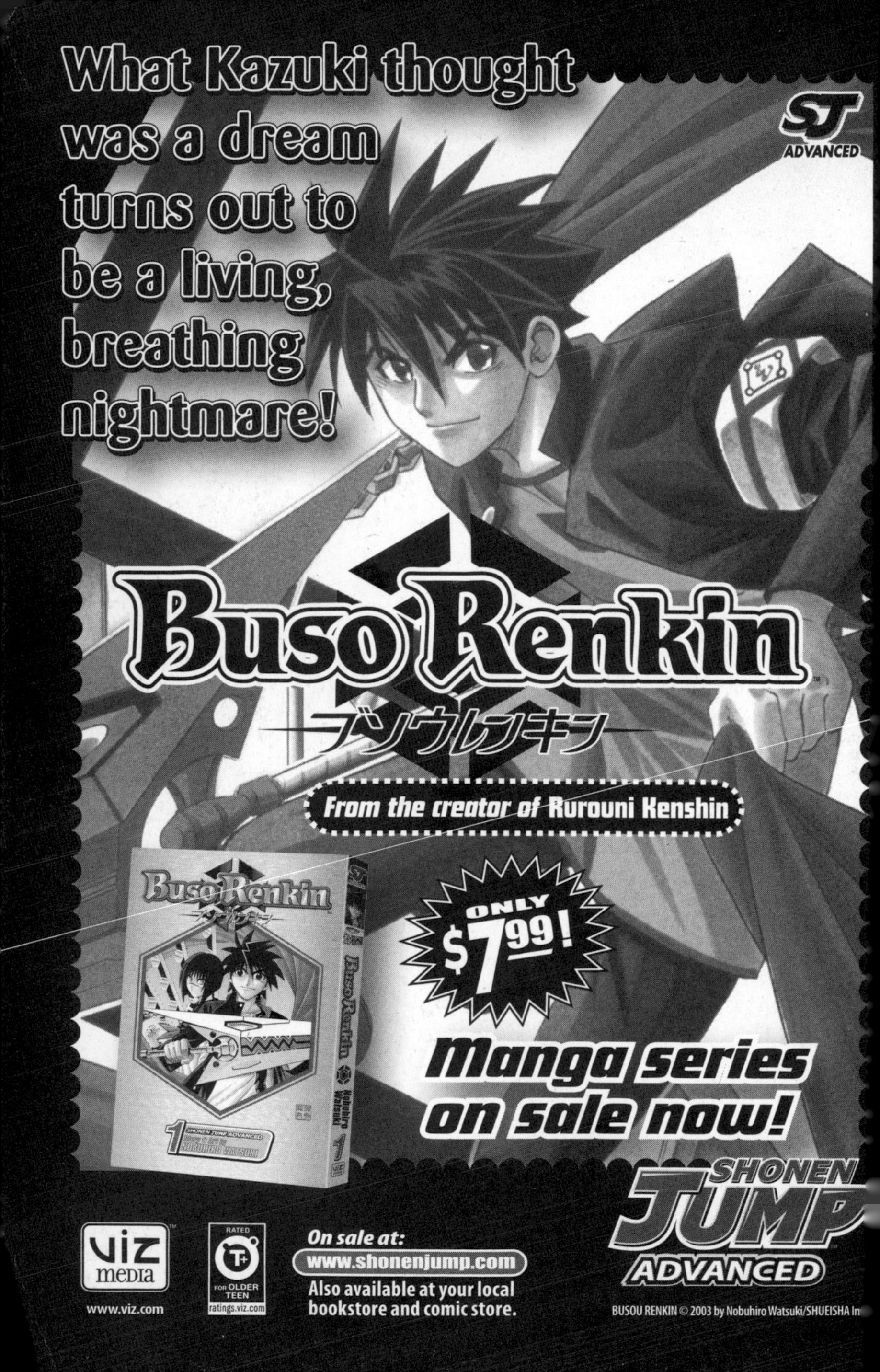
What Kazuki thought was a dream turns out to be a living, breathing nightmare!
SJ ADVANCED
Buso Renkin
ブソウレンキン
From the creator of Rurouni Kenshin
Buso Renkin
ONLY $7.99!
Manga series on sale now!
SHONEN JUMP ADVANCED
viz media
www.viz.com
RATED T+ FOR OLDER TEEN
ratings.viz.com
On sale at:
www.shonenjump.com
Also available at your local bookstore and comic store.
BUSOU RENKIN © 2003 by Nobuhiro Watsuki/SHUEISHA In

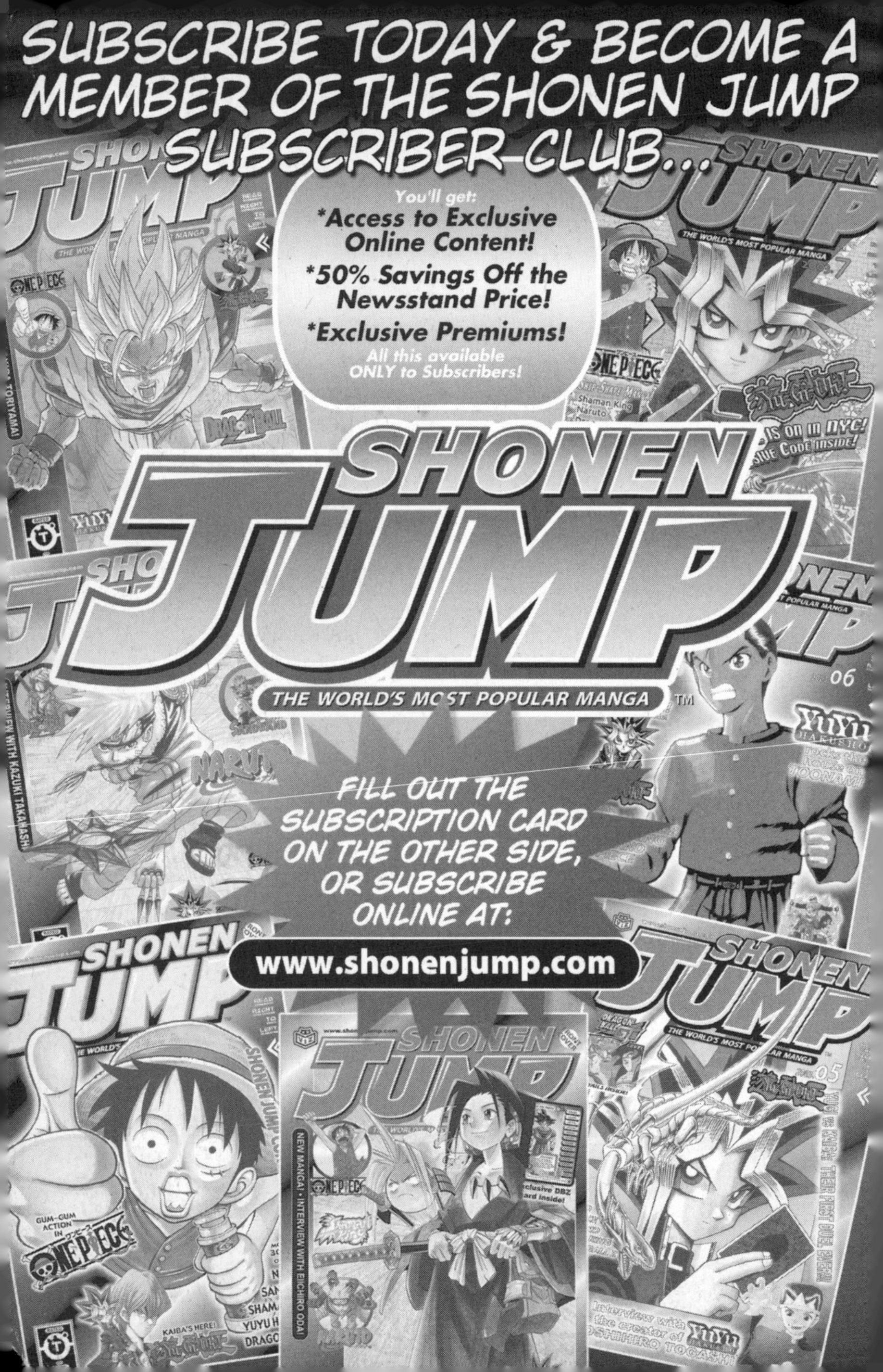
SUBSCRIBE TODAY & BECOME A MEMBER OF THE SHONEN JUMP SUBSCRIBER CLUB...
You'll get:
*Access to Exclusive Online Content!
*50% Savings Off the Newsstand Price!
*Exclusive Premiums!
All this available ONLY to Subscribers!
SHONEN JUMP
THE WORLD'S MOST POPULAR MANGA ™
FILL OUT THE SUBSCRIPTION CARD ON THE OTHER SIDE, OR SUBSCRIBE ONLINE AT:
www.shonenjump.com

Save 50% off the newsst...

SHONEN JUMP

THE WORLD'S MOST POPULAR MANGA

SUBSCRIBE TODAY and SAVE 50% OFF the cover price PLUS enjoy all the benefits of the SHONEN JUMP SUBSCRIBER CLUB, exclusive online content & special gifts ONLY AVAILABLE to SUBSCRIBERS!

☑ **YES!** Please enter my 1 year subscription (12 issues) to *SHONEN JUMP* at the INCREDIBLY LOW SUBSCRIPTION RATE of $29.95 and sign me up for the SHONEN JUMP Subscriber Club!

Only $29.95!

NAME _____

ADDRESS _____

CITY _____ STATE _____ ZIP _____

E-MAIL ADDRESS _____

☐ **MY CHECK IS ENCLOSED**   ☐ **BILL ME LATER**

CREDIT CARD: ☐ **VISA**   ☐ **MASTERCARD**

ACCOUNT # _____ EXP. DATE _____

SIGNATURE _____

CLIP AND MAIL TO ➤

SHONEN JUMP
Subscriptions Service Dept.
P.O. Box 515
Mount Morris, IL 61054-0515

Make checks payable to: **SHONEN JUMP.**
Canada add US $12. No foreign orders. Allow 6-8 weeks for delivery.

P6SJGN   YU-GI-OH! © 1996 by Kazuki Takahashi / SHUEISHA Inc.